Date Due

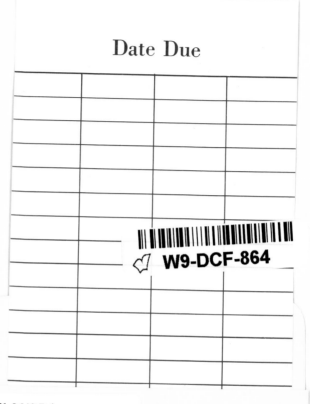

W9-DCF-864

SEARCHING FOR CERTAINTY

SEARCHING
FOR CERTAINTY

INSIDE THE NEW CANADIAN MINDSET

DARRELL BRICKER
EDWARD GREENSPON

DOUBLEDAY CANADA

Doubleday Canada and colophon are trademarks.

National Library of Canada Cataloguing in Publication Data

Bricker, Darrell Jay, 1961–

Searching for certainty : inside the new Canadian mindset

ISBN 0-385-25966-2

1. Canada-Economic conditions—1991– 2. Canada-Social conditions—1991–
3. Canada-Civilization—1945– I. Greenspon, Edward II. Title.

HN103.5.B75 2001   971.064'8   C2001-900754-X

Jacket photography: Peter Poulides / Stone
Jacket design: CS Richardson
Printed and bound in the USA

Published in Canada by
Doubleday Canada, a division of
Random House of Canada Limited

Visit Random House of Canada Limited's website:
www.randomhouse.ca

BVG IO 9 8 7 6 5 4 3 2 I

CONTENTS

PREFACE   1

Chapter 1
A NEW GOLDEN AGE?   9

Chapter 2
GLOBALIZATION IS US   45

Chapter 3
GOOD KING INTERNET   87

Chapter 4
MY FATHER'S TIE   118

Chapter 5
SCHOOL BY CHOICE   147

Chapter 6
THE CANADIAN EXCEPTION   174

Chapter 7
THE HEALTH CARE REVOLUTION   215

Chapter 8
HARD HEADS AND SOFT HEARTS   234

Chapter 9
WHOSE BODY IS THIS?   259

Chapter 10
THE NEW CAN-GLOBAL IDENTITY   279

Afterword
NAVIGATING THE NEW CANADIAN MINDSET   316

ACKNOWLEDGEMENTS   323

INDEX   327

PREFACE

We all know that Canada changed in the 1990s, but what about Canadians?

This book examines how the years of economic and social upheaval from the mid-1970s to the late 1990s shaped the way Canadians view their world, their country, and their own lives. The 1990s represented a particularly frustrating chapter in the history of this nation. Deficits and debt enfeebled governments, hindering their ability to assist citizens in times of need, such as during the recession that launched the decade. Taxes crept ever upward while social programs, especially our cherished health system, suffered neglect. Incomes stagnated. Family pressures mounted. Trust in bedrock institutions waned and confidence in the future, a leitmotif of our national existence, took a long holiday. Our very unity as a country came perilously close to vaporizing in the October 1995 Quebec referendum. "Canadians are losing faith in each other," the Department of Canadian Heritage declared in a typically pessimistic mid-decade report on public attitudes. To many of its inhabitants, blessed Canada had come to resemble paradise lost.

Searching for Certainty ultimately tells a story of redemption, perhaps even of paradise regained, as Canadians weathered the storms and emerged stronger for the experience. Policy analyst Judith Maxwell hit the nail on the head when she used the word resilient to describe Canadians in the 1990s. As the decade wound down, a renewed sense of purpose seeped back into the psychological outlook of the nation. Canadians expressed a determination to take control of their destinies. Abandoned by governments and the corporate sector, they turned increasingly to themselves for solutions.

Darrell and I were given the opportunity to jointly investigate the fundamental public opinion shifts of this period by grace of a strategic partnership between Ipsos-Reid, where he takes the pulse of the nation, and *The Globe and Mail,* where I get to tell Canada's stories. As the anxiety and pessimism of the 1990s began to recede, we took note of a fascinating slate of emerging trends: an unshakeable fiscal conservatism, a remarkable turnaround in attitudes toward free trade, an ideological devotion to public health care, a growing commitment to education, a renewed faith in social cohesion, a calculating consumerism, a celebration of diversity. We weighed the power of these factors alongside such meta-developments as globalization, multiculturalism, and the rapid rise of the Internet.

We wondered to what extent all these variables might have come together to forge a new consensus—what we came to call the new Canadian mindset—in the blast furnace of the nineties. And we were determined to find out. What we discovered both confirmed many of our suspicions and challenged many of our prejudices. *Searching for Certainty* recounts the story of our discovery.

Darrell is a "numbers guy" and I'm more of a "words guy." But we figured from the beginning that we're both, in our own ways, storytellers. And we wanted to make sure that any book we wrote about the evolving mindset of Canadians would comprise more than just a dry recitation of facts and figures. We were cognizant, therefore, of the need to lift our findings off the page through a judicious blend of anecdote and analysis. Darrell and I decided early on that a personal approach, one that related our own experiences in adjusting to the same realities as millions of other Canadians, would make the book a more pleasurable read. And on a more fundamental level, nothing in life is objective—not even polling. As we reveal something of ourselves, readers can see who we are and where we're coming from.

It all began with a series of long, spirited discussions over dinner, often at the Oyshi Sushi restaurant at Toronto's Harbourfront. From there, we dipped into the archives of the Angus Reid Group (now Ipsos-Reid) to test our suppositions about long-term public opinion trends. We also sought to get our hands on the publicly available research of other firms. In addition to Ipsos-Reid material, you will find in this book references to polls conducted over the years by COMPAS, Decima, Earnscliffe, Ekos, Environics, Gallup, Goldfarb, Leger, Pollara, and Strategic Counsel, among others. With this material in hand, we returned to Oyshi Sushi and again chewed over the meaning of it all. Only then did we put pen to paper—or, more accurately, fingers to keyboard.

The writing task fell mainly to me, but Darrell and I regularly convened late-night telephone debates as the manuscript unfolded. An early writing challenge emerged out of our desire to include ourselves in the story. Writing in the third person didn't seem appropriate, but neither could two authors share the first person. Readers will therefore notice that the book is written in the first-person singular, with me as the storyteller. References to Darrell are in the third person. But make no mistake: This book belongs to both of us.

Early in the process of our work on the manuscript, Pierre Trudeau died. His passing in the autumn of 2000 reminded us of the optimism that had characterized an earlier era in our national life. Neither of us had yet reached adolescence when Trudeaumania swept the country in the magical spring of 1968, but we, along with so many of Canada's current crop of decision-makers, came of age in the Trudeau era, the Age of Aquarius in Canadian politics. Trudeau burst on the scene with the country still riding the high of a hugely successful Centennial celebration. Although basic differences certainly could be ferreted out among Canadians, a strong consensus existed as to the way forward. The Trudeau consensus, more so than the man himself, was rooted in an easy confidence in the state as the vehicle for delivering the Just Society. From that basic premise flowed a gentle *dirigisme* and seemingly benign economic nationalism. Canadians felt confident in the road well travelled and put their confidence in their well-travelled new leader.

But a quarter-century of economic and social decline—beginning with the oil shock in the early 1970s and continuing into the late 1990s—fractured the consensus at the heart of the Age of Aquarius. For most of the 1990s, as Canadians began to notice the rot eating away at their idealized Canada, a core consensus no longer existed in the land. Thus the fragmented five-party Parliament of the past decade, reflecting a country riven regionally and ideologically by competing fears and passions. But the pendulum is swinging back. We will argue in the following chapters that a new consensus—a new Canadian mindset—is taking shape, one that builds on traditional foundations but takes them in new directions.

In his 1996 book, *Shakedown,* polling impresario Angus Reid, a charter member of the Trudeau generation, observed that "a unique era, which began in the 1960s, has ended." He went on to remark that "a new set of forces is moving swiftly into place—forces that will create challenges and opportunities we couldn't have dreamed of a decade ago." This book, published five years later, takes stock of the challenges and opportunities underlying the post-Trudeau consensus. Reid saw a new house under construction. We're now able to take you inside the edifice—to explore the interior rooms of the new Canadian mindset.

Through our research, we've come to believe that the transformation of Canadian public opinion is too often misunderstood, or purposely mischaracterized, as a neo-conservative outgrowth of our neighbours to the south, as some kind of alien ideological invasion. Nothing could be further from the truth. The new Canadian mindset is steeped in the traditions of the country. It reaches back into our past to reflect a national culture both parsimonious and compassionate, individualistic yet communitarian, innovative yet conserving—in other words, liberal and loyalist both.

A quarter-century of frustration has left us more fiscally conservative, more outward looking, and more personally assertive. We've rejected the controlling tendencies of the nanny state and the blind faith that it could right wrongs and square circles through the magic of a parliamentary appropriation. But our heightened self-reliance doesn't mean that Canadians have lost their distinctive sense of the collective good, nor their desire to reside in a cohesive community rather than a gated one.

As political scientist Gad Horowitz noted a generation ago, an unmistakable "Tory touch" is embedded in Canada's political culture. Drawn from the fragments of our melange of founding cultures, this Tory touch has created a unique political sensibility in the upper half of North America, one in which American-style individualism cohabits peacefully with European-style communitarianism. Unlike the Americans, who revel in an operating myth succinctly put on New Hampshire licence plates—"Live Free or Die"— Canada, by and large, can be safely characterized as a nation of life insurance holders. Perhaps unsurprisingly, Canadians are second in the world only to the Japanese in insurance coverage. Faced with a cash windfall, our idea of bingeing is to increase our RRSP contribution.

Our world-class companies, Bombardier, Nortel (for a time), and more recently Ballard Power, have been built through a blend of private enterprise and public assistance. The values of public education and public health care remain unassailable despite the stresses and strains of recent years. The Tory streak that runs through the centre of most Canadians constitutes a dominant national trait. We are preservers as much as creators. We value continuity even while accepting change. The classic Tory principles set out in our constitution of peace, order, and good government continue to resonate.

When actor and gun activist Charlton Heston ventured north from Hollywood to the relative wilds of Prince George, British Columbia, in the spring of 2000, he couldn't resist haranguing Canadians for being a bunch of wusses. He came north in his capacity as president of the National Rifle Association to rally opposition to Canada's new gun registry. "Why is your government doing this?" he thundered in the voice of Moses and Ben-Hur. "Because they can. And even worse, you let them."

He was right. This is, after all, a country willing to accept reasonable restrictions to our individual freedoms for the greater social good. It is right there in Section 1 of our Charter of Rights and Freedoms, which enables governments to restrain freedoms "to such reasonable limits prescribed by law as can be demonstrably justified in a free and democratic society." Canadians, by and large, view as perfectly reasonable what Heston—living in a less nuanced world—could only imagine as a fundamental abridgement of individual freedom.

At the same time, though, ours is also a society that has been exposed more thoroughly than most over the past decade to the winds of change. Canadians have come to accept that they reside in a global economy, and that it is better to confront the elements than seek permanent shelter from the storm. Our economic space is larger than our political space, which challenges us to make our political space the best in the world. This means getting health care right, getting education right, getting taxes right, getting tolerance right, and so on. Mediocrity is no longer an option for Canadians, especially our younger people. They demand excellence at home. Failing that, they will entertain offers from abroad.

In order to join us on the journey inside the new Canadian mindset, it is necessary to begin with an appreciation of three underlying trends in public attitudes: the decline of public trust, the rise of the knowledge consumer and knowledge citizen, and the search for certainty.

THE DECLINE IN PUBLIC TRUST

Comparisons over time show that practically every public institution and profession has experienced a significant decline in status with Canadians, a pattern that holds true for other countries as well. The institutions in which we once blindly placed our trust—our churches, our governments, our medical establishment, our teachers, our employers—are now called upon to prove their worthiness. We've lived through depleted cod fisheries and depleted government treasuries, through the *Exxon Valdez,* the Walkerton water system, and the Mount Cashel orphanage. Exhortations to "trust us," "have faith," or "accept that we know what's best for you" no longer suffice. Trust is no longer given but earned, and even at that it is dispensed only conditionally and situationally.

THE RISE OF THE KNOWLEDGE CONSUMER AND KNOWLEDGE CITIZEN

The term knowledge worker has become common in the modern lexicon, but we now live in the era of the knowledge consumer and the knowledge citizen as well. The decline of public trust has intersected with a rise in educational standards and the advent of the Internet to create an information-enfranchised society the likes of which has never been seen before. Canadians are breaking the knowledge monopoly that has traditionally separated the governors from the governed.

These new knowledge consumer/citizens tend to be opinionated, demanding, empowered, and ultimately disloyal. They expect results and are prepared to hold producers accountable for performance failures. They demand choices in everything they encounter. More than at any time in the past, we live in a meritorious society. A knowledge society values intelligence over capital, education over connections. We have no more time for Family Compacts and Vertical Mosaics. Ask the Eaton brothers: Pedigree alone doesn't cut it any more.

SEARCHING FOR CERTAINTY

The mantra of the knowledge consumer/citizen can be described something like this: "Since I'm not prepared to take what you say on faith, you (professional, public servant, politician, or business person) must make your case and persuade me why I should buy in. I want it in writing and I intend to hold you accountable for any failure to deliver." In the end, the knowledge consumer/citizen is searching for certainty—by which we mean as much assurance as can be mustered in a world of constant change that promises will be kept and commitments delivered upon.

This demand initially flows out of the economic upheavals of the past quarter-century. Canadians seek the certainty that they won't ever again be subjected to the rough recovery regimen imposed on them in the 1990s. But the search for certainty also reflects the return of social priorities to the top of the public opinion agenda. Canadians care far more about their quality of life than their standard of living. The latter is generally seen as a means to the former. In recent years, as the public has regained confidence in the state of the economy, it has turned back to issues such as health care, education, and poverty. Canadians insist upon having the comfort of knowing that the health care system will be kept in a state of good repair for when they eventually need it. And they demand the certainty that the accepted ticket to survival in the global economy—education and training—will be both accessible and of high quality.

Getting inside the new Canadian mindset is critical for the country's decision-makers, whether in the public, private, or not-for-profit sectors. Grasping the subtle interplay between the rise of individualism and the persistent Tory touch is a prerequisite to getting public policies and corporate strategies right in the twenty-first century. This book provides an important tool of understanding for our governments, our corporations, our unions, our religious institutions, our schools, our doctors, our financial advisers—indeed, anyone interacting with Canadians in their guises as citizens, consumers, or workers.

The line that once separated the private from the public has been erased in recent years. All institutions are public today. There was a time when governments were judged on trust and private firms on performance. That wall has been torn down. They are each judged today on both criteria. Governments are expected to deliver the goods in an efficient manner; corporations are expected to operate in the public interest. Both therefore need to be able to get inside the mindset of the increasingly assertive knowledge consumer and citizen and to understand their search for certainty.

Although he may not know it, Queen's University economist and public policy provocateur Thomas Courchene helped put a critical intellectual brick in place for *Searching for Certainty*. In a conversation in the autumn of 2000, Courchene generously provided a detailed preview of his coming oeuvre, *A State of Minds*. Courchene is a man of deep thought but pithy explanations. He recounted how in the book he cites Sir Wilfrid Laurier's famous declaration of nearly 100 years ago that the twentieth century would belong to Canada. Courchene had played off that to say that if we rise to the challenges of the new economy, the twenty-first century could belong not so much to Canada as to Canadians.

With Courchene as inspiration, this twenty-first-century book is more about Canadians than Canada. The two are, of course, inseparable, but the emphasis is on the people and their outlook—on public opinion more than public policy. In this spirit, we salute Canadians for the maturity and nuance of their mindset. Throughout our research, we couldn't help marvelling that no matter how complex the subject, Canadians can be counted on to work their way through to the sensible solutions.

We hope you will find reading *Searching for Certainty* as enlightening as we found writing it.

CHAPTER 1

A NEW GOLDEN AGE?

I n an odd way, the 1990s left us richer as a people. It was a lost decade, to be sure, a decade of reck-oning that compressed our pocketbooks as well as our spirits. We hunkered down through a prolonged winter of decline before finally, at decade's end, emerging from our shelters to breathe in the first stirrings of national recovery. The long journey tested our confidence in the country, its governments, our employers, and even ourselves. It left us wizened and wiser both. Sadly, we lost our innocence. But happily, we discovered a new inner strength.

Although the United Nations Human Development Index so beloved by Prime Minister Jean Chrétien continued to cite Canada as number one in the world, Canadians instinctively understood we were actually losing precious ground on most fronts. The decade began with a stubborn recession. Each time we seemed to escape its clutches, it overtook us again and dragged us back down. Economists introduced us to the term "dead cat bounce" to describe an economy that hits bottom but fails to snap back. We also learned the oxymoron "jobless recovery." Through it all, our employers were too pre-occupied with the challenges of the global economy to demonstrate even the remotest signs of noblesse oblige. And our governments—federal, provincial, and local—were too overburdened by debt to help ease our pain. We were on our own.

Canadians being Canadians, we put our shoulders to the wheel and pressed ever forward. We are a resilient lot, mixing the stoicism of the Russians with the optimism of the Americans. We are what we've always been—patient investors in our country. And our patience as we embark on a new century is finally reaping dividends.

For Canadians, an economic Groundhog Day arrived in February 1998. We poked our noses out of our dens and sensed that spring was finally in the air. That was the month that our national government delivered its first budget surplus in twenty-eight years. It was also the moment—symbolically and substantively—we regained our confidence in the future.

This book is about the years we spent hunkered down and the way the experience changed us. Canadians today are more fiscally conservative, less protectionist, less technophobic, more globally connected, and more self-reliant than at the onset of the lost decade of the 1990s. Yet they remain very much rooted in the political culture of the country they've carved out of the rock and snow, a nation deeply attached to the value of mutual responsibility.

Slowly but steadily over the past several years, a new Canadian mindset—less fearful, more hopeful—has taken shape. Globalization, once regarded with loathing, is accepted by most today as a creator of opportunity. A full quarter-century of self-inflicted fiscal wounds have finally been sutured. The economy began showing renewed energy near the end of the 1990s. Anxieties about job security abated. Our tax burden has finally lightened and investments are being made again in our most cherished social programs. Even the economic slowdown of 2001 failed to dent the underlying mood of public optimism. Like mountain climbers, Canadians know they will encounter mini-descents on their larger ascent. Overall, things are definitely looking up, at least for the vast majority of us.

It's quite the turnaround. I remember very clearly looking at our future from the other end of the telescope in the spring of 1991. I had been stationed in London as *The Globe and Mail*'s European business correspondent for three and a half years. In total, I had spent five of the previous seven years in Europe, first as a graduate student at the London School of Economics and then, after returning to Canada for twenty-two months in 1986 and 1987, back across the Atlantic with a spacious *Globe and Mail* flat and a corporate credit card.

Being away meant I missed out on many of the developments of the period that helped drive Canada ever deeper into a collective funk—Meech Lake, the introduction of the GST, the uncompromising anti-inflation policies of the Bank of Canada. But distance often confers advantage in grasping the larger trends and truths at play. My perch in Europe furnished me with a unique perspective on the state of my country, both good and bad. I could more keenly than ever appreciate Canada's great gifts of tolerance and civility and freedom. You couldn't travel extensively in eastern Europe, as I did, and fail to appreciate the freedom it was so easy to take for granted at home. Nor was Western Europe a haven of tolerance.

Less happily, my country's steady economic decline, a barely recognizable drip here and drop there to many Canadians back home, was blindingly obvious to an observer abroad. Europe was drawing closer together while the forces of political gravity in Canada appeared anything but integrationist. Even in the supposedly good times of the late 1980s, I could see the Canadian ship of state fading on the horizon. It reminded me of the British Empire, whose long, genteel decline could hardly be discerned at close quarters.

In those days, I was paid to travel around Europe chronicling political and economic change. I wrote about the economic dividers being knocked down among the liberal democracies within the European Community and the dramatic toppling of the political walls between east and west. The Berlin Wall fell in November 1989, preceded by the ascension of Solidarity into government in Poland in the same decade that the movement had been banned by martial law. The Velvet Revolution provided a stunning victory for soft power over hard power in Czechoslovakia. I was in Romania over Christmas 1989, as history caught up with the country's egomaniacal and ruinous dictator, Nicolae Ceausescu, and meted out the ultimate justice. I ate Christmas Eve dinner in a tiny apartment in Timisoara, the guest of a family that brought two journalists home from a fire fight to celebrate their emancipation. (Dessert was spent crouched on a darkened floor avoiding sniper fire from the apartment block across the way.)

For a young journalist, the Europe of that era provided a cornucopia of action, much of it historic in nature. I remember listening to Lester Thurow in the early 1990s saying that when the century was over, one of the three dates that would stand out forever would be 1989 (along with 1914 and 1945). He was right. In 1989, we all—not just the east Europeans—broke free of the rut of the Cold War.

Having a seat on the freedom train that rolled through the Soviet bloc countries was thrilling, but the place on the continent that most impressed me was northern Italy. It was rich in the best sense, pulsating with enterprise and style. Its creativity and energy were irresistible. The streets were clean and full of life. Everyone looked good in a sweater. Even the highway food stops looked neat, classy, and sumptuous. Italy had its problems to be sure. Its government was as lead-footed as its private sector was fleet of foot. The country was even more indebted than Canada, and public services (planes, phones, post) were a joke. But you didn't take much notice in the wealthy regions up north. Indeed, economists said that if one could fold northern Italy into its natural economic unit with the neighbouring parts of Switzerland and Austria and southern Germany, you would have the wealthiest nation in the world.

My wife and I were starting a family, so we thought a lot about the future. I recall one conversation in which we discussed how Canada in our parents' generation had provided opportunity for hundreds of thousands of Italian-Canadians. We had many friends among the offspring of these immigrants. Could it be, we pondered, that our children would in their generation become Canadian-Italians, economic refugees in search of a better life in Europe? Should we stay overseas at least long enough to ensure them a European Community passport?

These musings became quite relevant when I received a call in early 1991 from Margaret Wente, the newly installed editor of the "Report on Business" section of the *Globe*. She wanted to know if I would come home and run the business pages for her on a day-to-day basis. It was a wonderful opportunity, but home was a country halfway to hell in a handbasket. It had lived beyond its means for so long that Canadians seemed blind to the damage done. Nonetheless, it was home. We returned to an economy mired in recession and a country, psychologically, slipping into depression. There were times during the 1990s—the decade of reckoning—when I thought hard about our decision.

That explains, I suppose, why I was as astounded as everyone else when I picked up my newspaper on the morning of February 23, 1998, to read Finance Minister Paul Martin declaring us on the cusp of a new golden age. (Talk about Wiarton Willie leading with his chin!) As Ottawa bureau chief of *The Globe and Mail*, I knew Martin certainly wasn't immune to hyperbole. And he had good reason to be feeling particularly heady that week. The following afternoon he would bring down his fifth budget and announce that after twenty-eight years of profligacy, the deficit monster was finally slain.

So it was in his round of pre-budget interviews that he grandiloquently declared that Canada was embarking upon a new age of prosperity that would rival that of the booming post-war years, when his father had served in the Liberal governments of Mackenzie King, Louis St. Laurent, and Lester Pearson. "I believe unequivocally that the next ten to twenty years are going to be a golden age for Canada. Everything is coming together," he enthused. He pointed to the surging high-tech economy, a well-educated workforce and the country's wealth of natural resources. "On top of that, we're getting our fiscal act together so well that there is nothing that is going to stop us."

Golden age? Preposterous, protested the pundits. Martin was mocked and ridiculed for his partisan presumption.

February 23, the day the article appeared, is Darrell's birthday. At the time, he ran the Ottawa office of the Angus Reid Group. He remembers well the avalanche of calls from incredulous television interviewers wanting to know if Martin was out of his mind. Darrell held off his celebrations to make the rounds of their studios. He sagely informed audiences that a recession is a state of mind as much as a state of the economy and that Canadians certainly weren't basking in the optimistic aura Martin described. *He* may be saying it, but Canadians aren't feeling it, Darrell declared in the sort of pithy clip that television devours.

It's easy to understand the cynicism Martin's comment engendered. His own political advisers were gnashing their teeth. Besides the fact that it was so self-serving, his declaration also seemed to crumble under the most routine scrutiny. The country was hardly out of the woods yet fiscally. Martin was booking a budget surplus, but just as it had taken years for the public to twig to the fact of deficits, so it would take a long while before it sank in that the age of being in hock up to your eyeballs was ending. The debt clock maintained by the Vancouver Board of Trade sat at a record $583,500,000,000 on the Monday morning on which Martin's sunny statement was published. Taxes continued to climb. One report said the average Canadian was paying a confiscatory 55 cents in taxes on his or her last dollar earned. Economic growth was again on the wane in the wake of the Asian financial crisis. The dollar was falling. Personal incomes had been stagnant so long in Canada that paycheques seemed to emit an odour faintly reminiscent of blue cheese. The country continued to live with the horrible hangover from the Trudeau-Mulroney years.

Moreover, in the midst of this persisting fiscal mess, globalization had pretty well demolished job security. It seemed that every other day some major company or another announced layoffs—restructuring or downsizing, they called it. Job anxiety remained high among all classes. Up to two-thirds of Canadians—an astounding figure—would tell pollsters they felt they had lost control of their economic future.

Young couples found it impossible to gain any traction. They moved from dead-end job to dead-end job, putting off house purchases and hesitating about starting their families. Kids coming out of college or university complained—wrongly but sincerely—that they stood only a slightly better chance than those who had forsaken their education altogether. Youth unemployment for 1997 remained stuck at 16.7 per cent. Behind even the educated aristocracy were massive student loan debts (swollen by government cutbacks to post-secondary institutions). Ahead lay the prospect of several years flipping burgers. No wonder so many felt like the ground beef in the middle of the bun.

Golden age? Bah! Trudeau's children were unimpressed. All they had known for a quarter-century was less and less. They weren't amused hearing some pin-striped politician's loose talk of more and more.

But, as it has turned out, Martin's analysis got a strong psychological boost just two weeks later, when Statistics Canada reported an eight-year low in the unemployment rate. And his rosy prediction has stood the test of time pretty well. The 1990s were undeniably trying times for all Canadians, as we finally began to come to grips with a quarter-century of poor economic management. We call them the Nervous Nineties—a time of deep nervousness about making ends meet and ever again achieving a better tomorrow. It seemed for a long while that songwriter Gary Nicholson was right when he wrote, "The 90s are just the 60s turned upside down."

But we're past that now and Canada finally does appear launched toward a new tomorrow. Our governments have begun to refinance critical programs, cut taxes, and pay down the debt. The year 1998 was the tipping point. Economic growth chalked in at 3.1 per cent and then built on that with nearly 5 per cent growth in 1999 and again in 2000, levels not seen since the mid-1960s.

After years of stops and starts, the economy actually began to kick into high gear in 1997, but wary Canadians had seen this movie before. They weren't quite ready to believe it yet. Over the final four years of the decade— 1997 through 2000—more than 1.5 million jobs were created. The unemployment rate sank to lows not experienced since our decline began in the early 1970s, defying the prognostications of economists that we would never see the south side of 8 per cent again. The jobless rate fell through the 8 per cent barrier, settling in through 2000 at about 6.8 per cent, still well above the Americans but a damn sight better than the miserable 9.1 per cent average of the previous quarter-century. And most of the new jobs were full-time positions, overturning forecasts that the future would offer only the ball and chain of part-time and contract work.

February 1998 was certainly an important milestone in our history—the end of the long deficit war that had sapped our spirit and distorted our will. As they prepared for their budget that month, government strategists such as Peter Donolo, the prime minister's director of communications, weren't sure if Canadians would really understand the import of the moment. In some way, it had been so well telegraphed; in others, it was so abstract. He need not have worried. On the morning after the budget, Bruce Hartley, a fellow aide, picked him up for the short drive to the office. Hartley had the radio tuned to an FM station. The disc jockey came on and announced that the next song up would be "Here Comes the Sun" by the Beatles. Why? Because it had been recorded in 1969, the last time Canada had a balanced budget. The two of them looked at each other and broke out laughing. It had been a long cold lonely winter, and it seemed that Canadians understood.

Two other developments are noteworthy in chronicling the economic thaw that began in 1998. In June, the provinces and Ottawa launched a joint program to fight child poverty, the first new social policy initiative of any significance in a generation. The year also marked the end of the steady erosion of the public part of our health care system. The private portion of national health care spending had been rising for many years—from 25 per cent to 28 per cent to 30 per cent to 32 per cent. In 1999 and 2000, the public share, which fell to 68 per cent at its low point, once again rose above 70 per cent. The Nervous Nineties were drawing to a merciful end, and with an improving economy came the opportunity to address the social priorities of Canadians.

Moreover, inflation, which had wreaked such economic havoc in the 1970s and 1980s, continued to be down and out, averaging just 1.5 per cent in the final seven years of the decade. Among the apparent miracles of the new economy, if it proves out in the long run, is the way in which it appears to drive a wedge between economic growth and inflation. Central bankers have always operated under the immutable belief that at the point in the business cycle when the productive capacity of the economy is going at full tilt and everyone who wants to work is employed, prices and wages will shoot through the roof. The job of monetary authorities is to move in and apply the brakes—hopefully gently—through interest rate hikes designed to slow the economy before it skids out of control.

But the late 1990s in the United States seemed to disprove this iron law. Every time the economy should have hit its capacity, it broke through the barrier with little or no hesitation and little or no wage and price pressure. Unemployment fell to levels economists would have considered unachievable a few years earlier. As a conservative economist of the old school, Federal Reserve chairman Alan Greenspan was as flabbergasted as anyone by this extraordinary development. But as an evidence-based professional, he began to come around to the theory that the new information and communications technologies were having a historical impact on productivity and prices. The old measures of how high was up no longer necessarily computed.

Lawrence Summers, U.S. Treasury Secretary in Bill Clinton's final term as president, explained in a speech in the spring of 2000 that the old rules had been rewritten by "the move from an economy based on the production of physical goods to an economy based on the production and application of knowledge." The application of new and better ideas and technologies are continuously increasing productive capacity, easing, though certainly not eliminating, inflationary pressures. Inflation, with all its distorting signals, remained dormant even in the latter stages of the longest U.S. expansion in the post-war era. Same in Canada, which thankfully no longer has a need for the anti-inflationary boards on which Bank of Canada governor David Dodge cut his teeth in the 1970s.

Periodic head colds notwithstanding, the long winter of economic decline has clearly come to an end in Canada. A new mood of optimism—real and measurable—has gripped the country. In a January 2000 Angus Reid poll, 81 per cent of Canadians appraised the state of the economy as good versus 18 per cent who thought it was poor (1 per cent were undecided). That compared with just 36 per cent optimism at the time Martin brought down his historic deficit-cutting budget in 1995. Just about every group imaginable felt positive. Canadians of all ages held fast to that four-to-one ratio of optimists to pessimists. Lower-income Canadians judged the economy as being in good shape by 71 per cent to 29 per cent. Even that group of Canadians who have been widely written off as the flotsam of the new economic order, those with less than a high school education, gave the thumbs up to the economy by a two-to-one margin.

Nobody has been tracking public opinion as long as the Gallup organization. As the nineties drew to a close in December 1999, Gallup asked Canadians to review the progress of the economy over the previous six months and assess the next six months. Comparisons with 1995 were again instructive. Respondents thought the economy was better rather than worse and would continue to get better rather than worse by a three-to-one margin. In 1995, the pessimists drowned out the optimists by as much as four to one.

The same pattern held true on the employment front. The job anxiety of the previous decade was also fading away. Just one in five Canadians was concerned that he or she or someone in the household might lose his or her job over the next six months. That was the lowest figure since the Angus Reid Group had begun asking that question in 1990. Nor did Canadians dismiss the economic recovery, as they might have, as a mere momentary uptick on our long downward slide. Asked for their ten-year outlook, 50 per cent said the economy would get even better; 32 per cent thought it would be about the same; and only 18 per cent thought it would get worse.

The Nortel meltdown and all the talk of doom and gloom through the early months of 2001 failed to deflate this new mood of hope. Canadians accepted the distinct possibility that yet another decade might open with a recession, but they also felt that both they and the country were better equipped to weather a downturn. Most believed the economy would either slow down or contract ever so slightly and ever so briefly. Only two out of ten expressed concern that someone in their household would lose a job. One out of seven felt his or her own personal economic situation would worsen.

Optimism alone doesn't make for a new golden age. But the end of pessimism sure doesn't hurt.

It has been a long time coming, mind you. For a century that was supposed to belong to Canada (so proclaimed by Prime Minister Wilfrid Laurier in a Canadian Club speech on January 18, 1904), the last hundred years featured more than its fair share of ups and downs. They began well enough; economic growth was fuelled early in the century by the settlement of western Canada and strong foreign demand for its wheat. The so-called wheat boom lasted until the eve of the First World War. The war itself brought with it inflation (as well as a new form of government intervention called income tax, a temporary measure we were told). Prices rose 47 per cent from 1914 to 1918. As the war ended and inflation remained, new unions demanded recognition and recompense. The Winnipeg General Strike of 1919 was merely the bloodiest confrontation in a period fraught with unprecedented labour unrest. The post-war slump drove unemployment to double digits. You may have survived the trenches, but the restoration of peace delivered little personal security.

The economy recovered nicely in the 1920s. The numbers of Canadians living in urban areas inched forward every year, finally surpassing the rural population for the first time in 1931. A nascent consumer society was emerging, built around the automobile and a burgeoning entertainment industry. But the stock market crash of 1929 chewed off the head of the Roaring Twenties. The Great Depression hit Canadians with a heretofore unseen fury.

Farmers, fishermen, miners, factory workers all suffered terrible hardships. Fifty years later, as a young reporter on the Prairies, I heard the stories of lost farms, empty stomachs, broken families, and shattered dreams. Governments throughout the world responded to the Depression by erecting import barriers designed to protect their domestic industries. These beggar-your-neighbour policies proved an unmitigated disaster that hit particularly hard at Canada, which was even then heavily reliant on world markets. Gross domestic product plunged 42 per cent between 1929 and 1933. Personal disposable income melted away by an astonishing 44 per cent. Unemployment reached 24 per cent. Canadians ate into their savings in every year between 1929 and 1936. The deep recessions of the early 1980s and 1990s pale in comparison.

It wasn't until the Second World War that the economy regained its lost ground and then continued to surge forward, fuelled initially by borrowed money to finance the war effort and then by pent-up consumer demand. The war transformed Canada, completing the process of industrialization. The farms emptied and the cities flourished. New industries built around petrochemicals, aeronautics, and the like sprang up. Great public projects, from hydroelectric plants to highways to seaways, were initiated. Governments had gained great confidence from their wartime management. Factories had assimilated the lessons of mass production and were firing on all cylinders.

An anticipated post-war slump, mirroring 1919, never materialized. The next quarter-century represented Canada's halcyon years or, to borrow a phrase, a golden era. For twenty-five years, the standard of living of the average Canadian moved ever upward, doubling in real terms. Canadians, like others, had suppressed or been forced to suppress their desires during the Second World War. Afterwards, they sought to play catch-up. The age of the consumer took off. We purchased cars, refrigerators, and new homes in the suburbs. In little more than a dozen years, we went from a country where one in three families owned their own homes to a country in which only one in three did not possess a castle to call their own.

Canadians, joined by skilled refugees from Europe, flooded into the cities to feed the growing industrial sector. New jobs and new opportunities abounded. In 1956, unemployment stood at 3.4 per cent. Inflation remained in check, averaging about 2 per cent a year through the 1950s and 1960s. Periodic slowdowns occurred, to be sure, but they marked mere bumps on the highway to greater and greater prosperity. As a society, our wartime debts shrank to a pittance and we expanded our social programs. The post-war boom financed the expansion of old-age pensions and the adoption of hospital and then medical insurance. How good was it? Consider this: In the 1950s, the average income of Canadians recorded its strongest performance of the century, growing by 43 per cent. The 1960s produced another 37 per cent jump in average earnings. The post-war boom left us twice as well off.

Then there's the last quarter-century, a period characterized by slowing productivity gains; laggard economic growth; rising unemployment; the distortions and distractions of inflation and the ephemeral high that comes from living off borrowed money. The symbolic starting gun on this sorry era—the economy was already showing signs of wear—was fired in 1973–74 with the OPEC-led energy shock that followed on the heels of the Middle East war. Oil prices quickly doubled and doubled again. Even though Canada was a major oil producer—indeed, perhaps *because* Canada was a major oil producer—we fumbled the moment. All countries stumbled and suffered, but most adjusted more quickly to changed economic circumstances because they had no alternative. Canadian policy, in contrast, consisted of wrapping ourselves in the flag of political convenience. The rest of the world learned to cope with the new reality of international oil prices; we lived with our very own domestic one. Soon we were suffering from the supposedly impossible economic phenomenon, so-called stagflation. Keynesian economics posited that high inflation and high unemployment would not occur simultaneously. The 1970s turned Keynes on his head.

The consumer price index leapt ahead 12 per cent in 1974. The Trudeau government responded slowly to the challenge. The prime minister mocked Conservative leader Robert Stanfield in the 1974 election for proposing to attack the problem through wage and price controls. "Zap. You're frozen," Trudeau taunted his opponent. He should have taken the matter more seriously and sooner. (Ultimately, he would impose wage and price controls himself, which would provide only a temporary balm.) Once an inflationary psychology takes root, it is difficult to dislodge. Bank of Canada governor Gordon Thiessen explained in a 1999 speech, "High inflation exacts a heavy toll on an economy by making the future particularly uncertain." Long-term financing becomes difficult for businesses to obtain because of the imponderable of future returns. Lenders demand higher interest rates to cover their risk of higher future inflation. Moreover, speculative investments in areas such as real estate come to be preferred over investments of the type that will generate new economic activity and jobs. Political pressures build to protect first seniors and then everybody else through indexation that will keep them whole with the shrinking purchasing power of their dollars. But the economy is too complex an organism to cover all bets, and the impact differs, in any case, from person to person. The consumer price index becomes the arbiter of everything, supplanting profitability or productivity or even social justice considerations. The economy becomes an echo chamber of discordant notes.

It would be unfair, to be sure, to isolate Canada from international trends. For the world economy in general, the next twenty years would be tough ones as the easy productivity gains of the post-war era mysteriously melted away. The old verities prove themselves lacking everywhere at the same time. But Canada earned pride of place over the next quarter-century for taking a bad situation and making it worse. In the two decades up to 1973, productivity growth—the ability of the economy to produce more economic value from an hour of work—averaged 2.3 per cent a year. In the two decades afterwards, it fell to 1.1 per cent. The United States also experienced a drop-off in this period, but not as far and not for quite so long. Canadian productivity would drop by two-thirds compared to just one-third for the United States. Even after Canada's productivity began to recover in the back half of the 1990s, it grew just 1.6 per cent a year compared with 2.8 per cent for the U.S. By 1999, the average Canadian worker's output was just 80 per cent of a U.S. worker's and was even lower in the manufacturing sector.

Productivity is an often misunderstood concept. Many Canadians equate it to job losses—to being replaced by a machine. While that may be true on an individual basis, nothing could be further from the truth for a society overall. The world is a better place thanks to increases in agricultural productivity. The process threw thousands off the farm, but they found jobs at a higher standard of living in the new urban factories and the emerging services sector. In short order, they owned refrigerators and washing machines. Women were freed from a regimen of back-breaking, time-consuming chores. A simple test should suffice to make the productivity case, the one that advisers Peter Nicholson and David Dodge used to finally bring around a resistant

Paul Martin in 1994. They showed him with charts that when productivity gains were strong in the pre-1974 period, unemployment was lower. When it fell over the next twenty and more years, unemployment in fact went up. The relationship is like that of a see-saw. Low productivity brings with it high unemployment and a reduced standard of living. High productivity, over time, delivers the opposite results. The job deck gets shuffled, disorienting many, but the number of cards in the deck increases.

In his May 2000 speech, Gordon Thiessen listed the productivity slow-down as one of the main drags on the Canadian economy over the previous twenty-five years. He admitted to not fully understanding what went wrong. "But I am prepared to assert that high inflation and the large fiscal deficits through most of the past twenty-five years were not conducive to productivity growth. They led to high interest rates and considerable uncertainty about the future—both of which discourage the investment in technology and new equipment that helps to advance productivity increases."

Whatever the complete explanation—and nobody knows precisely why productivity gains vanished in the early 1970s—we know this: In the twenty-two years between 1953 and 1975, real economic growth in Canada grew by 5 per cent or more thirteen times. But in the two following decades, it bettered the 5 per cent benchmark just three times. Growth in the 1980s declined by half—to just 2 per cent. It vanished entirely in the first half of the 1990s. From 1980 to the late 1990s, the average incomes of Canadians utterly stalled—dipping sharply then rising gradually, dipping and then working their way slowly back to the starting point.

There had been a time when Liberals, who governed Canada longer in the twentieth century than the Institutional Revolutionary Party ruled Mexico, had been considered good fiscal managers. They had presided over most of the post-war period, when the implementation of new social programs was often purposely slowed to allow the finance minister of the day to cool down inflationary pressures and pay off war bonds. The Liberals had never forgotten the admonishment in Mackenzie King's 1919 party manifesto, a visionary blueprint, that universal social programs would be made the law of the land "so far as may be practicable, having regard to Canada's financial position." They drove the country with one foot on the accelerator and the other on the brake—cautious, Canadian-style.

Paul Martin's father, the health and welfare minister through most of the 1950s, was forever whining over how the fiscal conservatism of his big-L Liberal government denied him the necessary funding for his small-l liberal initiatives. "Too frequently, an all-knowing finance bureaucracy overruled the judgements of my officials and myself," he fumed in his diary. The Liberals even postponed the introduction of national medicare from 1967, Centennial year, to 1968 because Finance Minister Mitchell Sharp fretted over the cost. Sharp's protégé at the time, Jean Chrétien, would downplay reports of a left-right rift in his cabinet three decades later by telling me that the difference between a left-wing Liberal and a right-wing Liberal was medicare in 1967 or medicare in 1968.

By the late 1970s and early 1980s, though, Liberal appetites far exceeded the stocks in the pantry. Trudeau had once warned, "If government wants to do the popular things, it will ruin the economy—real quick." But Trudeau had fallen under the sway of professional political strategists in the wake of his near-defeat in 1972. Combined with his relative inattention to matters economic and the easy confidence exuded by the advanced democracies that the state could solve all problems, his governments opted increasingly for the popular course. Liberals seemed incapable of recognizing that the smoke in the hall was caused by a fire. They just kept revving the fans, hoping to clear the choking mist.

Throughout the Western world, big government was the rage. That suited Canada fine. Trudeau's governments leaned toward expensive policy options in almost all cases, whether a subsidized made-in-Canada oil price, unemployment insurance benefits generous enough to induce unemployment, or programs aimed at equalizing wealth in all regions of the country. Public spending in Canada began to eat up a larger and larger slice of the Canadian economy. Federal spending went from 14.7 per cent of gross domestic product in 1968 to 19.4 per cent in 1984, the highest level of spending for any year in post-war Canada. Today that figure is back down to 11.4 per cent—the same level as 1949–50. The spending of all governments combined edged up from 37 per cent of the economy in 1975 to 43 per cent in the 1992 recession. A six-point swing would translate today into $60 billion more or less of government spending.

In 1974, the jobless rate stood at 5.3 per cent, higher than it had been in the 1960s, but still within a tolerable range. Then it clocked in at 6.9 per cent in 1975, 7.1 per cent in 1976, and 8.1 per cent in 1977. And these were still relatively good times. Unemployment wasn't even considered the main economic policy challenge. Inflation still held that distinction.

The onset of recession in the early 1980s handed unemployment pride of place as *the* issue. The jobless rate hit double-digit figures and held there for four long years. The bank rate peaked at 21.03 per cent in August 1981. Paul Martin would finance his purchase of Canada Steamship Lines that year with a bank loan at 22.75 per cent. Martin somehow prospered, but under the stewardship of a Bank of Canada governor, Gerald Bouey, from the tiny farming community of Trossachs, Saskatchewan, thousands of farmers and small businessmen lost their livelihoods. In 1981, a mortgage renewal would set you back 22 per cent. Car loans cost 23 per cent.

The prolonged but shallow recovery of the late 1980s made a difference. Attending international economics meetings in that decade, I would hear people who should have known better suggest that the business cycle had been repealed. Evidently, our standard of normal, of acceptable, had somehow changed. Now the unemployment rate was 8 or 9 per cent in the good years, not the terrible ones. Few people batted an eyelash. When the country was subjected to its second deep recession in a decade in 1991 and unemployment again rocketed above 11 per cent, we seemed to accept it as our lot in life.

Social scientists spoke of the troubling trend of a hollowing out of the middle class, the mortar in any modern society. The economic upheavals of the period were pummelling the great middle classes. They were too well off to qualify for government support programs, particularly given all the cutbacks and clawbacks, but not well off enough to cope with the effects of negative income growth. A lucky few with a strong education and the right occupation (like currency traders), were being thrown upward, but a far larger group, the downsized industrial workers and managers, were being pushed into quicksand. Economic statistics clearly confirmed a steady shrinkage in the proportion of Canadians with middle incomes.

The polls spoke to the psychological malaise. A 1992 survey asked Canadians the classic polling question of how they compared their standard of living to what their parents had known. One-third felt neither better off nor worse off. Among the rest, 66 per cent said they were worse off.

A measly 2 per cent felt ahead of their parents a generation earlier.

In the summer of 1993, I travelled to Pense, Saskatchewan, for a story I was researching on the state of the middle class. I joined an extended family named the Crumps for a reunion on their old homestead. Ranging in age from four months to seventy-three years, the thirty-seven descendants of Kitty and Henry Neville Compton Crump provided a rich tapestry of the middle-class mindset.

I was particularly struck by the story of Tom Crump, a forty-three-year-old health care administrator restructured out of a senior management position at Vancouver's St. Paul's Hospital the previous March. The misfortune had befallen him of becoming the first Crump to lose his job to economic circumstances since the family patriarch, his grandfather, had been briefly laid off as a government surveyor during the Great Depression. "We were getting ready to lay off fifty people and my boss came in and said it was going to be fifty-one," he told me as we sat by a fence post on a sunny Saturday afternoon.

He related his take on the way in which Canadians suppress their emotions and bottle up their anger. "You can even take their jobs away from them and tax them heavily and they don't rebel. They grumble about it, but they accept it. Nobody speaks up. I think there's an awful lot of anger, emotion, and fear locked up in Canadians because they don't express it."

That conversation came back to me four years later when I attended a luncheon at the U.S. ambassador's residence in Ottawa in the spring of 1997. The guest of honour was a visiting Indiana congressman named Lee Hamilton, one of the most thoughtful members of the U.S. House of Representatives. It was the early days of the 1997 general election, which would see the Chrétien government re-elected with a reduced majority. Unemployment in Canada still stood at 9.5 per cent, but the issue hardly registered in the campaign. Congressman Hamilton marvelled at the political acceptance of our high unemployment rate. Any politician running on such a record in the United States would be subject to a firestorm of protest, he said, and an onslaught of television attack ads. He could kiss his job goodbye. But like the proverbial guy in the chronically tight shoes, Canadians had been in discomfort for so long that they no longer seemed to realize how much it hurt.

Then there was the deficit. Somewhere along the way, Trudeau's finance ministers had forgotten another of their Keynesian principles—that deficits were fine to combat economic slumps, but budgets should be balanced over the medium term. His revolving cast of finance ministers were deficit men for all seasons. Even in the 1984 Liberal leadership race, some candidates defended deficit financing by saying it didn't really matter since we were just borrowing from one another—a statement that was both untrue and wrong-headed.

In short order, the achievement of an earlier generation of Liberals in paying down the huge debts from the Second World War while rebuilding the economy and extending the social safety net were frittered away. In its final tawdry year in office, the spit-in-the-wind Trudeau government drove the deficit to an astronomical $38.4 billion, in relative terms the largest budgetary shortfall since 1945. (In today's terms that would equal an $85-billion deficit.) The national debt had stood at 104 per cent of gross domestic product at war's end. From 1947 to 1975, Canadian governments, usually Liberal ones, brought it down to 18 per cent, mostly through the benefits of strong economic growth. The national debt totalled just $19.4 billion when Trudeau took power and $26.2 billion when the oil shock hit. At the end of the Trudeau era, a decade later, the figure had vaulted to $208 billion. Even when discounting for inflation and the size of the economy, that represented an increase of two and a half times in just ten years. During his prime ministership, government spending climbed from $11 billion a year to $87 billion— from 14.7 per cent of the economy to 19.4 per cent. The unemployment rate tripled and inflation galloped along, finally restrained only by the most severe recession since the 1930s. At the start of the Trudeau era in 1968, the so-called misery index—unemployment plus inflation—stood at 8.8 per cent. In his last term of office, it peaked at 21.9 per cent. Unemployment and inflation, previously strangers, formed a double-digit partnership. Even the proud Liberal legacy of social programs stood bent and bowed. In time, the core principle of universality would be sacrificed in an effort to calm the raging deficit seas.

The Mulroney government followed suit. On the surface, Michael Wilson, the Bay Street poster boy slotted into finance, looked grim enough to dispense the necessary medicine. He even tried—for a while. But his early efforts to limit inflation protection for old-age pensions met with stiff resistance and the politically hyper-sensitive prime minister, Brian Mulroney, repeatedly undercut his minister's efforts and forced him to back down. Wilson would forever lament that when push came to shove, he couldn't count on his prime minister the way Paul Martin would later be able to count on Jean Chrétien's support.

It is amazing to look back on the number of commentators from the period who uttered Mulroney's name, usually critically, in the same breath as the neo-conservative giants of the day, Ronald Reagan and Margaret Thatcher. Mulroney was never, as Thatcher might say, "one of us." He couldn't carry Thatcher's handbag as a reformer and he couldn't ride with Reagan as a tax cutter. One could persuasively argue that he was simply a Canadian prime minister, hemmed in by the regional complexities of the country and the natural moderation of its people. Under those circumstances, you can argue that he did his best to muddle through.

Wilson gamely hung in. As the situation grew more grave, he turned to stealth tactics to curtail social entitlements, hike taxes, shift costs onto the provinces, and squeeze spending. He brought spending back into line with revenues, but he couldn't compensate for the interest payments on the ever-rising stock of debt. The conflagration was burning out of control. He was battling a five-alarmer with his garden hose. And Bank of Canada governor John Crow's high interest rate policies acted as knots in the line, driving up costs to the country's biggest debtor. Moreover, Wilson's supposedly conservative mates on the front benches kept diverting the water supply, responding to the siren call of an oil mega-project or any other high-profile scheme that held out the promise of jobs and might therefore save their seats.

The economy neared a danger point. Under Crow, the Bank of Canada's single-mindedness in snuffing out a resurgent inflationary outbreak threatened to bring the whole house of cards down. There would be benefits down the road from the central bank's price stability policies, but the process was brutal and the rhetoric so totally devoid of empathy that Canadians came to conclude that their economic stewards simply didn't give a damn about their welfare.

Crow's high interest policies would ultimately be held responsible by many commentators for exacerbating the depth and length of the early 1990s recession. Some even called it a "made-in-Canada" recession. The charge is not without an element of truth, but it is equally true that the severity of the recession was the inevitable outcome of a coddled country belatedly trying to cope with new economic realities afoot in the world. The United States had adjusted throughout the 1980s—the era of the rust belt. By and large, Canada resisted until the pressure became unbearable.

The recession in the early 1990s finally exposed the shilly-shallying passing for economic toughness in Ottawa. In 1989, the combined deficits of the provincial and federal governments clocked in at $33 billion. Within three years, the figure had doubled to $66 billion. In their last year in office, the Tories managed to even top the single-year Liberal deficit record from 1984–85, leaving behind federal credit cards maxed out by the sum of more than $42 billion. Despite the tax increases and program cuts, the accumulated national debt—Ottawa and the provinces combined—stood at more than $700 billion and counting. Not only did we have to pay the interest on that debt (40 per cent of it in the hands of foreign bondholders) but also lenders demanded a risk premium in the form of higher than necessary rates. The jobs picture was just as bad. Some 1.6 million Canadians were on the unemployment rolls, and that didn't count those who had given up looking or had fallen into provincial welfare programs. Government policy at least proved effective in wrestling inflation to the ground, to borrow another memorable phrase from Pierre Trudeau that he failed to deliver on. But not without considerable collateral damage.

In October 1992, Canadians voted down Mulroney's Charlottetown constitutional accord, thumbing their noses at the legions of political and economic elites who campaigned for it. The agreement had enough faults on its own, but it also presented the first real opportunity to register a wider protest. Canadians were simply acting out, the commentators said. Well, yeah. Like Tom Crump, they had been biting their tongues til they bled; now they had a chance to give some expression to their frustration over the failure of the economy and the failure of government. They were depressed, and with good reason. Governments had let them down for two decades. My wife, Janice, and I once again considered Italian language courses.

To be fair, Mulroney, ably assisted again by Wilson, also tasted victory in office. For more than a century, natural resource-rich Canada had prospered under the philosophical and policy precepts of Sir John A. Macdonald's National Policy. We used tariffs and other barriers to protect our industries, especially in central Canada. The concept was to fight the natural north-south gravitational pull of a continental economy and instead impose an east-west polarity in building the country. Western Canada, with its resource-based relationship to world markets, had always displayed a strong free trade streak, but lacked the political muscle to overcome the vested manufacturing interests in central Canada. Twice in the century, the Liberal party had either advocated or secretly negotiated to open up the economy. In 1911, Canadians were not ready and defeated Laurier's government. In the late 1940s, Mackenzie King got cold feet and never even disclosed his handiwork. In the final months of the Trudeau government, the free trade light flickered again. Talks with the United States were initiated in specific sectors and the government appointed a Royal Commission to examine our economic prospects. Its chairman, Donald Macdonald, a former Trudeau cabinet minister who had moved in the course of fifteen years from the left of the political spectrum to the right, would provide the intellectual spark that eventually brought on free trade. But by that time the Tories were in power.

By the late twentieth century, the thinking behind the National Policy was definitely showing its age. The world economy was reorganizing itself in the wake of a transportation and telecommunications revolution that had shrunk the globe and turned capital into a highly mobile commodity. National borders mattered less and less to large international corporations. Competition among nations became more cutthroat than ever, but Canada's manufacturers, sheltered from the pressures to keep pace with the best in the world, lacked the conditioning for big league play. As a country, we were being relegated to second-string status. We had always found refuge from any economic storm in the safe harbour of our natural resources bounty. But commodity prices were in a long-term decline as new deposits came on stream in the developing world and the world economy began to value human resources over natural resources. An uncompetitive industrial sector, the decline in commodity prices, and our burgeoning foreign debt left Canada with a huge balance of payments headache.

Moreover, the multinationals of old were reinventing themselves as global corporations. They no longer depended on carbon-copy subsidiaries in all major markets essentially spewing out the same products with the same processes. In the emerging global economy, a plant in Ontario now competed with a plant in Alabama or Lombardy or Surrey for a global mandate over a product line for all markets. Competition existed everywhere, even within companies. When General Motors was looking to restructure in the early 1980s, each plant had to make the case internally as to why it deserved to survive. The game no longer just pitted Canada against the United States, but Flint, Michigan, against St. Catharines, Ontario.

These more specialized industrial approaches implied even greater global investment and more international trade. A National Policy predicated on favouring domestic economic relations over international ones simply wasn't sustainable in the new global order. In December 1988, the Mulroney government finally ratified its hard-fought free trade agreement with the United States after an election campaign fought for the soul of the nation. The appeal for Canadians to take a leap of faith into the future prevailed, albeit with a huge helping hand from our first-past-the-post electoral system. It was free trade by a TKO.

With the free trade agreement, it was left ironically to a Conservative prime minister to drive a stake through the National Policy creation of his own political party. In so doing, Mulroney reversed his own earlier anti-free-trade stance. Like Donald Macdonald, he showed his flexibility in facing up to the new global realities. He recognized the transformation would be painful and promised to help Canadians cope with the inevitable adjustments. The 1990s recession that quickly followed was aggravated by that adjustment process as industrial advantage and disadvantage shifted from sector to sector. Predictably, the new realities of global business caught up with the old ways of doing things, but at the worst possible point in the economic cycle. Unfortunately, our governments were so fiscally ravaged by then that they found themselves incapable of delivering on their promise of adjustment assistance. Canadians were left to fend for themselves. Resentful, they defeated the Mulroney/Campbell government and installed as prime minister Jean Chrétien, who campaigned on a promise to address their economic anxieties.

Chrétien talked up his main electoral planks of "jobs and growth," but was soon consumed by the spreading forest fire of the deficit. What John Crow did to defeat inflation, Chrétien's finance minister, Paul Martin, would finally do for the deficit in his crusading 1995 budget. Except Martin, unlike Crow, was a politician. He wanted to get re-elected. He even aspired to greater things. So he worked hard to exude empathy and to bring ordinary

Canadians on board with his anti-deficit campaign. (By and large, they had come to the same conclusions earlier than he, which made an otherwise effective public relations campaign that much easier.) He was a Man with a Plan. Once Canadians accepted that, they invested him with tremendous credibility. At first they were dubious about the whole enterprise, at least so far as its prospects of success were concerned. In the months after the deficit-busting budget of that year, just 2 per cent of Canadians believed the deficit problem would be solved by 2000.

The listing ship of state had begun to take corrective action. But public opinion remained under water. The Nervous Nineties would continue to take their toll on individual Canadians with repeated cuts to programs and regular increases in taxes. One study showed that the average family's tax bill had risen 40 per cent—about $3,000 a year—between 1984 and 1994. Canadians felt as if they lived under the cloud of relentless threats to their economic security and well-being. Would they survive the economic restructuring? Would they qualify for the rapidly shrinking unemployment insurance program? Would the Canada Pension Plan go broke before they could collect? Would their take-home pay ever rise again?

Mid-decade marked the low-water mark. Ottawa and the provinces had finally got serious about their deficits and were slashing programs left, right, and centre. Taxpayers were lucky to be getting 70 cents of services back on their dollar. The rest was going to cover the interest costs on past overspending. In fact, interest payments on debt had shouldered aside such priorities as health and education as Canada's biggest public spending category. The recessionary gloom of the earlier part of the decade had never lifted. The Mexican financial crisis in December 1994 threatened, along with the effects of the February 1995 budget, to drive us back into a recession that only the economists, with their bloodless technical charts, had ever credited with officially having ended.

Job creation couldn't keep up with population growth. Martin's department had published an economic blueprint in late 1994, his policy bible, which stated in no uncertain terms that the floor for unemployment in Canada, the so-called NAIRU (Non-Accelerating Inflationary Rate of Unemployment) at which any more jobs created would simply drive up inflation and stall the economy, stood at 8 per cent. Officially, then, an 8 per cent unemployment rate was considered as low as it could safely go. The floor. Not a happy thought. Canada seemed condemned to a future as the land of perpetual high unemployment. One analysis showed that if Canada, in 1996, had been able to employ the same percentage of its population as the United States 1 million more people would have had jobs. This was the human toll from a sick economy.

At the end of 1995, veteran pollster Allan Gregg published his annual year-end pulse-taking in *Maclean's* magazine. The noxious combination of continued economic malaise and the near-miss in the Quebec referendum on October 30 produced "the blackest polling results" he had encountered in twenty years of measuring public opinion. Almost 90 per cent expected unemployment insurance and welfare to be less generous or eliminated entirely within five years. A similar number thought that young Canadians would find it even harder to secure meaningful work. About 80 per cent expected to see the collapse of the Canada Pension Plan. More than 60 per cent felt universal health care would bite the dust.

One of the *Maclean's* writers turned to Leonard Cohen's lyrics to express the mood: "I have seen the future, brother. It is murder."

How hard were the times? Consider this as a bellwether: From 1986 to 1996, the percentage of twenty-five- to thirty-four-year-olds living at home shot up from 23 per cent of females and 28 per cent of males to 33 per cent of females and 40 per cent of males. Young Canadians weren't making it on their own. They couldn't find traction in the poor economy.

The Angus Reid Group went into the field in the opening months of 1996 with a massive survey of 3,600 Canadians. The mood remained sour. Four in ten still worried about losing their jobs. A full 72 per cent said the federal government had done a poor or very poor job of meeting its commitment to create jobs. (They didn't think all that much either of Ottawa's record on economic management, national unity, or social programs.) As many Canadians felt the economy would worsen over the next year as believed it would improve, and nobody on the positive side of the ledger thought it would improve much. A majority said Canada had either "become weaker" or was in "serious trouble" in the aftermath of the October 1995 Quebec referendum. The discourse in Canada was so negative that among the questions that pollsters thought it reasonable to ask was whether military force should be used to keep Quebec in Canada. (Ninety per cent in Quebec and 84 per cent in the rest of Canada responded with a resounding no!)

Canadians still felt the great middle class was taking it on the chin. By 62 per cent to 10 per cent, they thought the middle class was worse off rather than better off than ten years earlier. Fifty-six per cent said the size of the middle class was shrinking, 17 per cent growing, and 27 per cent remaining the same. And these numbers held steady for all income groups. "Canadians no longer define middle class by the opportunity it presents, but the burdens it carries: high taxation, fear of the future and a feeling of being overwhelmed by events," the polling firm concluded.

This represented the fertile ground that an American economic theoretician named Jeremy Rifkin tilled. Rifkin's 1995 book, *The End of Work*, was gaining a following in Canada. Its apocalyptic vision was emblematic of the period. Federal cabinet ministers, who had put together a special jobs committee in late 1995 to study what they considered their number one economic vulnerability, chatted up the tome. In Ottawa, cabinet ministers are generally too busy to actually read books. Others tend to read for them and then summarize the books in what are called decks, essentially a stack of overhead transparencies. The ad hoc cabinet committee on jobs was shown a deck on *The End of Work*. Paul Martin actually read the book, which irritated his departmental advisers who thought it poppycock.

Rifkin's argument, boiled down, was that technology was killing jobs. Soon there would be no work left. Robotics had already, in his view, destroyed blue-collar manufacturing jobs. Now more advanced computers were cutting a swath through white-collar service jobs. Technology had chased workers from the farms to the factories and from the factories to the office. Now they had nowhere else to go. He wanted governments to underwrite a massive program to employ all these surplus workers in the so-called third (or voluntary) sector.

Some, like David Dodge, then deputy minister of finance and now governor of the Bank of Canada, dismissed Rifkin as an economic alarmist, someone who in an earlier age would have raged against "robotic horses" (tractors) and their devastating impact on farm jobs. Dodge was a specialist in labour markets. As a former professor, he tended to the long view. History proved, he said, that technological advances, after a few bumps and hiccups, actually created more jobs than they destroyed. Unfortunately, the destruction in what the great Austrian economist Joseph Schumpeter called creative destruction tended to occur first. And it was far more visible than the creation that followed. Dying industries get a lot of ink. Vested interests are at play. The buggy whip manufacturers have an industry association. So do the shipbuilders. They contribute to political campaigns. They operate plants the size of football fields. Their workforces are unionized. The unions contribute to political campaigns and organize marches when their membership is under threat. Journalists cover the press conferences of both the employers and employees.

Meanwhile, start-ups are silent. They work out of the back of garages, with two, then six, then twenty employees—none of them public relations specialists. That's how Apple, Hewlett-Packard, and Microsoft started in the United States. And Magna International in Canada. Although they worked out of scattered barns, the new auto manufacturers of the turn of the century, not the powerful buggy whip lobby, represented the future. Dodge thought the Rifkin thesis populist claptrap that would soon collapse under the weight of developments. However, the prevailing mood of pessimism was not conducive to arguing anything of the sort. In 1995, nobody was ready.

In early 1996, editors at *The Globe and Mail* asked me to write the opening article in a series on jobs. The economy was at least a year into steady positive growth but you wouldn't know it from speaking to ordinary Canadians. Eighty-two per cent of them told Environics Research that the country remained in recession.

I had read both the Rifkin book and an intriguing magazine piece by business guru Peter Drucker called "The Age of Social Transformation," in which he put forth arguments similar to Dodge's. Rifkin and Drucker agreed on one thing: The job market was being convulsed by revolutionary technological changes and the intensification of global competition. But from that common platform, their prognoses diverged sharply. Rifkin was essentially making the case for the probable losers in economic change; Drucker for the potential winners, those with marketable skills and entrepreneurial abilities.

I decided to test their competing theses by visiting an area in the midst of economic change. I settled on a strip along Eglinton Avenue East in Toronto's Scarborough suburb known as the Golden Mile. The industrial corridor had provided a good middle-class living to thousands of blue-collar workers in the decades after the Second World War. It was bounded on one end by a ball-bearing manufacturing facility and on the other by a General Electric factory and, across the street, a General Motors van plant.

The GM plant was particularly noteworthy. It had served for two generations as the biggest employer in the area before the announcement by General Motors two years earlier that it intended to close down in Scarborough. After lengthy decommissioning work, the facility now lay gutted and recently levelled. In fact, one of the local members of Parliament, Derek Lee, told me how he had been driving along Eglinton East a few weeks earlier when he suddenly realized the plant had vanished. "I looked and it shocked me," he related. "There were just these two mounds of dirt. It was like they had torn the heart out of the Golden Mile."

It wasn't hard to find plenty of people to testify to the decline of a once thriving local economy. Down at the Canadian Auto Workers clubhouse, I met a sad, fifty-one-year-old former GM worker named Craig Clements. He had worked for sixteen years on the assembly line, the last eleven on the Golden Mile, earning a good union wage. Initially thinking he and his family would join relatives in the United States, he opted for a buyout rather than a place near the head of the queue for jobs at GM plants in Oshawa or London. But the move fell through, and now he was among the ranks of the long-term unemployed, picking up odd jobs here and there, falling onto welfare at times.

Clements had six kids, five of them still at home. Three were nearing the end of high school and wanted to go on to college or university. He felt totally defeated. The tension of how to provide for his family was obviously eating away at him. I asked him what he thought the future held.

"Nothing," he said, barely containing his bitterness. "I see a very bleak outlook, really." I described him in the article as the sad face of the displaced aristocracy of labour.

The plight of Craig Clements was moving, but as always in life there was another side to the Golden Mile story. Even amid the destruction, one could discern the stirrings of re-creation. Across the street from the old GM site, in the building that used to churn out GE appliances, a wholesale food terminal catering to the restaurant industry bustled with activity. And a block and a half east, in the old ball-bearing plant, the Bank of Nova Scotia had established a technology and customer service centre that had replaced GM as the area's largest employer.

As Darrell and I were preparing this book, I called Derek Lee. He told me he had been to the barbershop that morning and the discussion had turned to the new Wal-Mart store on the old GM site and all the other big-box retailers along the Golden Mile. "Out of the ashes rises the phoenix," he said. "It's consumer oriented now. It's moved away from manufacturing, but it's still churning out dollars." Lee had just come through an election campaign and said that with one or two exceptions, nobody had raised job concerns over thirty-six days of door knocking.

I tried to track down Craig Clements, but failed to find him. I can only hope he joined the country in its recovery.

It took until early 1998—about the time Martin balanced the budget and predicted a new golden era—before Canadians finally began accepting that the national nightmare was over. Voting with their pocketbooks, they began returning to the shops and the car lots throughout 1997. Consumer sales, capped by a strong Christmas season, recorded their strongest growth in a dozen years. Anxieties about jobs fell 17 percentage points (from 49 to 32) between the summers of 1997 and 1998. The misery index—unemployment plus inflation—fell below 10 per cent for the first time since 1971. The number of Canadians telling Ekos Research that they felt they had lost all control over their lives peaked at 50 per cent in 1997 before beginning a gradual but steady downward decline. By a three-to-one margin, respondents judged the economy better rather than worse than five years earlier.

Concern about the deficit also declined significantly. But their near-death fiscal experience has not been lost on Canadians. They have become more conservative in their view of government intervention. Back in the 1980s recession, Canadians still looked to governments to insulate them from economic downturns. A 1984 report by Liberal pollster Martin Goldfarb concluded that "any attempt by government to deal with the deficit by curbing social welfare spending will not be well received by the public."

By the 1990s, expectations of government had altered considerably. The heroic attempt by Bob Rae's Ontario government to spend its way out of recession—in ignorance of the hard lessons learned a decade earlier by France's Socialists—succeeded only in digging the province into a $10 billion deficit hole and eventually destroying the NDP as a serious force. Canadians had become highly dubious of government rescue missions.

The Crump family had told me as much out in Pense, Saskatchewan. Nearly to a person, they spoke of the need to confront our economic problems head-on. They accepted that the deficit had to be wrestled down even if it meant the erosion of their standard of living. Shaken as they were by their experiences, Canadians from coast to coast told their politicians to stick with the cod-liver oil regimen. By more than a three to one margin, they felt the country would emerge stronger for it.

An international survey taken in 1996 found deficit-weary Canadians near the top of the heap in backing cuts to government spending. Eight out of ten favoured cuts versus 8 per cent who were opposed and 11 per cent neither for nor against. Canadians were also among the least receptive to providing support for declining industries in order to protect jobs. Thirty-nine per cent of respondents put their thumbs down versus 36 per cent in favour of such actions. That compared with half of Americans supportive of subsidizing declining industries and 65 per cent of West Germans.

An Angus Reid poll for *The Globe and Mail* in late 1997 captured this new fiscal conservative mood well. A solid majority of Canadians expressed skepticism at the government using its looming surplus to embark on new national projects such as providing jobs for young people or reducing child poverty. They suspected a lot of money would be spent with little accomplished. In the western provinces, this mistrust of government ran two-to-one.

When they were asked whether they would direct surpluses toward new spending, tax cuts, or debt repayment, the most conservative option of paying down the debt won out with 47 per cent. Tax cuts came next at 37 per cent and spending last at 13 per cent. Other pollsters found more support for spending when they specifically mentioned health care and education, both burgeoning public priorities in the post-deficit firmament. But the underlying message remained the same: Canadians wanted governments to proceed with caution on spending and to pay special attention to paying down the debts accumulated during the reckoning years. They tended toward the homespun metaphor of using a windfall to pay down the mortgage, thus reducing the chances of having to suffer the pains of economic retrenchment ever again.

The results were not unambiguous. Canadians drew no joy from their war on the deficit, only lessons. When prompted, 55 per cent said the federal government had cut too deeply, a number that grew larger among those living east of the Ottawa River and those with low incomes (groups that had felt the brunt of the pain). Still, even though three out of four Atlantic Canadians said the Liberals had cut too deeply, 54 per cent thought they would be better off as a result.

By 1999, now accustomed to surpluses and anxious over the state of medicare, Canadians nevertheless again evinced a conservative mood in a pre-budget poll for *The Globe and Mail*. Federal spending as a percentage of the economy had been hacked back to early 1950s levels. But only 14 per cent wanted the government to grow again versus 36 per cent who thought it should continue to shrink. Half thought it had probably reached the right size.

Debt reduction still came first with 39 per cent support, followed by tax cuts at 33 per cent. New spending on programs won favour with just 24 per cent of respondents. When asked about health care spending specifically, Canadians withdrew their objections to loosening the belt. But they expressed extreme wariness of granting the government much licence. "Their sense," Darrell told the *Globe*, "is that governments have become a bit out of control in the past. Their sense is that we do have an obligation to pay down some debt, and their sense is that they are not necessarily prepared, except in very specific circumstances, to see governments get all that active on the spending side." In fact, 62 per cent, reflecting on the previous few years, supported legislation making it illegal for future governments to record a deficit.

The Liberals understood there was no going back. The economic approach of the previous generation was thoroughly discredited. Canadians, having lived through rising taxes, social program cuts, and reduced economic security, had adopted an attitude toward deficits akin to—albeit probably milder than—the German aversion to inflation. Germany's two brushes in this century with hyperinflation have built a hard monetary mentality right into that country's political culture. In Canada, a national government that messes up our finances again invites swift public retribution.

From his perch in finance, Martin understood the danger well. He told associates he could never take the chance of slipping into deficit again. In a 1999 interview with *Policy Options* magazine, Martin's deputy minister, Scott

Clark, recounted how Martin had once challenged him when the debt-to-GDP ratio turned out, for technical reasons, higher than the department had publicly projected.

"Well, minister, we are talking about decimal points here on the debt-to-GDP ratio," Clark pointed out.

"I don't care," Martin replied. "I can never be wrong."

He's right. Canadians won't tolerate it.

They won't tolerate it because the poor performance of the past twenty-five years was no mere abstraction for Canadians. It didn't exist only at a governmental level. They lived the poor performance themselves.

They watched with bemusement at they fell further and further behind their American cousins, uncles and aunts, brothers and sisters. They watched as middle-class Americans invaded our summer holiday spots, chortling at the laughably low prices when translated into Yankee bucks. The American Century closed with the bang of an all-American decade. The incomes of Canadians lost a percentage point to the Americans in every year of the 1990s. At decade's end, the gap in real per capita income for each man, woman, and child between us and them stood at an impressive and depressing $9,000.

A report by Standard and Poor's DRI Canada showed that our disposable incomes, which had been 20 per cent above the average for all industrial countries in 1989, fell to just average in 1998. The OECD ranked our economy the twenty-fourth best performer out of its twenty-five member countries for the period 1988 to 1998. And it warned that unless we got productivity up, we were going to slip some more. Another study, this one by economist Pierre Fortin, pinpointed 1980 as the high-water mark for Canadian disposable income in relation to the United States. By 1998, Fortin calculated, the average Canadian could purchase just two-thirds as much as the average American, a difference that translated into a $6,000 (Canadian) shortfall for every man, woman, and child or $24,000 for a family of four.

A 2001 analysis by Andrew Sharpe, head of the Ottawa-based Centre for the Study of Living Standards, found that from 1989 to 2000 the personal income of the average Canadian fell from 87 per cent of American levels to 78 per cent. After-tax income fell from 79 per cent to 70 per cent, with the lion's share of ground lost between 1989 and 1996.

The worst cut of all: Even those Canadians in the richest provinces enjoyed less disposable income than Americans in the poorest states. A rank order of the fifty states and ten provinces found the Canadian jurisdictions holding down positions fifty-one to sixty. And it wasn't even close. "Alberta's real per-capita disposable income," the report stated, "is 10 per cent below that in Mississippi, the poorest U.S. state." Ouch!

The 1990s were, in the phrase of former Royal Bank of Canada chief economist and now Liberal MP John McCallum, a *decadus horribilis* (with apologies to the Queen's *annus horribilis*.) The 1980s, despite their reputation as fat years, were little better. Both decades featured long periods of economic growth after deep and protracted recessions. But the recessions were long enough and sharp enough to wipe out the income gains from the growth periods.

My first full year in the labour force was 1980. Average income in Canada, adjusted for inflation, came in at $26,670 in that year. Of that, $4,077 went to cover personal income tax payments, according to Statistics Canada. In 1997—nearly a generation later—average income had fallen back to $26,042 and income taxes now gobbled up $5,187. Seventeen years without income growth even outstrips the Dirty Thirties for a prolonged period on the economic treadmill.

These numbers are doubly revealing. Most commentators assume that the lack of income growth in the 1980s and 1990s can be traced directly to higher taxes. In fact, even without the tax hikes, Canadian incomes were stagnant. Between 1980 and 1997, average pre-tax income declined by 2 per cent while the average income tax burden increased by 27 per cent. The disposable incomes of Canadians therefore moved backwards by nearly 8 per cent. Canadians have a lot of lost ground to make up.

How did they manage? At least part of the answer can be found in the national savings rate and in credit card debt. We managed by squeezing our savings from 1982 onward and particularly in the 1990s. And we did it by running up our credit cards. Canadians sucked it in while governments got their act together. They won't countenance going through that again.

In early 2001, I caught up with Tom Crump, whom I had met on his grandfather's Saskatchewan homestead eight years earlier. He was living in Cloverdale, British Columbia, a suburb outside Vancouver. He cheerily recalled sitting together on the grass as we discussed his unhappy situation. The 1990s had been a tough time for him, but he had come through in great shape. When we'd last spoken, he had told me of his determination never to become beholden to a single employer again. "Our game plan," he had explained, "is to have multiple sources of mini-income."

He and his wife, Sue, had followed through by starting a couple of small businesses and by peddling his health administration expertise as a consultant. One of the ventures almost dragged them into bankruptcy, but eventually they regained their feet. Today, Tom has three sources of income. He runs a publicly funded seniors' home down the street from his home in Cloverdale. He and a couple of partners also own a private nursing home in Nanaimo. Finally, they own a software company that provides patient, payroll, human resources, and other record-keeping for health care facilities. At the start of the year, it employed about sixty people, including Sue.

He's optimistic for his two boys, aged seventeen and fourteen. The older one is taking a special two-year course in his high school that was put in place by Cisco Systems, the giant technology manufacturing company. Tom feels the skills the son is acquiring in the new economy will produce great opportunities. The Internet is already a big part of his own business.

He set out very purposefully to insulate himself and his family from the kind of external shock that brought them down in the 1990s. And he's succeeded. In less than ten years, he's gone from dependence to independence.

"Losing my job at the mid-point in my career was a shock that changed me mentally and emotionally," he says. "All of us grew up with great expectations that if you work hard, you will be rewarded. In the eighties and nineties that's not what happened." Back then, he recounts, moving upward in the organization—what he calls the status track—mattered most to him. Today, he's more concerned with controlling his destiny and enjoying the quality of his life. He walks to work and can see the boys during the day.

For Tom Crump and millions of others, the Nervous Nineties have come to a merciful end. But like a tornado that burns itself out, the damage doesn't get cleaned up overnight. In some cases, the scars last a lifetime. Even more than in 1993, Crump feels Canadians are too passive in accepting mediocre results from their governments. He's happy the economy has improved, but he shakes his head at all the lost opportunity. The United States enjoyed ten years of unprecedented growth, and what do we have to show for the 1990s, he sighs.

Others have computed the cost of our lost decade. The Business Council on National Issues reported in 1999 that our cumulative gain in real GDP per capita (that's the basic measure of our standard of living) came in at one-third that of the French between 1988 and 1998, one-fourth that of Americans, and an astonishing one-eighteenth that of the Irish, who nearly doubled their standard of living in the same decade ours stood still. Roger Martin, the dean of the Rotman School of Management at the University of Toronto and co-author with Harvard's Michael Porter of a 1991 report that warned of Canada's decline, undertook some of his own calculations. In 1991, he noted, Canada slipped to fifth place in the world in gross domestic product per capita after twenty years in third. We have vacillated ever since between fifth and seventh. "Had we simply maintained our standing at third, the average Canadian family of four would have had $13,000 more, or about $650 a month after tax in 1998."

In September 1989, before Canadians came to understand they were living on borrowed money and borrowed time, 74 per cent of them said they were better off financially than their parents had been at the same stage of life. This is a fairly standard expectation in a country like Canada—that a successor generation would enjoy a higher standard of living than the previous generation. It is what middle-class mobility is all about. But by October 1992—with the recession in full bloom and the country in gridlock over the Charlottetown accord—only 56 per cent considered themselves better off, 18 per cent the same, and 24 per cent actually worse off than their parents. The slide continued as the nineties went on: 47 per cent saying they were better off in November 1995; 44 per cent in July 1998. Canadians were nearly evenly divided between those who considered themselves better off than their parents and those who considered themselves worse off. That is an amazing attitudinal finding—the feeling of having made no progress over an entire generation. It also demonstrates a keen sense of reality.

Only in mid-2000 did we begin to see the first pickup, with 48 per cent saying they were better off and 33 per cent worse off. The improvement demonstrated that after years of tightening our belts, confidence, from a cumulative financial perspective, had tipped back in a more positive direction.

But the results also threw light on the extent of the damage done. Amid a profound economic recovery, just a minority of Canadians could still find comfort in this most profound of middle-class measures. Their incomes had returned to 1989 levels, but their perceptions of their relative standard of living still lagged well behind. Only older Canadians, the children of Depression-era parents, could resoundingly say they were better off than their parents (75 per cent to 12 per cent). Middle-aged Canadians (at 45 per cent to 34 per cent) had still not regained the ground lost relative to their post-war parents. Among younger Canadians, many of them the children of early boomers, just 29 per cent thought themselves better off than their parents when they had been young versus 50 per cent who considered themselves worse off. That represents a considerable amount of lost mobility. The return of growth was real. The new optimism was real. But so was the feeling of loss. We asked Canadians in the summer of 2000 how easy it was to make ends meets compared to five years earlier. Fifty per cent felt it was harder and only 17 per cent found it easier. Canadians are still not fully recovered from two decades of income stagnation, higher taxes, and reductions in government services.

Canadians emerged from the Nervous Nineties obviously chagrined about the time wasted and opportunity lost, but at least ready, once again, to embrace a future of promise. In some countries, there may have been a revolution. In France, truckers would have organized a blockade and farmers would have burned carcasses outside the National Assembly. In Canada, a nation accustomed to bad weather, we assessed the severity of the storm, headed for shelter, and hunkered down until spring beckoned. And when the weather did begin to warm, what did this nation of patient investors tell pollsters would be their top spending priority in 2000: putting money into their RRSPs.

As with Tom Crump, the experience of the twenty-five lean years has cured Canadians of dependence and fear. They are battle hardened and prepared to take on the world rather than hide behind the skirts of the state. Their attitudes toward free trade and globalization, as you will see in the next chapter, have turned on a dime. The most talented Canadians feel they can run with anyone else's best and brightest; indeed, they relish the opportunity.

At the end of 1999, Allan Gregg wrote in the same *Maclean's* space that had resounded with fear and pessimism just four years earlier about a confident nation at ease with its inner self: "The trauma of recession shook us out of our complacency. Our loss of faith in traditional leaders and authority nudged us towards greater self-reliance. The failure of the tried-and-true forced us to entertain new approaches and solutions. Looking into the abyss of national disintegration caused us to appreciate all that we had to lose."

CHAPTER 2

GLOBALIZATION IS US

A decade ago, while I was racing around Europe trying to understand the chain of events set off by the fall of the Berlin Wall, Darrell was considering the implications of the evolving new world order on behalf of the Progressive Conservative government of the day. Before joining the Angus Reid Group in 1990, Darrell served in the dual capacity as director of public opinion research for the PC party and for the Prime Minister's Office. He made lifelong friends and learned lifelong lessons.

These were heady days for a twenty-eight-year-old newly minted Ph.D. graduate. For fourteen months, he probed the deep-seated feelings of Canadians about their political leadership and the issues that mattered to them. One of Darrell's key mentors in this period was Michael Wilson, the

Tory's major-domo economics minister. Darrell considers Wilson one of the least understood politicians he has ever encountered. His patrician bearing and old-fashioned sense of noblesse oblige often set him apart from his more thrusting colleagues. He was studious and level-headed. The constant ego-stroking demanded by many politicians was decidedly not part of the Wilson character. While the public viewed him as having the mien of an accountant or funeral director, Darrell found him personally engaging and even funny in private.

Well, sometimes funny. Then there was the night he put Darrell on the spot. After joining Angus Reid in November 1990, Darrell continued to conduct research for Wilson. In April 1991, Wilson was shuffled out of finance and given a new super-ministry that combined both the Industry Canada and international trade portfolios. His marching orders, pretty tough ones, were to demonstrate to Canadians that the government wasn't totally preoccupied with constitutional issues (it was) and to put the infant free trade agreement into a context that would be acceptable to the public. To this end, Wilson launched the so-called Prosperity Initiative, which featured a major offensive to improve Canadian competitiveness, including an expansion of the Canada–U.S. free trade agreement into the North American Free Trade Agreement.

Darrell's research told an ugly story: Canadians were in no mood to listen to Michael Wilson, particularly when it came to NAFTA. They already felt sold down the river by the first free trade agreement (support for it, as you will see in this chapter, had been steadily falling), and they were unprepared to give a fair hearing to allegedly new and improved versions.

One evening in the summer of 1991, Wilson convened a meeting of advisers in the imposing Lester B. Pearson building on Sussex Drive, home of the Department of External Affairs, where he maintained an office among the diplomatic corps. About a dozen of his most trusted internal and external political advisers were arrayed around the table in the minister's personal dining room. Gloved waiters in black uniforms served dinner with heavy silver implements. Wilson sat at the head of the table. Darrell was to his immediate right. As the others ate, Darrell presented the results of the latest batch of NAFTA polling and analyzed how the government was faring in getting across its message. Now pollsters and journalists tend to be a similar breed, which is how, I suppose, Darrell and I ever got together on this book. We tend to be life's observers, not its doers. We can tell you what's wrong with something till the cows come home. But we wouldn't think of ever getting our hands dirty milking one of those cows.

So it was that Darrell got rather passionate in his critique of the government's salesmanship on NAFTA. He ranted on for a couple of minutes, oblivious to the effect he was having on the reddening Wilson. Finally, after listening long enough to this stream of critical consciousness, the normally dour minister turned to the young critic in his midst, crooked his finger, and intoned in a mocking voice, "Okay, smart-ass, do *you* have any better ideas?"

The room fell silent, save for the purr of the overhead projector and the quickened beat of Darrell's heart. Everyone looked at the smart-ass standing in the shadow. Mortified, the shrunken soothsayer mumbled some bromide or other. The answers, back then, weren't any more apparent to him than to anyone else. But now, with the benefit of a decade's maturity and, more to the point, hindsight, he knows precisely what he should have responded. "Sit tight. Canadians are going to completely change their mind on this issue. By the turn of the century, they will embrace free trade. They will, in the immortal words of Dr. Strangelove, learn to stop worrying and love the (globalization) bomb."

Nothing, but nothing, has shifted so dramatically in the past decade in public opinion as the attitudes of Canadians toward free trade and, by extension, toward the cluster of developments we have come to call globalization. It has been a ten-year journey from fear to respect, from loathing to acceptance. In the process, we have transformed ourselves as a country from the timid little Canadians of old into a new breed of voyageurs willing to test the fast waters of the new global economy. Beginning with the famous free trade election of 1988—which sounded the death knell of Macdonald's century-old National Policy—we have made our peace with the forces of globalization. We are not unencumbered by complaints and criticisms of the new world order, particularly its paucity of democratic accountability and its indifference to the have-nots it sows. But for the mainstream of the country—the 70 per cent or so of Canadians making a go of it in the globalized world—these represent concerns with the excesses or failures of a system we otherwise accept, even embrace. Only a small number among us think any more that they can keep their heads in the sand and hope to avoid the ugly truth that globalization is here to stay.

Canadians took their tentative first steps on this long and winding road in the second half of the 1980s after the Mulroney government thrust the bastard free trade issue—born without electoral parentage—onto the national agenda. In the opening rounds in 1987, the country was pretty well evenly divided in its opposition and support for free trade. By the time of the free trade election a year later, though, opposition had grown to 54 per cent versus 35 per cent support. These figures moved up and down over the next year as Canadians watched television ads of the border being erased and were subjected to the give-and-take of the free trade election. But through it all public opinion reflected a deep vein of skepticism.

Support for free trade would fall into the deep freeze with the recession that hit in the early 1990s. Canadians tended to associate their increasing economic insecurity and employment anxiety with free trade. They felt let down by a government that had failed to deliver on its promise to assist them in the difficult adjustment to the new economic order. Increasingly pessimistic, the country feared that NAFTA would deliver a future not as a mini-United States, but as Mexico North. Perhaps even the worst of both worlds—Mexico's economy and environment with U.S.–style social policies. Opposition to free trade soared to 64 per cent in 1992 against 31 per cent support. Canadians appeared invulnerable to the blandishments of the apostles of globalization.

Canada was never really an economic island. The country was developed largely by British then American capital. It was populated in the twentieth century by immigrants from all over Europe. We exported our wheat, fish, and lumber to the four corners of the globe. But as recently as 1982, we could still expect to remain relatively unaffected (Prairie farmers notwithstanding) by the currents and eddies of the international economic system.

When the Third World debt crisis broke with Mexico's inability in the summer of that year to service its $80 billion (U.S.) in foreign debt, Canadians were treated to a front-row seat thanks to the coincidental timing of the annual meeting of the International Monetary Fund and World Bank in Toronto. The Third World debt crisis would dominate international economics discussions for the better part of a decade. Even today, many developing countries continue to suffer from the fallout. But from a Canadian point of

view, the crisis never really hit home. It was a crisis for the borrowing countries and a crisis for the banks, many of them our own, which fretted over the
consequences of possible default. Not that we cried them a river. The recession was well underway in 1982. Interest rates remained stratospheric and the
banks were detested for their foreclosures on farms, small businesses, and
homes. If the banks were in some difficulty over bad loans given out on
springtime junkets to Buenos Aires, tough luck. Despite its magnitude, the
debt crisis wasn't seen as a Main Street problem.

That's because it occurred in the very early stages of the formation of a
global economy. Back then, an international economy certainly existed, particularly in the world of finance. Central bankers coordinated their policies,
and commercial banks from around the world were tied together through
syndicated loans. But, in large measure, the domestic economy operated sep-
arately—a second cousin of the world economy. Even the famed multinationals were largely creatures of their country of operation. They tended to
duplicate in country X the production, marketing, and other functions of
country Y. They still lacked the sophisticated communications systems that
would allow them to integrate operations across borders—to become, in
other words, centralized global entities rather than a federation of national
enterprises. In Canada, east-west trade patterns still mattered more than
north-south. We may have been a branch plant economy, but we were our
own branch plant, operating behind our own tariff walls.

As such, much of the domestic economic activity in this era was insulated from the trends of international trade and investment. And only a handful
of individuals participated directly in the risk of financial calamity through
the ownership of bank stocks. (Others paid a price without recognizing it as
the banks squeezed profits from other operations by raising service and other
charges.) Today, in contrast, international finance and commerce and communications are so tightly integrated and interwoven and shared ownership
so widespread that a head cold in Mexico City, as we are about to see, can
cause a runny nose in Ottawa.

Let's fast-forward a dozen years. On December 20, 1994, Mexico once
again rocketed to the top of the international agenda with another monetary
crisis. From 1986 on, after picking itself up after the debt crisis, Mexico
had served as a poster boy for the proselytizers of Third World economic

liberalization. It had discarded much of its protectionist garb and thrown open its economy to international investment and trade. The group of financiers and traders that *New York Times* columnist and author Thomas Friedman calls the electronic herd had rewarded Mexico with an investment bonanza. As foreign money flowed in, its middle classes swelled. Prosperity was in the air. But the money was hot, meaning it went into short-term speculative investments and could flow out as quickly as it flowed in. Nobody noticed, but the Mexican boom was melting down.

Suddenly, on that Wednesday morning, closet fears that the Mexican peso had become overvalued (and that the economy was really not so open nor growth easily sustainable) exploded into full view. The livestock that make up the electronic herd came to their independent conclusions, appropriately enough, at precisely the same moment. Mexico's central bank ordered a massive devaluation of the peso. Foreign investors ran for the nearest exit, laying waste to the Mexican miracle. The government, defenceless against the overpoweringly negative sentiments of the electronic herd, had no choice but to allow the peso to go into free fall.

Ottawa is 3,600 kilometres from Mexico City. In the 1982 debt crisis, the world economy respected that distance. Mexico's woes were not Canada's woes. In the 1994 peso crisis, the global economy viewed the same distance quite differently. Canada and Mexico were separated by the blink of a cursor. And so the peso crisis quickly became our crisis, a situation aggravated by our huge budgetary and current account deficits in that period. It took a couple of weeks to understand the significance of how the world had changed. Indeed, the federal cabinet met on the morning of December 20, its last meeting before the holidays, to discuss its plans to cut spending in the upcoming February budget. Finance Minister Paul Martin had been alerted to the Mexican devaluation by Bank of Canada governor Gordon Thiessen. But he didn't think to mention it to cabinet.

It was not until January that the lessons of globalization would make themselves utterly impossible to miss. The peso crisis begat the so-called Tequila Effect. The shell-shocked electronic herd frantically shifted its hot money to countries that offered the protection of hard currencies with little risk. Canada, a mid-sized economy with a major-league deficit and debt problem, failed to make the grade in this so-called flight to quality. The

Canadian dollar came under attack. The Bank of Canada felt compelled to raise interest rates by more than 1.5 per cent in the month after the devaluation, but still could not hold the value of the dollar. On January 11, the *Wall Street Journal*, the community newspaper of the global economy, published an editorial entitled "Bankrupt Canada," describing Canada's currency, like the peso, as a basket case. "Mexico isn't the only U.S. neighbor flirting with the financial abyss," the paper stated. "Turn around and check out Canada, which has now become an honorary member of the Third World in the unmanageability of its debt problem."

The point is this. The unrelenting spread of communications technology and the subsequent integration of economic activity has removed all the hiding places in the world. We now live in a global economy, both in finance and production. Japanese cars are produced in Canada. The Ford Villager van contains a Nissan engine. The Germans own Chrysler. Thousands of trucks a day shuttle across the bridge at Windsor, indifferent to political boundaries as they rush to make their just-in-time deliveries. Billions of dollars flash across computer screens without ever smelling the leather of a wallet. Pierre Trudeau's famous line about the elephant and the mouse was far more appropriate in the decade after his retirement than in the decade of his speech to the National Press Club in Washington.

An event like the peso crisis brought the fact of globalization home to Canadians. However it may have raised our dander when the *Wall Street Journal* trashed our fiscal policies or when New York–based Moody's Investors Services placed our bonds under review, it mattered. Firms like Moody's constitute the privatized police force of global finance—get on their wrong side and you are in trouble. Capital is more mobile than at any time in history and we, like all countries, are competing for our share of investment. The second peso crisis delivered the message that globalization is us. There was no avoiding it. There was only, with strong leadership and good policies, the hope of accommodating global realities to our domestic priorities and learning to accommodate our priorities to it.

The Asian economic crisis in the fall of 1997 and the related Russian ruble crisis the following summer completed the education of Canada about globalization. As Asian consumption collapsed, world commodity prices fell through the floor, hitting with particular fury at our Pacific gateway, British

Columbia. The dollar once again plunged. If Canadians still didn't fully appreciate the interconnectedness of the global economy, who could blame them? The gnomes in the federal Department of Finance still didn't entirely get it either. Displaying old linear thinking, they initially computed the economic effects on Canada in terms of direct trade losses with Asia. Only later, with the dollar battered and the stock markets in full retreat, did it become clear we were operating under a different set of rules. Other countries were even more vulnerable than Canada. Australia fell farther and harder than we did. In South Africa, Nelson Mandela, a political prisoner for most of his adult life, couldn't believe the swiftness of economic retribution meted out on a country still trying to recover from the legacy of apartheid.

Commodity-rich Russia, struggling after the collapse of the Soviet Union, also took a blow to the solar plexus. It lurched along for a while, but with the ruble falling out of bed, President Boris Yeltsin ultimately chose to default on debt repayments. The effects half a world away in Canada were instant and substantial. Before June 1998, the Canadian dollar had never traded below 68 cents U.S. By August, it was flirting with 63 cents. Late that month, the Bank of Canada hiked the benchmark bank rate a full percentage point, from 5 percent to 6 percent. For fifteen minutes, the dollar rallied before plunging again. The Toronto Stock Exchange composite index fell more than 20 per cent in August. U.S. Federal Reserve Board chairman Alan Greenspan expressed his sympathies for the innocent national victims of the Asian crisis, saying they "have experienced the peripheral gusts of the financial turmoil."

You might think from this grim catalogue of globalization crises that Canadians would have turned even more deeply against the process. Even billionaire financial speculator George Soros wondered in the midst of it all if the global capitalist system "is coming apart at the seams." But Canadians held fast. Their stoicism in the wake of the summer of 1998 stock market panic serves as testament to their new maturity and a salient lesson to investment industry professionals. Canadians are patient investors—both in the stock market and in their country.

Mutual fund firms braced for a flood of redemptions as the TSE 300 fell 28 per cent between April and August. A subsequent survey by Winnipeg-based Investors Group discovered that only 8.2 per cent of respondents redeemed part or all of their investment while 17 per cent altered their investment mix, presumably moving from stocks into more stable, fixed-yield instruments. Industry statistics showed that while gross sales in August fell by half from a year earlier, investors were still turning to the markets, albeit with greater caution. The Angus Reid Group asked respondents in the early fall about their reactions to the stock market slide. Seven out of ten said the value of their investments had declined versus two out of ten who claimed to have sailed through okay. What actions did they take? Seventy per cent said they held fast, doing nothing. Only 3 per cent headed straight for shore. Nine per cent adjusted their portfolios. Finally we have the brave—and ultimately smart—15 per cent. They used the downturn as a buying opportunity. On August 31, 1998, the TSE 300 index closed at 5530.7. Two years later, it would peak at about twice that amount before falling back to close the year at 8933.7.

The unflappability of investors, many of them recently enrolled in the market and unaccustomed to its sudden upheavals, took even political leaders by surprise. At a G-7 finance ministers meeting that fall at the Hilton Hotel near London's Heathrow airport, U.S. Treasury Secretary Lawrence Summers allowed that he, too, had expected a market panic from rookie investors and was heartened by their level-headed response.

It seems to be a trend. When the U.S. Department of Justice won its antitrust case against Microsoft Corp. on April 3, 2000—at a time when market exuberance and technology stocks were already deflating rapidly—investors remained calm. Once they might have dumped their stocks altogether and fled to the safety of tucking their hard-earned savings under the mattress. This time, they merely switched back into blue chips—their own flight to quality. The tech-heavy NASDAQ declined that day by 300 points. The Dow Jones Industrial Average rose by 300 points.

Canadians, among others, had stopped obsessing about the ugly face of globalization. Increasingly, they viewed it as a Janus-faced phenomenon. They were learning to roll with the punches on its scowling days and to take advantage of its more appealing side, the face of globalization that held out promise of new opportunities and greater choice. But when Nortel collapsed, investors were livid, not because of the vagaries of the market but because they felt they had been denied the basic right of timely disclosure. Trust matters big time in the rollicking world of the global economy.

What exactly is globalization? In one sense, it is merely the acceleration and intensification of trends that have existed for a long, long while. Marco Polo was an early global man. Christopher Columbus, too. Queen Victoria ruled an empire so vast that the sun never set upon it. In Canada, the movement of goods and capital and people over long distances represents the very essence of our history. Our European roots began with the fur trade, an early global enterprise. The world has been shrinking since people put sail to wind. It shrank further with the advent of the steam engine and the invention of the telegraph. Again with the development of the railway, the jet engine, direct dialling, and the Internet.

But the last twenty years or so have been characterized by a major qualitative and quantitative difference, one that moved us from the concept of "international" to "global." The key driver of this change can be found in the revolution in information and communications technology, and therefore the speed at which massive volumes of information can be sent around the world. This is as much the foundation stone of such intertwined concepts as globalization, the knowledge economy, and the new economy as steam was the foundation of the Industrial Revolution. Foreign exchange markets trade nearly $2 trillion (U.S.) a day in currencies, more than 100 times the daily volume of the 1970s. Foreign direct investment flows rose three-fold between 1988 and 1998, topping $600 billion a year. Trade flows increased about 50 per cent in relative terms over the same period.

Our modern pace is like nothing humans have ever experienced. Once time moved to the rhythm of the moon or the seasons. Today, it moves to the rhythm of an atomic clock. Consider the example of Irish-born journalist William Howard Russell of the *Times* of London, reputedly the world's first war correspondent. He lived and worked in the glory days of the British empire. In the 1850s, he was sent to provide eyewitness coverage of the Crimean war, a true journalistic innovation.

But geography still ruled back then. Russell's famous account of the ill-fated charge of the Light Brigade was published in the *Times* on November 14, 1854, taking twenty days to make its way back to London from the mile-long valley of death at Balaclava. Now contrast that with the Gulf War in early 1991 and CNN's just-in-time reporting from Baghdad. We watched as the bombs fell. Time and space had been compressed into tiny bits. And nearly anyone, anywhere has instant access to the goings-on at the front. The entire war took less time than the journey of Russell's dispatches back to London.

I'll never forget watching the outbreak of hostilities. I was in Moscow covering one of the key moments in the eventual collapse of the Soviet Union and staying with my friend, Canadian Press correspondent Jim Sheppard. He woke me in the early hours of the morning with the news that the bombing had started in Iraq. We took the elevator up to the apartment of CBC Radio correspondent Jeanette Matthey, an old schoolmate of mine, and sat up most of the night with her and her guest, CBC's Anna-Maria Tremonti, sipping cocoa and watching a war, live. Their building happened to be situated along the path that relayed CNN's signal to the Kremlin. Think about that—we were viewing the same pictures in the heart of the old Soviet Union as George Bush Sr. was watching at the White House. The world had definitely lived up to its billing as a global village.

In dramatically shrinking economic and social space, globalization has changed the way countries and corporations and individuals relate to one another. Among the victims have been diplomats, once the indispensable middlemen of relations between nations. Diplomats still serve an important function based on their pools of knowledge. But you don't need one to report back on the bombing of Baghdad if the event is carried live on CNN. Nor do you need one to carry a message in a diplomatic pouch from one world leader to another. When Prime Minister Chrétien was briefly moved to put together a peacekeeping expedition for central Africa in the autumn of 1996, he simply asked his office switchboard to begin connecting him to other world leaders. Over the course of a single weekend, he placed more than twenty calls. Not much of a role for middlemen there, even ones in pinstripes and top hats.

The roots of modern international financial markets can probably be traced to the so-called Eurodollars of the 1970s—several hundred million in American money that was left to grow in Europe rather than being brought back home to be taxed. As mentioned, currency trading alone now constitutes nearly $2-trillion-a-day activity, and stocks and bonds trade around the clock through various time zones. The power of financial markets is enormous. In the old international order, central bankers controlled the value of currencies. In today's global economy, they can only influence these values at the margins. The real decision-making power rests with a far-flung network of currency traders sitting in front of keyboards and computer screens in financial capitals around the world, no longer content to merely swap currencies to smooth trade in goods and services, but rather motivated by the desire to speculate in the values of currencies themselves.

Globalization is most associated in people's minds with the business world. Indeed, corporations have moved swiftly and definitively to exploit the advantages of the new information and communications technologies. In so doing, they have consolidated their power to an extent never seen before. The revenues of many global corporations exceed the gross domestic product of the majority of UN member countries. Nor do they feel overly constrained by the dictates of any single country. They can take their marbles and play elsewhere, much to the detriment of a nation's technological and economic prospects.

As we discussed in the last chapter, the multinationals of old have reinvented themselves as global corporations. They no longer replicate their operations from country to country, but rather place such functions as research and development, finance, marketing, and production where they make the most sense. Powerful new information technologies provide head offices with sufficient information to allow them to manage global companies from a central location, keeping track of sales and inventory and payrolls in far-flung locations around the world. The middlemen of national head office managers have been largely rendered redundant. These global corporate networks have also ushered in a period of unprecedented trade and investment, much of it existing within companies. Borders are nearly as irrelevant to global corporations as tall buildings are to Superman. Both can be leapt in a single bound.

The service economy, too, is increasingly global. Individuals and corporations peddle their expertise around the world. This global service economy is populated by a peculiar class of people who basically live on airplanes, the shock troops of U.S.–style capitalism. My brother-in-law, Rick Mills, used to work as an international management consultant before settling down to a corporate job. He constantly shuttled around Europe and the United States— one day in Madrid, another in London, yet another in Pittsburgh. Through most of this period, he and my sister-in-law, Diane, were based in Europe. But they spent one year in Boston at his consulting company's head office. Boston is a mecca for management consultants, probably because of the knowledge that flows from its great universities, particularly the Harvard Business School. People who don't understand the rise of global service industries should spend a single Monday morning at Boston's Logan airport, watching the travelling salesmen of the global knowledge economy fly off to peddle their brain-wares around the world. On Friday evenings, the jet aircraft bring them home, their briefcases bulging with wads of cash ready to take up residence in the greater Boston area.

The spread of communications technology has also changed the way individuals interact. It has shrunk the world not just for financiers but for brothers and sisters, mothers and children. When I first moved to Britain in 1984 to study at the London School of Economics, I earned some money on the side by writing stories for *The Globe and Mail*. I would have to type up the article in my student residence and walk down to the Reuters office on Fleet Street. There I would hand my story to a keypunch operator, who would re-type it into a telegraphic machine (at astonishing speeds) and transmit my precious words to editors in the *Globe* newsroom in Toronto.

When I returned to Europe as a *Globe* correspondent a mere two years later, I could file my stories over a phone line to the Toronto newsroom myself, albeit at 300 words a minute and sometimes only after hot-wiring the phone box in a German hotel room. Today, the *Globe*'s foreign reporters can transmit their reports over high-speed phone lines or e-mail them to the newsroom from anywhere in the world. Sometimes they take a small satellite phone into the field with them. More importantly, my wife can communicate directly and instantly with her sister in Uganda over the Internet.

After Pierre Trudeau died, I wrote a column for *The Globe and Mail* reminiscing about how I first met him as an eleven-year-old on election day in 1968. He signed the plaster cast of my friend, Richard Weinstein, who had broken his leg. A picture of the three of us outside Trudeau's riding headquarters appeared in the next day's paper. A few days after I wrote the article, I received an e-mail from Richard, whom I hadn't seen in twenty years. He is living in Australia, where he's a barrister. He read my column on the *Globe* Web site and figured it was time to reconnect.

These major technological advances in our own generation, while hardly holding a candle to the changes that have torn through the business community, are nonetheless opening up new vistas to "knowledge consumers" and "knowledge citizens." The word revolution is habitually over-used in this age of hyperbole to describe significant but incremental changes in society. But revolution is justified in the case of the radical changes wrought by information and communications technologies in our economic and social relations and even in our personal lives.

Commentators such as Thomas Friedman in *The Lexus and the Olive Tree* have traced the origins-of-species globalization to the fall of the Berlin Wall. In some senses, this analysis is true; in others, it's too neat by half. The technological seeds of a new order were already well established by the time the Soviet bloc crumbled. In fact, they played a huge role in the collapse of the empire. Having said that, there is much to recommend tying the two developments together.

Friedman tells the story in his book of a meeting with the chairman of a large Brazilian mining company. The businessman relates the tale of a militant and bitter strike that occurred in November 1988 at a state-owned steel maker. The workers took over the factory and insisted on huge retroactive pay increases and a reduction in their shifts from eight hours a day to six. The strike escalated into violent confrontations and eventually the army was called in. Five years later, the executive recounted, these very same workers were demanding the mill be privatized so it would remain competitive and keep most of them employed. "You realize the Berlin Wall fell here, too," he told Friedman. "It wasn't just a local event in Europe. It was a global event. It fell on Brazil. The big changes to the Brazilian economy happened at exactly the same time that the Berlin Wall fell."

Friedman is referring to what the Germans call *die Mauer im Kopf*—the wall in the mind—an expression I learned in Berlin in the months after the bricks-and-mortar wall fell. The fall of the physical wall clearly changed geopolitical realities from Angola to Mongolia. Countries that lived off the avails of Cold War intrigue discovered they now had to find a day job. They quickly got with the new global economic program—showcasing their wares each January at international capitalism's trade show in Davos, Switzerland. But the message burrowed even more deeply into the public mind. With the dead hand of socialism so thoroughly routed as an alternative, reconsideration was given at many levels of society to the merits of the invisible hand of free markets. Social democratic parties around the world sought to fit their communitarian values into a free market context.

In Canada, the Liberal party began the process at its Aylmer policy conference in November 1991 of backing away from the strong anti-free trade positioning of the 1988 general election. Leader Jean Chrétien closed the two-day conference by stating, "Protectionism is not left-wing or right-wing. It is simply passé. Globalization is not right-wing or left-wing. It is simply a fact of life." Within a month of taking power in 1993, the new Liberal government signed NAFTA and Prime Minister Chrétien went on to promote a free trade zone for the Americas.

The end of the Cold War opened minds and opened markets. But in reflecting on the relationship between this epochal event and the spread of globalization, it is important to remember that the effects cut both ways. It wasn't just that the end of the Cold War that removed impediments to globalization; the process of globalization also made a major contribution to the end of the Cold War. For despite the consolidation of corporate power, the forces propelling globalization are inherently democratizing.

Anyone who spent time in eastern Europe in the late 1980s could witness first-hand how the new communications technologies undermined the central command-and-control modus operandi of the communist authorities and put those countries at a fatal competitive disadvantage. The Soviet countries maintained their domestic power first and foremost by controlling information—whether by dint of ideology or propaganda or censorship. They lied to their people about the world outside their borders and, indeed, the world within. Only when that failed did they resort to coercion.

The authorities spared no effort in the struggle to monopolize the flow of information. In early 1989, I was in Poland to cover the power-sharing talks between Solidarity and the Jaruzelski government. One Sunday, I decided to make the rounds with my translator of church services around Warsaw and visit some of the private markets popping up around the capital. The two forbidden religions, Christianity and capitalism, emerging from the cellars together seemed somehow an irresistible story.

The priest at St. Andrzej's Church happened to deliver a sermon on the topic of how Poles will work hard once they are given some control over their labour. Proof of his acumen could be found in the various marketplaces

I visited. I was particularly taken by a group of young computer fanatics swapping their wares in the gymnasium of a nondescript secondary school across from the church. They were buying and selling Commodore, Atari, and Astrad equipment. The hottest items on offer were pirated computer games such as Indiana Jones and Zorro, goods a command economy would never even think to supply.

I asked the traders about official tolerance for their activities. They were hardly operating underground. They told me an interesting thing: that the authorities didn't mind them having computers so long as they didn't hook up modems. I turned that over in my mind for a long time. The fear of the authorities was not so much that these teenagers would have their minds poisoned by action heroes or even be whipped into an individualistic frenzy by Indiana Jones as it was that they would connect their computers to one another. In order to suppress the revolutionary potential of geeks of the world uniting, the sclerotic state was willing to sacrifice the economic creativity and advances in the standard of living that informal networks engender.

It was all for naught, as will ultimately prove the case with Chinese government efforts to control the Internet. The truth bubbles to the surface eventually, especially when transmitted by technologies easier to hide than a printing press. The Soviets educated their people, and then tried to keep them ignorant. It was an unsustainable concept in the information age, both politically and economically. In the industrial age, the goals of information control and industrial development could be made to co-exist. But not in the information age. A nation cannot build a modern economy while suppressing the creative energies of its population. You can't command a million flowers to bloom. That's why the Soviets lost the Cold War—their system was incapable of adjusting to the global age. Its loss of technological and economic competitiveness inevitably eroded its ability to compete militarily as well. That's how empires generally collapse.

In Canada, the free trade battle is over, at least with regard to public opinion, this year's protests in Quebec City notwithstanding. The globalizers have won. Canadians agonized over free trade for over a century and then turned on it with a vengeance once it was adopted. In the early days of the Canada–U.S. free trade agreement, respondents would tell pollsters by a ten-to-one margin that the arrangement had hurt Canada more than benefited it. By late 1997, however, Canadians had switched their mindset sufficiently to conclude that the benefits of free trade actually outweighed the harmful effects. Seventy-one per cent of them told the Angus Reid Group they now supported free trade. Opposition had fallen to just 25 per cent. In the summer of 1999, with heavy news coverage of U.S. takeovers of Canadian companies, just 16 per cent of respondents thought Canada should reduce its economic ties with the United States, although a majority still wanted to vet foreign takeovers. Chaviva Hosek, Prime Minister Chrétien's chief policy adviser for seven years and organizer of the 1991 Aylmer conference, once told me the public's dramatic *volte-face* on free trade represented the most stunning public opinion shift of the 1990s.

Even more than its direct economic impact, the free trade agreement served as a powerful symbolic statement of the new imperatives of the global economy. The message to business was that the curtain had fallen on the era of the state serving as wet nurse to the huddled masses of domestic industrialists—David Lewis's corporate welfare bums. There was a message for government as well: Canada had lived too long off its natural resource endowment, like a scion running down the trust account, and would have to adapt to new realities. Natural resources alone couldn't sustain a high-income nation in the emerging knowledge economy. Canada therefore would have to grow up quickly. Governments would be required to spend less time fixated on the redistribution of our God-given wealth and more time serving as midwife to its creation. Industry would have to condition itself to run with the best.

The adjustment process was brutal, heaping more woe onto the Nervous Nineties. The free trade agreement put our tariff walls on a crash diet, setting in motion a process that over the next ten years would expose numerous business sectors, but not all, to the cold shower of competition. Canadian carpet manufacturers, safe behind a 20 per cent tariff wall, were one among a multitude of industries that approached free trade with misplaced bravado. Industry leaders blithely predicted their U.S. competitors would eschew the hardships of life as northern carpetbaggers. "Canada is just small potatoes to the American industry—they're not going to give us a lot of thought," an industry executive predicted in 1988. "But for us free trade means opportunities we've never had before."

Three years later, another industry executive was describing the experience to *The Globe and Mail*'s Bruce Little as "total absolute disaster." The Canadian manufacturers of carpet had seen their domestic market share plummet from 92 per cent in 1988 to 64 per cent. Employment fell by almost half. Between the recession, a high dollar, low productivity, and the new competition, the Canadians found themselves covered in wall-to-wall losses. "How the carpet makers got it so wrong," Little wrote, "is a classic case of an industry protected for so long from international competition that it lost touch with reality. It thought it was good when it was really only coddled."

In comparison, the U.S. manufacturers were lean and hungry. They had gone through the same bloodbath in the 1980s that their Canadian counterparts experienced ten years later, the so-called rust belt era. Economies of scale—and therefore lower prices for consumers—were realized through mergers and acquisitions. New technologies, such as computerized distribution systems that allowed them to respond rapidly to consumer demands, delivered enhanced productivity. The carpetbaggers came to Canada after free trade and brought with them lower prices and greater choice.

A decade later, just six of twenty-two Canadian carpet manufacturers had survived the onslaught. They did so by abandoning the low-cost mass market to the bigger guys from down south and carving out niche markets in which they could compete both domestically and internationally. "We have had to adjust, slim down, and become more efficient. We have had to broaden our lines and improve our product offerings," Yvon Hebert, a Quebec-based manufacturer and president of the Canadian Carpet Institute, commented. "We have also reacted positively by expanding our own export base."

In the decade after free trade, a new outlook emerged among the best of Canadian businesses. The post-free trade business elite learned to run with the best. They no longer cried out for shelter from the storm. Remember how everyone said Canada's protected wine industry would get smashed by international competition. Instead, it found its niches, upgraded its quality, and thrived. Even the Business Council on National Issues, the lobby group for Big Business, admitted in the spring of 2000 how coddled its members had been a decade earlier. "We freely acknowledge that many Canadian business leaders have in the past been too willing to hide behind trade barriers and to lean on the protective crutches of subsidies and a weak currency. We have been too conservative in evaluating opportunities, too slow to expand abroad, and too defensive in our strategies at home."

The sledding was tough, but we persevered. The experience stripped us of our smug superiority and easy answers. In November 1999, amid a new outbreak of fears that the domestic economy was being gobbled up by rapacious U.S. companies, *The Globe and Mail* surveyed Canadians on the growing integration of the two economies. Although they wanted the government to act more aggressively in reviewing whether individual deals served Canada's national interests, seven out of ten cited the closeness of the two economies as a positive rather than negative trend. The new dominant mindset did not automatically seek refuge in protectionism nor cloak itself in old-fashioned anti-Americanism. As the century drew to a close, we felt we could be global and pro-Canada at the same time.

Remember the arrival of Wal-Mart into Canada in the early 1990s. It was described in the media in terms of an invasion. You would have thought they sold tanks instead of tank-tops. Wal-Mart's famous greeters could well have been Green Berets. John Heinzl, *The Globe and Mail's* retail reporter at the time, employed the invasion metaphor on the morning after Wal-Mart swallowed 120 Woolco stores. "The worst fear of Canadian retailers became a chilling reality yesterday," he reported, "when Wal-Mart Stores Inc., the world's largest and most powerful merchant, announced that it is invading Canada by swallowing 120 Woolco stores." One analyst remarked that "Godzilla has arrived" and another chimed in that the move marked "the most phenomenal change in retailing since World War Two." No Canadian retailer would remain unaffected, he prophesied. Shares of Canadian retailers plummeted on the Toronto stock exchange.

The quintessential Canadian store of the era was, and may still be, Canadian Tire. We were called upon as a nation to rally around the corporate flag, to rush to the barricades to defend our very own big-box outlets. Several retailers experimented with buy-Canadian loyalty programs, emphasizing their patronage of Canadian suppliers, as a competitive tactic. Even Wal-Mart responded by promoting its use of Canadian suppliers. This was retail war and so a call to patriotism was to be expected. "Johnny got his credit card!"

Re-reading the media coverage a few short years later, it is almost quaint to see how Wal-Mart's move into Canada was framed as threatening our very national identity, as if we were somehow defined as a people while passing through the checkout counter. But Canadians couldn't be bothered with such silliness. They didn't insist on a heritage litmus test for either Canadian Tire or Wal-Mart. They were seeking the best quality at the lowest prices. The nationalist outpouring soon gave way to good old-fashioned consumerism. Retail citizenship was on its last legs. The Wal-Mart greeters were not border guards.

Four years later, the great Canadian icon, Eaton's, fell to its own inbred lack of business acumen. Again, the headline writers tried to squeeze the story for a nationalist angle. But it was hard to find anyone under eighty who truly cared. When it came to shopping, Canadians think and behave as consumers, not citizens. Angus Reid surveyed them about the demise of Eaton's and got back an earful. Nine out of ten found nothing special to attract them to an Eaton's store. The biggest rap against the chain was its perceived high prices followed by poor management. Six out of ten respondents proved themselves, whether they knew it or not, to be disciples of Schumpeter's creative destruction. They felt that "Eaton's didn't keep up with what shoppers want and industry changes—its closing makes room for better stores and Canada's retail industry will be stronger for it."

The story line, as it turned out, had little to do with nationalism or nostalgia. The new knowledge consumer had done his and her comparison shopping in the wide-open mall of Canadian retail and found Eaton's lacking. The decline of loyalty being experienced in other areas extends, quite naturally, to shopping patterns as well. Consumers swim in a sea of choices these days and are only too happy to exercise their choice. They have the means and they have the will. Japanese management guru Kenichi Ohmae considers globalization nothing more or less than "consumer sovereignty." That's certainly over-generous, but it contains an undeniable element of truth.

Once Eaton's, the producer, held all the power. Remember the reaction of Roch Carrier's mother in his classic Canadian story, *The Hockey Sweater*. He's a Montreal Canadiens' fanatic, more to the point a Maurice Richard fanatic, growing up just after the war in the small Quebec village of Ste. Justine. One day, his mother decides his hockey sweater is too small and too torn for him to wear any more. She goes through the Eaton's catalogue and orders him a new one.

Unfortunately, instead of delivering the red, white, and blue of the Montreal Canadiens, "Monsieur Eaton" mistakenly sends the boy the blue and white of the Toronto Maple Leafs. He is horrified, but his mother forces him to wear the enemy's uniform, explaining, "If you don't keep this sweater which fits you perfectly I'll have to write to Monsieur Eaton and explain that you don't want to wear the Toronto sweater. Monsieur Eaton understands French perfectly, but he's English and he's going to be insulted because he likes the Maple Leafs. If he's insulted, do you think he'll be in a hurry to answer us? Spring will come before you play a single game, just because you don't want to wear that nice blue sweater."

Yes, those were the days when consumers didn't want to offend the all-powerful producer. But the pendulum has swung. Nobody should count on the timidity of consumers for their continued prosperity. Nor should they base their business plans on an equation in which inferior service is tolerated for nationalistic reasons. Canadians remain nationalistic. And all things being equal, they prefer Canadian options. But they won't make sacrifices merely to line the pockets of Canadian businesses living off the avails of their citizenship rather than quality of their service. Globalization has liberated the consumer.

By the way, guess who came first when Angus Reid Group asked these knowledge consumers in 1999 which stores have been improving by keeping up with what Canadian shoppers want? Wal-Mart, that's who!

A look back at Darrell's work is instructive in understanding the massive transformation that has occurred in the Canadian economy and dominant mindset. Economic optimism was in free fall in the early 1990s and confidence in government ability to manage the economic challenges rested on the sea bottom. Canadians felt profoundly pessimistic about our prospects to compete in the global economy against the likes of the United States, Japan, and Germany. Even though one could detect underlying sentiments that going global was the thing to do, this appreciation was overwhelmed by a sense of powerlessness to make the grade.

Canadians displayed ambivalence toward free trade in the course of negotiations with the United States in the late 1980s and in the aftermath of the deal being struck. Polls through the period showed support for an agreement hovering in the mid- or high forties, not too far off the 43 per cent of the popular vote the Mulroney government amassed in the 1988 "free trade" election. Canadians were divided and wary, uncertain of the impact of free trade on their economic well-being, social safety net, and cultural identity. With the jury still out, the whole issue became ensnarled in the early 1990s recession.

As the economic reversals took their toll, 73 per cent of Canadians rated the Mulroney government's management of the economy as poor or very poor. Only 2 per cent thought it very good. Moreover, two-thirds of Canadians felt the federal government had no ability to control the national economy and 61 per cent felt it was incapable of protecting them from the expected onslaught of international competition. Ninety per cent believed that becoming more competitive would make Canada more prosperous, but eight out of ten lamented that compared to countries such as Japan, Germany, and the United States, Canada was falling behind.

The fallout effect on the main plank of the mistrusted government's economic agenda—free trade—was as might be expected. As the economy started heading south in 1990, 40 per cent of Canadians felt the country had been hurt by the free trade agreement and 45 per cent felt it hadn't had an impact. Very few people thought it had been helpful. Public judgement would get worse. By the spring of 1992, the negatives shot up to 72 per cent with only 19 per cent saying the agreement had not made a difference. Those with positive feelings would be hard-pressed to find each other outside a confab of the Business Council on National Issues. They represented just 6 per cent of the population. Only 10 per cent felt the oversold FTA had actually helped Canada versus 60 per cent who felt we had been hurt. Looking ahead, though, nearly as many Canadians thought there would be long-term gains as long-term losses. So even at the height of the storm, Canadians sensed this was the direction to go. They weren't so much against competing internationally as they were mired in low national self-esteem. They didn't think they or their governments could cut it. They were frightened of the journey ahead and doubted their elected sherpas would keep them out of harm's way.

In the fall of 1992, as the recessionary gloom persisted and Canadians grew ornery over the Charlottetown accord, Darrell delivered another sobering report to Wilson's department. Only three in ten Canadians approved of the government's performance in helping Canadians adjust to change, and these tended to be the people least in need of help. More and more, the public associated the free trade agreement with job losses. By a two-to-one margin they

felt it had destroyed more jobs than it had helped create. They feared companies would move to Mexico for lower-cost labour and those that remained
would be unable to compete. When asked in an open-ended question to
describe what NAFTA meant to them, twice as many Canadians described it in
terms of lost jobs and low Mexican wages as saw it simply as free trade among
three countries.

These attitudes, particularly anxiety over the loss of manufacturing jobs,
were fostering a protectionist form of nationalism, with 56 per cent of
Canadians urging their government to protect Canadian industry by limiting
the amount of foreign goods allowed into the country even if it meant
Canadians would pay more for products. They judged the agreement a miserable failure in its stated aim of relieving trade disputes. We overwhelmingly felt the Americans were getting the better of us. Even the earlier split view
on long-term impacts took a turn in the other direction, with nearly a two-
to-one view that the long-term impacts would be harmful.

Darrell picked up the same messages, unfiltered and unabashed, in talking directly to Canadians across the country. He still marvels over a focus
group he conducted for Wilson's department in Vancouver in the spring of
1991. This is where he learned the banjo theory of Canadian economics.

One of the participants argued that Canada really didn't need to worry
about international trade or globalization. Instead, British Columbia could
cut down its trees and sell the lumber to Ontario. Artisans there would craft
the wood into banjos, which could then be sold to musicians across the country. The country would thus be inoculated from international economic
trends. An autarchic Canada built around a banjo economy. Even John A.
might have blushed, although other participants in the focus group found
comfort in the argument. We've certainly done a lot of economic growing up
in the past decade.

The equation that globalization equals job losses no longer computes in
the wake of the strong job creation of recent years. Not so long ago, globalization to many still meant lay-offs at K-mart and dim job prospects for our
kids. Today, it brings together an odd blend of economic insecurity and
opportunity. Canadians are realists. They understand the future cannot be
avoided. They accept it can be both destabilizing and beneficial. They hope it
will be well managed.

Interestingly, the turnaround in attitudes toward free trade began to register well before the general pick-up in economic confidence in the late 1990s. The federal Department of Foreign Affairs and International Trade has monitored the free trade issue since it became a public issue in the mid-1980s. In late 2000, it asked Queen's University academics Matthew Mendelsohn and Robert Wolfe to review the archive. "The changes in support for liberalized trade since the late 1980s," they said, "are startling. One rarely see changes of this magnitude and abruptness in public opinion time series data." Support for free trade, they point out, was weak even before the early 1990s recession. Moreover, opponents of free trade felt much more passionate about their positions than supporters did. Certainly, the recession had its impact, with support for free trade falling to its low point in 1992. In that year, only 32 per cent of Canadians told Environics Research that they strongly or somewhat supported the FTA between Canada and the United States. Over the following three years, though, that figure first returned to its pre-recessionary levels in the mid-forties and then shot up to 54 per cent in 1994 and 59 per cent in 1995. By 1999, support for NAFTA had climbed to 73 per cent.

Canadians have come to accept that free trade produces positive economic returns. Somewhere along the way, they severed the automatic connection in their minds between free trade and job destruction, and began to associate trade agreements with opportunity instead. According to the government research, in 1991 only 20 per cent of respondents felt the trade deal helped job security and 66 per cent thought it hurt job security. The remaining 12 per cent felt free trade made no difference to job security. By 1999, the number who believed trade deals helped job security had risen to 57 per cent, with only 14 per cent finding them harmful and 28 per cent figuring they had no impact.

That is not to say that free trade attitudes are not at least partially tied to economic performance. Support is higher among more economically secure and optimistic individuals—they are younger, wealthier, better-educated, more urban, and male. Their opposite numbers tend to be less supportive, but not necessarily opposed. Support for free trade notably is weakest in British Columbia, where economic confidence badly lagged behind other provinces in recent years.

Clearly, though, the country has undergone a profound reversal on free trade—one conditioned by economic performance but not dependent on it. What precisely caused the turnaround in attitudes falls into the realm of conjecture, but certain factors are apparent. The elections in 1992 and 1993 of Bill Clinton in the United States and Jean Chrétien in Canada certainly played a major role. Free trade had been badly tainted by the poor economy and the even poorer reputation of the Mulroney government. Tory strategists understood their own negative credibility was dragging down the entire edifice, which was why they tried putting forward such non-governmental free trade champions as Harvey Kirck, the ex-CTV News anchor.

When it comes to U.S. politics, Canadians are strong Democrats. Thus Canadians took note in 1993 when the new Democratic president fought hard to save George Bush's NAFTA deal from congressional oblivion. They liked the fact he added an environmental and labour market component— whatever that truly meant. Then came Chrétien's election in October 1993, at a time when the fate of the NAFTA deal hung in the balance. The Liberals had promised to renegotiate NAFTA, but they sent private signals in mid-campaign to the Clinton White House they would not kill the agreement if elected. In one of his first acts in office, Chrétien met with Clinton in a Seattle hotel and threw Canada's support behind the deal.

Many commentators thought Chrétien's action would rebound against him given the party's strong anti-free-trade stance over the previous half-dozen years. The opposite actually happened. Canadians concluded that if even Jean Chrétien and the Liberals accepted the inevitability of free trade then they too had better get with the program. Public acceptance almost immediately began its inexorable march upwards. Today, the public rates the Chrétien government more highly on its handling of trade than anything else it does.

Other factors have continued to propel free trade and globalization acceptance forward: the return of economic optimism; the positive image of the Internet (a theme we will return to in the next chapter), and, most importantly, the fact that Canadians reside, day in and day out, in global space. To them, globalization is no abstraction.

Let's take a few examples from our everyday lives. Hockey is Canada's national game. Like Roch Carrier, my youth was spent worshipping the

Montreal Canadiens. The Rocket was long retired. But the Pocket Rocket served as ample inspiration to a scrawny kid obsessed with learning to stick-handle. Jean Beliveau reached down over the heads of the bigger kids after my first ever game at the Montreal Forum to give me his autograph. "*Ah, le petit garcon*" were to me the most famous words he ever uttered. I collected hockey cards and hockey Coke caps and insisted that my father buy his gaso-line from Esso, which sponsored "Hockey Night in Canada." When it became clear I would never handle the puck like the Pocket or shoot like Boom Boom, I took to being a pest, modelling myself on number 14, Claude Provost, whose job it was to check Bobby Hull into submission.

I still know the number of every Hab from that era. Then again, it was a far simpler era. Until I was ten, the National Hockey League only had six teams. There were eighteen players per team—a 108-man NHL.

The truly amazing fact was that, with the exception of an American here or there (two in the first year of expansion), all the players came from Canada. Stan(islaus) Mikita, the Chicago Black Hawks playmaker born in war-time Czechoslovakia but raised in St. Catharines, was as exotic as it got. Back in 1972, when Canada and the Soviet Union played their historic eight-game series, the guys with the Russian names really were foreign. Today, foreign is local. My youngest son, Jacob, adores his Ottawa Senators. His favourite player is a Swede named Daniel Alfredsson, the team's captain. The most notorious player in Ottawa was a Russian named Alexei Yashin. Today, every dressing room from Vancouver to Florida constitutes a mini-United Nations.

A record number of non-North American players now play in the NHL. Canadians account for only half the players in the league today, with Europeans making up a third. The process really got going after the end of the Cold War, with the proportion of European players tripling over the next ten years. In the 2000–2001 season, the *Hockey News* reported that for the first time, non-North Americans made up more than half the new intake in the NHL. The captain of my beloved Montreal Canadiens is a little Finn named Saku Koivu. The captain of the dreaded Leafs is a Swede. In early 2001, the country took stock of the global realities when an American entrepreneur named George Gillett Jr. purchased the fabled Habs from Molson's. Globalization comes home.

Canadians are also globalized in their travel. In the summer of 2000, my wife and I took our kids, aged ten, eight, and six, to Paris and London for a millennial vacation. (Given the cost, it's something we plan to do every thousand years or so.) I was sixteen the first time I went to Europe, and even at that the entire trip consisted of five days in Spain accompanying my father to a life insurance convention. My parents were married fifteen years before taking their first European vacation. My maternal grandparents came from Europe, but once they made the long ocean voyage in 1928 there was no thought of ever going back for a visit.

Today, jet travel and higher living standards make European vacations and business trips relatively commonplace. According to Tourism Canada, in 1999 Canadians took 4,252,000 trips overseas. If you want to get exotic, you have to explore the upper reaches of the Asian subcontinent or deepest Africa.

The workplace presents yet another first-hand encounter with globalization for most Canadians. Darrell has been brushing up on his French oenology ever since Angus Reid Group was purchased last year by the French public opinion giant Ipsos and renamed Ipsos-Reid. The global economy has exposed more and more Canadians to either the experience of foreign ownership or the job of penetrating foreign markets. Moreover, the office towers and shop floors of the nations themselves are increasingly diversified. Nearly everyone knows somebody at work or at church or at school who has come from a different country. Globalization Is Us.

But we are not really true globalizers yet. While the world has stridden into the Canadian parlour, our corporations have been tentative in venturing forth into the world. Business leaders have been picking up the pace in the new global economic race, but only after starting from way back of the pack. International trade at mid-decade remained largely the preserve of the largest and most sophisticated companies. John Manley, the industry minister through most of the 1990s, discovered at one point that just five companies accounted for 23 per cent of Canadian trade and the top fifty companies accounted for half. The call went out for small and medium-sized companies to join in the game, although some of them were probably already feeding into the products of the larger companies.

As a country, we are far more reliant on external factors than ever before, with the weight of the export economy quickly approaching that of the domestic economy. But so far, we have largely limited our horizons to the

United States. Exports last year accounted for an astonishing 45 per cent of Canadian gross domestic product, a steep increase from the 23 per cent trade reliance at the time the Canada–U.S. free trade agreement came into force in 1989. Fully 86 per cent of those foreign sales go into the U.S. market, meaning the performance of the U.S. economy has a direct impact on nearly 40 per cent of our annual economic activity. In 1997, two-way trade volumes surpassed $1 billion a day. About 18,000 trucks a day cross the border between the two countries.

In the first decade of free trade, our economies drew more closely together than at any point since Confederation, as trade with the United States grew an astounding 140 per cent. That probably explains Jean Chrétien's faux pas on the White House lawn in the spring of 1997. He was attending a press conference with President Clinton in the Rose Garden, when a question was thrown at him literally out of left field by a veteran Washington journalist, Sarah McClendon, who was in a wheelchair and therefore far from the rest of the press corps. She wanted to know about the increase in drugs coming across the border from Canada into the United States.

Chrétien, not hearing her well, shrugged. "It's more trade," he said, obviously pleased. Clinton, quickly realizing his guest had misheard the question, interjected, "More drugs, she said."

"More drugs? I heard 'trucks,'" Chrétien recovered, having already offered the real insight into the modern Canadian opinion. The more trucks, the better.

It's a far cry from thirty years ago when Pierre Trudeau came up with the so-called Third Option policy designed to lessen our reliance on the United States by building trade relations with Japan and Europe. Back then, our exports to the United States accounted for a mere, in relative terms, 12 per cent of GDP, or 65 per cent of our total export basket—and that was considered too high. In the final Trudeau years, international trade and trade between provinces were roughly equal at about 27 per cent of GDP each. Today, international trade, at 45 per cent of GDP, has surpassed inter-provincial trade, 20 per cent of GDP, as the prime source of wealth in every province of Canada except Prince Edward Island and, in some years, Nova Scotia and Manitoba. Ontario's exports of goods and services to the United States account for more than half the province's GDP, three times its level of trade with the rest of Canada.

Overall, the country is more than twice as dependent on international trade as inter-provincial commerce. Ours is a truly open economy.

In investment, too, Canadians are more plugged into the world, and particularly the United States, than at any time in history. In fact, the traditional equation of Canada as a net recipient of foreign direct investment has been turned around in recent years. We now invest more outside the country than flows in. Increasingly, we're willing to venture beyond our own backyard and take our shot at conquering the world's highest peaks.

Remember the Wal-Mart invasion. Well, late last year another Canadian icon was targeted—Tim Hortons, the doughnut chain that now sells soup and sandwiches. The gauntlet was thrown down by Krispy Kreme, a U.S. contender in Winston-Salem, North Carolina, which announced on the eve of New Year's eve that it would add 32 new outlets in eastern Canada to the 175 shops it already operated in 28 states. The new Canadian CEO spoke not of a regular doughnut shop but of providing "a doughnut-making theatre," with the product baked right in front of you in huge factory-like stores. "It's a multi-sensory doughnut experience," he declared.

What's the difference between the Wal-Mart assault on Eaton's and Krispy Kreme's plans for Tim Hortons? About a decade's worth of experience with free trade and globalization.

Tim Hortons had already stolen a beat on Krispy Kreme. It was the market leader, not some meek Canadian pushover. The chain numbered 2,000 stores and already competed head-to-head against Krispy Kreme in four U.S. states. In fact, Tim Hortons boasted nearly the same number of outlets in the United States as its sugar rival. How the battle will ultimately turn out is anyone's guess. But one thing is certain—Tim Hortons, a product of the global times, would rather expand than protect.

Our cultural industries are undergoing a similar transformation. Canadian policy has traditionally played an active role in protecting and promoting cultural expression in the face of the seductive onslaught of American information and entertainment. We've nurtured a national broadcaster and a multitude of other instruments to ensure that Canadian stories will be told to Canadians despite the difficulty of achieving economies of scale in a country of 30 million people, situated on the doorstep of the American information and entertainment juggernaut.

But the interesting evolution in recent times has been the success of Canadian producers in selling their works abroad. The export of cultural goods and services totalled about $4.5 billion in 2000, nearly a 40 per cent increase over five years. "The Road to Avonlea" has been seen in 140 countries. Margaret Atwood's *Alias Grace* was published in two dozen countries. The Cirque du Soleil thrills the world, and Canadian recording artists such as Celine Dion, Shania Twain, and Bryan Adams now bring more royalty money into Canada from abroad than flows out to benefit foreign performers. Increasingly, the cultural industries are stepping out into the global economy, seeking access to foreign markets as much as protection from foreign producers. After decades getting fat behind tariff walls, Canadians are shedding their fears and becoming voyageurs again.

As we've seen, ten years ago Canadians perceived the opening of our economic borders and the adoption of new technologies as certain job losers, indeed as imperilling our national being. But their experiences over the past decade and their growing economic sophistication have given them cause to reconsider. By a seven-to-one margin, they now believe that trade is positive rather than negative with regard to technological development. By two to one, they see it as positive with regard to jobs. In March 2000, Ekos Research Associates asked Canadians to describe their attitudes toward globalization. By 52 per cent to 17 per cent, they said they were optimistic rather than pessimistic. By 50 per cent to 20 per cent, they described globalization as rewarding for Canada rather than damaging for Canada.

Ekos also polled them on their attitudes toward "change," a word that comes straight out of a globalizer's lexicon. Asked whether change was generally a good thing or a bad thing or neither good nor bad, 66 per cent cited it as a good thing. Only 4 per cent said it was a bad thing. The respondents were then asked how much change they and their household had experienced over the previous five years. Not surprisingly, nearly everyone said either a moderate amount of change or a great deal of change. Then they were asked whether this change had been mostly for the better or mostly for the worse. By a six-to-one margin, people said it was mostly for the better. Imagine that! Moreover, looking ahead over the next five years, they also overwhelmingly believed Canada would undergo great changes and that these, again, would be mostly for the better. Ekos president Frank Graves concluded that Canadians have put "future shock" behind them, a thesis that will naturally have to be tested through an economic downturn as well, but quite a departure nonetheless.

As with deficit fighting, a consensus on globalization was a long time coming in Canada. But once forged, it has rapidly entered the realm of the commonplace. Some commentators have written pessimistically of the juxtaposition of an extraordinarily dynamic, flexible, and productive economy with an unstable and fragile society and increasingly insecure individuals. We feel that view sells short the extraordinary dynamism and flexibility of the modern knowledge worker and knowledge consumer.

In early 2000, the Toronto-based Pollara Group also asked Canadians their views on increased trade and globalization. About three in ten said these trends had helped them, twice as many as said they had been hurt. The majority felt they had not been affected. But looking forward to how globalization *will* affect them, the result was far more telling. Fifty-eight per cent said it will help them versus 22 per cent who think they will be hurt. Only 12 per cent said they will not be affected. Nearly everyone accepted that the global economy will change their life, most of them for the better.

An Angus Reid survey in early 2000 of 9,000 adults in seventeen countries, including Canada, found Canadians near the top of the world in their positive attitudes toward free trade. This is good, given that Canada, an economically advanced nation of 31 million people, is as dependent on trade as any country in the world. Whereas the United States, with its huge domestic economy, relies on trade for just 12 per cent of economic activity, the corresponding figure in Canada is 45 per cent.

Over the past ten years, the public has developed a very nuanced and sophisticated understanding of globalization—the good and the bad, the opportunities and the costs. There are concerns, to be sure—very real concerns over globalization's potentially corrosive effects on national sovereignty and identity and over the plight of those ill-equipped or simply unable to paddle in the fast-moving global economic waters. But these concerns exist within the context of overall acceptance of free trade.

In the run-up to the Summit of the Americas in Quebec City in April 2001, the Centre for Research and Information on Canada administered a detailed questionnaire on Canadian attitudes to free trade. By a ratio of five to one, respondents thought Canada should have more rather than less involvement in negotiating new trade agreements. The poll uncovered more support for new trade agreements than for Canada's peacekeeping role. By 45 per cent to 17 per cent, respondents wanted to see Canada encouraging even more rapid globalization. (Thirty-eight per cent declined to register an opinion.) At about the same time, Environics Research participated in a twenty-country survey on globalization. Asked about the effects of globalization on themselves and their families, 55 per cent of respondents cited it as positive. In Canada, the positive mentions came in at 68 per cent.

But the results were not unambiguous. Whereas 71 per cent of respondents felt that Canada as a country benefited from trade agreements, they had far more trouble identifying the precise benefits for their local community or for social programs and the environment. While this may be subject to revision in a recession, Canadians exhibit a strong consensus that globalization is good for the economy and our standard of living. But the public is also attracted to arguments (perhaps flowing from their economic contentedness) for a globalization with a human face—one that respects social programs and cultural identity, stands up for human rights and the environment, and speaks to our democratic impulses.

Canadians don't want to lose their identity to globalization, and they certainly don't want to sacrifice those aspects of their national personality that give them the most pride and sense of purpose. The compilation of past free trade research for the Department of Foreign Affairs and International Trade to which we referred earlier was commissioned to take stock after the Seattle demonstrations in November 1999. Mendelsohn and Wolfe set out to answer the question "Was it an isolated event, or was it part of a trend toward great unease about globalization?" To truly understand latent attitudes toward trade, they concluded, required understanding the underlying value structure of Canadians. Increasingly, Canadians want their trade relations to reflect their sense of self.

Unlike the great free trade election of 1988, the debate in future will not be limited to simple questions such as "Free trade, good or bad?" As governments move forward with a Free Trade Agreement of the Americas, a General Agreement on Trade in Services, and other extensions of free trade and globalization, the debate will centre increasingly on free trade with whom and to what end? Are we dealing with countries that can be reasonably considered democratic? Do they respect human rights? Does our relationship with them further or hinder these causes? Are the agreements themselves models of democratic values? Have negotiations been open and transparent? Are trade decisions accountable? Do they still leave us the political space to pursue the sorts of social programs that we desire? Are our values protected at home and projected abroad? If Canadians are satisfied their political beliefs are reflected in trade agreements, they will be more inclined to support these agreements. If they see their values being contradicted in such areas as environmental degradation abroad or lack of democratic accountability at home, their support will be far less easily secured. Ultimately, free trade agreements are political documents. Governments—and global corporations—had better remember that and ensure that these agreements reflect Canadian values.

In their work, which they called "Probing the Aftermyth of Seattle," Mendelsohn and Wolfe concluded that Seattle was about more than just trade. "The WTO is a lightning rod because it seems to displace Parliament by being a forum for decisions about the environment, human rights and lots of other policy domains—telecoms, competition, health, education, magazines, asbestos, beef hormones and on and on. People may have no qualms about 'trade,' yet have no interest in letting the WTO dominate these policy domains. If Canadians believe that the government acts on their own core values (for example, in the fight against child labour) they are likely to believe that the method the government chooses is the most effective one (for example, the reduction of trade barriers). On most issues, the public does not have a preferred plan of implementation; instead they have goals and values, and so long as they believe that the government shares these goals and values, they will support the government's actions to implement them."

Clearly, it would be premature and foolhardy for proponents of globalization and free trade to declare victory and leave the field of public opinion combat to their critics. The battle for public opinion never ceases and the cause of free trade is not without several Achilles heels. Globalization may have the wind of economic logic at its back. It may have powerful supporters in the business community and in government. But it will not be safe if it cannot broaden its constituency and make the case convincingly that the process serves more than special corporate interests. As we've shown in this chapter, Canadians, like others, have learned in recent years to live with globalization. But they have not yet come to love it.

Some economic historians refer to the current period as the second global economy to distinguish it from an earlier global era. While lacking in the immediacy and interactivity of today, the first global economy thrived in the latter part of the nineteenth century and into the early twentieth century. This was a period in which distances were also reduced substantially by transportation advances and engineering breakthroughs. The steam engine became the dominant motive force of the era. The first transatlantic cables were laid. The Panama Canal was constructed.

Trade and investment flows surged and the world was treated to the sort of long economic growth periods some economic commentators think we may again be experiencing. Talk about the power of the private sector. By and large, central banks did not yet exist at the time of the first global economy. (The Bank of Canada only came into being in the 1930s.) Private commercial banks controlled monetary policy. The power financial markets once again exert—including the ability of traders to gang up and overwhelm central bankers—marks as much a return to the past as a brand-new development.

But the house of cards came crashing down. Economist Paul Krugman has argued that this first global period holds out important lessons for our current global economic revolution. Support the first time around didn't extend beyond a cosmopolitan elite. "The political foundations for a global economy were never properly laid, and at the first serious shock the structure collapsed."

The shock in that instance came in the form of the outbreak of the First World War. The moorings continued to crumble in its aftermath: Hyperinflation in Germany took its toll, as did isolationism in the United States. The 1929 stock market crash was followed by a disastrous retreat into protectionism. Krugman reports that world trade did not return to its pre-1914 level until the 1970s and large-scale investment in so-called emerging markets, akin to the Canada of the early twentieth century, would not be seen again before the second global economy was well established in the 1990s. The big question for this century, Krugman writes, is really political: "Can the Second Global Economy build a constituency that reaches beyond the sort of people who congregate at Davos?" Exactly. We call it Davos Man versus

Seattle Woman syndrome. Canadians bore personal witness to the conflict at the April 2001 Summit of the Americas in Quebec City.

Davos is the ski resort high in the Swiss Alps where the cream of the global set—business chieftains, politicians, and the odd jet-set celebrity—gather every winter behind a heavy security cordon for a week of networking, deal-making, and general intellectual recharging. It amounts to a blowout annual "trade show" for global capitalism.

Seattle, of course, was the scene of the anti-globalization riots in November 1999 that scuttled the launch by the World Trade Organization of a new round of global trade talks. A rag-tag coalition of interests comprising environmentalists, trade unionists, animal rights activists, anarchists, raging Grannies, and militant lesbians took to the streets and politically roughed up Davos Man, trapped in pricey hotel suites above.

Consumer rights activist and U.S. presidential candidate Ralph Nader was reported to have joined the protestors in the streets of Seattle carrying a sign that read "Say No to WTO, Say No to World Government." The *Wall Street Journal* took affront. It responded with an op-ed piece headlined, "The WTO is not world government." *The Economist* chimed in that "the WTO is not a global government." Technically, these like-minded publications are right. But they protest too much. The WTO and a grab-bag of related organizations with an eye chart full of mesmerizing initials often do resemble a nascent world government, sans the nuisance of democratic accountability.

The WTO, the International Monetary Fund, the World Bank, the Group of Seven (or eight when Russia is included), the Bank for International Settlements—together these organizations represent a primitive form of technocratic-led world government. Their activities remain stubbornly opaque and largely beyond the ken of all but the ablest elected officials. To make matters worse, bodies such as the World Trade Organization often seem to act like self-replicating computer viruses, continually invading areas of national sovereignty not previously contemplated by our political leaders. Their rulings and those of NAFTA panels may disemploy an asbestos worker or overthrow the auto pact, or pronounce upon the legality of beef hormones. They may be used to disallow a magazine policy or open the tap on freshwater exports. Clearly, they matter to the lives of Canadians, but their rulings are often beyond the reach of voters.

The Europeans have an expression for this: democratic deficit, a term they have employed over the years to describe the accountability problems faced within the European Union. It applies even more aptly to the institutions of the new global order. Canadian finance minister Paul Martin has described the challenge of global governance as the issue of our times. That might be a bit wonkish, but it's not far off the mark.

Canadians don't get much of a look inside the WTO, or the IMF, or the NAFTA panels that determine whether a law banning a gasoline additive is fair or whether a California company deserves hundreds of millions in compensation for a Canadian ban on water exports. Indeed, the NAFTA panels tend to be so secretive that, unlike any other judicial proceeding, statements of claim and defence are not normally published and proceedings are held in private. Even the location of a hearing isn't automatically disclosed. (These restrictions are currently being challenged by non-governmental organizations.)

In 1998, the three-years-in-the-making Multilateral Agreement on Investment, a kind of Charter of Rights for global capital, collapsed and died thanks to the efforts of anti-globalization activists led by Canada's Maude Barlow. The MAI's medical chart would have cited a number of reasons for its sudden demise: general concerns over globalization; the lack of a compelling reason for an investment agreement in the first place; the ineptitude of bureaucrats in duelling with Ms. Barlow and her cohorts. But among these reasons, and those behind whatever support can be found in the general population for the now-famous protests in Seattle, lies one compelling concept: the democratic deficit. Just who are these people making these rules that affect us all? They may be the representatives of democratic governments, but they operate far removed from normal parliamentary debate and public input. And their handiwork, once entrenched, is difficult or impossible to amend in future.

Remember the American colonists dumping tea in Boston Harbor to protest against taxation without representation? Well, today we have globalization without representation, at least not direct representation. The Seattle demonstrators understood this historical link, which is why they took a break from the streets to dump Chinese steel and hormone-treated beef in Seattle harbour. Many of the demands and positions of the protestors in Seattle— our favourite was the placard calling for an end to interest rates—are barely disguised challenges to democratically elected national governments. The same was true in Quebec City, where participants in an alternative summit of self-selected non-governmental organizations demanded a summit-to-summit meeting with the heads of thirty-four hemispheric governments. Clearly, the elected officials inside the meeting halls enjoyed greater democratic legitimacy than the protestors outside. But that doesn't mean they necessarily enjoy greater credibility or that the message of the streets lacks resonance.

Modern-day democracy entails more than governments running for election every four or five years. Voters today demand transparency and accountability between elections. They want to be able to influence decisions being made that have an impact on them and they want to be able to hold those decision-makers to account. In the run-up to the Quebec City summit, six out of ten Canadians expressed confidence in the ability of the government to protect our national interest while negotiating trade agreements. But they weren't prepared to give anyone carte blanche. Nine out of ten insisted the public must be consulted and kept well informed, with three out of ten going so far as to demand "a big say" for ordinary citizens in negotiations of trade agreements. Another poll showed that non-governmental organizations are more trusted than their governments and corporations to operate in the best interests of society.

Canadians may be prepared to live with, or even embrace, globalization, but they are not ready to do so at the expense of their democratic traditions. The knowledge citizen is justifiably suspicious of anything that smacks of knowledge suppression. The challenge for the proponents of globalization is to open the doors of institutions such as the WTO and ventilate them with the sort of transparency and accountability the public has rightly come to expect at home.

In short, we must get our political structures and economic structures into alignment.

Davos Man is perhaps best personified in Canada by Thomas d'Aquino, the long-standing chief executive of the Ottawa-based Business Council on National Issues. The BCNI is the lobby group for Canada's largest and most outward-looking corporations. D'Aquino, a former staffer in Trudeau's first and least interventionist term, has served his bosses well as an influential voice for the globalization agenda. He helped Brian Mulroney push through free trade and prodded the Liberal government that followed to join the parade. In May 2000, he travelled to Tokyo and signed a pact with his business counterparts there to work toward a Canada-Japan free trade agreement—no government apparently required.

For Seattle Woman, our nominee is Maude Barlow, the chairwoman of the Council of Canadians, a nationalistic voluntary group with more than 100,000 members. She, too, worked briefly in Prime Minister Trudeau's office as an adviser on women's issues in his final and most interventionist term. She came to prominence in the late 1980s, with her impassioned opposition to the free trade agreement, including some memorable television debates with her arch-nemesis, d'Aquino. She lost that round, but later bested Davos Man in killing the MAI. At the so-called people's summit in Quebec City, she argued on the one hand that free trade was eviscerating governments and, on the other, that by their very interest in a Free Trade Agreement of the Americas, those same governments lacked legitimacy.

When d'Aquino departed in January 2001 on his annual Swiss Haj to the World Economic Summit in Davos, Barlow boarded a plane for the alternative World Social Summit in Porto Alegre, Brazil. She's even harder to get hold of than he is. They were both in Seattle in November 1999. They might even have shared an Air Canada flight. While d'Aquino looked down from his hotel suite on the violence on the street and lamented the public relations black eye for the cause of free trade, Barlow marched with her comrades and demanded the WTO be either fixed or nixed.

It's no wonder the two hold such special contempt for each another. They are mirror images, practically attached at the hip. What Davos Man d'Aquino proposes, Seattle Woman Barlow opposes. Global government demands a global opposition. The former lacks proper democratic institutions; the latter thinks protest is a substitute for parliament.

Technology and jet travel have done for the "official global opposition" what they've done for all other organized segments of society. Barlow today is as much the total global animal as d'Aquino. When Australian television was looking for someone to debate with the head of the Paris-based OECD (incidentally another Canadian, Donald Johnston) over the MAI several years ago, they linked her up by satellite from Ottawa. One week she can be found in Stockholm banging the drum to keep water within public and national control. The next week she'll be in Cairo talking about the Nile Delta or in Melbourne speaking at a conference on globalization and the live performing arts. Then it's back home to Sydney, Nova Scotia, to draw attention to the tar ponds and then off to Japan for an eight-city tour with local activists. Like Shania Twain, Barlow has grown beyond Canada. She's a global superstar now—and she has the frequent flyer points to prove it. Like Shania among music fans, Barlow is universally recognized in her milieu simply by her first name. She's Maude to anti-globalization activists the world over.

The irony of her globalized, jet-set existence isn't lost on Barlow. She believes the only way to stand toe-to-toe with business is by building global coalitions. As such, she works closely with groups such as Ralph Nader's Public Interest, Amnesty International, Sierra Club, and Europe's anti-genetic food movement. In preparation for Seattle, she participated in conference calls involving representatives from dozens of countries and organizations as they tried to hammer out a compromise position between those who merely wanted to fix the WTO and those who aimed to nix it. They cobbled together a platform called Shrink or Sink.

The tools of globalization are her tools, most notably the new information and communications technologies. The MAI would never have been defeated without the Internet. It allowed the front benches of this global opposition movement to rapidly disseminate information among themselves and out to the public. The turning point in the battle came when Barlow received a leaked copy of a draft agreement and posted it on the Internet for all to see. Governments at that point were still denying such a draft existed. The apostles of globalization within the free trade industry, accustomed to going about their business beyond public scrutiny, weren't up to the task of fighting against the tools of globalization. "We could never have organized to stop the MAI with snail mail and faxes," she says.

In late 2000, Barlow immersed herself in the cause of the remote Bolivian village of Cochabamba, trying to help the locals regain control of their water supply from privatized foreign interests. Her gang of global activists learned of the issue and were kept abreast of developments by two American nationals who had married into Bolivian families and were Internet savvy. As Barlow tells it, in the olden days of a few years back the authorities may well have moved to suppress protests against this local water movement. "But Amnesty International was able to tell the Bolivian government, we are watching every move you make. We've totally adapted to global realities. If a government is up to no good, we can mobilize instantly."

As nearly everyone, including d'Aquino, now accepts in the wake of the Seattle protests, globalization must guard against a populist backlash by making itself more inclusive. In a speech last year in Banff, he described Seattle to other business leaders as "a wake-up call." He warned that nothing is inevitable, reminding his listeners how the earlier flowering of internationalism in the late nineteenth and early twentieth centuries had withered under the political pressures of the day. Today's believers in globalization needed to be conscious of the need to include interests other than business in the global equation.

In public opinion terms, the anti-globalization forces have the wind at their back when they talk about accountability and democracy. But when their rhetoric froths over—as it did in Porto Alegre and again in Quebec City—with anti-capitalist invective and their actions degenerate into violence, they simply come across as warmed-over revolutionaries. The objective of Porto Alegre was to show that the opposition party to globalization could actually muster an alternative vision and not just a negative one. On that score, the meeting failed. They are unified, like many populist opposition movements, by a common enemy, not a common vision. The T-shirt of choice in Porto Alegre depicted Che Guevara, everyone's favourite revolutionary. Talk about yesterday's man!

Still, in a dozen years the Council of Canadians has gone from being a stand-alone organization concerned with made-in-Canada issues to a key cog in a global web of activists. With 100,000 paid-up members, it dwarfs the New Democratic Party, the old standard-bearer of the Canadian left. Yet it is sometimes difficult to discern Barlow's ultimate objective. In her more moderate moments, like the hour and a half we spent over lunch together in late December 2000, she presents the reasoned face of a global opposition leader. I asked Barlow the overall objective of her activism. She didn't say the defeat of globalization. Rather, she is working, she told me, toward a "globalization from below."

On this particular day, you might call her a social democrat rather than a communist, which means reforming globalization not overthrowing it.

However, several weeks later in Porto Alegre, she got caught up in the rhetoric of "war against our governments" and admitted to being "pretty ashamed of my government." In Quebec City, she disavowed violence for her organization but refused to condemn it by others. She and her adherents must be mindful that these governments they oppose are democratically elected, which provides them a first line of credibility not available to a self-appointed opposition. It's worth remembering that the Parliament of Canada or legislatures in other developed countries have very few elected members articulating a Seattle Woman agenda. Meanwhile, representatives of these same institutions, even social democratic ones, find it easy to identify with Davos Man.

I have a friend named Tessa Hebb, who used to be the research director of the federal New Democratic Party and was briefly the chief of staff to the leader. Today, she is one of those people on the left trying to reconcile social democratic values with global realities. She's not finding it all that difficult, at least in her personal life.

After her party's drubbing at the polls in 1993, she took stock. She concluded that the NDP simply didn't live in the same world as most Canadians, who use bank cards, are plugged into a global financial system, and are coping with change. The NDP was for turning back the clock, not making a better future.

So Tessa headed for Harvard University and the Kennedy School of Government, where she satisfied herself there was a role for the left in the global economy. After all, most of the money coursing through stock markets comes from employees' pension funds. She has worked in the capital markets ever since—for the workers. Shortly after returning to Canada, her job took her to the Toronto office tower that housed the Toronto Stock Exchange. While she was working there one day, her path crossed that of NDP leader Alexa McDonough, the woman who first recruited her to the party years before. McDonough was participating in a protest outside the building, shaking her fist and denouncing the high priests of capitalism. Tessa was horrified. "She was coming with a very traditional view that didn't reflect reality. I thought, 'I need to make sure that she understands that the money in here is

the workers' money. They want a return on their dollar. It's for their retirement. She needs to think about that.'"

Left-wing critics of globalization do need to give more thought to these
matters. The public has moved a great distance over the past decade. The old
auto-kinetic opposition to all things global is over. The global economic system bears intense scrutiny and certainly needs to become more transparent
and accountable, in keeping with the expectations of the knowledge citizen
and consumer. But Tessa's message is clear: Canadians live and work and play
in the global world. It is their reality and to deny that is to live in an unreal
world. Social democratic reforms that give globalization a more human face
may resonate, but simply chanting "Down with Global Capitalism" is passé.
Globalization Is Us.

The Nervous Nineties taught us, as Darrell wishes he had told Michael
Wilson a lifetime ago, to stop worrying and, if not love the bomb, at least
accept it as a fixture in our lives, one that creates new opportunities as much
as it upsets the status quo. The challenge now is two-fold—to humanize and
democratize the governance of the global order and to make Canada a win-
ner in the global world.

CHAPTER 3

GOOD KING INTERNET

It wasn't until the summer of 2000 that I first realized the Internet had changed my life. In some ways, it's surprising the recognition came so late. After all, I had been a major advocate within *The Globe and Mail* from the spring of 1999 forward of the need for us to log on to this exciting new information delivery system. I subscribed to the dictum of the publisher of the *New York Times* that "it's not the paper in newspaper that defines us. It's the news in newspaper." As a former paperboy, I figured you deliver the news any which way the reader wants to receive it.

I remember very clearly coming back from holiday that summer and sitting down with my publisher, Phillip Crawley, to discuss the state of the newspaper war between the *Globe* and the *National Post*. At one point in our conversation, I remarked, "What if we've got it wrong and the biggest strategic challenge facing us over the next three years isn't the *National Post* but the Internet?" Crawley has this wonderfully sonorous voice overlaid with a broad northern England accent. He speaks slowly and deliberately, kind of like a Newcastle-upon-Tyne version of John Wayne (except he looks more like Alan Ladd). His wit is quite a bit drier than his isle of birth.

"You may be right," he responded after a long pause, "but do you think for the next three months you could concentrate on the newspaper war?"

"All right," I replied, "but if you say that every three months, three years may go by."

"I won't," he promised.

I returned to the noble cause of fighting the newspaper war. Six months later, Crawley approached me and said the time had arrived to pursue an Internet strategy for the newspaper. He wanted me to work with Lib Gibson, the new media pioneer heading up Globe Interactive, to come up with a plan for an Internet news operation. My assignment was to move the editorial department in the direction of "the newsroom of the future."

Talk about a kid in the candy store. I visited news operations in the United States to study how they had structured and organized their Web operations and fit them together with their traditional newsrooms. And, of course, to see which content worked and which didn't work for them. I had never been a big techie, but I possessed a huge curiosity about this new medium, and had a faith in its potential. I regarded the Web as the early explorers in Canada must have regarded the lands flowing out of Hudson's Bay—virgin territory that cried out to be mapped and settled. I ran across a quote I liked from a guy named Tod Johnson, chairman and CEO of Media Matrix Inc. "With motion pictures, it took thirty years before someone thought of doing a close-up," he said. "On the Internet, we probably haven't discovered the close-up yet."

In any case, the point being that by the summer of 2000 I was already deeply immersed in the Internet at work. We had switched over at home to Sympatico high-speed service, which suddenly made the Web nearly as accessible as the telephone. And we moved our PC from the attic to the family room, graduating it from the ranks of the rarely used sewing machine into prime mindshare territory alongside the TV set.

Still, the Internet remained far from a way of life.

That came in short order. I probably should have clued into the fact that something significant was up when my mother began sending me e-mails rather than phoning. But three further events would transpire before I fully appreciated the transformation underway in our lives.

The first event occurred over the winter when I put my RRSP and RESP holdings onto Globefund.com. Suddenly, I found myself sitting atop a motherlode of information. And the ore body lay right on the surface; no digging required. I had always enjoyed a nice enough relationship with my financial adviser. But the nature of it changed dramatically. Suddenly, I had direct access to information about the performance of my portfolio: how I did yesterday; how I'd fared year-to-date; how my funds compared with others. And most importantly at that stage, how my MERs, those nasty management fees charged regardless of performance, ranked with the alternatives. All readily accessible. I found the MERs particularly revealing. I had been bugged for a long while by the feeling I was being charged usurious rates. But the rising stock market had tended to dampen down my concerns, and who could find the time to obtain comparable information anyway. Now, my fingers did the walking.

I was no longer just a client. I had morphed into a knowledge consumer. Same level of education. Same amount of time on my hands. Same curiosity quotient. What had changed was my ability to access and manipulate relevant information on a timely basis. Now, I could run with the information monopolists on Bay Street.

My second revelation can be traced to a flight home from New York City, where I had attended an Internet conference as part of my *Globe* work. I sat next to a lovely woman with a raspy voice who waxed lyrical about Napster, the Internet music-swapping operation. I had heard of Napster, of course, but had never used it. Coincidentally, my daughter, Bailey, told me that weekend that Madonna had recorded a version of "American Pie," a classic song from my teenage years. Somehow, Madonna and "American Pie" didn't compute in my crotchety mind. I wanted to hear her rendition myself, but I didn't have time to visit a record store (I still call them that) and didn't think I would ever be mentally ready to purchase a Madonna CD. So I downloaded the song on Napster. I didn't have to wait for it to come on the radio. I didn't have to drive downtown. Two minutes on the computer and I knew with absolute certainty that one of the great anthems of the rock and roll age had been ruined.

Within a few weeks, my kids, then aged ten, eight and six, had become big Napster users. One Saturday morning, I awoke puzzled that they weren't watching television. Instead, I found them gathered around the computer downloading just about every Weird Al Yankovic song ever written. For months afterward, my weekends weren't complete without "Star Wars Cantina" or "Livin' La Vida Yoda."

Finally, there was the infamous oil filter incident. Early in the summer of 2000, just before we were to head off on vacation, the engine in our minivan seized after the bottom of the oil filter was shorn off for the second time in a matter of weeks. The $3,000-plus bill did not amuse us. My wife did a search on the Web, keying in the words Villager (the model of the van) and oil filter. Within seconds, she had plugged into a network of Villager owners with similar tales. We sent e-mails to the people who had posted their oil filter horror stories on the Web. Soon we were commiserating—and conspiring. We had tapped into the oddest community of interest I could imagine, one that extended from Ontario to Nova Scotia and down to Tennessee.

Connecting up with a far-flung network of like-minded oil filter victims really got me thinking about the extraordinary power of the Web. A couple of words typed into a search engine and presto—the world gives birth to an interest group, a political action committee, a consumer revolt. (Not that we got anywhere, but that's a different story.) The tools of globalization now rested in the hands of us, the little guys. Producers had always enjoyed an upper hand because of their command over information. The Internet served to level the playing field considerably.

Darrell's introduction to the Web was a little less utilitarian, but no less instructive in appreciating the reach and influence of this new medium. As with me, his work life had already been transformed by advances in information technologies. In his early days in the polling business, Darrell worked at Decima Research, the Tory polling firm founded by Allan Gregg. Decima was retained in 1987 by a New York public relations firm to provide polling for the Ma'arach Party in the upcoming Israeli election. The survey work took place in Israel itself. A local office conducted the interviewing, but the data-processing capacity existed at Decima's headquarters in Toronto. These were the days before commercial networking and so after each sampling, an employee from the Israeli end would board an El Al plane in Israel carrying little more than a 5.5-inch floppy disk full of results. If the data had been downloaded incorrectly or somehow become contaminated en route—as happened twice—the employee, who had already returned to Israel, would re-board the plane for a second round trip. The computer age's equivalent of carrier pigeons! Even in the 1988 free trade election, Darrell recalls that Decima's polling results were tallied by paper and pencil from overnight reports phoned in by field supervisors around the country. Last year, in contrast, Darrell's company conducted research in eighty-five countries, with data flowing hither and yon instantaneously over the Internet.

So much for the workplace. On the home front, his life as an Internet geek didn't really take off until three and a half years ago. Most evenings, after putting his daughter to bed, Darrell would descend into the basement of his house for some late-evening unwinding time. A generation ago, he might have indulged his penchant for woodworking or his fascination with butterflies—solitary pursuits appropriate to the subterranean surroundings. But this was 1998, and Darrell's relaxation took the form of a computer game called Age of Empires, in which players with Napoleonic pretensions but suburban lifestyles set out to conquer the world electronically. Oftentimes, he would find himself battling for world dominance against fellow mercenaries from faraway Argentina or Thailand or nearby Markham or Ajax. His cellar provided not so much a place of escape from the wider world as, thanks to the Internet, a portal into it.

And so the Internet has insinuated itself into our lives, moving from nothingness to the periphery and then the core over a five-year period. Last winter, Janice and I purchased a new home in Ottawa. While we found our place through good old-fashioned word-of-mouth, we turned to the Web to get a sense of the prices in the neighbourhood where we were looking. We also used the Internet to purchase appliances after quickly discovering that no showroom contained the kind of selection we sought. We typed our desired features into a search engine and suddenly dozens of choices appeared before us. Again, with wallpaper, we thumbed through samples on the Web. The opening hours of the neighbourhood decorating store didn't mesh with our schedules. Our shopping expeditions on the Web took place at ten at night.

We haven't abandoned the old bricks-and-mortar world to be sure. We wouldn't have purchased wallpaper without also seeing it in the flesh. But we saved valuable time by researching the possibilities over the Web and we gained invaluable insight into the range of reasonable prices. Darrell did the same with his and Nina's spring vacation to Italy. They checked out their hotel rooms on the Net and arranged their bookings without a single long-distance call. In fact, six out ten Canadians with Internet access are researching their holidays on the Web and two out of ten are using it to make reservations.

A decade ago, Canadians had never heard of the Internet. The fledgling technology was the sole purview of elite government and academic researchers, often involved in defence work. Its mainstream appeal remained far from apparent. By the fall of 2000, however, 70 per cent of adults—more than 15 million individuals—told the Angus Reid Group they were connected to the Internet at home or work or school, with 12 million of them active users. By the end of 2001, four out of five Canadians will probably enjoy access.

Perhaps most tellingly, despite ongoing security concerns and difficulties with its complexity, the proportion of Canadian households with Internet access passed into majority territory for the first time in September 2000. Unlike access at work, which is a matter of necessity rather than choice for most employees, household connection represents a purely voluntary act. Individuals actually choose to pay money out of their own pockets so Internet service providers will connect them to the Web. By that act, they have passed judgement on the value and importance of the new medium. They are committed. And their level of commitment deepens by the month.

The growth in Internet access is nothing short of breathtaking. In September 1995, only 10 per cent of Canadian homes were connected to the Web. By September 1997 the figure had risen to one-quarter. Two years later, it had surpassed one-third and a year after that penetration broke through the important 50 per cent barrier.

Usage is growing even faster than access. In the summer of 1998, 38 per cent of Canadians told the government in a survey that they had used the Internet over the previous three months. The next summer the figure was up to 51 per cent. By the summer of 2000, it reached 63 per cent. Half of

Internet users now report spending more than four hours a week on-line, a figure that creeps up with every quarterly survey. Meanwhile, television viewership has gone into decline. Although growth will inevitably level off, the Internet already represents the most popular use for personal computers. Moreover, the uses to which it is being put are changing. It is rapidly evolving beyond just e-mailing, chat groups, and Web sites and into electronic business transactions. Although e-commerce remains in an infant state—and, like children learning to walk, can be expected to take its fair share of tumbles— 5 million Canadians reported in 2000 having made at least one purchase over the Web.

Figures such as these speak to the most rapid spread of a technology in the history of humankind. Lag times always exist between the introduction of a new technology and the point at which it achieves critical mass. According to figures compiled a couple of years back by the United States Internet Council, it took seven years for Internet usage to reach 30 per cent in homes. In comparison, personal computers didn't reach that level of penetration for thirteen years after their introduction; radios for twenty-two years; television for twenty-six years, telephones and automobiles for thirty-five years, and electricity for fifty years.

Among the Internet's many qualities, two stand out: immediacy and interactivity. Time never slows in the modern world. Actions that used to transpire over days or months or years have been truncated into far briefer time spans. The high-tech Gulf War lasted but a hundred hours. Massive stock market falls can occur in a morning with the bounce back beginning after lunch. An election campaign claim, counter-claim, and rebuttal can occur within ninety minutes. The Internet lives in that world of the immediate, distributing information to all comers in an instant. It then adds the interactivity—allowing information recipients to respond to the information producer or communicate with one another. Just as immediacy reflects the "new" way of the world, interactivity hearkens back to an older age of the town square. This something-old, something-new quality can be seen in the way the Internet has revived the time-honoured practice of letter writing (at least its contemporary version) after several decades of decline. E-mail is by far the most utilized feature of the Internet; it is as immediate as a phone call, but both more permanent and less expensive. The Pew Institute in the United States found last year that more than half of Americans reported that e-mail exchanges had improved their connections to family members and friends. The institute's report also lauded the Internet for rekindling moribund relationships. It suggested that 26 million Americans had reached out to relatives with whom they had not previously had much contact and that 24 million had used the Web to locate or hunt for a missing family member or friend. In my own family, cousins, some of whom have never met, are now in touch through a group mailing list. Some cousins have built a family Web site with photos and a family tree. A large reunion took place last summer. All courtesy of the Internet.

Just how popular is the Net? Consider the great cable comeback story. In the early stages of our research on this book, I happened to be channel surfing one night when my attention was caught by the sight of John Tory, the president and CEO of Rogers Cable Inc. I know John from his days as a Progressive Conservative political operative and so sat back to watch for a few minutes. What he said made my jaw drop. It seemed even more preposterous than some of the spin he had fed me during the 1993 federal election campaign.

The program turned out to be a re-broadcast of the cable industry's annual association meeting on CPAC, the Cable Public Affairs Channel. John was on stage with several others, including the association's pollster, discussing the industry's image. As far as I was concerned, you didn't need to spend much on polling to understand the cable industry's image problems. They must be among the most detested companies in Canada. Canadians are allergic to monopolies and resent both their ever-rising monthly cable bills and the unwillingness of the cable operators to allow consumers to pick and choose which channels they desire. And that was before the cable companies dreamed up their infamous negative-option marketing campaign of late 1995 and early 1996. Their attempt to force a back-door rate hike onto unwary subscribers through a marketing trick precipitated an extraordinary consumer revolt. Long-suffering customers let Rogers and Shaw and Videotron have it. Faced with an unmitigated public relations disaster—and with populist politicians moving in for the kill—the cable companies backed down in abject surrender and apology. But not before the industry's reputation went from bad to awful.

Now, just four years later, John and his colleagues were making the incredible assertion on my television screen that the industry's image had turned up. And to what did they owe this welcome development? They had no hesitation: the Internet.

I phoned John a couple of days later to find out more. He told me that cable's move into high-speed Internet had definitely pushed up both customer satisfaction ratings and overall industry approval ratings. Thanks to the Internet, customers now viewed the cable companies as competitive rather than monopolistic. Unlike with television offerings, they had a choice of where to purchase Internet service; subscribers liked being freed from consumer servitude. The cable companies, previously viewed as stodgy and remote utilities, suddenly looked sexy and connected and relevant. "People are intrigued by the Internet and some of that has rubbed off on us," he said.

A copy of the public opinion study from which these conclusions were drawn reinforces the point. It reported consistent feedback from focus groups linking the industry's involvement with the Internet to improved perceptions of cable companies, a softening of historical negatives such as lack of choice and monopolies, and a perception of the industry as a technological innovator that utilizes its presence in homes and its "wire" to deliver new and up-to-date technologies to households. The study noted that very few participants actually purchased Internet services from their cable company, but awareness of cable Internet connections was high and the availability of such services is seen as "a clear demonstration of the versatility of the cable wire, the ability of the industry to capitalize on new services and position the industry as 'up-to-date,' 'progressive' and able to harness the new technologies that are in demand today."

The cable companies have experienced problems with their high-speed services, but their bump up in public estimation still provides a telling answer to the question of just how popular the Internet is. Popular enough, it seems, to lift even the dead weight of the cable industry's negative image.

The origins of the Internet go back to the mid-1960s, when top thinkers in the U.S. military-industrial complex put their minds to the challenge of building a communications system that could withstand nuclear attack. Any system with a central clearinghouse would obviously be vulnerable. So what to do? The most intriguing idea to emerge came from the RAND Corporation, the think tank of choice in the Cold War era. A RAND analyst named Paul

Baran proposed a network with no central control, one that would be "designed from the beginning to operate in tatters" because its very conception would be anarchic. All nodes in the system would be equal to all other nodes, and each would possess its own ability to originate, pass on, and receive messages. Each message would be contained in a separate "packet of information." These packets would bounce along like bottles in the sea, always moving in the direction of shore but not via a predetermined route.

The first step toward actualizing this concept of a decentralized communications system beyond anyone's complete control occurred in 1969 under the sponsorship of the Pentagon's Advanced Research Projects Agency. It sought to link researchers together by networking their computers. The first node of the ARPANET, as it was known, went into operation in September 1969 on the campus of the University of California at Los Angeles. In short order, nodes were also set up at Stanford, the University of California at Santa Barbara, and the University of Utah. With these four sites—all devoted to highly classified defence work—the forerunner to the Internet took flight. By 1971, the ARPANET had fifteen nodes and a year later thirty-seven.

The ARPANET continued to grow and even sprouted a public profile. But in 1975, security imperatives convinced the Pentagon to bring the operation even more closely under its control. Academic organizations that fell outside the ambit of high-level defence work felt abandoned and aggrieved. They decided to form their own networks. Electronic mailing lists burst forth in all sorts of disciplines, and some of the leading scientific minds on the planet began devoting their extra-curricular time to finding ways to upgrade communications with one another.

Indeed, one of the most charming aspects of the Internet is how, right from the beginning, its anarchic conception imbued it with an untamed, frontier character. Early on in its development, the computer-sharing usages intended by ARPA had to duke it out for computer space with the electronic mail dispatched around the network by its community of scientific users. In addition to collaborating on projects, scientists used the system to swap gossip and tend to personal matters. Soon they constructed mailing lists, one of the first big ones being devoted, perhaps unsurprisingly, to the subject of science fiction. The ARPANET administrators weren't pleased by these unauthorized uses but the genie would never be put back into the bottle.

On June 1, 1990, the U.S. government "deinstalled" the twenty-one-year-old ARPANET, and private providers began peddling Internet connections to its users. Founded by government, the Internet had already taken on the freewheeling character of the private market system. Hundreds of small, independent innovations propelled its evolution forward. *New York Times* writer Steve Lohr has described the Net as "informal and individualistic, decentralized and hard to control." He attributes to it a very American character, one that reflects the very same ingredients that make up U.S.–style entrepreneurialism—"venture capital financing, close ties between businesses and universities, flexible labour markets, a deregulated business environment, and a culture that celebrates risk-taking, ambition and getting very, very rich." We would add civic-mindedness. The Internet is probably the greatest public-private partnership in history, and many people pushed it forward for no better reason than they believed in it.

By the late 1980s, the Internet had developed its own version of urban sprawl. The frustrations experienced by users trying to navigate its byways and side streets inspired a series of navigational innovations, including the "archie" program developed in their free time by a trio of McGill University computer scientists. The popularity of "archie" attracted so much interest that at one point it accounted for half the computer traffic into the university.

But the big breakthrough in taming the wild growth of the Internet was taking place in the shadow of the Swiss Alps on the other side of the world. A thirty-something Oxford-educated physicist named Tim Berners-Lee of the CERN physics laboratory outside Geneva began devising a system to organize information and resources required for his research. Berners-Lee was not unfamiliar with innovation. Both parents were English mathematicians who had worked in the 1950s on the world's first commercial stored-program computers.

Berners-Lee set to writing the now standard software protocols for addressing, linking, and transferring multimedia documents over the Internet: URLs (uniform resource locators); HTTP (hypertext transfer protocol); and HTML (hypertext mark-up language). Think of the Internet up to then as a library with the thousands of books piled on the floor. It would be nearly impossible to find what you wanted. His programs, quite basic and very functional, served as a sort of Dewey Decimal System, putting each text on a shelf that could be easily located itself and in reference to related texts.

At first Berners-Lee thought he might call his system Mines of Information, but the acronym MOI (French for me) seemed too self-centred. He flipped the words and got The Information Mine, which led to TIM, also a tad egotistical. Eventually, he settled on the name World Wide Web, the www designation so familiar to Internet users. The basic architecture of the modern Internet had taken form. In 1990, the University of Toronto and National Research Council launched the .ca network, creating east-west linkages on the information highway for Canadian researchers as well as three exit ramps into the American NSFnet. Two years later, the public pulled onto the new electronic expressway. Now, a decade into the consumer stage of the Internet's existence, it has become an integral part of our lives.

What do Canadians think of this increasingly ubiquitous communications innovation? Quite a lot, according to a February 2001 Angus Reid poll.

- By 75 per cent to 15 per cent, respondents judged the Internet to be having a positive impact on job creation.

- By 66 per cent to 20 per cent, they thought it was having a positive impact on Canadian content in entertainment and news.

- By 79 per cent to 10 per cent, they thought it contributed positively to Canada's ability to compete internationally.

- By 57 per cent to 18 per cent, it's a good news story on prices for shoppers.

- By 70 per cent to 16 per cent, it's a good news story on choices for shoppers.

- By 68 per cent to 23 per cent, it's seen to enhance the quality of education for our children.

- By 85 per cent to 6 per cent, it improves our ability to know what's going on in the world.

- By 61 per cent to 24 per cent, it brings us closer together as Canadians.

- By 54 per cent to 23 per cent, it helps us communicate with government.

- By 84 per cent to 8 per cent, it assists people in finding others with similar points of view on important issues.

- An astounding 94 per cent of Canadians agree, most of them strongly, that the Internet will be as ubiquitous in the near future as the telephone today.

We will deal a little later with some interesting caveats to this optimistic mood. This very real affection for the Internet is not completely unfettered. But the numbers, nonetheless, convincingly demonstrate that Canadians view the Internet as an enabling technology that opens up new vistas of opportunity.

One of our favourite advertising banners of recent years posed the question: "What do YOU want the Internet to be?" I walked by a Nortel billboard bearing those words at least once a week at Ottawa Airport for a year, and they would always dance around in my head. They play both to the youthfulness of the Internet and its continued openness to innovation and participation. It remains, as it embarks on its second decade as a popular medium, far from fully formed. And individual users will continue to shape its development, just as they have all along. "What do you want the Internet to be?" Well, Tim Berners-Lee gave us his answer in 1990. Nearly a decade later, he reflected on his creation in the pages of the *New York Times*, looking upon the World Wide Web with a mixture of parental pride and concern. "I think of the Web as an adolescent," he said. "It has started realizing it has a new-found power. No one knows if it knows how to use it responsibly. And maturity is a long way off."

The Internet is many things to many people, but we believe its true revolutionary potential lies in its ability to universalize access to information and share it anywhere at any time. The notion of information control doesn't compute in the Internet age. Take the experience of Tony Soprano, the gangster-cum-family man of the cult television show "The Sopranos." Tony is in the waste management business in New Jersey, or so he wants his son to believe. Tony's daughter can't convince her younger brother of their father's true calling until she takes him on a visit to several gangster sites on the World Wide Web. Dad is revealed.

The Internet is a great leveller, perhaps the greatest in history, furnishing members of the public with timely information on everything from new cancer treatments to the voting records of elected representatives and the trail of a toxic cargo to the true nature of your dad's work. It is opening vast territories of information to the most educated population in Canada's history. The Internet has formed a catalytic bond with this educated cohort to create the knowledge citizen and knowledge consumer. Information plus education equals knowledge, and knowledge, as we know, is power. Educated Canadians now have the informational and communications tools at their disposal to assume greater control than ever before over their private and public lives. The Internet expands the range of choices and allows these choices to be better informed. It is shifting power from governments and corporations to citizens and consumers.

These knowledge consumers and knowledge citizens no longer need rely on a hierarchical informational structure. The Internet empowers them to communicate not just with authorities, but with one another. You can talk to fellow users about the safety record of a given car, the reliability of a computer, or whether other travellers have experienced the same problem as you with the cruise line that served bad food on your holiday. The customer, historically captive to a paucity of good information, now enjoys the means to achieve self-liberation from the yoke of corporate and government control. This new capacity to form their own communities of interest is well expressed by Nortel's decision to build its marketing campaign in better times around the Beatles song "Come Together." The telecommunications company initially promoted the song as a metaphor for bringing telephony, video, data, and wireless together with the Internet. But in a socio-political sense, "Come Together" speaks of a much more ambitious Internet agenda.

As a technology born in Cold War laboratories, it is indeed ironic that the Internet has evolved into a powerful instrument of democratization, writ large and small. And not the Internet alone. It's merely the most important manifestation of a larger trend. Let's consider a small example to start. Many of us take taxis from time to time. You've probably noticed that most cab drivers these days are outfitted with cell phones. For decades, drivers have been captive to their dispatchers for fares originating at homes and businesses. And consumers have been captive, as well, to the happenstance of whichever driver arrived—good or bad, they had no choice.

These days, I rarely call the central taxi exchange. I have two or three drivers I know and like and I tend to phone them first. (It actually eats up less time than being put on hold by the dispatchers.) I can get the drivers I prefer, and I can count on them to give me the straight goods as to whether they can pick me up in five minutes or twenty-five. The faceless dispatchers, with their infuriating habit of filling me with misleading assurances, are decreasingly a part of my life. One of the aspects I like best about these developments is that the good drivers are rewarded with increased business from their loyal cadre of customers. The bad drivers are penalized by drawing on a diminished pool. The communications technology of the cell phone creates a win–win situation: Consumers win by being able to exercise choice, and the ultimate provider of the service wins by loosening his shackles to the middleman.

The Internet is ushering in an era of similar upheavals in all relationships between consumers and producers. The recording industry has been among the first to feel the pressures to reform its modus operandi. The industry's successful intellectual property rights lawsuit against Napster in early 2001 should not be misconstrued, however, as anything other than a rearguard action; the new Web-based distribution channels will not be denied.

Artists are divided. The heavy-metal band Metallica threatened to sue its own fans for swapping music over the Internet. That's the old command-and-control mentality at work. The geniuses at Metallica had better get used to the new consumer age; sue your fans at your peril. Others performers, such as Neil Young, Courtney Love, Sheryl Crow, and Limp Bizkit leader Fred Durst, have embraced the Internet as a way of challenging the oligopoly of the big-five recording companies. They're tired of being dominated by the guys in the suits. They regard digital delivery of music as a means of breaking free.

In reality, both sides are missing the point, which is that one way or another the Internet will overthrow the classic distribution models for the music industry. But it will have to do so within an economic model that strikes a balance between the rights of artists to earn royalties and the rights of consumers not to be gouged.

The practice of manufacturing CDs and selling them at obscenely inflated prices—a blank CD costs 25 cents and then is sold with music added for about $20—will not remain sustainable in the Internet world. Several recording companies have arranged to download music for on-line purchase at an outrageous $3.49 (U.S.) a song. This diehard effort to preserve profit margins rather than adjust to new realities is destined to fail. The recording companies need to get with the program. They should be mindful of what economy guru Robert Reich calls the Age of the Terrific Deal, an Internet-enabled era in which "choices are almost limitless and it's easy to switch to something better."

Given a choice, consumers will eventually rebel against the current arrangement. In coming to the defence of Napster earlier this year, U.S. comedian Dennis Miller complained that the recording companies have been ripping everybody off in the music industry for decades and the time has finally arrived for consumers to horn in on the action. "Considering how many times you get fucked when you go to the record store," he said, "I have to assume Richard Branson was being ironic when he named the place Virgin."

Unless the record companies learn to marry their song lists to newer and less costly distribution channels, they can expect that Napster will be followed by Gnutella, which also shares music, but without using a central server—making it even harder to control the swapping of songs. At some point the combination of the Internet and knowledge consumers will blast the old order's eardrums to smithereens. And once again, the middleman is most vulnerable. Artists and Internet music providers are no longer totally dependent on the suits, as they will soon discover. CDs are merely a delivery system for digital music. The Internet will provide a superior delivery system, with sound and video combined and an added cataloguing function thrown in for good measure.

Television producer and media visionary Mark Starowicz has heralded an age in which we will witness the death of what he calls linear time, another liberating experience, to hear him tell it. He describes linear time by comparing television and radio to magazines.

"Imagine if I sold you a subscription to *Maclean's* and said to you: Here's the deal—I will come to your door every Tuesday at 8 p.m. and hand you the current copy of *Maclean's*. Then, regardless of whether you're having a fight with your spouse, your mother called or the bathtub overflowed, I will return in precisely one hour, at 9, and take the magazine back. What do you think this distribution theory would lead to? The readership of *Maclean's* would plummet by 99 per cent.

"Yet I have just described the fundamental distribution system of television programming. 'The Fifth Estate' will appear on your TV set at 8 p.m. and regardless of what else is happening in your life, it will end in an hour. Same for 'w5' or 'Witness'."

Unlike print, he continues, broadcasting is completely hostage to linear time. And that impels producers, who face enormous hurdles agglomerating economic audiences, to aim their content at the largest audience possible. Starowicz foresees a time in the not too distant future when viewers will sit down in the living room at 8 p.m. and through voice-recognition software order up the six o'clock news and last Tuesday's 'West Wing' and yesterday's 'Fifth Estate'. The television might even tell the viewer it has retrieved an item broadcast earlier in the day on a favourite subject. Television, he predicts, will acquire the flexibility of print—to be consumed at a pace that suits the consumer, not the producer.

Not only will time constraints be lifted, but minority tastes also will be better served. The current scarcity of prime time hours—twenty-one a week—will become irrelevant with the demise of linear time. The economic imperative of catering to a fast-food audience will be overturned. "For forty years," Starowicz says, "this economic law suppressed hundreds of program constituencies—you don't program to children in prime time, you're certainly not going to do a book show, and you don't even schedule the news in prime time on commercial networks."

The advent of specialty cable channels and the popularity of video stores has already significantly increased choice. We're in the throes of a transition from a world of broadcasting to narrow-casting. The new Internet-driven media world, freed of the burden of linear time, will carry this movement further down the field. "Commercial television and radio under the Darwinian law of linear prime time," Starowicz tells us, "resembled the choice you find in an airport paperback rack. The new radio and television digital spectrum, liberated from linear time delivery, will be eventually as rich in sections and shelves as the largest bookstore you can imagine. And if you're skeptical, think of the video store today, compared to your choices before the VCR. The choices between twelve movies playing in theatres that week twenty years ago versus thousands of films available today through cassette."

We've seen in the previous chapter how anti-globalization activists have used new media tools to organize themselves and broadcast their cause. The Internet simplifies the ability of citizens to congregate and re-congregate in virtual political movements, like Hollywood producers assembling a team for a new film, disassembling it afterwards and then bringing together some of the same people as well as new ones the next time out.

Commentators who conclude that Canadians are seized by apathy when it comes to matters in the public realm should think again. When governments get in the way of the right of Canadians to use herbal remedies or medicinal marijuana, citizens organize themselves very quickly and make their views known. When governments spend taxpayer dollars on unpopular causes, such as subsidizing hockey teams, Canadians have the means to make themselves heard loud and clear. And then they retreat into their private lives until they feel the need to assert themselves again. But assert themselves they will.

What has changed is the nature of public participation, not that participation itself. Like everything in modern society, public participation is more episodic and fleeting than in past. It is also less institutional. For those who want to involve themselves with more than a vote every four or five years, joining a political party is no longer the only ticket in town. In another age, Maude Barlow, chairwoman of the Council of Canadians, would have run for Parliament. Indeed, in another age, back in the late 1980s, she even tried. Today, she hammers her point home from the outside.

In his recent book, *A State of Minds*, Canadian economic thinker Thomas Courchene talks about the emergence of "a new, exciting and empowering global citizenship/democracy driven by information-empowered, like-minded individuals from all corners of the globe." The ultimate impact of the Internet, he foresees, will be to privilege citizens individually and collectively with a degree of information, influence, and power heretofore unimaginable—and impossible for any government to ignore or suppress. Playing off *New York Times* writer Thomas Friedman's "electronic herd" of hyper-connected bond and currency traders, Courchene labels this emerging global network of information-privileged activists the "electronic citizen-democracy herd." In his view, this second herd is evolving into an important countervail to the first. They are hearing the message of "Come Together." "One thing I can tell you is you got to be free."

The corporate sector as well should pay attention to the electronic democracy herd. The lines between public and so-called private behaviour are blurring to the point of near invisibility. Just ask Nike or Shell or any other company under global boycott in recent years. I was astounded a year ago when my six-year-old son Jacob piped up from the back seat of the van to say he had a problem and didn't know what to do. He really liked Nike because he likes Tiger Woods but he really didn't like Nike because he's heard from his older sister and brother that Nike uses child labour. Apparently my kids aren't alone. In an Angus Reid survey last year, 35 per cent of respondents said they were currently boycotting a product or service because of concerns over corporate ethics. And 44 per cent said they had been involved in a boycott over the previous year. The Internet has greatly enhanced the ability of these people to find one another, educate themselves on issues, and then organize their actions.

Consider one example—that of Home Depot and an environmental campaign in favour of old-growth forests. If you put Home Depot into an Internet search engine, the second site that pops up is homedepotsucks.com. It is part of a long-running campaign to convince consumers to boycott the do-it-yourself retailer's lumber products. The campaign, which has included in-store protests, has wrung a commitment out of Home Depot to phase out the sale of lumber products from old-growth forests by 2002.

Think about that for a moment. A generation ago, environmental activists would have petitioned governments to protect old-growth forests against rapacious capitalists. Now they initiate, organize, and carry out their own campaigns. They've cut out the middleman—governments. Indeed, only after the activists made use of old-growth wood painful enough for the end seller did the British Columbia government and forestry companies feel the need to restrict harvesting in 1.4 million hectares of the province's coastal forests.

The history of technology in Canada has been one of private enthusiasm and public suspicion. Deeply ingrained in our national psyche is a techno-ambivalence rooted in the belief that new technologies serve private interests over the public good. Futurist Alvin Toffler reflected in an interview with *Business 2.0* magazine in September 2000 on the redefinition of the place of technology in society. "The dominant assumptions about the future by geniuses such as Orwell and endless numbers of science fiction writers, sociologists and other scholars and so on were simple: more technology equals more bureaucratization." But now it's become obvious, he went on, that one of the defining changes has actually been "a shift to increase diversity rather than uniformity."

To put it another way, both Darrell and I can remember reading Orwell's *1984* as teenagers. In Orwell's world, authorities used technology to spy on the people. In the emerging Internet world, people use the technology to spy on the authorities.

The Internet has managed to leap the tall doubts historically associated with new technologies in a single bound. Even in its adolescence, it already stands out as an extraordinarily popular and populist technology. So popular, in fact, that we believe it may even be challenging the assumptions of Canadians about technological progress in general.

Ten years ago, Canadians could be fairly labelled technophobes. The public generally equated new technology with job losses. Scratch any innovation and you would discover it benefited the big guys over the little guys and producers over consumers. Pollster Allan Gregg used to tell a wonderful story about a focus group his firm conducted in the early 1990s. As a prompt to get people talking, the moderator showed them a variety of slides. One slide featured a young woman wearing a headset. "Poor lady," snorted one of the participants. "She's about to lose her job."

"Why do you say that?" asked the moderator.

Everyone else in the group seemed to understand. "Voice-mail," they explained. She didn't know it but technology stalked the woman in the picture, like a new economy version of an old-fashioned movie thriller. She may as well have been Janet Leigh in the shower. Technology, amoral and out of control, would take her livelihood.

Voice-mail was viewed back then neither as a consumer convenience nor an employment creator (think of the programming jobs). It was an enemy of the people.

Compare that with e-mail, still the number one attraction on the Internet. Does anyone complain about its dehumanizing effects, the way they do with voice-mail? Is anybody standing up for the rights of postal workers in face of the threat to snail mail from electronic mail?

For the past generation, Canadians have lived through a period of unprecedented change. The Nervous Nineties produced the perfectly understandable reaction of "change-phobia" as a never-ending stream of economic and technological changes roiled our jobs, families, communities, and emotional health. The famous Moore's law—that computing power will double every eighteen months—produced a human flip side in the exponential growth of stress. Yet although the pressure stream continues to rush forward unabated, we seem to have come to terms with it.

In the summer of 2000, pollster Frank Graves, who does extensive work for federal government departments, tapped into the same attitudinal vein that got Darrell and me excited about this book in the first place. He asked Canadians if generally they thought change was a good thing, a bad thing, or neither good nor bad. Twenty-eight per cent considered it neither good nor bad. Among those with a strong opinion, it was judged a good thing by 66 per cent and bad by just 4 per cent. Graves was so astounded he double-checked and triple-checked the numbers.

Respondents weren't talking abstractions. The vast majority said they personally had been subjected to extensive changes over the previous five years. But they didn't think, as one might suppose, it had all been pointless torture. Seventy-one per cent thought there was a high need for change in the country versus 5 per cent who thought there was a low need.

Graves mulled over his data. Canadians, he remarked as if a bit surprised himself, had turned away from being "change-phobic and future-shock types" to becoming not just accepting of change but actually positively predisposed toward it. Having passed through a vale of tears, they were pumped to meet the future. They cited the Internet by a five-to-one margin as a positive force for change. In the Internet, Canadians see a technology that creates more opportunity than it destroys. In January 1999, 85 per cent of Canadians told Industry Canada that young people with access to the information highway probably have a brighter future than those without. By similar proportions, they felt the new electronic communications technologies would generate business opportunities in rural areas and for small businesses, improve employment prospects, and enhance access to health information.

At roughly the same time, Toronto-based Pollara asked an interesting set of questions on technology. Six out of ten respondents said they had been helped by advances in technology and only one in ten felt he or she had been hurt. The rest were neutral. Looking ahead, 67 per cent said technological advances would help the next generation versus 19 per cent who felt they would be harmful.

Take the example of the human genome project. In August 2000, shortly after the announcement that the gene map had been completed, Angus Reid found that nine out of ten Canadians believed, most of them strongly, that this breakthrough would lead to discoveries that "will greatly increase our quality of life." When read the statement "I think genetic testing will have more negative effects than positive ones," two-thirds of respondents turned thumbs down. Their support for genetic research tended to be very personal. They foresaw advantages for themselves—for example, testing to know if they were at risk of developing a hereditary disease as well as other medical uses. At the same time, they expressed misgivings about what might happen if genetic testing of fetuses became commonplace.

But the really interesting issue arises over control of information. Canadians are adamant that genetic information is no business whatsoever of their employers, their governments, or their insurance companies. They see no reason for these institutions to have access to such private information. They felt differently when it comes to professionals with whom they interact. They believe by 96 per cent to 4 per cent their doctors should have this information and are evenly divided about nurses and pharmacists. For them, genetic mapping and testing, like the Internet, is favoured when it serves their interest. But don't try to divert the benefits or infringe on their privacy.

The Ontario government has heard the same messages over and over again in recent years. Residents of the province can see the overall benefits of so-called smart cards in reducing fraud and duplication. But how does that outweigh the potential infringements of their personal privacy? Darrell recalls similar sentiments emerging in focus group testing he conducted a few years back on Ontario's controversial toll thoroughfare, Highway 407. The government wanted to gauge reaction to the idea of embedding chips into licence plates—"smart plates"—in order to keep track of payments. It explained the interests of car owners would be served by such a move since it would be far easier to find their vehicles in the case of auto theft. The focus group participants looked at Darrell like he was Big Brother himself. Why should we let the government know where we are at any given moment!

Although science and technology have come a long way in public estimation, nobody is willing to grant carte blanche. Angus Reid has found 57 per cent of respondents expressing concerns that science and technology in general (not the Internet), while providing better products at lower costs, still threaten jobs. So while the Internet is widely viewed as a positive development, and one we believe is lessening autokinetic responses against innovation, its spillover effects certainly are not limitless. Rather than reflexively believing, as a friend of mine wrote in the opening line of a college essay on urban sprawl, that "progress is a dirty word," Canadians will judge each innovation on its merits.

Appropriately, the public believes in good technology and bad technology. They're more willing than ever before to embrace good technologies, especially the ones in which they can see benefits for themselves, but they aren't inclined to take anything on faith. Theirs is a show-me mentality. On the Internet and the human genome project, with some misgivings, they've been shown.

In other areas, the show has flopped. There is probably no better example of bad technology, at least with regard to public opinion, than genetically modified foods. Unlike with the Internet or genetic testing, consumers see little benefit for themselves in the trend toward GM foods. It comes down to risk management—why take a chance if all the benefits accrue to producers and none to consumers? So far, the benefit balance sheet looks like this: Producers increase yields and profit margins. The only upside consumers can count is that fewer pesticides are used. Meanwhile, what about the health and safety risks? Until producers of genetically modified foods can identify strong consumer benefits to offset the perceived risks of "Franken-foods," the chances of winning over the public will remain slim.

Awareness of GM foods increased significantly between 1998 and 2000, from 61 per cent to 79 per cent, most of the rise driven by negative portrayals in the media. In a 2000 survey, 58 per cent cited the trend toward such foods as negative versus just 45 per cent two years earlier. Fewer than one-third of Canadians are confident that GM foods that reach the marketplace are safe even though seven out of ten largely trust the food industry to provide safe products.

Two developments, in particular, have undermined the case for genetically modified foods. The first concerns the changing context of the discussion.

In 1998, 40 per cent of Canadians viewed GM foods as a science and technology issue, 27 per cent considered it a health and safety issue, and 21 per cent considered it a moral or ethical matter. Two years later, 55 per cent put the question in the context of health and safety. Those viewing it as a science and technology issue had fallen to 22 per cent and only one in ten Canadians still considered it a moral issue.

Public health and safety issues obviously have garnered a great deal of publicity in Canada. In the summer of 2000, the story of deaths from contaminated water in Walkerton, Ontario, shocked the country. As well, the continued global scare over mad cow disease (and the failed assurances of government and industry) has taken a natural toll on public confidence.

The second issue eating into public confidence has to do with labelling. The food industry has steadfastly opposed suggestions to label GM foods as such. Part of the argument is that so much genetically modified material finds its way into food processing these days that almost everything would end up carrying the label. To the public, this sound disingenuous. In fact, surveys show that shoppers are purchasing increasing quantities of organic produce, meat, and eggs—so labelling obviously serves a purpose. The true reason for the resistance to labels, Canadians suspect, is that industry research shows that a GM food label, fairly or unfairly, would scare away significant numbers of buyers.

Labels matter to the public. They are part of the information revolution, the transfer of power to knowledge consumers. Canadians are assiduous readers of labels. Amazingly, one-third claim to always read the labels on food products, another third say they usually read the labels. Only 3 per cent admit to never reading labels. When it comes to genetically modified foods, a convincing 84 per cent of Canadians say they should be clearly labelled.

The Internet world is all about transparency. Science that sets out to obscure or obfuscate simply won't cut it with the public. If the Internet were an entertainment program, it would probably be the Jetsons, the chirpy, futuristic cartoon of our youth. On genetically modified food, Canadians think more in terms of *Bladerunner,* the dark 1982 Harrison Ford thriller set in the urban genetic cocktail of 2019 Los Angeles.

The Internet itself is not without its own challenges, although these at least are framed against the backdrop of widespread acceptance of its consumer and societal benefits. The private sector has done well with this public offspring, but at least two of the public's issues will require government intervention.

First, there is the so-called digital divide, the term generally employed to describe the uneven pattern of Internet access and usage. The statistics tell the tale of the tape quite convincingly. Internet access among eighteen- to thirty-four-year-olds in the fall of 2000 stood at 85 per cent while for those fifty-five and over it was 45 per cent; 88 per cent of higher income Canadians are connected versus 52 per cent of lower income Canadians; 85 per cent of university-educated Canadians had access to the Net as compared with 46 per cent with high school or less. The prototypical Internet user, therefore, is a university-educated young adult earning more than $60,000 a year. The prototypical non-user would be a low-income pensioner who never completed high school. One other peculiarly Canadian aspect of the digital divide: It mirrors the east-west divide of so many economic indicators. Internet access east of the Ottawa River was less than 60 per cent and west of the Ottawa River was more than 70 per cent. Quebec, probably due to the predominantly English character of the Web, has the lowest penetration rate in the country. A strong rural-urban split also exists.

Remember the incredibly bullish Internet poll we showed you earlier in the chapter? Well, despite the overwhelming numbers heralding the Internet as a positive force in society, only 55 per cent of respondents ultimately described themselves as more hopeful rather than fearful about its impact over the next ten years. The most fearful tended to be over fifty-five, with incomes of less than $30,000 a year and education levels below high school leaving. In contrast, Canadians better positioned to prosper in the economy of the future—the university educated and the young—felt more hopeful than fearful by a two-to-one margin.

How to interpret this? Well, wide swaths of Canadian society—generally the older and under-educated—remain insecure about the impact of new communications technologies not on society so much as on themselves. They display a grudging respect for the new technology, accepting that it creates jobs and spreads social benefits. They don't hate the Internet. They just don't feel they have the tools to cut it in this changing, fast-paced world. It's probably safe to say that two classes of Canadians are emerging in the Internet age: those who want in and those who fear being left out.

We have identified at least three digital dividing lines of interest to government policy-makers (besides Canadian content issues):

- **ECONOMIC EXCLUSION**
  Individuals can't afford either a computer or an Internet server and therefore are being left behind

- **GEOGRAPHIC EXCLUSION**
  Individuals live in an area, usually rural, that private-sector Internet companies have little inclination to wire, particularly with the broadband capacity necessary to realize the Internet's potential

- **EDUCATIONAL EXCLUSION**
  Individuals are excluded because they lack the skills or educational attainment necessary to work the Internet

The statement "Some people may benefit from having access to the Internet but it won't be me" elicits very revealing results. Respondents disagree by 47 per cent to 30 per cent, with the rest neutral. It is those 30 per cent—nearly all living on the wrong side of the digital divide—who obviously are of the greatest interest to government policy makers. The first and third divides are part and parcel of broader social issues; the geographic divide is the most open to a market solution.

To some extent, the digital divide already is narrowing. Early gender differences in access already have nearly vanished. As well, governments have taken commendable actions on the economic front to level out equality of opportunity. All of Canada's 15,000 public schools now have Internet access as do 3,400 libraries and thousands of community centres. The federal government now is looking into underwriting the cost of subsidizing broadband access outside the commercial and metropolitan centres that attract private-sector providers.

For us, the most troubling aspect of the digital divide concerns education. The issue with the Internet is much the same as that motivating the early childhood education movement, the idea being to ensure that children are ready to learn by the time they arrive in Grade 1. When it comes to the educational divide, the issue has nothing to do with government providing computers or connections. It comes down to the much more vexing panoply of policies required to prepare Canadians for a fast-paced global world so as to raise their level of prosperity and enhance their quality of life.

The second major challenge for the Internet emerges out of its very essence as a free-wheeling, hair-in-the-wind, pedal-to-the-floor, born-to-run medium. Early Web-heads liked to portray their electronic plaything as a no-go zone for government and regulation. They dismissed the very idea of a regulatory hand as contrary to its spirit. This early Web culture idealizes the Internet as a libertarian island in an over-governed ocean. The unfortunate presence of pornography and hate alongside sites of higher purpose elicited a shrug. The price you pay for freedom.

But as the Internet goes from the preserve of the young and connected to a common household fixture, this Wild West character will be reconsidered. American political humorist Bill Maher captures this mood well when he scoffs at those who liken the Internet to an electronic version of the public library. "Sure," he shoots back, "except the librarian happens to be a Nazi pedophile."

Canadians side with Maher, the man in the middle on the program "Politically Incorrect." By a two-to-one margin, they disagree with the statement "Material on the Internet should not be regulated." The true Web-heads feel differently, but as the masses take over the Internet, the dominant mindset undergoes change. For Canadians at large, the quintessential national principle of peace, order, and good government prevails—even on the Internet.

It's not only the obviously nasty sites that jeopardize the good name of the Internet. The Web overflows with junk and dross, frustrating and confusing users and diminishing the overall credibility of the medium itself. Which health sites should they believe? Which should they disbelieve? We are living in the age of the intangible—information. It comes without a Canadian Standards Association label. Songwriter Kris Kristofferson wrote "Freedom's just another word for nothing left to lose." Perhaps the pervasiveness of poor-quality information is an unavoidable price to pay for the freedom of the Internet. Then again perhaps freedom's just another word for something critical to lose—trust.

Canadians are evenly split—49 per cent to 48 per cent—on the reliability and trustworthiness of information found on the Web. This is well below the level of confidence normally associated with traditional media such as newspapers, radio, and television. The trust issue is bound to become larger and larger as the Internet continues to insinuate itself into everyday lives.

The flip side, of course, is that providers with well accepted "trustmarks" should enjoy tremendous comparative advantage in the information jungle. This exact issue was the subject of strong debate within *The Globe and Mail* in the early months of 2000. Should our Internet strategy build on the high trust quotient already invested in *The Globe and Mail* name (a position I held) or should we create a new brand that would not be "weighed down" by the stodgy image of an old-growth business? Others certainly had chosen the latter route, both within the Globe and other media organizations, such as the Chicago-based Tribune Group. Canoe, a website owned by the Sun Media Group, gave away no tell-tale signs of its corporate parentage, nor did it even bother leveraging off the organization's existing news-gathering infrastructure.

Remember the giant AOL-Time Warner deal in late 1999? AOL, the upstart Internet portal company enriched by the irrational exuberance of the market, was widely portrayed as the victor in bagging old-line Time Warner, owner of such famous brands as *Time* magazine, *Sports Illustrated* and Bugs Bunny. New media triumphs over old, rang out the headlines.

But whereas 1999 had been the year of AOL, it seemed obvious a few months later that 2000 would be the year of Time Warner. The great brands, the names that inspired trust, had ironically been catapulted into even greater importance by the prevailing dot-com gold-rush mentality. All around us, cocky Internet entrepreneurs launched new sites aimed at cannibalizing the audiences of the old-line companies. They spent millions not so much on content as on what they called customer acquisition—circulating their names through advertising and promotion in hopes of attracting "eyeballs" to their sites. The real contest in the 2000 Super Bowl game took place between start-up Internet companies promoting their names between passes, runs, and punts. But the more of them that joined the fray, the more futile their efforts. One ad was as good as another, albeit increasingly expensive. The marketplace had become hopelessly cluttered. Consumers had gone from swimming in a sea of choices to drowning in them. Ever been in a restaurant with a seven-page menu? It's hard to know what to order. You begin looking for external signals, perhaps the specials, perhaps advice from the waiter, perhaps your companion who has eaten there before. An abundance of choices is basic to the Internet, a medium limited by neither time nor space.

In the over-crowded Internet world, the best signals come from brand names we trust. In this atmosphere, who was better positioned to win the battle for mindshare with, let's say, the family audience: wearefamily.com or Disney.com? No contest. In our case, we felt globeandmail.com would carry a lot more weight than hereisthenews.com.

As the Internet economy ushers in an era of rapid business changes, Canadians will increasingly look to companies with established trustmarks. In his recent book, *The Future of Success*, U.S. economy guru and former Labor Secretary Robert Reich describes these brands as "trustworthy guides to what's good." A trustmark goes well beyond a good brand name. The brand provided the entry point to the product. Frito Lays are good corn chips. Mercedes-Benzes are serious cars. But today people are seeking guidance of a higher nature. They want to know if the information coming their way is authoritative, credible, reliable. They aren't seeking a signal about the quality of the product as much as the trustworthiness of the producer.

In Reich's view, the old business model was predicated on creating distribution oligopolies. The new business models will be built around "oligopolies of trustworthiness"—names, he says, that "will dominate psychic space, not shelf space." Moreover, he sees these new-style oligopolies as portals through which all sorts of related enterprises can reach the consumer marketplace. It's not really important that Disney itself provides all the components along their value chain. It can contract out or partner. But all the players along that chain know they are relying on Disney's good name to get them in the door, an asset of considerable value to the trustmark holder.

If you've got a trustmark in the Internet economy, you sure as hell want to make use of it. And preserve it. Trustmark stewardship should be seen as one of the top tasks of modern CEOs. It probably takes a great deal of incompetence to squander a trustmark advantage, but nothing near the massive quantities of competence that would be required to re-establish it.

Trust is the lubricant of all economic relations, and the Internet must strive to enhance its trust quotient. Users need to trust its offerings in their informational transactions and they need to trust its security for their commercial transactions.

In her 1996 book, *Systems of Survival*, urban planner and philosopher Jane Jacobs suggests that two inter-related groupings (or moral syndromes, as she puts it) prevail in modern society, merchants and guardians. The merchants make up the business class; the guardians the political class. Each has its own important function.

The book opens with a story from Armbruster, one of five characters involved in a running conversation. He recounts the story of a consulting engagement in Hanover in which he was sorting out the international rights for an autobiography on behalf of a German-American family. From there, he was heading to Switzerland on holiday. "I took my fee to a local bank for transfer to my bank here. Commonplace sort of transaction, but this was one of those occasions when the commonplace suddenly seems extraordinary. It hit me that I'd handed over my fee to a total stranger in a bank I knew nothing about in a city where I knew almost nobody, and where they spoke a language I didn't understand. What I had going for me, I reflected as I dashed to catch my train for Zurich, was a great web of trust in the honesty of business. It struck me with awe how much that we take for granted in business transactions suspends from that gossamer web."

It is his friend Kate who comes up with the idea of the two moral syndromes or survival systems, which flow from two distinct ways of making a living. There are those who exchange goods and services and those who take what they want. The merchant class is associated with honesty, voluntary agreements, competition, respect for contracts, inventiveness, efficiency, and collaboration. The guardian class, not just government but all those operating in the public sphere, is associated with loyalty, obedience, discipline, tradition, hierarchy, and administration. One is meant to create value in society; the other to protect the values of that society.

What Jacobs seems to be saying in her book is that you can't have one of these without the other. They are competitive but complementary. Each has its role.

The Internet is a product of both spheres of influence—founded by the public, fostered by the private. As it evolves, in Berners-Lee's phrase, from adolescence to maturity, important roles remain for both merchants and guardians. They need only be mindful of which is which.

The history of communications meta-innovation is replete with unpredictable effects that often take many years to reveal themselves. Gutenberg's fifteenth-century printing press led inexorably but unknowingly to Martin Luther's treatise and the Protestant Reformation. Ultimately, all this created the conditions in which capitalism thrived. Television came of age as an entertainment medium, but within a generation was credited with having ended American involvement in the Vietnam War. The Internet is still in its grainy, black-and-white stage. We are in television's equivalent of 1949 and so far the best programmers have come up with is to take "Amos & Andy" from radio and put them in front of a camera. As broadband access and wireless delivery advance, someone is going to think up the Internet's answer to the motion picture close-up. The power of the medium will undoubtedly have huge social consequences.

"What do *you* want the Internet to be?" Count on it being hugely influential in ways we cannot yet contemplate.

CHAPTER 4

MY FATHER'S TIE

I remember when my dad finally got a job that called for him to wear a tie. It was a pretty big breakthrough for a guy who, as the oldest son, had been forced to drop out of high school at sixteen when his father died suddenly. He went in to my grandfather's automotive parts business, plying the back roads of western Quebec and eastern and northern Ontario for a while before eventually opening up his own auto parts store on the west island of Montreal.

I was eight or nine when he sold the store (I couldn't fathom why anyone would want to give up those wonderful tailpipes in the basement). After some stops and starts, he ended up selling mutual funds and life insurance. It was a big leap from persuading an operator in a greasy garage to buy your spark plugs to persuading first-time parents seated around the dining room table to take out an insurance policy. A big enough leap to require an entirely new uniform.

My father went to visit his friend Burt, who manufactured suits in Montreal's garment district. My father was proud of his made-to-measure suits and proud to have the kind of job that society deemed worthy of a necktie. To him, it was a badge of honour. To me, a generation later, it's literally a pain in the neck.

I was reminded of all this one day when Darrell and I met for lunch to discuss this book. He was decked out in a turtleneck and leather sports coat. I, the more formal one, was wearing a long-sleeved crewneck shirt under a sports jacket.

I was very conscious at that point of workplace dress codes. *The Globe and Mail* had recently asked me to organize an Internet news service. This was a step up for me. I could get rid of that damned tie.

I received some good-natured kidding at work about my new Internet-wear, but nobody took it too seriously. (On the days I wore running shoes, my impeccable publisher would mutter about the further deterioration of my appearance, but I chose to interpret this as simply a manifestation of his dry sense of humour.)

Not every organization, however, was coping well with the move to informality. One of the young guys I interviewed to work for our news service, Richard Bloom, arrived at my office for a midday interview in a tie, a humorous tie as I recall, but a tie nonetheless. I, of course, was without one. I teased him about his attire. Richard told me how the financial industry Web site for which he worked had been taken over by a bank. The Web operation was moved into one of those soaring Toronto bank towers; the young Webbies were placed in a sprawling space they shared with such disparate departments as purchasing and stock records. Shortly after they moved in, one of the bank's stuffed shirts made a point of letting the Web-heads know they were expected to wear ties. This was a bank, after all. Harrumph!

I guess that's why banks will never be very good at the new economy. It was an invitation for all their bright young Web-heads to look for work elsewhere. A friend of mine who worked with the banks on their failed merger proposals of a few years back said the experience reminded him of his time in government: a lot of smart people trapped in a dumb organization—and therefore behaving stupidly.

Richard now writes about the stock markets for globeandmail.com. He tends to wear an open-necked sports shirt or jersey over a white T-shirt. He's a great worker and seems perfectly content. In his first summer, he dyed his hair a weird shade of orange. I thought it looked off-putting, but who cares. The inside of the head is in fine working order.

The point is that the workplace is changing in style and substance—and corporations had better keep up with the expectations of their newly self-styled workers. The best employees are in great demand these days. (Even average employees are in demand and will continue to be so as baby boomers reach retirement age.) I was struck last year by a headline on ROBTv. "Paine Webber to spend $800 million to retain staff," it said. That was retain, not recruit. The New York brokerage firm had recently been taken over by a Swiss bank. It didn't want its most prized assets walking out the door. Paine Webber well understood the value of the knowledge worker in the new economy.

John Wright, Darrell's colleague at Ipsos-Reid, likes to recount the story of how Scott McNealey, the founder of Sun Microsystems, came to fully appreciate the shift in the balance of power between employers and employees. One night, John happened on the powerful high-tech executive on television. He was asked when had the world changed for him. That's easy, he replied. It was when I flew to Boston two years ago on a job recruitment exercise at MIT.

One of the applicants he interviewed was a young guy in jeans and a neat shirt. The CEO asked the young man if he knew much about the company. The applicant said that he knew a lot about the company. He had visited its Web site and he had read the reports of the financial analysts who follow Sun Microsystems. Moreover, he had looked into which divisions were doing what work and had communicated directly with people in those divisions to see where the really interesting work was happening and where the good managers were.

He went on to tell the Sun Microsystems chief executive which division he wanted to work for and what he wanted to do there. Moreover, he said, "I have a hobby that's called rock climbing. And I want two months off every year so I can do some serious rock climbing. And if that's not acceptable to you, I have two other offers in my pocket so I can make another choice."

For McNealey, it was clearer than ever the rules of the game had changed; the balance of power had shifted in the world of work. As with other areas of society, the workplace has undergone sweeping changes in recent years. Workers have new expectations and toughened attitudes.

Now, not all employees fall into the category of the most highly prized knowledge workers. These lucky people constitute the new aristocracy of the labour market. Individual brains are replacing the collective brawn of organized labour as the true power-broker in employer-employee relations. While most apparent in new economy industries such as telecommunications and bio-technology, the same forces are at work in old economy and new economy industries alike. None are immune to the revolution that has vaulted human capital over even financial capital as a source of competitive advantage. And with the early baby boomers approaching retirement age, all skilled workers are finding themselves in demand today.

Ted C. Fishman, writing in the July 2000 issue of *Esquire* magazine, recalled that it wasn't too long ago that downsizing was all the rage. "In those days, managers aspired to nicknames like Chainsaw," he wrote. As a business journalist through much of that period, I remember it well, too. I recall once interviewing the chairman of British Coal, Sir Robert Haslam, at his London headquarters. He told me a story of being at a dinner party several nights earlier and how his friends around the table, also corporate chieftains, enumerated one after another the numbers of workers they had laid off.

"One was saying they had done extremely well," he recounted, "because they had reduced their labour force by one thousand last year. And the other chap sort of clapped his shoulder and said, 'We have done rather better than that: we dropped two thousand.'"

Sir Robert's British breeding served him well as he resisted showing them up with his far greater prowess of having slashed his workforce from 221,000 miners to 92,000. "Well, I was biting my tongue," he told me. "We have been doing that before breakfast."

I described the conversation in my article as "a curious executive-edition game of 'Mine is bigger than yours.'" That's how CEOs measured their manhood a decade or so ago.

But as Fishman says, "Judgement Day, however, has come for the job-slashers. Lately, they've been having to beg for workers." Companies in the United States, he reported, now offer pet care, elder care, child care, and even dry-cleaning services on site for employees. "Getting the boss to clean and press your gym clothes," he declared, "feels like karmic justice to the once downsized." Of course, even high-tech companies aren't immune to layoffs as Nortel so convincingly demonstrated in the first half of 2001. But few Nortel casualties can be expected to be counted among the ranks of the long-term unemployed. An employee with the right skills and experience will continue to enjoy advantages in the new workplace.

While some companies in Canada, particularly in high tech, have also offered everything from child care to fitness facilities for top workers, the real key to attracting and retaining the workforce of the twenty-first century—in whatever industry and at whatever level—is education and training. How it got to be so is an interesting story in itself.

In the run-up to the recession in the early 1990s, no single issue truly dominated the Canadian public policy agenda. For a while, free trade held the number one position. With the Meech Lake crisis, national unity took over top spot. The Oka crisis had a similar effect. For a while, the environment moved up the charts, driven by major media reporting on events such as the shocking PCB fire in Saint-Basile de Grand, the ozone conference in Montreal, and the *Exxon Valdez* spill.

But no issue had real staying power. Then the recession hit, making unemployment the number one preoccupation of Canadians. It stayed firmly in place until July 1998.

As the recession deepened and Canadian job anxieties grew, the government fell into a state of paralysis. The years of fiscal profligacy had robbed it of the ability to act, even to undertake the sort of spit-in-the-wind, dig-a-ditch, I-feel-your-pain programs traditional in such circumstances. In fact, Ottawa did worse than nothing. Broke and self-absorbed, it moved to curtail unemployment insurance benefits at the very moment job losses were spinning out of control.

The sense of abandonment would get worse. Just as Canadians were going out of their minds with economic anxiety, the Mulroney government came out with the Charlottetown agreement. The attempt at constitutional peace sent the wrong message at the wrong time. The government appeared totally distracted from the issue that mattered most to Canadians, jobs. Instead, it made a massive fuss about a federal-provincial power-sharing arrangement, a matter of marginal utility to an economically insecure population. As we've seen elsewhere, Canadians expect their governments to come up with plans to confront the real problems of the country. As patient investors in their country, they'll hold their breath and play with pain if they think their long-term interests are really being pursued. Instead, it looked to them as if Prime Minister Nero was fiddling while Rome burned.

That error of judgement, turning back to national unity during a serious recession, would help lead to the defeat of the Charlottetown accord in the October 1992 referendum and the rout of the Conservative government a year later. And it would help nail down a major plank in the new dominant mindset.

Essentially, the economic security of Canadians rests on three pillars: their employers, their governments, and themselves. Their employers had let them down throughout the 1980s with their aggressive downsizing policies, even as profits soared in the latter part of the decade. Canadians believed up until that point that they enjoyed an implicit contract with their employers: They worked hard in exchange for reasonable job security. Many had launched their working lives in a more paternalistic age, a time in which companies offered subsidized cafeteria meals and spoke with pride of how they had held onto their employees even through the Depression. Remember back then: IBM was an employer for life. It was not unusual for grandfather, father, and son to have worked in the same mine or factory. The long growth years following the Second World War gave corporations the opportunity to present themselves as caring creatures. No pressure existed to trim workforces; companies tended to portray this fact as an act of munificence.

All this made the breakdown in the 1980s of the post-war workplace compact—loyalty in exchange for job security—an even more bitter pill to swallow for working Canadians. But swallow it they did, force-fed by the corporate sector. Shareholder value was all the rage. Employees suddenly amounted to a mere cost of doing business, an accounting entry like any other. The first pillar had fallen.

The early 1990s recession toppled the second pillar. Government was not there for Canadians, either in substance or symbolically. It cut the safety net just as people were falling off the high wire, and it failed to provide hope at a time of mounting fear. Sometimes even a hug helps when you're in pain, but tired and out of touch, the government had even lost its sense of empathy. In her brief moment in power, Prime Minister Kim Campbell famously declared, as she called an election in September 1993, that unemployment wouldn't dip below 10 per cent for the rest of the century. She said she was speaking the hard truth and wouldn't resort to the old politics of false hopes. As it turned out, she was off by five years. Two years after her solemn pronouncement, unemployment dipped below 10 per cent. But the gaffe really lay in her failure to project hope and a plan of action. The Liberals under Jean Chrétien ruthlessly exploited the opening. Chrétien made jobs *his* top issue, speaking endlessly about the dignity of work and promising a $2-billion infrastructure program to kick-start the economy. "The Tory priority is to create jobs for the year 2000. The Liberal priority is to create jobs in 1993, right now, and we'll start in November." Six weeks later, he was prime minister.

Canadians were grateful that someone had at least acknowledged their anxieties, but they understood enough economics to know that broke governments weren't going to make much real difference. An improved mood certainly didn't hurt, but $2 billion represented just one-quarter of 1 per cent of the Canadian economy.

That left only one pillar on which to rely—themselves. What emerged from the recession was a new attitude of resiliency and self-sufficiency. Focus group research in the mid-1990s began picking up growing signs of acceptance among individuals that they would have to make it on their own. As in that Elton John song, they wore their war wounds like a badge. Left to sink or swim, Canadians learned to swim. In the space of a few years, these recessionary survivors reached for the controls over their own economic destinies.

The confidence Canadians now articulate about their economic futures is clearly the most striking feature of this transformation. In late 1998, with economic fear well on its way to economic hope, 34 per cent of employed Canadians still worried they might lose their job over the next couple of years, according to the first annual Personal Security Index compiled by the Canadian Council on Social Development. By late 1999, just one year later, that figure had fallen to 26 per cent. In some other polls, job insecurity has fallen even lower (21 per cent in April 2001) despite all the chatter about an impending recession. Even more telling was the fact that just 27 per cent of Canadians in 1999 said they lacked confidence they could find a new job within six months if they lost theirs, an improvement of a full 10 percentage points in a single year. So even if they did get knocked down, they felt optimistic they would quickly get back on their feet.

The anxious worker about whom one constantly hears certainly exists, but this segment of the population constitutes significantly less than a majority of the workforce. Unsurprisingly, older workers, single parents, and those with less than high school education are the least confident of finding a new job if they were to lose their existing one. All told, this anxious segment probably makes up about a quarter of the workforce. Yet even among them confidence has been growing.

The more interesting, and bigger, story lies with the majority. Canadians have emerged from more than two decades of economic pain with their bodies erect and their heads held high. Ultimately, the experience has been cathartic. They resemble high school athletes suddenly finding the heart to reach up and compete at that next level. The best of them are ready to run and throw the javelin on Mount Olympus. But they want the training it takes to compete effectively in the economic games of the global economy.

Pollara asked Canadians in 2000: Do you have the skills necessary to succeed in the new economy? An emphatic 68 per cent replied yes. Just 28 per cent said no. Pollara went on to inquire whether advances in technology had helped them: 61 per cent said yes versus only 11 per cent who felt hurt by technological advances. The figures were even more striking when they considered the impact of technological change on the next generation. Young workers, higher-income workers, and the better educated lead the way in confidence. But really this is a broad phenomenon, extending right through the middle classes. By April 2001, the numbers had increased further, to 88 per cent who agreed they have the necessary skills to succeed.

So much for a population cowering in the face of a technological onslaught. Bring on the future, Canadians seem to be saying.

Pollara posed one more, quite intriguing, question. They asked people to choose between the importance of remaining on the cutting edge of technology and protecting traditional jobs. By 59 per cent to 31 per cent, respondents opted for the new technology alternative, for the future over the present. Full-time, part-time, self-employed—it didn't matter. The only groups that felt differently were those out seeking work and those feeling very insecure about their jobs. And even they were pretty much evenly divided. Canadians understand there is no going back. That the only hope of economic security requires moving forward.

Although the foundations of these new, forward-looking, self-sufficient attitudes began taking form in the mid-1990s, it was not until late 1997 and into 1998 that the fear finally lifted. Only then did the new dominant attitude among Canadians begin coming into focus. As we've noted before, it often takes time for a public opinion trend to crystallize. Only after years of fiscal profligacy and dire warnings of the unsustainability of governmental actions did Canadians come to accept that deficits mattered. And then it took quite a while—long after the deficit was actually eliminated—for the public to embrace that triumph as something other than propaganda. In the spring of 1998, a couple of months after the big balanced budget announcement, 80 per cent of Canadians expressed surprise upon being informed by Liberal pollsters that the deficit had been eliminated. For the Canadian worker, the tipping point from pessimism to optimism occurred some time in 1998.

Today, with several years of sustained economic growth under our belts and strong demand in place for skilled workers, a new mindset holds sway in the workplace. Liberated from fear and dependency, workers are increasingly seeking out three factors in their relationships with their employers: education, rewards, and freedom. These reflect both their search for certainty and the arrival of the new consumer into the job market.

Education and training come first with employed Canadians. They represent the new passport to economic security, replacing the income support programs of old. Canadians don't want a social safety net anymore as much as a jobs springboard. They accept the fact the economy is constantly changing around them and therefore they must adapt with it. Corporations are engaged in a perpetual effort to define and redefine themselves. New process and product technologies alter competitive standing, and new entrants in the marketplace, often coming out of nowhere, make for continuous upheaval. As the Prime Minister's Advisory Council on Science and Technology reported in March 2000, the accelerated rate of economic change means "we are always trying to hit a target that moves at a rapidly increasing speed. This is a very different situation from the old economy, in which skills had a much longer shelf life."

The new worker understands it is as impossible to stand still in the economy as on a bicycle. In both cases, you risk toppling over. You always have to be moving forward. Since workers can't depend on their employers or governments to protect them in unstable times—and all times are unstable with globalization—they are relying on themselves for the peddling power. As authors Jim Botkin and Stan Davis wrote in *The Monster Under the Bed*, in the knowledge economy you don't earn a living, so much as "you learn a living."

In its 1999 Personal Security Index, the Canadian Council on Social Development, reported, "In the wake of changes brought about by technology, liberalized global trade and new management philosophies, the average Canadian felt that the ground shifted during the 1990s. For many people, traditional job security has been based on working for one firm for a long period of time and being protected by seniority. Today, this has been replaced by the prospect of holding many jobs during a lifetime and by more self-employment. The extent of employment security no longer depends on seniority, but rather on workers' skills and education."

If you understand one thing about the workplace, make it this. Nothing matters as much to Canadian workers as continuous education and skills enhancement. What they are seeking out of the workplace is a skills-ocracy. It is their vaccination against the scourge of unemployment. It provides both a defensive strategy against economic uncertainty and an offensive strategy of investing oneself with economic choices and thereby gaining a seat at the buffet table of the global economy. It is the way in which Canadian workers manifest their search for certainty, or at least the greatest measure of certainty they can possibly hope to find in the uncertain environment of the global economy.

Next in the hierarchy of new workplace expectations comes reward, which includes but is not limited to monetary rewards. Interesting work and the opportunity to expand one's horizons—all these count, too. Even when it comes to pure money matters, Angus Reid Group research shows the most highly prized workers—those frequently referred to these days as "the talent"—desire more than just high salaries. They expect to participate in the success of their companies and are confident enough of their abilities to want to be judged on their individual performance. They see themselves as entrepreneurial and therefore expect to share in the rewards of the entrepreneur. The polling firm asked employees which of the following two options would attract them to a new company or keep them working at their current organizations: an average salary with an opportunity for bonus or compensation based on performance or an above-average salary with no bonus opportunities. By a staggering four-to-one margin they opted for the average salary and performance-related bonus.

Finally, they want the freedom to manage their affairs within their corporation. A good working environment matters big-time. Again, the same survey asked if employees would prefer a very positive work environment with average compensation or an average work environment with above-average compensation. The result was 67 per cent to 31 per cent for work environment over compensation.

The new workers have been labelled intrapreneurs by some commentators, meaning they bring entrepreneurial instincts and values to corporate organizations. Their self-image is not that of the assembly line, with its punch clock and hourly wage. These new workers feel they are part of the organization—indeed, they are the organization—and therefore demand to be treated with a different degree of respect. They willingly put in long hours, but expect their employers to show them flexibility. They are independent minded and they are seeking the head space and elbow room to do their jobs as they see fit. A necktie if necessary but not necessarily a necktie, sums up their frame of mind.

These three desires—opportunity for growth, participation in success, and freedom to excel—are obviously intertwined. Keeping current on knowledge is also a ticket to freedom and money. An intrapreneur seeks the means to participate in success and perhaps gain a measure of economic freedom. The best of workers are looking for enabling employers. They have witnessed first-hand disloyalty in the workplace. They or some member of their family were most probably victimized by it during the downsizing phase. It has hardened them. Now that power has shifted in their direction, at least for the best of workers, they won't hesitate to be loyal, first and foremost, to themselves.

As Carolyn Clark, vice-president of human resources for the Fairmont Hotels & Resorts unit of Canadian Pacific Ltd., told *The Globe and Mail* last year, "In the late eighties and early nineties, Gen-Xers saw their parents working hard and losing their jobs. Today when people work for a company, they want to know: 'What's in it for me.'" Ditto for just about anyone among the three-quarters of workers in the confident classes.

An international comparison made last year suggests that Canadians have emerged from their two decades of disappointment as among the more disloyal employees in the world. The Hudson Institute, an American think tank, measured attitudes in thirty-two countries. Canada sat right in the middle of the pack with regard to employer loyalty and satisfaction. Only 14 per cent of Canadian workers described themselves as "truly loyal" to their companies compared with an international average of 34 per cent. American workers came in at 24 per cent.

After all they've been through, workers are primarily loyal to themselves. That doesn't mean they're dissatisfied, just self-interested. The overwhelming majority of Canadians are satisfied with their work and employer. But the battle to keep them engaged is waged every day and on many fronts. Within Canada, the Royal Bank of Canada has been plumbing the depths of workplace attitudes for several years now. Its studies confirm many of the trends we have discussed in this chapter. As early as the fall of 1997, the bank began picking up early signs of an emerging optimism in the Canadian workplace. At that point, close to seven in ten Canadians said they felt they had what it would take to succeed in the twenty-first-century economy. They were registering for courses and pursuing educational opportunities. They were upgrading their knowledge and skills to better manage their jobs. They were well on their way to assuming control over their futures.

Sixty-two per cent reported they had taken at least one course over the previous year, the majority paid for by their employer and many during work hours. They were working longer and harder to right-skill themselves for the economy of the twenty-first century. The breakneck speed of change was hard on them, but most expressed confidence that they—and their employers—were moving in the right direction. The evidence suggested that employees felt better and were more productive when they could exercise a measure of control over their work. Being equipped effectively imbued them with greater resiliency to live with constant change. These workers were really throwing the gauntlet down to their organizations and governments: Give us the tools, make us feel appreciated, care about us—and watch us take off for you.

At about the same time, the bank put out a separate report exploring the outlook of the so-called Gen-Xers, the age cohort born between the early 1960s and late 1970s. Popularized by Vancouver writer Douglas Coupland in his 1992 novel *Generation X: Tales for an Accelerated Culture*, these were the people, a quarter of the Canadian population, widely viewed as our lost generation. They had the misfortune to come of age right behind the oxygen-hogging baby boomers and in the midst of our long economic decline. Even if they were so inclined, none would have been able to recall the fat years.

If you look back on the writing of academics and commentators in this period, concern over the fate of the Gen-Xers was one of the most omnipresent of all hand-wringing exercises. Despite their high education levels, the economy had failed to accommodate them. In fact, the length of their education was seen as a defensive measure as much as anything: They stayed in school only because they couldn't find work. The youth unemployment number proved an immovable object; the only work possible was in dead-end jobs in the service industry, the so-called McJobs; the incidence of poverty among young families was alarmingly high.

Coupland's pessimistic vision of a lost, aimless, cynical, and ambivalent generation seemed all too real as the early 1990s recession was followed by little in the way of economic vital signs. We all worried for the next generation. In November 1995, a mere 12 per cent of Canadians thought this younger generation would enjoy a financial future better than themselves. Sixty-two per cent figured the future for young people would be bleaker than their own.

But was all that pessimism justified? Had we reduced a diverse generation to a single stereotype, just as we had in typecasting every kid who grew up in the sixties as a long-haired, pot-smoking, anti-war demonstrator? Were the Gen-Xers, like others adjusting to new circumstances, actually more optimistic than the media portrayal allowed? Were they Olympians rather than deadheads? The Royal Bank study certainly suggested so. Contrary to public perceptions, the majority of these young Canadians perceived their own quality of life as high and assessed their situation as improving. Moreover, their optimism was strongly linked to their job and career perceptions. Sure enough, a significant portion of them, about 20 per cent, fit the marginal and wayward stereotype, but the rest bubbled over with enthusiasm about butting heads with the vicissitudes of life. Even the easy assumption that they were stalled despite their education didn't stand up to scrutiny over the medium term. A 1995 study of post-secondary students from the class of 1990 found them doing as well as an earlier generation of graduates five years after leaving school.

Robert Barnard, a Gen-Xer himself and president of d-Code, a consulting firm dedicated to understanding this cohort of Canadians, never ceases to be amazed at the simplistic stereotypes thrown at the group. Alternative adjectives that could be used to describe this generation, he offers, would include adaptable, skeptical, optimistic, and savvy. He's attempted to rechristen them the Nexus generation, which he and his co-authors describe in their book *Chips & Pop* as "a distinct group of people growing up at a unique point in history, sandwiched between two significant generations, linking an exciting future to an important past." Nexus, he allows, certainly came of age at an economically gloomy time, but also in a period when it would experience computer chips and global media in its formative years. It combines many of the attributes of the baby boomers, including a surprisingly conservative impulse for purchasing RRSPs (perhaps a result of its early economic uncertainty and its lack of faith in government pensions), and the so-called Net generation behind it. The Gen-Xers or Nexus generation encountered the first video game, Pong, at seven and had started using PCs before hitting the workplace.

The Gen-Xers were different, to be certain, although largely for the good. Their experiences had left them better educated, more at ease with technology, and less perturbed by mobility demands than the rest of us. They were environmentally conscious, and tolerance was no more a value for them than oxygen is an element for you and me. It was second nature. They were, as Trudeau's children, post-liberal in that sense. Contrary to popular belief, the workplace was important to them. It represented the hub of their social, as well as economic, existence. But they did not suffer corporate bureaucracies and hierarchies gladly. They preferred flexible, entrepreneurial organizations in which to express themselves. Nor did they have much time for the traditional ways in which we express community, through governments and political leaders. They certainly possessed a sense of community, but one that reflected their own values, not those of their elders. No wonder everyone misdiagnosed them as alienated!

Consider this:

- Forty-one per cent said they were completely satisfied or very satisfied with their overall quality of life versus only 4 per cent who described themselves as very dissatisfied.

- By 41 per cent to 13 per cent, they said their quality of life had improved, not declined over the previous six months.

- Fifty-four per cent agreed with the statement "I am in control of what happens in my life" versus 5 per cent who disagreed.

- Only 27 per cent agreed with the statement "I know that at any given moment everything in my life could fall apart" versus 37 per cent who disagreed.

Remember how we all fretted that these Gen-Xers would be the first generation in our history to be worse off than earlier generations. Again, they didn't see it that way.

- Only 13 per cent disagreed with the statement "You will be better off financially than your parents." Forty per cent agreed.

- Forty-five per cent agreed that "You will meet or exceed your career expectations." Only 7 per cent disagreed.

- By six to one, they felt their children would be better off than they were, the classic Canadian dream.

Ultimately, the researchers divided them into three subgroups. The first group, comprising about half of Gen-Xers, expressed satisfaction with their circumstances, felt in control of their lives and optimistic about the future. The second segment, about a third of the overall group, felt similarly optimistic, but had a greater distance to journey to achieve their financial aspirations. They tended to be at the younger end of the generation. And then there was the final group, the one about which we tend to hear most and the one clearly in the most need of our public policy intervention. They made up about one-fifth of Generation Xers. They confessed to being in difficult financial straits and imagined little prospect for improvement. They voiced negative and pessimistic views about most aspects of their lives. They tended to be a bit older (thirty to thirty-five), with low incomes and often had gone through a marriage breakup. They didn't feel at all in control of their lives.

As we've mentioned, the renewal of Canadian optimism began showing up in late 1997 and gathered force in 1998. When the Royal Bank went back into the field in 1998, the can-do attitude was even more pronounced. From the boardrooms to the mailroom, workers expressed an overwhelming sense that a tornado of change had blown through their workplaces. Amazingly, they stated that its effects had been for the better, not the worse. Precisely two-thirds agreed with the statement "I like things changing all the time. It keeps things exciting and challenging." Only 18 per cent agreed that things are changing so fast that it's hard for them to keep up. Indeed, 63 per cent of employees thought change had been for the better, not worse (the figure rose to 72 per cent in 2000). Two-thirds gave their employers credit for helping them prepare for change, lauding them mostly for improved training and education programs and for keeping up with new technologies.

Three out of ten workers still felt very vulnerable to these changes. Thirty-one per cent said they "have little control over things that happen to [them] at work." This was especially true among older workers, junior employees, and low-income Canadians. Thirty-two per cent said they have more to do than they can comfortably handle.

Again, it was the majority that told the story. Most were taking courses as a coping measure to regain control. More than that, employees were looking on their workplaces as a type of family; they put enormous stock in companies that cared about them and that gave them the freedom to soar. Overwhelmingly, by 85 per cent to 8 per cent, respondents said they prefer to make their own work decisions rather than having them made for them. The same with initiating their own work regimen as opposed to having someone lay out a structure and schedule for them. The message: Employees don't want to be mindless automatons or armchair cynics, even if they are well compensated for it. They want to be involved, in the thick of things.

They were read the statement "I work just for the pay." Only 25 per cent agreed.

Business guru Tom Peters did a nice job when he set out to describe the attributes of the new-style worker. He wrote:

> She is turned on by her work!
> The work matters!
> The work is cool!
> She is "in your face"!
> She is an adventurer!
> She is the CEO of her life!

"I work just for the pay." Not on your life. But, by the way, don't try to rip me off.

Darrell and I have both managed divisions within our knowledge companies and have interviewed hundreds of prospective employees in recent years. The shop mentality is gone. Rarely do we discuss salaries until long after we decide they are right for us and, more importantly, we are right for them. This transformation of work from a standard-of-living mentality to a quality-of-life mentality must be understood by employers or they will fail in their number one challenge of today: attracting the best and brightest who will power future prosperity.

In April 2000, Angus Reid and the Royal Bank waded back into the pool to test the waters of the new worker once again. This time, they decided to concentrate on university students on the cusp of entering the workforce, interviewing 3,000 of them from twenty different universities. The importance they attached to the quality of work life was striking. They are "more in pursuit of interesting experience than the almighty dollar," the report concluded. Eighty-one per cent said they would rather have an interesting job than make a lot of money. Three-quarters would be more attracted to a company with a very positive work environment and average compensation over above-average compensation and an average work environment. The opportunity to experience a variety of tasks and opportunities ranked well ahead of job security as a priority. Mind you, they were not anti-money. Of all the factors that would influence where they would work, two stood out—the opportunity to learn and the salary. So money matters, but only as part of the whole package.

Workopolis, Canada's biggest Internet job site, arrived at similar conclu-sions in a major workplace study in early 2001. It identified as the top five reasons for staying in a job: like the work (78 per cent); like the co-workers (68 per cent); like the mission and activities of the company (61 per cent); learning a lot (57 per cent); salary satisfaction (53 per cent). With regard to what it would take to entice them away, a salary increase of 10 per cent ranked ninth. Salary certainly matters, but not first and foremost. Just 12 per cent of respondents said they work just for the pay.

And guess who were the most confident about finding a job and the most optimistic about their future career opportunities? Young workers, many of them those supposedly forlorn Gen-Xers.

It has become almost a cliché of the corporate world to pay lip service to new workplace realities. But after all those years of discarding employees in the pursuit of being lean, mean profit-making machines, Canada's corpo-rate leaders have something to prove: that they really do place a premium on the care and development of their most important asset, their human capital. Economic theorists agree that what separates the winners from the losers in the new economy is more often than not the brains employed in the organ-ization. Can you attract the best? Can you retain the best? Can you lead them or, better yet, create an environment in which they take the lead?

The better companies have started treating their employees with the same care as their customers. And with good reason: Success in the knowledge economy is increasingly reliant on your talent pool. But the real test will come through a downturn more painful and protracted than we experienced in the first half of 2001—will talent be protected or, once again, thrown overboard?

Ultimately, the companies that show a genuine commitment to lifelong learning will enjoy a competitive advantage as employers of choice. The Conference Board of Canada found in one of its studies that augmenting stu-dent programs with cooperative work placements and the like was the single most important factor in a company's success in recruiting the graduates it required. The other top finisher: the sincerity of its commitment to a culture of lifelong learning and its willingness to show the colour of its money when it came to all the rhetoric surrounding training and workplace development.

While employees obviously desire corporate support for improving themselves and are on the lookout for these attributes, interestingly, they are not counting on employers to deliver for them. Fifty-two per cent of employees in the fall of 1998 said that individuals should be mainly responsible for ensuring they have adequate education and job training. Thirty-one per cent say the job should fall mainly to government with just 16 per cent pointing to the private sector. This is further evidence of the self-sufficiency of the new dominant mindset.

They have heeded the advice of Andrew Grove, former chief executive of Intel Corp. and author of the best-selling *Only the Paranoid Survive.* "The sad news is nobody owes you a career," he wrote. "Your career is your business. You are a sole proprietor. You have one employee—yourself."

We like to call this the baseball-ization of the labour market. An employee with anything on the ball wants to be a free-agent these days. And it is those super-talented employees who make the real difference in the success of a company. Employers have got to start facing up to the free agent world. No more one-size-fits-all compensation structures for the stars. Some people prefer rock-climbing to pensions. They don't mind being measured on their batting average and slugging percentage. And they won't hesitate to jump to another team, not just for the money, but for the chance to win the pennant.

High-tech workers are at the vanguard, and their attitudes are revealing. As the most highly sought after employees in the new economy, they have been showered with fitness facilities, on-site child care, flex time, telecommuting, stock options—whatever it takes. But according to a 1999 study of 2,000 Canadian employees by the human resources firm, AON Consulting Inc., high-tech employees display a fascinating paradox. On the one hand, they are more likely than employees in other industries to agree that their organization is one of the best places to work (56 percent). On the other hand, they are the least likely (33 per cent) to say they would remain with their company if offered a better paying position elsewhere.

They are self-confident. They are mobile—even across national boundaries. They are, like baseball players, part of a free-agent market. Their first loyalty is self. They are the CEOs of their lives. And it's not just the power-hitting post-graduate electrical engineers and computer programmers. Take the case of Ben Chartrand, who was laid off in June 2000 from Corel Corp. in Ottawa. He was a twenty-one-year-old software developer with a degree from Heritage College in Hull. Just eighteen hours into his first day of unemployment, Ben was driving down Highway 417 when his cell phone rang. It was a recruiter from Syndesis Ltd., a telecommunications software company. He happened to be one exit away from their office. "It was thirty seconds and I was there," he told *The Globe and Mail*'s Simon Tuck.

When we checked in to see whether Ben had landed the job, he told us he hadn't been quite as unworried as one might have thought. His wife, Amy, also worked at Corel and they fretted over a double layoff. However, he was confident his education, skills, and personality would hold him in good stead. "Take someone who got laid off from Chrysler," he said. "They're going to have a really hard time because maybe all they did was assemble Colts. Where people are skilled, and obviously high tech is one of those, there's a huge job market right now and a lot of job openings."

As it turned out, Ben's skill set in commercial software wasn't a good fit with Syndesis. But two days later, he landed a job at Netactive Inc., a company he'd been watching even while at Corel. He holds one of only two research positions in the far smaller company and therefore enjoys greater responsibility. "It's a huge step forward from what I did at Corel. If I were to go back to Corel, I would have a huge list of demands, and I'm sure Corel would never be able to meet them." Ben continued to thrive even during the high-tech retrenchment in the first half of 2001.

Ben's a pretty good representation of the opportunities open to a new generation with the right skills and a capacity to live with risks. His father never obtained a high school diploma. The choices before him were either grunt work or a military life. He opted to enlist and spent his career as a weapons technician. He had wanted Ben to either learn a mechanical trade or go for the security of a public service job. But despite a close relationship, they're different people. "The contrast between me and my father is enormous—we're worlds apart," Ben says. "He can't understand that in my first job I made more than him in his last days at DND. He can't get over how well I'm doing."

Ben certainly didn't enjoy the experience of losing his job and wouldn't relish going through it again. Last time out, he feared he and Amy might lose their townhouse. But he's philosophical about the possibilities and takes comfort in the fact that his skills can't be taken away. In any case, job security has to be balanced out with the work environment and the satisfaction that comes from seeing your work produce results. "You have to enjoy going there each morning and also the people you work with."

Author and human resources consultant Barbara Moses talks of the logical next step after niche marketing being the niche workplace. Organizations competing for talent will increasingly do so by differentiating themselves because of their unique corporate cultures. She counsels companies to become employers of choice. "Employers will compete to attract and retain the best and brightest new workers. The winners will be those who can offer work-life balance, scope for decision-making, learning opportunities, friendly culturally rich environments, and a socially responsible approach to business. Individuals ask: 'Why should I work here, what will I learn, what will I walk out with at the end of the day that I didn't have before?'"

Moses sees the changing psychological profile of the new worker coupled with the growing demand for talent creating an equality mindset in employees. Not among themselves, like the old union mentality, but in their relationships with employers. The new worker wants to enter into reciprocal relationships. They no longer feel beholden to their employers or dependent on corporate largesse. They demand their worth be recognized. And, once again, they are looking for a new form of security. "Whatever your official work status, there is no security other than what you create for yourself—which is to say, the security of knowing you are employable in other settings."

The new motto of the new workplace for the new economy could be "Self-reliance brings its own rewards." For employers, it also brings its own risks—if you don't connect with the true desires of these workers.

We can't stress this point enough. As we discussed in Chapter 2, Canadians have come to accept the reality of the global economy. The best among us, the people whose intelligence and motivation truly drive innovation and economic growth, in particular see themselves swimming in a global pool. Economic Olympians, they are more excited than daunted by the opportunities of competing at the highest levels possible. They want to win the pennant.

Robert Prichard stepped down last year after a decade as president of Canada's largest post-secondary institution, the University of Toronto. A natural-born optimist, he is generally pretty bullish on Canada's prospects. In the early to mid-1990s, he worried that Canada was falling out of the first rank among nations. Today, he believes the country is back in the hunt.

But he worries about our human capital. The very attributes of the new worker make them harder to hold on to. In the spring of 2000, as he prepared to leave the university, Prichard participated in fourteen U of T convocation ceremonies. As each student came forward, he shook their hand and asked them what they intended to do. "It was downright scary," he told me a few weeks later. It seemed to him that wave after wave of his graduates was heading for the United States. "It was amazing to me. It was scary, scary, scary." This exodus of talent was most pronounced among electrical and computer engineering graduates. But it extended into law, medicine, nursing, and other disciplines.

"I think they are seeing opportunity," Prichard reflected. "They take globalization seriously. They want to compete at the highest level in their chosen fields. They don't want any false ceilings." He found that those leaving Canada were departing with an excitement about the opportunities ahead, but devoid of any genuine joy. "They are proud of Canada. They love Canada. They are not happy about leaving." It is not about taxes or debt or anything tangible, he says. It is about opportunity.

Though disappointed by their loss, Prichard is not totally surprised. He has encountered the same sentiments in trying to retain and recruit university faculty members. Their central question is invariably "If I come to the U of T, will there be any artificial limit to my ability to succeed in the global world?" They want to be known as the best. They don't want to have to play second string to someone else who happens to benefit from the support structures of a Princeton or MIT or Stanford.

In its early stages, the debate in Canada over the brain drain revolved around two issues: whether it really existed and, if so, whether tax cuts or new spending on such items as research was the best way to reverse it.

Although it took the government, and particularly Prime Minister ean Chrétien, quite a while to smell the coffee, the evidence is really straightforward, although a quick glance can be misleading. There is nothing unusual about several thousand Canadians hopping the border each year for opportunities on the other side. Canadians have become accustomed to making up this deficit, and then some, through the immigration of skilled workers into the country. Thus brain drain becomes brain gain.

Having said that, the deeper trends of recent years are more disquieting. First off, no Canadian parent is going to be happy to hear that yes, their kid may have decided this country lacked the opportunities in fields of interest to them, but someone from somewhere else is taking their place. We're talking here of human beings, not cattle. Someone else's kids won't be coming over for Sunday brunch. As well, any loss is a loss. You don't want to lose the next Bill Gates no matter how many others you gain. Although this flies in the face of old-fashioned Canadian egalitarianism, the danger of the brain drain is not in the quantity but the quality of the individuals departing. In order to succeed in the global economy, Canada needs to attract, as we've discussed, not just skilled workers but the most skilled workers as well—both domestically and internationally. The top layer of talent in the country largely determines competitive advantage these days.

The evidence unfortunately shows that we are losing a disproportionate share of graduates and workers with highly specialized new economy skills. A recent survey, less anecdotal than Prichard's informal head counting, showed that just 1.5 per cent of university graduates were choosing to move south. But among them were one in eight doctoral graduates. Those with graduate and post-graduate degrees are more likely to go south by a factor of three to one. Among 1995 Canadian graduates emigrating to the United States, 44 per cent said they had been in the top 10 per cent of their class.

Prichard is among those who feel the main priority for policy-makers interested in hanging on to our most talented individuals comes in creating challenging opportunities in Canada. He's encouraged by such policies as the federal government's creation of 2,000 university research chairs, which will multiply by more than ten-fold the number of endowed chairs in Canada, as well as other increases in research funding. Recruitment is going on around the world, with top priority on repatriating Canadian brains. "Creating Opportunity," by the way, was the title of the Liberal Red Book in the 1993 election campaign.

Increasingly, Canadian workers, like our Olympic athletes, want to run with the best in the world. They've been brought up to go for gold. Life in a bronze-medal country holds little appeal.

Think of two figures we've related in this chapter. As early as the fall of 1997, with the fear barely lifted, nearly seven in ten Canadians told Angus Reid Group they had what it takes to succeed in the twenty-first century economy. The following year, 68 per cent told Pollara they possess the skills necessary to succeed in the new economy. These are large numbers that stand in defiance of the presumed doom and gloom coming at the time from media commentators. The optimism and sense of determination have only grown more pronounced since that time.

Nobody can predict the future course of the economy. But there is no denying we have entered into a golden age for skilled employees. Industries of all sorts, from automotive to telecommunications, are so concerned about recruiting good employees in the future that they are setting up programs in high schools to begin developing relationships with the workers of the future. Law firms are increasingly being forced to offer up permanent positions in order to recruit top articling students.

The ever-innovative Cisco Systems, one of the world's top Internet manufacturers, announced in the summer of 2000 that it was giving stock options to its 1,300 interns and co-op students in order to tie them into the company. It's also busy in high schools, along with other high-tech companies, fostering the coming generation of knowledge workers. Tom Crump, the health services manager we met in Chapter 1, recounted with satisfaction that his seventeen-year-old son had been through a two-year Cisco program at his high school. "When he comes out of high school with that background, he's going to have great opportunities before him."

Nor is this just an issue for high-tech workers such as the demanding applicant at Sun Microsystems. Take the case of automotive mechanics. A few years back, I visited a fascinating training program on Highway 404 north of Toronto. Young men, many of them high school dropouts, had enrolled for a rigorous course in automotive repair, one meant to break the cycle of despair of being unable to get a job without experience and being unable to get experience without a job. Everyone accepted in the program was guaranteed a position if they could get through the three sixteen-week cycles. I learned that in the old days, fixing a car required little in the way of formal training. Some people had mechanical aptitude and some lacked it. Your average farm boy could fix what was under the hood. But cars, like everything else, are less mechanical and more electronic these days. They are akin to computers on wheels. Aptitude doesn't count nearly as much as knowledge. Dealers were finding their veteran mechanics ill-equipped to cope with the highly technical diagnostic equipment at work in their service bays. And so they set out to finance the training of this cohort of new economy automotive engineers, providing them with technical and business knowledge and working on their interpersonal skills. Chrysler had already promised a job to all graduates of the class I visited.

I met a young man named Eric Batsford. He was working on the differential of an old Chrysler New Yorker while we spoke. As we bent under the hood of the car, he told me he was twenty-three and had bounced around between teaching skiing in the winter, putting in some hours on landscaping projects in the spring, and collecting unemployment insurance in between. He wasn't interested, just as with the research we saw earlier on Gen-Xers, in spending his life whining and crying about his situation. "I felt bad collecting unemployment," he told me. "I didn't want to suck the system for the rest of my life. I don't want to be that person. I want to be marketable and I want to be self-sustaining."

I looked Eric up as we were preparing this book. He was working for a Chrysler dealership in Calgary. When I phoned him at home one evening, he was giving his two-year-old daughter a bath. He told me that after graduating in 1995, he had moved from dealership to dealership in the Toronto area—with some time-outs in the body repair business—before finally ending up out west. "I never went back on pogey," he said. "My skills have provided me something I can always do." He was enjoying his middle-class existence—he made $60,000 a year, owned a home, two cars, a boat. And his job allowed him the opportunity—indeed, forced him—to constantly upgrade his skills. "I'm extremely computer literate," he said.

But he was far from satisfied. He was happy enough with his standard of living, but not the quality of his work. He didn't get to interact with customers and he didn't see much chance for advancement. Too much of his time was spent on basic repairs such as oil changes well below his skill level. Simply put, his employer wasn't challenging him. He'd been talking to a friend in his neighbourhood about buying into his garage and convenience store operation. "Maybe my generation always wants more," he said. "I envisage my future as an entrepreneur."

All employers today are desperately seeking workers with skills. Ken Georgetti, president of the Canadian Labour Congress, warns that we had better prepare now for a looming skills shortage, or be sorry later. The average age of journeymen in the construction trades is nearing fifty, he points out. Georgetti is trying to shift attention from the obvious demand for glamour jobs such as software programmers and Web page developers and draw attention to the fact that the country also desperately needs carpenters, electricians, and instrument mechanics. Even public administration is facing the crunch of a jobs shortage. The federal government announced last year that it will have to recruit upwards of 12,000 people a year to replace those baby boomers, with their years of expertise, starting to leave its midst.

All of these future employees, no matter what their field, will be looking to upgrade their skills, to make themselves, like Eric Batsford, marketable and self-sustaining. There really are very few low-tech jobs left. As one commentator recently said, it's not so much a situation of people looking for jobs as jobs looking for people. Bell Canada, one of Canada's largest companies, spent most of the 1990s, shedding thousands and thousands of positions. Now it offers cash bonuses to technical employees willing to upgrade their skills.

We talk a lot in this book about the new economy. But the biggest single classification of male jobs in the 1996 census, according to Statistics Canada, was truck driver. There were 222,795 of them. (The top female job was retail salesperson.) And know what? Truck drivers work in the new economy, too. Trucking is a critical component in the highly developed knowledge network known as just-in-time delivery—the circulation system of the modern economy.

Truckers belong to the new economy in two ways. First, thousands of them work for new economy companies, delivering the e-commerce products ordered over the Internet, and second, tens of thousands more employ new economy techniques in their trucking operations. A study at the height of the Chapters Online experiment found that 42 per cent of its employees were either truck drivers, warehouse workers, or call centre operators—the old economy embedded in the new. But there aren't many old jobs in any case. Even today's truck driver is a knowledge worker. He, or increasingly she, plies the highways between Winnipeg and Toronto in a rig equipped with a global positioning system. The driver may be processing orders right in the rig and using a computer to advise on optimum routes. New sensing equipment attached to a dashboard screen is being used to warn of heightened dangers of truck rollovers. The industry talks of "smart trucks," "twenty-first century trucks," and "offices in the cab." About half of today's rigs are Internet connected, and voice-activated or touch-screen computers are more and more commonly found mounted on truck dashboards. Have you seen a FedEx driver lately? Each one runs around with a hand-held computer, one that probably contains more computing power than was available to entire corporations thirty years ago. And, judging by the Tom Hanks movie *Castaway*, FedEx delivery guys in Moscow carry the same device.

David Pecaut, who used to run the Boston Consulting Group's global e-commerce group in Toronto before moving into the venture capital business last year, recalls a visit he made to Xerox PARC in California. He was shown a system called Eureka that contains thousands of tips on what may be wrong with your copier. Every Xerox repair person in the world is equipped with a diagnostic kit that includes a device to plug into this system. The truly amazing thing is that the system is dynamic. If the repair person encounters a new wrinkle with a sticky roller, his report will be automatically consolidated into the tip sheets. You may not see it, but when the photocopy repair person comes to your office, the brains of thousands of his colleagues are packed in his case.

The lines are blurring between old economy and new economy. Today's knowledge workers come in all shapes, sizes, occupations, and—of course—uniforms. The old rules no longer apply between white collar and blue collar. The Xerox repairman might be in a tie; the programmers back at Xerox PARC in polo shirts.

The necktie challenge may well remain the simplest litmus test for how companies and governments are facing the workforce challenges of the future.

In the summer of 2000, the federal department of finance, of all places, decided to go casual. Housed in the high-rise L'Esplanade Laurier in downtown Ottawa, the finance ministry has traditionally given a higher meaning to the word stodgy. But on July 4, 2000, an edict went out—relax. No more shirt and tie required. (Being the government, this was announced as a pilot project to be evaluated at the end of the summer.) The Treasury Board, the government's bean-counters, quickly followed suit—if you will.

The edict moved *The Globe and Mail's* Mark MacKinnon to write:

"There comes a point where every revolution dies and becomes merely the institution.

"The record will some day show that the casual dress revolution—the gift of scraggly computer geeks and engineers to an overdressed world—died today when civil servants in the Finance Department left their three-piece suits in the closet and arrived at work attired in golf shirts and khakis.

"While that may not seem like much of an event, it's notable because today is a Tuesday, not a Friday. Even in Ottawa in the summer, the week doesn't end this early."

The finance department said it was taking the step because it wanted to catch up with the private sector. But really it meant catch up to the high-tech sector, which increasingly sets the tone for our entire economy. The fact is that old-world companies are only beginning to get the message that the old rules of the workplace no longer compute.

In the spring of 2000, the Canadian Imperial Bank of Commerce officially shucked its button-down image in favour of extending its casual Fridays policy to every day of the week. (Tellers were excluded for the time being until the bank could gauge the probable reaction of customers, none of whom, we can assure the bank, are going to protest. My bank tellers already have pierced tongues and noses.)

As Karen Howlett reported in *The Globe and Mail*, CIBC, in true banker-ly style, had sent a memo to all 46,000 employees worldwide the day before with a list of fashion dos and don'ts. On the banned list: any clothing made out of Spandex; T-shirts; shorts; and anything with rips or tears. The acceptable "business casual" included chinos and polo shirts for men, khaki pants, casual dresses and blouses—with sleeves—for women.

Perceptively, Howlett traced this new relaxed trend on Bay Street not to an internal liberalizing mentality—let's treat our workers like adults—but to an external business rationale. These "banks and law firms increasingly deal with clients in the dot-com sector—folks who ditched their ties long ago," she noted. The changed dress codes reflected efforts on the part of these so-called old economy players to look as new economy as possible. Sort of like the year your father wore a Nehru suit.

Indeed, she quoted an executive at Torys, one of the most prestigious law firms on Bay Street, fessing up about the true reasons behind its plans to introduce a business casual dress code for the summer months. Many of the firm's clients are in the high-tech sector, said Patty Grimes, director of client services. "There are so many changes in business dress. We really feel we have to adapt."

But not go crazy. Down the Bay Street glass canyon, at Osler Hoskin & Harcourt, another blue-blood Toronto law firm, a business casual dress policy had been in effect for the previous two summers. It was fine for lawyers to dress casual when they met high-tech clients, said managing partner Terry Burgoyne. But most kept a suit and tie at the office to meet with clients who arrived in town from New York for a mergers and acquisitions deal.

Howlett's article ended by noting the CIBC's new dress code had evoked a bit of envy at Montreal-based National Bank of Canada, which had yet to introduce even casual Fridays. "Oh, lucky them," exclaimed spokesman Jean Robillard.

I looked at that article and laughed. National Bank was where my young colleague Richard Bloom, the one now without the tie, used to work.

CHAPTER 5

SCHOOL BY CHOICE

In early 1999, Toronto's Humber College accepted an invitation to compete in a four-team basketball tournament at the University of Ottawa along with McGill University and the University of Prince Edward Island.

Humber, a community college with two campuses and 11,000 students, enjoyed a reputation for having a pretty good basketball program. It had taken home four Canadian Colleges Athletic Association titles in the previous eight years. During the twelve-year tenure of head coach Mike Katz, his Humber Hawks had posted the enviable record of 223 wins and just 43 losses.

Perhaps that's why the Hawks found themselves abruptly disinvited with just two months to go to the November tournament—bounced in favour of the University of Western Ontario. Then again, perhaps this ill-mannered

treatment flowed from Humber's humble status as a community college. It
seems the tall pointy-heads on university teams simply didn't want to reduce
themselves to the level of their low-brow college counterparts. "It's two
different streams, two totally different types of people, two totally different
types of athletes," McGill's coach, Ken Schildroth, told *The Globe and Mail's*
Robert MacLeod.

"It's not the same academic philosophy," he added, as if basketball resided
in the department of humanities.

Coach Katz responded with the kind of straight talk he evidently employs
to good effect in the dressing room. Noting that Western had withdrawn from
a tournament a year earlier because of the participation of Mohawk College,
he surmised that colleges were being victimized by "a real elitist attitude that
some schools are hanging on to." Then he really stuck the knife in. "I can't tell
you the number of [university] graduates that come back to Humber College
because they need more specific training to get the jobs they want."

The incident serves as a telling reminder of how badly the educational
establishment lost touch with public opinion developments in the 1990s.
Through much of the decade, public schools and universities—the least
consumer-driven and therefore most insulated of the educational institutions—proved to be the slowest to grasp rapidly evolving trends in education.
They clung to rigid and outmoded attitudes—witness the Humber College
incident when all around them Canadians were adapting to new realities and
looking to their increasingly vital educational institutions to lead them safely into the new economy. When it came to a match between colleges and
universities, Canadians tended to give the nod to the college boys, who were
seen as being more in tune with changing economic times.

The public believed in different strokes for different folks—and that no
strokes should be interpreted as inherently superior to any others. Coach Katz
was right: The number of university graduates attending Humber, though still
relatively modest, had doubled over the previous five years. University-college
crossovers were increasingly commonplace. Some enlightened institutions
had even taken to recognizing one another's course credits in specified areas.
College kids and university kids no longer represented, if they ever had, "two
totally different types of people." They were all simply kids trying to better
themselves in one way or another.

The 1990s gave rise to a new Canadian attitude to education, as in so many other areas. The neat pillars of old—Johnny goes to university and Billy goes to college; education occurs between the ages of six and the early twenties; math is learned at school and values at home—collapsed into a disorderly pile. In the earlier part of the decade, a sense of economic panic pushed parents into survival mode—they focused narrowly on the needs of their own children and the perceived shortcomings of the system as a whole. But as the decade entered its later stages, the persistent Tory touch in Canadian life prevailed: All kids deserved the best possible education, parents came to conclude, but also the most appropriate for their particular circumstances. They insisted that the educational system treat Johnny and Susie equally but, if their needs so required, differently.

The new mindset on education that emerged over the course of the Nervous Nineties demanded tougher standards, greater discipline, and heightened accountability. Their confidence in education tested, parents felt the need to be able to judge for themselves whether the system was working. But they never abandoned the principle of the public system, nor lost faith in its ability to reform. And through the ongoing wars of attrition between teachers and governments, parents, at least, never lost sight of the point of the exercise: to prepare their children to prosper in the economy of the future and make a contribution to society overall. The new mindset combined a desire for the system to better reflect the individual needs of children with an understanding that we're all in this together. It believed in choice, but choice in the form of options within a common public school system—I need help with English, you want computers, she prefers French immersion. Canadians took little interest in the radical choice agenda favoured by right-wing reformers, fearing such schemes would weaken the public system and produce losers as well as winners. And as the decade closed, it became evident that the public continued to view schools as critical agents of social cohesion, the common glue that binds society together.

Not surprisingly, the story in education flows out of the same tributaries as the story of the workplace. The public is searching for certainty. In an era of unprecedented change, Canadians in the 1990s bought into the idea of a good education as a passport to economic security and social mobility. The education system can be viewed as one of society's primary institutions, providing the framework that supports a better tomorrow. It gives form, even more so today than in the past, to the important things in life: good citizenship, a decent standard of living, high quality of life. There's an aphorism in the foreign aid world that says if you give someone a fish, you can feed them for a day; if you give them a fishing rod, they can feed themselves for life. Education has become the fishing rod of modern society.

The foundation of public anxiety over education was poured in the 1980s and 1990s. Two devastating recessions within ten years—and the rise of the so-called knowledge economy with its polarizing effect on incomes and opportunities—left parents more inclined than ever to think of the educational system as a vaccination against economic smallpox. Canadians assimilated all the talk of the growing importance of a good education in the unfolding world order. An education could be regarded as a social investment, much like a government bond, producing a real and measurable rate of return in the form of greater economic security, higher wages, more personal choice. Slowly at first, but with greater conviction as the evidence mounted, they came to accept that workers, in the wonderful line from the book *The Monster Under the Bed,* wouldn't so much earn a living in the economy of the future as "learn a living."

Think of contemporary Canadian society as a skill-testing version of snakes and ladders. The next generation has the opportunity to climb faster and higher up the ladders of opportunity than any previous one. But the game board is also more full of snakes than ever before. Few of today's young people are likely to live in the same house with the same family and work in the same job their entire adult lives. Instead, they can expect that somewhere along the way—and probably more than once—they will lose or change their job, their career, perhaps even their family and community. They will go back to school or move across the country or around the world. The ability to climb up the ladders and to minimize encounters with the snakes depends very much on the quality of one's education.

The players, our children, will need all their wits to persevere. A return to the basics represents to parents a necessary but insufficient response. Rote won't do: Children will have to learn how to learn, since they'll never stop doing it. They'll also have to develop coping skills so as to manage the vicissitudes of life in a less stable world. Parents, therefore, expect schools to graduate students well versed in the fundamentals, but imbued as well with the personal attributes and learning habits that will allow them to dust themselves off when they land on a snake. Resiliency, says social policy analyst Judith Maxwell, has become a critical quality for survival in the modern world.

In late 2000, the Ontario government released the results of six months of polling and focus group research on education. A summary read as follows:

> Ontarians are torn on this issue. On the one hand, most believe in many of the major assumptions behind the government's reforms of the education system. Most participants believed that not enough is being done to ensure students master basic skills like reading, writing and arithmetic. Most participants believe the underlying cause of that failure is not how much the government spends, but rather changes in how students are taught compared to previous generations. Ontarians don't believe going back to the future is the only answer in education. They do want a recommitment to the 3R's, but they believe education has to be more. They want a balanced curriculum that exposes children to the arts, sports and the broader community. They believe life is much more complicated for today's youth and believe they may need additional support to cope with those social complications.

At the outset of the 1990s, Canadians had yet to become consumed by the education issue. The Nervous Nineties lay ahead. The uncertainty would creep up on them as the decade unfolded, slowly at first, and then at a quickened pace before finally slacking off. The Angus Reid Group began asking Canadians to volunteer their "top-of-mind" priority issues in 1986. Typically, education rated a mention by 5 per cent or fewer respondents. In October 1996, it reached double-digit numbers for the first time. By March of 2000, it had leapt to 29 per cent, second only to health care as a national priority.

This heightened attention to education should come as no surprise. Times of profound economic change are historically also times of equally profound anxiety over education. In a speech on education and work last year, Guy Saint Pierre, chairman of the SNC-Lavalin Group and a former education minister in Quebec, uttered the following words: "Upon the education of the people of this country, the fate of this country depends." The same sentiment could have been expressed by any of hundreds of commentators concerned about the greater demands being placed on education by the changing economy. Except that these words were actually spoken by Benjamin Disraeli in the middle of the nineteenth century. Saint Pierre noted that in Disraeli's era, ground-breaking technologies such as the telegraph and steamship were reshaping the world. History has a habit of repeating itself.

Compulsory public education has been part of the Canadian fabric since shortly after Confederation. But standards have undergone massive changes since that time. Until the late 1920s, Canada remained primarily an agrarian society, and farm work, even for children, tended to take precedence over school work. Many parents saw little advantage in educating their children and even less in pursuing higher education. (In fact, they were wrong: Not only did an education provide the second, third, and any subsequent children with the means to make a living away from the farm, it gave farmers themselves the requisite literacy and numeracy to deal with grain elevator operators and general store merchants.) At the turn of the century, enrolment in primary and secondary schools—free and supposedly obligatory—amounted to about 1.1 million children, but classrooms were little more than half-filled on any given day of the week. Educational attainment did not even merit inclusion as an official census item until 1951.

In the period after the First World War, most provinces introduced truancy laws in an attempt to counter attendance problems. Still, according to a Statistics Canada study published last year, many children did not begin school until they were seven or eight and often completed their education at fourteen. In 1921, only half of six-year-olds attended school. A 1930 survey found that one in three children enrolled in Grade 1 was eight years old or more.

The post-war boom in industrial production and human reproduction ushered in the more structured era of education with which we are familiar. School construction took off as enrolment grew year after year, finally peaking at 5.9 million children in 1970—the year I studied in a portable classroom. Kids almost invariably started school at seven and continued until at least sixteen. High-school graduation rates surpassed the 50 per cent threshold about the time Pierre Trudeau became prime minister in 1968. By 1986—two years after he left office—seven out of ten students were completing high school.

Post-secondary education followed the same general curve. In 1901, the student population at Canada's eighteen degree-granting institutions numbered 6,800—two-thirds the size of present-day Humber College. The public purse provided minimal financial support for colleges and universities, especially in the wake of the Depression. Access to a post-secondary education was generally the preserve of the offspring of moneyed families or exceptional students fortunate enough to find a benefactor.

A different pattern began to take hold during the Second World War. The military effort demanded a great deal of technical expertise. Parliament passed the Vocational Training Co-ordination Act in 1942 for civilian and military workers and oversaw the training of some 700,000 military personnel during the course of the war. The effort carried through into the post-war environment. The Veterans Rehabilitation Act offered payment of tuition and other fees for any veteran enrolling in a university or university preparation within fifteen months of discharge. Two years after war's end, 32,000 ex-service personnel engorged the nation's campuses. Shortly thereafter, the Massey Royal Commission recommended the federal government become directly involved in financing post-secondary institutions. The age of accessibility was upon us. University tuition was inexpensive, and a whole new category of community colleges sprouted up across the country. By the time the baby boom generation reached its late teens, the middle classes were streaming onto campus. But even then, they represented just a small minority of Canadians. As recently as 1996, fewer than one in seven Canadians could hang a university degree on his or her walls.

As the product of a cultural milieu in which the benefits of an education went unquestioned, I never appreciated that a different viewpoint existed. Not until 1979, when I landed my first newspaper job in Lloydminster, a farm and oil community straddling the Saskatchewan-Alberta border. My time there, though brief, was rich in the exposure it offered me to Canadians from a different region and with a different world view. I was especially close to my publisher, Fred Baynton, a foul-mouthed, big-hearted born-again Baptist shit-disturber whose family had published the Lloydminster *Times* for decades and whose brother was one of the city's leading lawyers. Fred and I carried on rollicking arguments over lunches at the Dairy Queen on just about every subject imaginable, including education. He didn't want his kids—I still have trouble accepting he was serious—going off to university and becoming infected with the sort of radical ideas he found rattling around my brain.

What you're really saying, I would challenge him, is that you don't believe in social mobility—in your children enjoying a broader range of experiences than you and your contemporaries. That argument didn't faze Fred a bit. "Exactly, Greenspon," he growled. "You're not such a dumb bastard after all."

I would encounter the same attitude in the industrial and mining centres of Britain and continental Europe in the late 1980s. In the coal towns, an economically endangered class of soot-faced miners would tell you they were fighting for their birthright so that their children could follow them into the mines, just as they had followed their dads. That constituted the extent of their dream for their kids—the same sooty existence.

I remember as well visiting the Krupp steelworks in Rheinhausen, Germany, as workers took to the picket line in the winter of 1988 in an attempt to stave off a closure of the historic plant. I sat in a seedy beer hall around the corner from the factory gate with a baby-faced forty-eight-year-old steel worker named Heinz Behmenburg. He mournfully recounted how thirty-three years earlier, he had informed his father that he wanted to be a sailor. The older man, a third-generation Krupp steelworker, wouldn't hear of it. "My father said, 'Son, stay with Krupp. You will have the most secure job.'" His wife, brother, and brother-in-law also worked there.

Krupp was their life. They had been raised in Krupp houses, attended Krupp kindergartens, frolicked in a Krupp swimming pool, had their tonsils removed in a Krupp hospital, shopped in Krupp stores, and now this large, beer-bellied man was drowning his sorrows in a Krupp bar. He and his mates called themselves Kruppiana and lived in close-knit communities on streets named after members of the steelmaking dynasty. A few years earlier, Behmenburg's son had become the family's fifth generation to earn his living from the giant fire-spitting blast furnaces that dominated and defined the community. Like his father before him, my drinking companion had failed to imagine a different dream for his son. Now, with little education outside their steelmaking training, the clan felt ill-equipped to cope with a changing world. The idea of these Kruppiana taking up jobs at a second steel plant 800 metres across the Rhine was as foreign to them as being asked to move to the coal mines of northern England.

I mention this because Darrell and I—and most readers of this book—are probably atypical of traditional attitudes in this country toward education, particularly higher education. Darrell has three university degrees; I have two (but try harder). To us a good education is its own reward. But millions of Canadians in the decades of plenty after the Second World War felt confident they would land and hold decent-paying jobs in the post-war manufacturing plants or the mill towns and fishing boats of far-flung Canada. A higher education—or even completion of high school—represented a luxury they could do without. The country largely lacked an educational culture. Today, even those manufacturing jobs require math and language skills and often a post-secondary degree. The blossoming of that educational culture through the 1990s marks a seismic shift in the dominant Canadian mindset.

When Darrell was in Grade 13 at Glenview Park Secondary School in Cambridge, Ontario, his lab partner in biology was a fellow named Scott Dykeman. Neither liked biology that much, especially the day they had to dissect a cat. Scott always prattled on about how biology wasn't going to help him when he became a production worker at Babcock & Wilcox, one of the main employers in the area. His horizons extended only as far as the big employer down the road. After high school, Scott fulfilled his plan, getting on with Babcock & Wilcox, the best work available in the region for an unskilled labourer. He had a good time there, forging lifetime friendships. Today, he works as head of receiving for a medium-sized auto parts manufacturer. He joined the company when it was young and rode the 1990s automotive boom in Ontario. "I got fortunate. I got into a small company that took off," he says.

Scott looks back without regrets. His Grade 12 education has provided him a decent enough living. He's lived in the right part of the country and been in the right industry at the right time. "I'm not going to end up in the best neighbourhood. But if you work and use common sense you end up all right, I guess."

But he certainly doesn't think it will be enough to sustain his son and daughter. "They were different times. Those days are over. Kind of like a single-income family. Those days are gone, too." In fact, his oldest, Ryan, is currently attending the University of Waterloo. What's he studying? Biochemistry, as it turns out. "I didn't help him with his biology homework, let's put it that way," Scott laughs.

Scott is typical of a whole generation of parents who have looked over the new economy and figured a survival plan for their children includes the post-secondary education they never had. In his generation, a higher education fell into the category of a luxury one could afford to do without. Today, after the Big Fear of the 1990s, it is seen by nearly everyone as a necessity. You can see the trend clearly enough through the regular polls taken in Ontario since the late 1970s by the University of Toronto's Ontario Institute for Studies in Education. In 1979, just 34 per cent of respondents cited a college or university education as very important. By 1992, the figure had grown to 75 per cent. To us, the remarkable fact is that a belief in higher education could have been so low in 1979, when both Darrell and I were undergraduate students. But it was, and the massive change in half a generation is dramatic.

This massive transformation in attitudes toward an education as a necessity precipitated a sharp reversal in the early 1990s in public confidence in the education system. This negative trend line can be readily discerned from two different public opinion snapshots, one taken in 1988 by Decima Research and the other by Angus Reid in 1999. In the first pre-recession snapshot, 60 per cent of respondents described the education received by young people in their area as either excellent or good. A similar proportion judged the quality of education as higher than that provided to the parents of these young people.

Fast forward eleven years to the summer of 1999, when *The Globe and Mail* undertook a massive study of parental opinion as part of its Family Matters series. A staggering 82 per cent of parents worried about the quality of education received by their children. That's not to say that their opinion on the quality of education received by their children had deteriorated that sharply. The bigger factor may well have been the "demand" side of the equation rather than the "supply" side. In other words, the times simply demanded a better education than ever before. Indeed, we would argue that the real public opinion story in education is more about changed expectations than decay in the system. Consumers of education felt the status quo no longer sufficed; they expected far more from the education system than ever before and were unconvinced it could deliver.

The evidence suggests that these growing expectations were responsible for the cratering in the early 1990s of confidence in the system. Confidence in all institutions in our society suffered significant reversals in the early part of the decade—in part because of the overall decline in deference in all Western societies and in part because of the specific economic problems of the era. But education fell faster and harder than any other institution. In 1989, 62 per cent of respondents told the Gallup organization they had a great deal or quite a lot of confidence in the school system. By 1993, confidence had dropped to 44 per cent in Canada. The decline in confidence was markedly higher in English-speaking Canada, where it fell approximately 25 per cent.

Dissatisfaction with the education received by children rose early in the decade—to 56 per cent in 1992 and 58 per cent in 1994. Satisfaction bumped along at a little over one-third. As for intergenerational comparisons, the number of Canadians telling the Angus Reid Group that the quality of education had worsened over the previous twenty-five years rose sharply from 35 per cent in 1986 to 46 per cent in 1993.

Debate raged in most provinces as to whether these negative public sentiments actually constituted a "crisis" in education, or whether certain ideologically driven players were seeking to foment a crisis for their own purposes. At one point, Ontario education minister John Snobelen was caught on videotape saying he would invent a crisis to whip up support for a radical overhaul of the system. He needn't have bothered. The numbers suggest that education—while never degenerating into the sort of genuine crisis in public confidence we've seen in health care—had reached a sufficiently negative standing to open it up to serious reform efforts.

At one point in the Nervous Nineties, two-thirds of Canadians expressed fears that private schools were providing students with a much better education than the public system attended by 95 per cent of children. Only 38 per cent of respondents agreed that high schools adequately prepared kids for the modern workforce. Two out of three Canadians believed high school graduates lacked essential reading and writing skills. The Big Fear was on.

As the 1990s progressed, the public treated education with a demonstrably heightened seriousness. The OISE researchers asked Ontario residents in both 1984 and 1996 if high school students, whether in preparation for university or the world of work, should be required to take subjects such as mathematics, English, science, French, and history. The changed attitude is profound. Take a look at the numbers for students presumed to be headed directly into the labour force: Support for math to be made compulsory jumped from 65 per cent to 96 per cent; English from 43 per cent to 97 per cent; science from 21 per cent to 68 per cent; even history shot up from 15 per cent to 45 per cent.

Clearly, the ground had shifted on the public's perception of the material value of an education—and with good reason. In early 2001, Statistics Canada reported that the average family headed by a high school graduate enjoyed a net worth of about $65,000. A family headed by a university graduate was worth closer to $120,000. For a professional degree in law, medicine, dentistry, and the like, net worth shot up to about $320,000. The proportion of Canadians feeling a high school education is adequate "in order to get along in this society" fell from one-third to one-fifth in the ten years from 1988 to 1998.

The same pattern holds true when it comes to standards. Asked in 1996 whether they favoured the imposition of higher graduating standards even if it meant fewer students would graduate, 64 per cent of Ontarian respondents said yes versus just 25 per cent stating no. More than three-quarters in both 1996 and 2000 felt high school students should not be allowed to graduate without first passing province-wide tests on all compulsory subjects. Only one-quarter agreed with the suggestion that it would be important for the social development of students to be passed onto the next grade with their classmates even if they hadn't mastered the material. An education in and of itself didn't cut muster any more in the age of the knowledge consumer. It needed to be a high-quality education.

Despite these deepening public concerns over education in the 1990s, Canada's record actually demonstrates a good news, bad news story.

As recently as 1951, slightly more than half of the adult population of Canada hadn't completed Grade 9 and just 2 per cent had attained a university degree. Even at the dawn of the Trudeau era in the late 1960s, nearly a third of adult Canadians had not got past Grade 9 and only 5 per cent had graduated from university. Just one-quarter of Canadians had completed high school. Incredible as it may seem, as recently as 1991, the percentage of adult Canadians without Grade 9 completion still remained higher than the percentage with a university degree. The numbers of university degree holders surpassed the badly under-educated for the first time in the 1996 census, according to Statistics Canada.

It looks like a woeful record, but it beats out most of the world. Although Darrell and I far prefer output measures over input measures (how much grain was produced over how many tractors worked on the harvest), it is worth noting that through most of the 1990s, Canada devoted a greater share of its overall economy to education spending than any other industrialized country and came second only to the wealthier United States in spending per student. More importantly, today we enjoy the highest rate of post-secondary participation within the Organization for Economic Co-operation and Development. No country has as high a proportion of eighteen- to twenty-one-year-olds enrolled in colleges and universities or as big a percentage of twenty-five- to sixty-four-year-olds with college diplomas or university degrees.

When the OECD last took a snapshot in 1995, 48 per cent of working-age Canadians reported post-secondary exposure of some kind (with colleges leading universities by about 2:1), more than twice the OECD average. By now, we are well over the 50 per cent threshold. For the first time in our history, a post-secondary education is more the norm than the exception. Nor does learning cease any more when people are in their early twenties. In 1998, some 1.4 million adults twenty-five and over were enrolled in formal education programs. Millions more trained at work or studied informally at home. Lifelong learning is a reality, not a theory.

While we're relatively good at making the leap from secondary school to post-secondary learning, we're just beginning to get better at actually getting kids through high school. Latest figures show that one-quarter of Canadian kids still drop out of high school, the second-worst record among the seven largest industrialized countries. We're on the right track, though. Thanks to the success of programs aimed at giving dropouts a second chance, the percentage of twenty-five- to twenty-nine-year-olds without a high school diploma fell from 20 per cent to 13 per cent between 1990 and 1998. One-quarter of the dropouts identified in a 1991 study had gone back and completed high school when revisited four years later. The record suggests even high school dropouts are getting the message that there's little future on the boats or in the woods.

The bad news is that more than half of the kids starting high school still don't progress to college or university and, even among those who do, a third don't complete their post-secondary studies. This has serious ramifications in a world in which experts say the majority of jobs will require at least sixteen or seventeen years of formal education. The 1990s, with their cutbacks in funding and tuition increases, were not good times as far as access to post-secondary education was concerned. Enrolments actively declined between 1995 and 1999, in sharp contrast both to the records of other industrialized countries and the rhetoric of the knowledge economy. Nor are we attracting enough students into the sciences, despite the obvious importance of the discipline to the economy of the future. Science graduates tend to fare very well in the labour market and make a disproportionate contribution to the overall economy. But the cohort of Canadian youth opting for science actually fell between 1987 and 1997 from 21 per cent to 20 per cent.

Quality also remains a big problem. More than one-third of Canadian youth fall short of the literacy requirements for entry-level jobs. In international comparisons, Canada ranks in the middle ranges on literacy, better than the United States but worse than many Asian and European countries. One in six Canadians is severely limited in his or her ability to deal with printed material and another one in four is weak. On science and math scores as well, Canada's marks are decent but far from outstanding—generally topping European nations but trailing the advanced Asian countries.

Even where we are doing well—in keeping youth in school for longer periods—success is highly uneven. A post-secondary mentality has spread through the middle classes, but low-income Canadians are still experiencing difficulty in breaking into colleges and universities. The impediments begin right at early childhood. Low-income mothers tend to give birth to lower-weight babies, which in turn leads to all sorts problems down the road. Low-income children also tend to be less well nourished and don't have as many opportunities at early-age stimulation. All this feeds on itself, making them less ready to learn when they finally enter the school system. Studies in recent years have shown that the wiring of the brains of young children is heavily affected by their experiences between birth and six years of age. Governments in Canada are therefore increasingly turning their attention to equalizing opportunity from the outset of life. Early childhood education is one of the hottest areas of public policy, appealing to politicians on both the left and the right.

Aboriginal Canadians are particularly excluded from the education revolution, lagging overall trends by a generation or more. More than four out of ten don't complete high school and only 6 per cent of Aboriginals between twenty-five and fifty-four have university degrees.

The record of new Canadians is more mixed. Those whose mother tongue is neither English nor French show both a higher rate of university participation and a higher rate of failure to finish high school—probably reflecting the dichotomy in the immigration system between the well-educated newcomers Canada seeks out and the refugees who seek out Canada.

All this points to a system that has kicked into gear, but still has significant ground to make up—particularly in the quality of outcomes and equality of opportunity for disadvantaged groups.

The pattern of public concern over education has been uneven and, at times, unpredictable. Unlike with health care, it never truly reached crisis proportions, even in Ontario, where the Harris government and the teachers' unions have been engaged in a six-year-long schoolyard brawl. No single player has emerged without scars. While certain aspects of the reforms—accountability and discipline, in particular—have proven popular, the government has never overcome the suspicion that its actions have been motivated by ideology and money rather than what's best for kids.

Although confidence in the system has clearly lost ground over time, the middle stretches of the Nervous Nineties showed a paradoxical bounce back in satisfaction levels in Canada's largest and most disputatious province. David Livingstone, principal investigator for the biennial OISE surveys, thinks he knows why: Ontarians felt a strong need during the period of spending cuts to rally around their embattled public system. "In all regimes where there has been a cutback agenda, there has been a trigger reaction, with the public reasserting its support for education," Livingstone says, citing evidence from Britain, the United States, New Zealand, and Alberta. "They see it as a basic entitlement, and they don't want to see it cut back."

Canadian devotion to a public system cannot be overstated. Oceans of ink have been spilled over the flight to private schools. In fact, the movement amounts to a trickle. In 1993, more than 5 million kids were enrolled in public elementary and secondary schools versus 265,000 who opted for a private education—many of them for religious and language reasons having nothing to do with confidence in the public system. Four years later, public school enrolment was up by 25,000 and private schools by 18,000. Even at the low point of their provincial education wars, Ontario residents turned thumbs down by a three-to-one margin to the notion of allowing private, for-profit businesses to operate public schools. Most opponents felt very strongly on the issue, unlike supporters, who were just lukewarm. In the United States, too, so-called voucher systems to open public schools to competition were resoundingly voted down by electors in states where they appeared on the ballot in the fall of 2000.

Despite widespread fears, the connection in Canada has not been severed between the affluent and the public education system. In fact, support for public funding of education generally builds as you move up the income and education ladders. The vast majority of parents cannot afford—nor are they interested in—private alternatives. Their strong preference is to inject greater differentiation and greater choice into the public system itself: performing arts schools, computer programs, middle immersion, special needs, and so on. The knowledge consumer seeks options. But Tory-touched Canadians also want a socially cohesive system, one that does not leave potential losers in its wake.

As the Nervous Nineties drew to a close, public anxieties over education began to subside. Perhaps this flowed from the abatement of economic insecurity or perhaps from a belief that public schools were truly undergoing a transformation. Whatever the explanation, public opinion became more contented—and more generous. The "My Kid First" syndrome came to be replaced by an "All Kids Together" mentality.

In March 1999, Gallup reported that satisfaction with the education system had climbed back to 44 per cent from its 35 per cent low during the recession. Dissatisfaction fell below 50 per cent for the first time in the decade. Respect for and confidence in the education system, which had dropped sharply to 44 per cent in 1993, slowly clawed their way back to 50 per cent in 1996 and then up a further point or two each year thereafter. It still remained below the 62 per cent level at the outset of the Nervous Nineties, but it was moving year by year in the right direction. By the summer of 1999, Angus Reid found that those who thought education was in worse shape than twenty-five years earlier had fallen to 37 per cent, almost even with the 35 per cent who thought it was better.

In their search for certainty, Canadians seemed to be telling teachers and government alike: "Yes, we're concerned about the educational system. We want to be assured it's keeping pace with the new challenges being thrown its way. But don't use this as an excuse to pursue ideological or fiscal agendas. We believe in our public school system. We want it strengthened, not gutted. And we want to be able to sleep comfortably, knowing it's working for our kids."

Looking back over the past decade or so, several lessons can be drawn. First, Canadians detested the ongoing warfare between governments and teachers' unions. Even when they backed one side or the other, they feared the price being paid in teacher morale and therefore the classroom environment. At the same time, they strongly supported initiatives aimed at instilling greater discipline and respect into schools, and they believed overwhelmingly in school and teacher testing. Clearly, they feel the education system must be more attuned to preparing students for the workforce of the future, but this must consist of more than a simple exercise in vocational training. And finally, they believe we're all in this together.

Let's take a quick look at each of these in turn:

DISRUPTION

The cutbacks and reforms of the 1990s sparked an ugly, decade-long civil war between teachers and provincial authorities. Civilian casualties were high. Many provinces were plagued by lockouts, strikes, and work-to-rule campaigns as governments and unions clashed over money, control, and competing visions of what's best for students. To parents, it often seemed a bewildering battle that excluded them, like some old industrial age dispute between the bosses and workers that paid little heed to the customer. Except these disruptions weren't about steel ingots or coal seams. They were about the welfare of our kids.

The overwhelming verdict of parents has been a pox on both your houses, accompanied by an abiding fatigue with labour-management matters. Even where strong support exists for educational reforms, there is a hesitancy about prolonged periods of implementation and the disruption that has entailed. That probably explains why Ontario parents, after railing about teachers' unions and the withdrawal of extra-curricular services, finally

conclude in focus groups and polling that they would oppose provincial legislation to force teachers to participate in after-school activities. They don't relish Pyrrhic victories, ones that will come at the expense of further demoral-
ization of the front-line workers so critical to a child's educational experience.

Indeed, the Ontario government focus group report we referred to earlier in the chapter contains an interesting tidbit on this. It goes on about the
public's inability to reconcile the assertions of teachers' unions that the good
of students is their paramount concern with their decision to withdraw support for extra-curricular activities. Parents can't understand the teachers on
this—how, the parents wonder, can refusing to provide programs serve the
best interests of the kids. Then the report delivers the *coup de grâce*—to the
government. "On the other hand, participants wonder if any reform is worth
the price of ongoing disruptions."

Parents simply want a good, functioning system. That is more important
to them at this point than heroic efforts at reform.

TESTING

Parental anxieties were stoked throughout the 1990s by reports that Canadian
students were achieving only middle ranks in international math, science, and
literacy comparisons. Parents clamoured for improved performance and a
means of public accounting. But teachers and school boards stoutly resisted
reforms meant to re-introduce province-wide standardized testing, which
could then serve as a basis for assessing school performance. The teachers
said these tests would be misapplied by failing to take into account socio-
economic differences between schools.

I once got into a very public argument over the issue with Council
of Canadians chairwoman Maude Barlow. We were appearing together on a
CBC Radio "Morningside" panel with Peter Gzowski. The other participants
were arrayed across the country. Maude and I were crammed into a tiny
Ottawa studio.

I was probably unduly frustrated at the time. My wife and I have three
children. It never ceases to amaze me how such differentiated creatures
can emerge from the same genetic stew. But there is no doubting that their
needs vary. My oldest has done well in a French immersion environment and
my youngest appears to be following suit. But my middle child, who is an

introverted perfectionist, didn't feel comfortable in the same school. (The school calendar that year happened to be interrupted first by a province-wide school strike and then later by the ice storm, but that's another story.) We discovered just how poorly he was faring in late fall of Grade 1 when my wife and I asked his teacher on parent-teacher night about the progress of his oral French. She confessed that she had no idea since he had never uttered a single syllable in class. That made sense (although we certainly would like to have known earlier). He was shy enough to begin with. Add to that the requisite willingness to publicly make mistakes that is part and parcel of learning a second language—well, he was lost.

We quickly concluded that this particular school did not work for this particular kid. So we began shopping for a new school. It proved a highly frustrating experience, in large part because parents are expected to choose schools with far less information at their disposal than when shopping for a car or a CD player. We did what research we could and made a change. Fortunately, he's never looked back. Unfortunately, the public school system lacked the flexibility to meet our needs. The worst part for knowledge consumers like ourselves had to be the paucity of information on which to begin to judge a school.

No matter what arguments Maude Barlow made—her basic point was that one school could never be compared to another—I could not credit resistance to testing as anything other than ideological and self-serving. Surely allowances could be made for socio-economic or pedagogical differences. Polling shows that Ontarians, and we suspect Canadians in general, concur. Indeed, one of the most striking findings in our research is the overwhelming level of support for student and teacher testing. The time is well past when parents accepted as an article of faith that their children were on the receiving end of a good education and that teachers and schools were equipping them for the challenges of the future. The decline of public trust and the concurrent drift of schools from social institutions to economic institutions has ushered in an evidence-based, show-me age. Parents are insisting upon independent, objective, and measurable information. Without transparency, there cannot be accountability. And without accountability, the search for certainty is futile.

In a May 2000 poll, we found 86 per cent support for standardized,

province-wide tests for students. The vast majority of respondents felt strongly about the issue. As well, more than eight in ten Ontario residents favoured
compulsory and regular testing of teachers. A similar proportion felt high
school students should have to pass a literacy test and a standardized province-
wide knowledge test in order to graduate. Without equivocation, they considered testing an idea whose time had come around—again. The OISE
researchers have also found high levels of support for testing over the years
and a strong rejection of the notion that individual schools should be allowed
to opt out of testing if they think the results would be unfair to their students. Inquiring minds want to know.

DISCIPLINE AND RESPECT

Canadians have spoken with a clear and consistent voice about their desire
for greater discipline and respect in schools. To some extent this reflects
society-wide trends; to some extent it reflects the critical role schools play in
the lives of today's work-stressed families. In 1994, 74 per cent of respondents
told Gallup that elementary schools were not strict enough and 79 per cent
felt the same way about secondary schools, up from 48 per cent and 54 per
cent respectively in 1988.

It is difficult to fully appreciate rising anxiety in the 1990s over education without reference to anxieties over family life altogether. Parents repeatedly cried out to social policy researchers about the stresses and strains they
felt in balancing the cross pressures of home and work life. These sentiments
came through clearly in *The Globe and Mail's* 1999 Family Matters series.
Fully 62 per cent of parents with children living at home said one of the
biggest worries in their lives is whether they are raising their children properly. Of the key child-bearing group aged eighteen to thirty-four, the figure
was 70 per cent. Mothers, particularly, felt deeply conflicted between their
desire to express themselves through paid work and their accompanying feeling that this ill-served their children. How to deal with getting home from
the office late and tired and ensuring that the kids were well fed and had help
with their homework? By one American estimate, "contact time" between
parents and children fell 40 per cent between the late 1960s and the early
1990s. Natalie Lacey, the vice-president who worked on the Family Matters
project, put the Canadian data through the analysis spinner and concluded

that 80 per cent of Canadian parents were utterly torn about what to do.

The same survey also underscored the severe stress caused by this impossible balancing act. Two-thirds of respondents admitted to irritability in the previous six months. Half suffered from sleep disturbances. Nearly a third reported depression. One in ten admitted to taking medication to control depression over the previous two years. Five per cent had thought of committing suicide. All these figures were higher for Canadians with children at home than for others. And higher for women than men.

In the quarter-century between 1961 and 1996, the double-income family had gone from a third of all families to 63 per cent, whereas the Ozzie and Harriet one-parent-at-work, one-parent-at-home family fell from 60 per cent to under a quarter. Meanwhile, the incidence of single-parent families grew from less than 10 per cent to about 15 per cent. That suggests that nearly eight out of ten families were highly vulnerable to work-home pressures.

Judith Maxwell, president of Canadian Policy Research Networks, has noted that for many families the issue comes down to the dilemma between those forced to work long hours to maintain a passable income and those whose incomes are strong but whose jobs demand ever-increasing hours. If real poverty doesn't get you, then time poverty surely will. In *The Future of Success,* Robert Reich argues the trend is worsening—and that success is no protection. "The richer you are the more likely it is you are putting in long and harried hours at work, even obsessing about it when you're not doing it. A frenzied work life may or may not make you better off, but being better off definitely seems to carry with it more frenzy." Moreover, the line between work and home has blurred. A survey of white-collar workers in the spring of 2001 for Workopolis found that 81 per cent accept business calls at home after hours, two-thirds check their business e-mail after hours, and six out of ten check their work voice mail.

Middle-class parents and single working mothers might well dispute the upper-class spin Reich puts on this phenomenon, but they wouldn't disagree with the general point. In early 2001, a poll commissioned by the Canadian Union of Public Employees found that 71 per cent of organized workers wanted their unions to give high priority to work-family balance issues in bargaining. Most were working extra hours and one-third reported having personal difficulty coping with the twin pressures of home life and work life.

Given these external stresses, parents have increasingly looked to the schools to serve as "safe havens" and to teachers and principals to act as "proxy parents." Maxwell's group travelled the country in 1998 and met with small groups in an exercise dubbed "The Society We Want." When it came to children, the groups were presented with three choices: giving children a debt-free society, trusting families to raise their children, or greater public investment in child development. The groups frequently used the expression "it takes a village to raise a child," by which they meant a collective approach that built on the efforts of individual families. These parents are counting on the education system to fill in some of the gap they personally feel in raising their kids. Their expectations of schools have grown; at the very least, they need to know their kids are in a safe and stable environment.

In the 1999 Ontario provincial election, Conservative leader Mike Harris exploited this search for certainty within the school system to deflect attention from his government's policy shortcomings in the education field. He couldn't talk up labour peace or spending on new textbooks, given the record of the previous few years. But he could put forward a program to rebuild respect, one built around codes of conduct in schools and a pledge of allegiance to start the day. These antiquarian policies actually resonated with a substantial cross-section of Ontarians.

The Angus Reid group probed this agenda of respect. An overwhelming majority of Ontario residents (91 per cent) declared themselves strongly supportive of a code of conduct that would require students who vandalize school property to either repair the damage or provide some sort of offsetting service to the school. Another 7 per cent were somewhat supportive. Two-thirds of respondents favoured automatic suspensions for students who swear at teachers.

Nearly eight out of ten respondents also favoured a dress code for schools that would prohibit jeans, clothes that reveal too much bare skin, and T-shirts with foul language. Seven out of ten respondents supported beginning each day with a pledge to show respect for parents, teachers, and others as well as to affirm the intention of the students to behave responsibly in their day-to-day dealings.

Interestingly, Ontarians were evenly divided on whether they thought schools were as safe as or less safe than five years earlier. But that missed the point: Their needs had grown. They required greater certainty, given the other pressures in their lives, about a positive school environment than ever before.

Nor was this new respect agenda a purely Harris Ontario creation. At the very same time, Quebec schools introduced a novel approach to the back-to-respect agenda by reversing the post-1960s trend of addressing teachers with the familiar *tu*. Henceforth, they decreed in a direct repudiation of the egalitarian principles that had prevailed for a generation, the more formal *vous* would be employed. Public school leaders expressed increasing solidarity with the approach of private schools—that familiarity can breed rudeness and bad behaviour.

The educators felt a return to formal titles would create a respect barrier between student and educator and thereby reduce verbal abuse and even violence against teachers. "The child is less aggressive than when they call you *tu*," said Fernand Dulude, secretary of a Montreal association of school principals. "Calling the teacher *vous* creates a climate of respect. Before you can instill knowledge, you have to instill respect." Indeed, *Globe and Mail* reporter Ingrid Peritz quoted one student remarking on how difficult it is to swear at someone you address as *vous*. Think of it in English, too. It's a lot easier to say "Screw you, Fred" than it is to say "Screw you, Mr. Johnson."

Respect is making a general comeback in Canadian society—from the outpouring surrounding the return of Canada's Unknown Soldier from northern France in May 2000 to renewed attention to our national history. The public yearns for a world that values decency and politeness, a world that honours its fathers and mothers—not the deference for authority of a generation ago but a genuine respect for accomplishment, sacrifice, and history. Few parents want a return to a time when teachers stood at the front of classes dictating lessons and hardly interacting at all with their students. Our society has evolved past the point of embracing authority figures and allowing them to operate beyond scrutiny. Nobody is suggesting that teachers be given rulers with which to rap the knuckles of slow learners.

But we also are rejecting the notion of the teacher as buddy, no different from anyone else in the classroom. Increasingly we believe that a more respectful classroom produces a better environment in which to learn and a better social foundation for the future.

EDUCATION AND THE WORKFORCE

We've already seen in Chapter 4 that increasing numbers of Canadians have embraced the notions of higher and lifelong learning as a means of surviving and thriving in a labour market beset by constant change. By more than a three-to-one margin, they think economic gain rather than personal growth is the best reason to go on to university after high school.

But government and business leaders often misinterpret this sentiment as meaning that Canadians approach the education system as a simple tool with which to acquire a job. While economic functionalism figures strongly in the way the public evaluates the education system, Canadians actually take a more rounded approach. Even in its economic guise, parents and students accept that no single job or skill will provide certainty on its own. They view a good education therefore as the prime route to future employability, not future employment.

As such, they are keen to direct any new funds for education into employability measures, such as expanding apprenticeship and work experience programs for high school students and funding adult-entry high school diploma programs. Indeed, support for spending more on adult education is higher than for additional spending on the formal school system.

By and large, Canadians have come to accept the simple equation that more education equals more secure employment and higher earnings. In 1995, Canadians with a bachelor's degree earned $43,600 on average. Those with only a high school diploma earned $29,700. Level of education represents the greatest divider in an increasingly polarized world. Economists say that the majority of jobs to be created over the coming years will require 16 or 17 years of education.

This helps explains the high relative standing in public opinion surveys of colleges, which are widely perceived as more labour-friendly than universities. In September 1998, just as this new dominant mindset about education's importance was gelling, six in ten respondents told Angus Reid they expect skilled, technical training will be the most valuable type of education to have ten years from now. Fewer than one in three thought a university education would be more valuable. Respondents were given six options to choose among. Here are their preferences:

- College diploma in a technical occupation (38 per cent)

- Apprenticeship in a skilled trade (23 per cent)

- University degree in science (17 per cent)

- High school education and lots of on-the-job training
  (12 per cent)

- Professional graduate degree such as law or social work
  (5 per cent)

- University degree in arts (4 per cent)

This same gap in favour of acquiring a trade or skill as opposed to a more general university education shows up time and again in polls. The biggest variation is based on educational status. Individuals without a high school education would encourage young people to get a trade or a skill over university by more than two to one.

The OISE studies show that Canadians understand that a university graduate is more likely to obtain a better job with higher income than a college graduate. But they consistently get wrong the fact that university graduates also are less likely to become unemployed. The Angus Reid Group found the same result in a major 1998 research project. Darrell's report read: "The general public is largely unaware that, on average, university graduates are more likely to be employed than college or trade school graduates. Moreover, after being told the statistics, many do not believe the 'facts'—they continue to feel that in the long term university graduates are more employable, but in the short term (i.e., just after graduation) college and trade school graduates are more likely to find employment."

Largely, this is as false a dichotomy as that of university basketball versus college basketball. The facts quite convincingly show that while a university education offers greater economic security than a college one, a post-secondary education of one type or another is absolutely imperative to win at snakes and ladders in the economy of the future. Therefore, access to higher learning will continue to be a leitmotif of public opinion over the next decade.

SOCIAL COHESION

The final point of consensus on education is as old as mass education—and Canada itself. Canadians want their education system to lift all boats. Not necessarily equally—at least not in equality of outcomes—but everyone must be given the same opportunity to succeed in the most appropriate manner for their individual needs. Canadians accept the presence of winners in society, but they still feel badly about the production of losers. You can see this sense of cohesion expressed in several ways:

- In strong concerns that the needs of low-income Canadians are not being adequately addressed through the education system. There is strong support for early childhood development programs, which are intended to level the playing field so all kids are ready to learn when they arrive in Grade 1. The public wants schools to serve as equalizers and not as perpetuators of class differences. Seven out of ten Canadians think children from low-income families don't have the same chance for a post-secondary education as those from upper-income backgrounds.

- In the continuing support, even during the period of cutbacks, for special education programs for children with learning disabilities. Three-quarters of Ontarians in 1998 rated this one of the best ideas for improving overall student achievement, second only to more emphasis on the basics and getting parents involved in reading to their children and helping with homework.

- In the public's underwhelming support (20 per cent) for streaming students in Grade 9, despite the expert advice of the educational establishment. Canadians fear that would lock in choices—and winners and losers—at too young an age.

- In the widespread discomfort with American-style ranking of schools by performance. Internal Ontario government polling shows a far greater preference for a rating system in which all schools could achieve 5 stars.

- In the strong belief that access to college and university must remain a key concern. Cost and affordability are the dominant issues in post-secondary education. Canadians overwhelmingly believe that merit should be the only criterion in determining access to higher learning, not financial means. By a two-to-one margin, Ontarians have told OISE researchers they believe every qualified person who wants to attend college or university should be guaranteed a place even if it means spending more tax money. Indeed, their number one priority if more money were found for education would be to bring university costs down. In an early 2000 Angus Reid poll, eight out of ten respondents opposed increasing tuition fees, most of them strongly, in order that students pay more of the actual cost of their education. In a world in which education matters more than ever, Canadians view reasonable access to higher learning as a social must.

Education represents the foundation block of the changed Canada we describe in this book. It protects us from insecurity and affords us opportunity. We are a wired people living in a wired world. We are knowledge workers, knowledge consumers, and knowledge citizens. We have a greater willingness and capacity than ever before to assert ourselves. The prerequisite for all this has been universal education and its increasing extension into postsecondary study. In twenty years, we went from 1 million Canadians over the age of fifteen holding a university degree to over 3 million in 1996.

More so than at any time in our history, we live in a meritorious society. A knowledge economy values intelligence over capital, education over connections. We have no more time for Family Compacts and Vertical Mosaics—just ask the Eaton brothers. Pedigree alone doesn't cut it any more. In his sociological profile of American society, *Bobos in Paradise*, writer David Brooks points out the way in which the *New York Times*' famous wedding pages reflect the changed social order. In the 1950s, brides and grooms were described by their inherited social status. In the 1990s, their place in the pecking order was determined by the universities they attended and the degrees they attained.

Canadians accept and understand these changes. They want all our young people to benefit from the most fundamental social policy a society can confer, a good education. They aren't rigid about this—if you want to play for Humber rather than McGill, that suits them fine. Just so long as everyone gets a fair chance to get into the game and play a position that suits them.

CHAPTER 6

THE CANADIAN
EXCEPTION

In the days leading up to the 1999 federal budget, the so-called health care budget, Deputy Prime Minister Herb Gray and his wife, Sharon Sholzberg-Gray, head of the Canadian Healthcare Association, briefly lowered the defences on their closely guarded private lives. Gray is one of the great survivors in Canadian politics, the longest-serving member of the House of Commons, beating out even Prime Minister Jean Chrétien. An extremely reserved man, he maintained a stoic silence when dropped from cabinet by Pierre Trudeau and left to languish on the backbenches through much of the 1970s. He was restored to cabinet in the 1980s and later, after his party lost its second consecutive election in 1988, he served as its interim leader until Chrétien took over. In 1993, the Liberals were returned to power, and Gray was restored to a position of respect in the new governing pantheon as solicitor-general of Canada and government House leader. And then, two and a half years after becoming the most senior minister in the new government, he was diagnosed with cancer of the esophagus.

Even at the best of times, Gray looked sickly. His hushed monotone and undertaker's pallor belied a lively mind and an aficionado's appreciation of rock and roll music and other manifestations of the *Zeitgeist*. Within the cloistered world of Parliament Hill, he had emerged, resplendent in his powerfully anti-charismatic personality, as something of a cult figure. He was widely and affectionately known as the Herbivore, a more pleasant nickname than his earlier handle, Gray Herb. Press gallery dinners were incomplete without drunken chants of "Herb, Herb, Herb."

As word of Gray's cancer spread in the spring of 1996, even close associates figured the end of the line had prematurely arrived for the venerable politician. But once again, he would prove himself a survivor.

Sharon Sholzberg-Gray had been around health care a good part of her life. She, like her husband, was a strong proponent of public health care, Canadian-style. A lawyer by training, she had been drawn throughout her career to the health policy field. In the late 1990s, she, too, would have a close-up experience with the frustrations of the system as she waited for months, bent and in pain, for hip-replacement surgery.

Their adventure began on a parliamentary break in April 1996. Herb Gray did what senior politicians do on their off weeks, flying to Manitoba to speak at a fundraising dinner for Ron Duhamel, a rookie backbencher from St. Boniface. He returned home on Saturday, feeling a bit under the weather. He figured he was fighting flu and spent the day in bed.

His wife called up to him in the early evening to come down for dinner. He got out of bed and collapsed. She thought it was his heart. Flustered, she failed to call the police or an ambulance. In Gray's position as solicitor-general, the RCMP fell into his ambit of responsibility. The force had installed a special panic button in the couple's Ottawa home that would summon the Mounties in an emergency. Sholzberg-Gray didn't think to hit it. She struggled to get her husband into the car and drove to the Ottawa Civic Hospital.

The diagnosis shocked them: He was suffering from small-cell carcino-
ma of the esophagus, a rare tumour that is difficult to treat. Over the following weeks, Gray's life entailed a judicious blend of chemotherapy treatments
and cabinet business. He refused to stop working, so briefcases of files shuttled back and forth from his Parliament Hill office. But his illness and journey through the health care system would provide him greater insights than
could ever be gathered in a cabinet document, insights into the real-world
challenges of emergency rooms, acute care wards, outpatient clinics, home-
care systems, and prescription drug coverage.

Indeed, over the next three years, this first couple of medicare would
experience, up close and personal, the inner workings of Canada's public
health care system, a structure that had taken decades to construct, only to
begin displaying signs of decline in its twenties. That's why I had requested an
interview with them on the eve of the 1999 budget. The country was in the
midst of a major panic attack about health care. With the budget deficit finally slain, sentiment was growing that governments had carved too much out of
health care. Canadians expressed deep anxieties over waiting lists for elective
surgery, emergency room responses, and shortages of hospital beds. Gray was
on the mend that February from emergency prostate surgery, his second
encounter with the health care system in a little over two years. Sholzberg-
Gray was inching her way up the waiting list for hip replacement surgery.

I went to visit them in their well-appointed home in the middle-class
Ottawa suburb of Alta Vista. Gray still showed discomfort from his most recent
surgery. The doctor had instructed him not to sit in one place for more than
an hour, and he became concerned when he realized he had lost track of the
time. Sholzberg-Gray required a cane to move around. She was bent at the
waist like a proud willow in a strong wind. She looked as if she might pitch
forward at any moment. They spoke eloquently and openly for several hours.

Our discussion was fascinating in how closely it mirrored overall
Canadian public opinion—the fears and the hopes. They were frustrated by
the perceived shortcomings of the system and troubled over its future. But
each felt they personally had received good care. Neither could put their finger on any egregious failures, certainly in Gray's case at least. (Having to wait
months for surgery was getting on Sholzberg-Gray's nerves, especially given
that her doctor was constrained by a cost-saving measure to two operations

a week.) Both praised the nursing care, but fretted that the nurses lacked the necessary time to do their jobs well. And they could not imagine that private solutions would do anything but imperil the health care system. Indeed, they didn't treat health as a service industry at all. More than a government program, medicare to them represented a birthright, an icon, an identifying mark of our Canadian-ness.

"What I've seen," Gray reflected, "is a system under stress but one that's working. And I want to make sure not only that it continues to work but that the stress is removed. We've got to act quickly before one of the glories of being Canadian is severely damaged."

Gray obviously was no ordinary patient nor an ordinary advocate of public health care. After all, as he liked to recall, he sat on the government benches under Lester Pearson when the Liberals passed the Medical Care Act in 1966. Still, his attitudes and those of his wife mark as good a place as any to begin plumbing the depths of public opinion on Canada's health care system. Gray and Sholzberg-Gray faithfully echo the findings of poll after poll and focus group after focus group that Darrell has conducted for the Angus Reid Group in recent years. A quick sampling:

"My son had recently been in for surgery, and I just found that, a lot of times, if I hadn't been there to help out, he wouldn't have received care at all. Now, I'm not blaming it on the staff, I am blaming it on the fact that there wasn't enough staff." (Saskatoon)

"There's less time for the nurses to take care of you. They are very busy, or at least they appear to be very busy. They want to do more for you, but they just don't physically have the time." (Calgary)

"The [hospital] personnel now can't function because you have one person doing the work of ten who used to do the same job. Patients are not getting beds because there are no beds. So people are lingering in emergency for days sometimes until they get a bed. Hospitals are just dysfunctional." (Toronto)

"Once upon a time there was a belief that if you were in Shorty, Nova Scotia, and you were in Shorty, Alberta, and you were in Shorty, British Columbia, it didn't matter where you travelled, you had that access to universal health care, and I don't think we have that any more." (Bridgewater)

"If I have someone in the hospital now, I want someone there with my loved one on a twenty-four-hour basis—a relative—because the nurse, it's not that they don't care, it's just that they're overworked." (Saskatoon)

Make no mistake about it, feelings on health care run deep, very deep in this country. We have seen elsewhere in this book the way in which Canadians have grown suspicious of government solutions to their problems. We have seen that they don't necessarily equate more spending with better quality. We have seen how twenty-five years of economic decline usher in a self-help attitude.

Forget it when it comes to health. We call it "the Canadian exception," in that all the rules go out the window when discussing this particular matter. Remember Tevye, the devout Jewish milkman in the Broadway musical *Fiddler on the Roof*? He loves his daughters and is repeatedly called upon by them to rethink his convictions and traditions to permit them to marry the men they love. Tevye engages in personal conversations with God. He looks to the one hand and then to the other hand as he rationalizes his support for the marriage of Tzeitel to Motel, the poor tailor, and the marriage of Hodel to Perchik, the idealistic agitator. But when his third daughter, Chava, falls in love with the gentile Fyedka, Tevye determines in his inimitable fashion there is no way to countenance this treachery. Some things simply go beyond the boundaries of our belief systems. "There is no other hand!" Tevye thunders.

Canadian attitudes toward health care transcend the strict bounds of rationality. They stray deeply into the territory of belief systems. Our support for public health is beyond mere rationality, but is not irrational. It is embedded in our values of fairness, identity, and social cohesion. We don't want to consider the alternatives because we can't imagine any are better. That would be outside our frame of reference. There is no other hand. Ninety-two per cent of Canadians disagree with the statement "If I had a serious illness or injury, I would prefer to be treated in the United States." They believe ours is the superior system. It is an article of faith. In 1997, at the height of public complaints that the health care system had deteriorated beyond acceptability, 90 per cent of Canadians still boasted that their country's health care system was one of the best in the world.

As much as anything, the genesis of a universal public health care system in Canada can be traced to a bone disease that afflicted a young child in Winnipeg early in the last century. The boy lay in the hospital off and on for three years, his parents unable to afford a decent surgeon and fearful he would lose his leg. Years later, having survived his ordeal but his knee never fully recovered, he would recount in his Prairie legislature how "I had my leg hacked and cut again and again without success. The only reason I can walk today is because a doctor doing charity work . . . came into that hospital one day with a group of students, took an interest in my case, and took it over."

The boy's name was Tommy Douglas, and in 1944, the residents of Saskatchewan elected him their premier, putting him in charge of North America's first social democratic government. From the outset, Douglas threw his energies into achieving the objective contained within his party's Regina Manifesto that "every civilized community" owed its citizens a properly organized public health care system. He found it unacceptable that citizens of a modern society would have to depend on the kindness of strangers for something as basic as their health care. Doctors liked to boast that they would never turn away a patient for lack of financial resources, which was true in many instances. But it was equally true that many maladies went without treatment and that the medical profession made liberal use of collection agencies.

The construction of a New Jerusalem in the health field took many years. Under Douglas's leadership, Saskatchewan pioneered free access to hospitals in 1947. But his province's ever-precarious fiscal health deterred him from pressing forward with a more comprehensive system until the early 1960s. Douglas looked to Ottawa for support for his schemes, writing to Liberal prime minister Louis St. Laurent in 1952 that "there is no longer any cause for delay." Paul Martin Sr., the national minister of health and welfare and a childhood polio victim, was also pushing in the same direction. But extreme fiscal caution characterized the Liberal government of the day, and neither man could make much headway.

By the late 1950s, though, a critical Martin breakthrough helped smooth the way forward for Douglas in Saskatchewan. The federal minister persuaded his colleagues in Ottawa to adopt a national hospital plan that would make hospital stays universally available in exchange for 50 per cent financing by the federal government. This first foundation stone of our universal health care system went into place on July 1, 1958, with Martin by then on the Opposition benches and Conservative John G. Diefenbaker in government.

This windfall from Ottawa along with a nice run-up in resource revenues finally gave Saskatchewan's CCF government the fiscal space in which to fulfil its long-held ambitions. Douglas announced his intention to proceed with a full-fledged medicare system—encompassing doctor and hospital care—in 1959. "If we can do this—and I feel sure we can," he declared in a pre-Christmas radio broadcast, "then I would like to hazard the prophecy that before 1970 almost every other province in Canada will have followed the lead of Saskatchewan." He foresaw a public system that would eventually expand to cover dental and optometric care, drugs, and whatever new health services evolved.

But Saskatchewan's doctors were not enamoured of any system that would restrict their independence. As many as one in five had come from Britain; they looked upon themselves as refugees from the National Health System. They were adamant that socialized medicine would not follow them across the Atlantic. The doctors decided to take Douglas on during the 1960 provincial election campaign. As recounted by Norman McLeod and Ian McLeod in their 1987 biography of Douglas, the Canadian Medical Association helped the provincial branch raise $100,000 for election advertising, outspending any of the competing parties. The ads were vituperative in the extreme, warning voters that doctors would flee the province and Douglas would be forced to bring in "the garbage of Europe" to tend the sick. Medicare bureaucrats, they contended, might well commit women with menopausal problems to insane asylums. Douglas came back with a majority, the episode once again underscoring the difficulty of buying elections in Canada.

By this time, another populist Saskatchewan representative had picked up the medicare cause. Having already implemented Martin's hospitalization scheme, Prime Minister Diefenbaker rose in the House of Commons on December 21, 1960, and announced that he intended to establish a royal commission on the health needs of Canadians. Dief clearly viewed himself as a champion of the downtrodden but could also be fairly described as a politician with a nose for a winning policy. He knew that Douglas, his political rival from Saskatchewan, would soon move to Ottawa to lead the fledgling New Democratic Party. And he had watched as reformist Liberals such as

Tom Kent had moved their party to the left at the Kingston policy conference three months earlier. If a national health plan was destined to win the hearts and minds of Canadians, Diefenbaker figured he and not they should be its benefactor.

At that point, the direction that a national health care plan would take remained unclear. The doctors supported Diefenbaker's initiative, figuring a Conservative prime minister would build upon the private insurance plans they already administered and leave them free to set fees as they saw fit. All they sought was the status quo plus government subsidies for the poor and indigent, whom the doctors had been left to carry in the form of either charity cases or bad debts. The doctors foresaw a means-based system, not the universal set-up proposed by Douglas in Saskatchewan.

In his choice to head the royal commission, Diefenbaker turned to a third Saskatchewan giant of the era, the independent-thinking judge, Emmett Hall. In his 1985 biography of Hall, *Establishment Radical,* author Dennis Gruending recounts how Diefenbaker phoned his former law school classmate while the judge was presiding over a criminal trial in January 1961. Hall called a recess, during which the prime minister persuaded him that he would be perfect for the job, given his background as trustee of a Catholic hospital. When Hall went over to the Assiniboia Club for lunch a short while later, the national radio news was already announcing his appointment as chairman. Diefenbaker didn't plan to waste much time.

Meanwhile, challenges to the Saskatchewan government continued. In 1962, the province's physicians and surgeons organized Canada's first and most bitter doctors' strike. It lasted a tense twenty-three days and attracted worldwide attention. The province fought back by flying in replacement doctors from as far away as Britain. The NDP government ultimately prevailed in this titanic struggle. The doctors had everything going for them—money, authority, prestige—everything except public opinion. Right from its inception, medicare would prove to be a favourite of the people.

Emmett Hall used his royal commission to sit in open-minded judgement on the merits of the competing national health care visions. He listened as medical associations, private insurers, and various business interests continued to argue for a premium-based private insurance system with the doctors in control. The doctors attempted to portray themselves as the guardians of

Canadian values, arguing that freedom, individual initiative, and the Canadian way would be violated by a universal public system. The Canadian Medical Association warned that a government-led plan would amount to "a measure of civil conscription . . . contrary to our democratic philosophy." But a different set of values already animated the public when it came to health care.

The Hall commission's twenty-three volumes of research provide a useful reminder of the state of health coverage two generations ago. It discovered that 30 per cent of Canadians—7.5 million people—were without any medical insurance in 1961, and many of the rest had only partial coverage. For many Canadians, a trip to the doctor had to be weighed against the cost of groceries or a winter coat. Private insurers, of course, evinced a strong preference for the healthy and the young as their clients. In a breathtaking act of stupidity, the insurers drove this point home to Hall when he turned sixty-five in the middle of his inquiry. The other commissioners threw a party for him. "After the dinner," Greunding writes, "he read aloud a polite letter from his private insurer. He was no longer covered because of his age." Over the years, he had filed only one claim.

By the time Hall reported on June 20, 1964, the Liberals under Lester Pearson had been restored to power in Ottawa. The commission called for the same sort of universal, compulsory, tax-supported health plan as Douglas had created for Saskatchewan. While favouring a government-run plan, Hall shunned straight-up state medicine, though. Doctors would still charge a fee for their service and would negotiate their fee structure with governments. They would not be relegated to salaried status. And patients would remain free to choose their doctors and doctors free to choose their patients. Tommy Douglas expressed pleasant surprise at the report's public-mindedness. John Diefenbaker was equally laudatory. The new prime minister, Lester Pearson, reacted with far greater reserve, as befits those actually in power.

Over the next few years, the embryonic national medicare system would confront and overcome stiff resistance from the provinces of Quebec, Ontario, and Alberta, as well as a rearguard action by fiscal conservatives within the federal Liberal cabinet. Finance Minister Mitchell Sharp feared the scheme would break the bank. In his memoirs, he recounts that the governor of the Bank of Canada even spoke to him about the adverse effects of such an expensive social program "upon international confidence in the financial position of the government and in the Canadian dollar." Sharp, whose parliamentary secretary at the time was a young Quebec MP named Jean Chrétien, has always maintained he personally favoured medicare and was merely concerned over timing. He pushed in cabinet for delay, precipitating a bitter debate and threatened resignations.

Ultimately, a Pearsonian compromise saved the day. The Medical Care Act passed third reading and received royal assent in 1966, but Sharp was granted a one-year reprieve (less than he sought), which delayed implementation until 1968. A year after Canada's centennial, with Pierre Trudeau now prime minister, the country's modern medicare system was finally in place.

The next medicare crisis hit before the plan was barely ten years old. In the late 1970s, Ottawa decided to change the funding formula through which it sent money to the provinces for health care. With the economy slowing, Ottawa revived Sharp's concern about costs. Moreover, the federal government complained that the system of automatically reimbursing the provinces for half their medicare expenses was unpredictable and open to abuse. The finance department, wanting to regain control over its own budget, moved to replace cost-sharing with a combination of expanded taxation authority for the provinces and a lump-sum annual grant from Ottawa.

One of the unintended consequences of this new formula, however, was a weakening of Ottawa's influence over how the provinces spent health care dollars. In fact, it became impossible to track whether federal health transfers were actually going to health services. Before, federal bureaucrats vetted every dollar to make sure the provinces conformed with the 1966 law. If they had evidence that something wasn't right, they withheld a portion of the federal transfer. Now, the only weapon remaining in the federal arsenal when Ottawa felt a province might be violating the terms of medicare was to deny the province all its health care transfer, even for a minor breach. Such a disproportionate response would be politically unsustainable.

At the same time that Ottawa lost its policing power, the medical profession was feeling the ill effects of wage and price controls and, as economic growth slowed, of provincial austerity programs as well. Frustrated by the erosion of their incomes, doctors, particularly specialists, increasingly resorted to a practice known as extra-billing, insisting that patients pay them directly for services at prices above the provincial fee schedule. The patient could then submit a claim for partial reimbursement from the provincial health plan. The right to extra-bill had been contained as part of the peace pact ending the Saskatchewan doctors strike in 1962 and, even though Hall had opposed this wrinkle, it had been replicated in other provincial plans.

The doctors maintained that extra-billing in fact protected medicare by acting as a safety valve. Since governments refused to adequately compensate its medical practitioners, this direct levy on the patient kept the system from sliding into disrepute, or so the argument went. Moreover, doctors remonstrated that the total amount of extra-billing represented a pittance—only 1 or 2 per cent—of total health expenditures.

Enter Monique Begin, the modern mother of medicare, a passionate champion of the poor and downtrodden whom Trudeau named federal health minister in 1977. Begin had experienced frustration and difficulty with her own cabinet in holding provincial feet to the fire on medicare in the wake of the November 1976 election of a separatist government in Quebec. Try as she might, she couldn't make headway against Ottawa's aversion to handing René Lévesque any leverage by intruding onto provincial turf.

Ironically, Begin's moment in the sun finally arrived with the brief removal from power of the Liberals in 1979, which liberated her to transform her private misgivings over the direction of health care into a public crusade against the new Conservative government. In quick order, she made a name for herself by denouncing the new health minister, David Crombie, for allegedly allowing the provinces to misdirect their federal health grants from medicare and for failing to shut down extra-billing by doctors and hospital user fees.

Crombie turned back to Emmett Hall, now retired and in his eighties, to investigate the charges. By the time he completed his second medicare report, the Liberals had been restored to power and Monique Begin to the position of health minister, marking the second time he had been commissioned by a Conservative government and reported to a Liberal one. Hall found the provinces not guilty of diverting health dollars, as Begin had charged. As for extra-billing and hospital user fees, he condemned the practices for eroding universal access and leading to a two-tier system.

Hall's report handed Begin the ammunition she required to push ahead with what eventually became the 1984 Canada Health Act. To this end, she was ably assisted by the stubbornness of the Canadian Medical Association's crusade in favour of extra-billing and by an ill-timed new round of hospital user fees introduced by the Alberta government. Her new act reaffirmed the five principles of medicare—universality, accessibility, comprehensiveness, portability, and public administration—and it outlawed extra charges. The act gave Ottawa the right to deduct one dollar from health transfers for every dollar a province allowed in extra-billing or user fees. It now possessed a proportionate weapon with which to enforce the rules of medicare.

Even at that, winning passage for the Canada Health Act, today an icon of Canadian nationhood, proved tough sledding. The provinces, even the NDP ones, and the various health associations stood opposed. At one point, Begin's staff organized a political briefing for the Liberal caucus. Her advisers constructed a massive grid listing the sections of the act down one side and naming all the interested parties across the top. Then they put red dots in the boxes for those opposed to a particular section, yellow for the neutrals, and green for supporters. A sea of red dominated the sprawling grid at the front of the caucus room, with just a small sprig of green running down the column titled "the public." One of the participants later recalled Pierre Trudeau shaking his head at the grid and saying, "Let me understand this, everybody's opposed except the people?"

The people, by now, had fully embraced medicare, a program only sixteen years old but already at the centre of our identity as a nation. Polling conducted in the middle of the extra-billing crisis found deep support for medicare. Canadians could readily list what they liked about the program— its universal nature, its comprehensive coverage, its easy accessibility—but they drew a blank when asked about the negatives. They were adamant that "the principle of equal access for health care should be maintained at almost any cost" and that user charges discouraged the sick from seeking treatment and would over time undermine the foundations of medicare. Three-quarters of respondents said they personally would hold off going to the doctor because of extra-billing. Perhaps the *coup de grâce* was this: Nearly 80 per cent said they would look for a new doctor if theirs turned to extra-billing.

The Conservatives could read the polls, too. One of the motivations of the Liberal government in proceeding with the Canada Health Act was to try to trap the new Tory leader, Brian Mulroney, on the wrong side of public opinion. But Mulroney and his caucus wisely chose to support Begin's bill, which, like the 1957 and 1966 legislation before it, sailed through the Commons without a dissenting vote. By 1986, every province, including Quebec, had passed legislation to put itself in compliance with the terms of the new act by outlawing extra-billing and hospital user fees. The second medicare war was over.

And there things basically stood until the Nervous Nineties, when deficit-strapped governments began hacking away at a health care system that many commentators thought had grown fat and unfocused. Hall had expected health care spending would take up about 7.5 per cent of the Canadian economy by the early 1990s, but by 1992 it gobbled up more than 10 per cent of economic space, second in the world only to the United States. Health care experts increasingly fretted that we weren't getting the bang—measured by such indices as infant mortality rates and life expectancy—to justify the big bucks. In fact, the Canadian system had become Soviet-like in its penchant to measure success by the input of dollars rather than the output of good health.

Nonetheless, it was fiscal imperatives rather than policy reforms that came to the fore early in the decade. Led by Saskatchewan, the most fiscally distressed province in the country in the wake of the gross mismanagement of the Grant Devine years, the new Romanow government reluctantly began cutting and hacking at health care expenditures. When the cradle of medicare announced the closure of fifty-two rural hospitals, the public across Canada paid attention. In the 1970s and 1980s in Saskatchewan, a small town could expect to lose its grain elevator. In the 1990s, it lost its hospital.

Alberta followed suit with three consecutive years of massive cuts in the early 1990s, noteworthy both for their scale and their unapologetic nature. Stories abounded in the national media of personal tragedies flowing from the so-called Klein Revolution. But the issue didn't really gain critical public opinion mass until 1998, ironically the year deficits were finally slain. Emergency room overcrowding, out-of-country cancer treatment, and hospital closures conspired to push the public beyond its tolerance level. The massive implosion in early October of Calgary General Hospital served as a powerful symbol that something precious was being lost. One moment the hospital was there; nine seconds later it had been reduced to rubble. That pretty much summed up our diminishing sense of certainty over health care in general.

By the mid-1990s, every province except British Columbia had ratcheted back its health expenditures. Government leaders spoke soberly of moving to a new model of care that would promote health rather than treat disease. In the meantime, sick people who hadn't had a chance to read about the new "wellness model" were lined up in hospital corridors or sat on waiting lists, like Sharon Sholzberg-Gray, for medically necessary but elective surgery. And then just as the provinces began slowing down their exercise in bloodletting, Paul Martin, son of one of medicare's founding fathers and the most fiscally endangered finance minister of them all, decided to extract his pound of flesh.

Ottawa's unilateral cuts to provincial transfer payments were accepted at first, but over time they nearly destroyed the Liberal government's reputation as the champion of medicare. The Liberals cut and then cut again. Then, even as the federal budget moved into balance in 1998, the government refused to restore the grants. Its preferred option was to expand medicare into new areas such as home care and pharmacare, where it felt its contribution would stand out in the public mind. But the public was clear: It wanted the old system fixed first. No wellness models. No boutique programs. Just repair the damage to the core services provided by doctors and hospitals. For three years, the federal government dragged its feet about restoring the level of its grants back to 1995 levels until finally, with an election in the offing in the fall of 2000, it relented and promised an increase of $21.5 billion over the next five years. And even that wasn't enough to restore federal health care transfers to the level of 1995.

Public anxiety with the cuts began to build in the early 1990s, but it was accompanied by a general appreciation that the country had lived beyond its means and needed to pull back. By the end of the decade, though, anxiety turned to anger. Governments again were debt-free—most had even begun cutting taxes—and yet the quality of the health care system continued to erode. From 1990 to 1998, real expenditures on health, the program about which Canadians care the most, actually fell; eight long years on the down slope before finally starting to rebound near decade's end. During that period, the private sector share of our health care system—comprising such things as drugs, dental care, eyeglasses, home care, and chiropracty—inched up just about every year, peaking at 32 per cent before finally beginning to turn downward in the final two years of the 1990s. Canada was the only country in the industrialized world that refused to allow a private parallel system to operate in tandem with its public one, yet it featured the highest proportion of private health spending, at $800 a head, of any other nation save the United States.

The Nervous Nineties proved an incredibly anxious period for sick Canadians and Canadians anxious about getting sick.

- The numbers of doctors and nurses fell in the face of increased retirements and the cutbacks in the system, which encouraged emigration to the United States. Moreover, new graduates were actively discouraged. From 1993 to 1997, admissions to nursing schools were cut from 12,621 to 5,063, according to the Canadian Nurses Association. Medical school enrolment was cut by 10 per cent.

- The supply of acute care hospital beds was reduced from 175,000 early in the decade to 122,000 near the end. Meanwhile, the great promise of home-care programs to pick up the slack failed to live up to its billing, as Herb Gray and many others learned the hard way. Allan Rock, national health minister during much of this period, has spoken often about his disappointment with the home care his parents received while battling cancer in the mid-1990s.

- Investment in new medical technologies was so radically curtailed that an OECD study would later rank Canada in the bottom third among twenty-nine countries in physician access to sophisticated equipment.

In light of all this, it isn't surprising that Canadians became increasingly disillusioned by health care performance as the decade progressed. Ever larger numbers reported difficulty gaining access to specialists, emergency treatment, and hospital care. A five-country international comparison in 1998 found Canadians the most vocal in citing their frustration over the difficulty of getting to see a medical specialist. Only family doctors remained relatively accessible, but deterioration could be seen here, too.

Depressing stuff. And yet no matter how agitated they became through-out the Nervous Nineties over the state of their health care system, Canadians never really doubted the system itself. Against all odds, they wanted, even demanded, more government intervention. The principles of medicare, espe-cially universality at 90 per cent and equality of access at 80 per cent, retained strong public backing. Canadians rejected the notion forcefully put forward in some quarters that the private sector could deliver health care more fairly or efficiently. The drift in public opinion toward individualism took an abrupt halt when the conversation turned to health.

Indeed, health care is the perfect expression of the Tory touch at work in Canadian society: Canadians lost confidence in the government's ability to manage the health care system, but they remained resolute in their belief in a collective approach. Not that changes in the dominant mindset weren't at play in the health care field. The knowledge consumer was eating away at the privileges of the medical elite. Patients arrived at the doctor's office armed to the teeth with their own files, with information often downloaded from that newly subversive force (at least to the previously knowledge privileged), the Internet. As we will discuss in the next chapter, Canadians wanted a consul-tation, not a visitation. They saw themselves as consumers of a service, not supplicants at the altar of the high priests of medicine.

Let's look at the numbers. It comes as no surprise that health care is the public's number one policy preoccupation. But the extent of that concern is breathtaking and probably out of all proportion to the actual performance of the health care system. From 1993, when the Chrétien Liberals won their first election, to March 2000, the percentage of Canadians citing health care as a top concern grew ten-fold—from 5 per cent to 53 per cent. It became the number one issue on our radar screens only in 1998 when we put the fiscal and unemployment and national unity crises behind us. Health care has since demonstrated an impressive endurance as the public's top policy issue; other issues might flit in and out of our consciousness with the news of the day or month, but health care remains at the forefront. Even after the September 2000 health care accord, with its $21.5 billion in addi-tional funds, health care kept growing as a priority, reaching 64 per cent as a top concern just before Christmas.

How predominant is the health issue? By historical standards, it is right up there. In 1988, in the midst of the great free trade debate, that issue was the top concern of just 37 per cent of Canadians. In 1990, as the collapse of Meech Lake shook the country, the national unity issue was tops among 52 per cent of Canadians. In the teeth of the recessionary 1993 election, jobs were the top issue of 58 per cent of Canadians. That's the kind of company that today's health care issue keeps.

As we have seen, Canadians began regaining confidence in the economy in the late 1990s. But their economic optimism stands in sharp contrast to their outlook on health care. The health care recovery has not yet permeated the public consciousness. Looking ahead ten years, 58 per cent of Canadians think the state of health care will get worse versus 24 per cent who say it will get better. It often takes years and years for issues to crystallize in the public mind. The deterioration of the nation's finances that began in the mid-1970s and worsened in the 1980s did not capture the public imagination until the mid-1990s. Similarly, health care worries are making their greatest impression today, even though the system has been deteriorating and public confidence has been waning for years.

Public assessments of the state of health care have been declining rapidly for a good decade. The number of Canadians rating the system as very good or excellent has shrunk like a cheap cotton sweater in an overheated dryer— from 61 per cent in 1991 to 25 per cent in 2000. Those judging the system poor or very poor increased three-fold over the same period. Negative ratings surpassed positive ones in February 1998, the month Ottawa virtually forgot health care in its first post-deficit budget.

Indeed, even in the wake of the federal government's so-called 1999 health budget, with the first promises of reversing billions in cuts, three out of four Canadians maintained the system was in crisis. Seventy-three per cent said the situation would get worse over the next five years versus just 5 per cent who thought it would improve. Those are very large numbers on an issue of such great import to the public. And Darrell's tracking shows that these concerns continue to grow.

Throughout the 1990s, Canadians judged the system as going from bad to worse. They saw waiting times for emergency care increasing. Same with waiting lists for elective surgery and for tests such as MRIs. They complained about the deterioration of nursing care in hospitals and reduced access to specialists. The cutting may be over, but the legacy persists. A key lesson: It is very difficult to clean up a disaster of your own making.

Those who think services available to their family have worsened:

- Waiting time in hospital emergency rooms: (1998) 73 per cent vs. (1996) 54 per cent

- Waiting time for surgery: 72 per cent vs. 53 per cent

- Availability of nursing care in hospitals: 70 per cent vs. 58 per cent

- Waiting time for tests such as MRIs: 61 per cent vs. 43 per cent

- Access to specialists: 60 per cent vs. 41 per cent

- Availability of home care: 30 per cent vs. 25 per cent

- Access to services from your family doctor: 27 per cent vs. 14 per cent

Then the great paradox—this growing sense of unease with the overall health system is accompanied by relative satisfaction on a personal level. In early 2000, amid the annual influenza crush on emergency rooms and media depictions of patients lined up in corridors, 72 per cent of Canadians said they were confident they would get the health care services they needed if they had a serious medical problem. Even after all the pounding the system has endured, two-thirds of Canadians in one poll agreed with the statement that Canada's health care system is one of the best in the world. Only one in four disagreed. And only one in nine truly despaired that the system was beyond repair. The rest divided neatly into those who thought solutions were at hand and those braced for more deterioration before solutions would be found.

For all its shortcomings, the publicly funded, universal system still comforts the afflicted and those apprehensive of affliction. In international comparisons in 1998 and 1999, Canadians were the least concerned people in the world about their ability to pay if a family member had to be hospitalized. Two generations ago, as we've seen, this represented a very real worry.

Research in Alberta—widely characterized as the national hotbed of private medicine—reinforces the point. The Alberta Advantage Surveys were undertaken in 1995, 1996, and 1999. As reported in the May 2000 issue of *Policy Options* magazine, the further one gets from the Klein government's early years of cutting health care expenditures, the sharper opinion becomes on the damage done. In 1995, 66 per cent of Albertans thought the cuts, then at their height, had been too deep. By 1999, this figure had risen to 78 per cent. Interestingly, too, as with other research, the Alberta Advantage Surveys show the greater the personal experience with the system, the more confidence there is that it is not crumbling before our eyes. Concerns over access to care, quality of care, and funding are less pronounced among those who have recently received health services than among those without first-hand experience.

Apparently Herb Gray is not atypical in concluding that the system worked for him but is under severe stress generally. On close examination, it appears Canadians are not so much unhappy with the health care system of today—though it has clearly fallen in their esteem—as they are fearful of the state of the system of tomorrow. Let's remember we're talking mostly about baby boomers, a generation that has come to expect instant and absolute gratification and a group increasingly concerned with health. When it comes to health care, the baby boomers are searching for certainty. They demand assurances the system will be there for them, whenever they may need it. These sentiments prevail across all income, education, regional, and age lines. It even perseveres regardless of political orientation, which is why the old Reform Party and now the Canadian Alliance also made health an exception to its general rule that tax cuts are (nearly) always superior to government spending.

The strength of the consensus is striking in a country as diverse as Canada. While perhaps one-quarter of Canadians would accept—some even welcome—the expansion of the private sector into the health field, there's no truly identifiable constituency in Canada for private medicine. The public views medicare as the first clause in the social contract that defines them as Canadians. They want the system repaired, not reconsidered.

———

Throughout the 1990s, Canada's physicians and surgeons continued to fight battles within their own ranks over the key question of whether medicare should be merely stitched up or more radical solutions considered. The popularity of medicare has created a constituency in its favour within the medical associations. Many doctors have grown fond of the fact that the system provides access to health care for all and that it frees them of administrative burdens such as bill collecting. And while the age-old question of control was exacerbated by the attempts of cash-strapped governments to reel in health spending, Canadian doctors felt relieved that they were less constrained under public insurance than were their counterparts in the United States under private insurance. Still, a ginger group of doctors continued to fight the last war. And so, as the public health care system came under increased strain in the mid-1990s, the debates among doctors strayed beyond mere calls for more government money and into such controversial territory as whether private medicine should be allowed to exist alongside the public system, as in some European countries.

Some advocates of a mixed public-private system complained during this period that Canadians have been victimized by group-think when it comes to health care—and that a little exposure to counter-arguments would prove convincing. Well, perhaps. But the propaganda exercise, if that is what it is, has been damned effective. In the mid-1990s, the Canadian Medical Association, representing more than 50,000 physicians, came close to endorsing a private sector approach to healing the ailing medicare system. A group within the CMA argued that by creating a parallel private system, as in Britain, pressure would be reduced on the public system. (The very same argument would be put forward by Alliance MP Jason Kenney in the November 2000 election campaign, tarring leader Stockwell Day with the dreaded phrase "two-tier health care.") The argument always put forward in favour of a parallel system is that richer Canadians might get into a shorter queue for paid health services, but by so doing waiting lists would shrink for everyone.

In the summer of 1996—with provincial cutbacks well advanced and federal ones just kicking in—the CMA was scheduled to hold its 129th annual general meeting, one for each year of Confederation, in Sydney, Nova Scotia. The locale happened to be home to Cape Breton kingpin and federal health minister David Dingwall, a strong opponent of private medicine. The CMA's radical elements intended to use the "Parliament of Medicine" to push their proposals onto the conference floor. Mr. Dingwall, sensing political opportunity knocking, was loaded for bear. An interesting confrontation loomed.

It took an impassioned intervention by the association's soft-spoken president, Jack Armstrong, to avoid a vote in favour of a parallel system. After a briefing from his pollster, our Darrell, he pleaded with his members not to be the "first ones over the trench." He feared the entire organization was about to take a bullet to the head. An assault on medicare led by doctors, no matter how well-intentioned, would look to the public like a transparent bid to increase their not insubstantial incomes, the Winnipeg pediatrician argued.

Armstrong won the day, but only by agreeing to let the issue live on. In the wake of the meeting, the CMA asked Darrell to test whether the private medicine propositions would fly with the public. The doctors sponsored so-called public dialogue sessions, in which randomly selected members of the public were polled up front on their attitudes toward health care and then invited to participate in sessions in which they would be "educated" on the issue. Indeed, in an interesting twist on classic focus groups, doctors themselves were to moderate the sessions. Some of them, long contemptuous of polling on medicare as unsophisticated, intended to show that a little public education would go a long way to challenging the status quo.

Sessions were organized in six centres across Canada. Participants filled out questionnaires at the start and then joined in these doctor-led discussions on the future of health care, with particular emphasis on the wisdom of allowing private money to pick up the slack. The participating doctors felt strongly about the issue. They were imbued with the credibility of front-line practitioners. They were confident they would prove an irresistible force.

As it turned out, the irresistible force of the doctors proved no match for the immovable object of public opinion. In fact, the tables were turned on the participating physicians as they were personally exposed, and in no uncertain terms, to the extraordinary attachment Canadians have for their public health system. Going into the meetings, of those who expressed an opinion, 62 per cent of participants said they disagreed and only 32 per cent agreed with the use of private funding as a method for improving our health care system. (Let's remember that this was at a time when it looked like governments would never be able to come back to the table with more money.)

After listening to the hour-long blandishments of their doctors, 60 per cent still disagreed and 34 per cent agreed. A little education went, as it turned out, a very little way. Public opinion researchers often like to say that given an hour with each respondent, they can turn around attitudes on just about any issue. Not, it seems, on medicare. Nobody measured the doctors, but many of them had their assumptions shaken by the experience.

Listen to some of the voices from the sessions. Pay special attention to the ideological nature of their attachment to medicare.

> "I'm worried about the Canadian system being Americanized, and I don't want that." (Saskatoon)

> "I've been all over the world, and you don't even know what you have until you go and look around and see what's out there. The States, you don't get sick in the States, period." (Saskatoon)

> "It's excellent in comparison to the American system or other models." (Vancouver)

> "We're getting more towards the tragedy known as the American health care system. Basically, if you are wealthy, you get better care." (Calgary)

> "I'm afraid that those who are able to pay will have their needs addressed promptly while those who are unable to pay will have to wait or go elsewhere." (Vancouver)

> "The idea of going to a two-tiered system: if you've got money, you're going to get good care. So if you don't, you won't. So we are really creating a class structure there." (Toronto)

> "The services they provide are good services. We can't complain as Canadians. I've had four children. If I lived in the States, I'd be committing suicide because I'd be in debt $100,000 or whatever. We've got it all." (Saskatoon)

> "I think that undermines everything that Canadians want and everything that we believe in. I think everyone sitting at this table would rather wait three months than have our entire system undermined, and I think that is what they would do." (Bridgewater, Nova Scotia)

> "Obviously doctors that go into the private system are going to be paid more and I think that more doctors are going to work in that

direction and the public's level of availability is going to decrease because of it." (Vancouver)

Surely, this must be unique in the world, where people cite a government program as a major part of their national identity. Canadians cherish the ideal of a single-payer, public health care system. They don't want their system "Americanized"; they don't want to sacrifice this last bastion of universality; they can't countenance a two-tier system in which care would be based on something other than need. In a 1998 study for Merck Frosst Canada, 25 per cent of Canadians cited the health care system as what makes us unique from other countries, more than three times as many mentions as other characteristics such as multiculturalism (7 per cent), freedom (7 per cent), and tolerance (7 per cent). "Of those who feel health care is our most differentiating characteristic, nearly three-quarters cite public funding and universality as especially defining features," according to the study. There's not a lot of room for debate here.

Indeed, moving beyond the nationalist arguments, the major objection that Canadians have about an increased role for private money is that it will lead to differences in quality and access in the delivery of the services their families receive. Darrell summed up these concerns in a note to one of his public sector clients:

- Ability to pay will become more important than need in determining access to quality health care;

- The facilities and doctors available to those with private money will be of a much higher quality than the ones available in the public system;

- The problems in the current system will not necessarily be solved by bringing in private money; and

- Private money will only put more cash into the pockets of those in the system who want to increase their incomes; it won't deal with the problems being experienced in facilities or services.

Clearly then, health care is not just another government program that can be amended and adjusted to suit the times. It is a major symbol of what we've accomplished together as a people, an expression of our common values. As such, debates about the future of our health care system are weighed down with symbolic and ideological baggage that militates against reasoned dialogue. For example, the debate about expanding the use of private money in a mixed health care system, taken from a British model, quickly transmutes into accusations about the "Americanization" of our health care system. The prevailing view in Canada is that anyone suggesting that pay-as-you-go should be an option is at best unpatriotic, and at worst a Yankee in sheep's clothing.

Doctors, the priests in the temple of medicine, had better pay attention. They've historically been on the wrong side of public opinion, articulating values such as freedom and independence that are way out of kilter with the communitarian instincts related to the "Canadian exception." Consider this for being on the wrong wavelength: In a survey in late 1999, doctors were presented with two contradictory statements. The first was "It is important to have a publicly funded system that allows universal and accessible health care to everyone, regardless of income or status." Just 38 per cent of physicians agreed. The other 62 per cent opted for the second statement: "Even in a publicly funded system, those who are willing to privately pay for higher levels of services and treatment should have the opportunity to receive them."

That is decidedly not the way Canadians feel. The wonder of it is how little damage the doctors have actually inflicted on themselves, especially in comparison with, say, teachers.

Deep Throat, the secret hero of the 1970s Watergate scandal, counselled the Washington Post reporting duo trying to crack the case of White House wrongdoing to follow the money trail. It's good advice as well for anyone wanting to understand the health care issue. It all comes down to money.

Even the most superficial economic and demographic analysis suggests that the demands on the health care system will continue to grow in the coming years. Everyone knows about the aging population; policy-makers shudder as the baby boom cohort inches ever closer to physical deterioration. The Conference Board of Canada estimates the health costs of the average fifty-five-year-old at $1,100 a year. The costs roughly double for a sixty-five-year-old, double again for a seventy-five-year-old and then double yet again for an eighty-five-year-old—reaching about $16,000 a person. Some commentators argue that the baby boomers have taken relatively good care of themselves and won't turn out to be the burden on the system widely forecast, or that technology will provide a fix. But with so many of them—and with such high expectations for the best and latest in treatments—policymakers have to prepare for a cost explosion.

The system is already gobbling up nearly $100 billion a year, more than one dollar out of every eleven that courses through the Canadian economy in a given year. Canadians are currently the fourth-largest spenders on health care, per capita, in the world, after a brief stint in second spot. We tend to always compare ourselves to the Americans, but advanced countries in Europe and Asia spend less on health care and not necessarily to the detriment of their populations. In fact, a World Health Organization report in mid-2000 put Canada into thirtieth spot in the world in with regard to the efficiency of its health care spending.

The experts will tell you that the combination of new medical technologies and aging baby boomers poses grave challenges for the sustainability of our publicly funded health system. Provincial governments also worry that an insatiable demand for health care will crowd out such other needs as education, highways, welfare, or environmental enforcement.

In the spring of 2000, James Frank, chief economist for the Conference Board of Canada, took the population profile of British Columbia in 2020 and superimposed it on the province's 2000–2001 provincial budget. The impact of a more aged population immediately added $1.7 billion to health care spending, driving the province's deficit from its projected $1.2 billion that year upwards to nearly $3 billion. Now the first rule of economics is that all things are never equal. Having said that, Frank wonders if the health care system we know and love is, under the circumstances, economically sustainable.

But one can just as easily wonder if Frank's very pertinent question of financial sustainability is politically sustainable. The acrimonious finger-pointing the federal and provincial governments have engaged in over the past several years has been highly effective in convincing the public that health care is under-funded. A pox on everyone's house! In its first term in government, the Chrétien government sponsored the National Forum on Health Care. It concluded that the $12.5 billion the federal government was then transferring to the provinces was ample. The salient question was really the disbursement of the money. Reform before cash went the rallying cry of the tall foreheads. Today, no politician intent on re-election would entertain such a thought. Even allegedly fiscal conservative governments in Ontario and Alberta are throwing mega-bucks at increased health care spending.

In the public mind, the most telling point about health care is that we probably wouldn't even be discussing the issue if governments would just fund it properly. The health care battles of the 1990s were all about money. At that juncture, governments could credibly argue they had the will, they just lacked the wallet. But with surpluses now the norm, talk of reform cannot hope to proceed without the opening ante of more cash. All those millions of government dollars spent on attack ads have created a situation where increased funding is required to even begin opening one's mouth about health care reform.

Again, let's look at the numbers. Three-quarters of Canadians still think the health care system is facing a major funding crisis. Moreover, half of those who don't think we're in the midst of a crisis today do believe we are heading for one in the next five to ten years. So that's nearly nine out of ten who say the crunch is here or is fast approaching. And most of them blame government mismanagement at all levels—poor management of the system outpolls an aging population as the main culprit by more than a two-to-one margin. Ask Canadians the major priority for the health care system, and just one-quarter opt for a reform model. The rest believe that funding alone is the priority or that some mix of increased funding from governments and policy reforms are required. It takes a fistful of cash to get to first base with this public.

The funding issue cannot be overstated. Eight out of ten Canadians agree with the statement that there will have to be an increase in public funding allocated to health care, even if it means reducing spending on other government programs. (Mind you, ask if increased taxes should cover this added health care spending and support drops to 37 per cent. Canadians think governments tax enough already; they just don't have their spending priorities right.)

Funding concerns colour everything. Consider the "wellness models" advocated by everyone from Alberta premier Ralph Klein (who has added the word "wellness" to the title of his province's minister of health) to federal Health Minister Allan Rock. The logic of the wellness approach is this: You can spend hundreds of thousands of dollars treating a smoker for emphysema and congestive heart disease or you can invest far less up front to discourage smoking in the first place. A second example: You can deal with the hugely expensive lifelong health consequence of low-birth-weight babies, or you can spend hundreds of dollars in prenatal care to monitor high-risk pregnant women.

Canadians buy into the logic of this new health approach, by and large. But not before the "old" health care system is fixed. By 60 per cent to 36 per cent they opt for ensuring that hospital and medical services are sufficiently funded to treat diseases, illnesses, and injuries after they occur, even if it means cutting spending on health promotion to reduce the number of diseases, illnesses, and injuries that occur. Governments that want to use new funds to move toward a "wellness" model had better beware. Public support is not there. The public, like Herb Gray, believes that "one of the glories of being Canadian is severely damaged." They've done their own mental triage: Emergency surgery on the system they've come to love takes precedence over the health care agenda of the future. Think of health care as a kind of insurance policy in a nation of insurance policy holders. Rightly or wrongly, cancer treatment takes precedence over cancer prevention.

First and foremost, Canadians are searching for certainty. And to them more health spending equates greater certainty. Even non-life-threatening illnesses translate into a loss of control for ordinary people. Depending on how sick you are, you can't work, or play with your children, or walk around the block. Health is central to our concept of quality of life, and quality of life dwarfs any other over-arching objective for Canadians.

That's one of the reasons why MRIs—magnetic resonance imaging machines—have become such an important flashpoint in the health care debate. Health authorities can argue, as they do, that waiting lists don't exist for those in extreme distress. But the argument falls flat with the public. While Canadians certainly still believe very much in triage—those most in need should jump to the head of the queue—that doesn't mean they are willing to wait at the back of the line indefinitely. Waiting for an MRI scan has a high personal cost associated with it. A delay in treatment reduces the quality of your life. And as we have seen over and over again, Canadians are not prepared to surrender the prerogatives of control and choice just so that governments can trim some costs, especially governments now apparently awash in tax dollars.

How supreme is good health? Consider this piece of research from the Canadian Council on Social Development, which asked Canadians what form of security was most important to them. They were given three choices: the economic security of a job and decent income; the physical security of feeling safe from crime; and the security of access to good health care. Health security came first at 55 per cent followed by economic security at 36 per cent and finally physical security at 8 per cent.

Governments don't want to get on the wrong side of this powerful sentiment. In Ontario, the Harris government learned first-hand in the run-up to its 1999 re-election campaign how difficult it is to shake negative perceptions of health care once they become entrenched. Over their four years in power, the temperature of the health issue had gone from high to higher. At its lowest point in the Tories' tenure (October 1997), 43 per cent of Ontarians surveyed identified health as the issue "that should receive the greatest attention from Ontario's leaders." In the run-up to the spring 1999 election, that figure rose to an unprecedented 73 per cent.

The Harris Conservatives were clearly in trouble on health care as they prepared their re-election campaign. Not only did it represent the most important issue facing the province, only 34 per cent approved of the government's performance in managing its health responsibilities. Usually, this double-whammy would constitute a fatal blow in politics. It is nearly impossible for a political party to win power when the public is so resolute about the precedence of a single issue, and one on which so few rate its performance as adequate. Conservative strategists understood this danger and determined they would have to hammer down this high spike before going to the people.

They began by conducting a series of research projects to help them understand the nuances of public opinion. The research was then used to shape a paid advertising program designed to take the starch out of the health care issue. Government strategists accepted that it would be nearly impossible to better the opposition parties on the "who cares more" about health care front or on who would do a better job of protecting it. Therefore the objective became to neutralize the issue as much as possible. In other words, wipe health care off the agenda so that another issue (hopefully an economic one) could take its place. In a nutshell, they set to work to change the ballot question for the up-coming election campaign.

Two major conclusions emerged out of the government's research: that before Ontarians could even begin to accept the good intentions of the Harris Tories on health care, they would have to be convinced the government was spending more rather than less money. And what the public really wanted from the government's management of health care was certainty. They wanted to know the system would be there for them when they needed it and that the government had a plan to ensure that.

In trying to change perceptions, the government decided to manage the man rather than the puck. It couldn't fix the underlying problem; that is, it couldn't change the way the public thinks about health care. Instead, the Harris government poured millions of dollars into advertising the fact that provincial expenditures on health care were actually higher that at any time in the history of the province. Their ad buy was one of the heaviest in Canadian history. An estimated 90 percent of Ontarians heard the message at least twenty times over the winter of 1998–99, enormous numbers for a government public relations campaign. On top of that, senior government figures trotted out a series of good-news announcements: $375 million to hire 12,000 additional nurses; $75 million over two years to increase emergency room capacity; $56 million in new funding to relieve waiting lists for cardiac care and cancer treatment.

But try as they might—and they certainly made a Herculean effort—the Tories could not escape their image as black-hearted accountants. To quote Oscar Wilde, the public believed the Tories knew the price of everything and the value of nothing. The Tories had spent the early years as proud hackers and slashers and were forever stuck with that image. The public refused to accept that they actually had a plan for improving health care. Focus group discussions convincingly demonstrated that the public couldn't get past the money question: How can you be serious when all you're about is cutting spending?

The Harris government never re-established its credibility on the health care issue. For all its advertising, it managed to convince just 4 per cent of the people of the fact that spending had gone up rather than down over the previous three years.

The following statistics "tell the tale of the tape."

- Straight-up approval of the government's management of health care: (December 1998) 39 per cent vs. (April 1999) 36 per cent.

- Among those who cited health care as the most important issue facing the province in July 1997, 34 per cent approved of the government's performance. In April 1999, it was still 34 per cent.

- Approval of government's performance in preserving our health care system: (July 1997) 41 per cent vs. (April 1999) 41 per cent.

- "I'm confident that if I had a serious medical problem I'd be able to get the health care services I need." Those who agreed with this statement: (October 1998) 57 per cent vs. (April 1999) 57 per cent.

- "Amount the government spends on health care has gone up over the past three years." Those who agreed: (October 1998) 33 per cent vs. (April 1999) 37 per cent.

Amazingly, though, the Opposition failed miserably in landing a telling blow in the subsequent election campaign. Even though health care remained the top issue throughout the spring campaign, neither the Liberals nor New Democrats could persuade voters they had a more credible plan. The point is important in that it shows that even on an issue as vital to Canadians as health care, they are a discriminating lot. They don't simply throw their support behind the highest bidder. Although Canadian attachment to our health care system is as much a right-hemisphere phenomenon as a left-hemisphere one, when it comes to the politics of health care there is little room for sentimentality or wishful thinking. Federal New Democrats have been frustrated for years by their inability to get traction on the issue. They have convinced themselves that nobody is as favourably disposed to public health care as themselves and therefore votes should fall their way from a medicare-obsessed public. During the fall 2000 federal campaign, NDP leader Alexa McDonough uttered health care, health care, health care incessantly for thirty-six days. Her party couldn't crack 10 per cent support. In pre-election polls, the public savaged the Chrétien government for its stewardship over the health care system, with a large majority of Liberal supporters including themselves in this attack. Still, the Liberals were deemed to have greater credibility than any other challengers in the election campaign when it came to protecting medicare.

Medicare is not a simple left-right issue. At some level, it is not even a fertile partisan issue. First off, all parties can read polling numbers. None are going to run against the angels. Moreover, the public views health care as more a matter of good government than of partisan politics. They won't succumb to cheap promises or born-again converts. Credibility is key. They know their health system was put through the wringer because of poor fiscal management and therefore they will assess such matters as fiscal credibility alongside an ideological comfort level in deciding which party to trust with their precious medicare system. That's how the Alberta, Ontario, and federal governments have survived the health care crisis. Simply caring more isn't enough. You've got to care credibly to satisfy the search for certainty.

A final point on this. The public's firmness on the principles of medicare should not be mistaken as an absolute aversion to change. In that five-country study in 1998, only 20 per cent of Canadians deluded themselves that minor changes would suffice in making the health care system road-ready for the journey ahead, down from 56 per cent in 1988. Eight out of ten felt either that while our health care system is good, fundamental change is required (56 per cent) or that it is so flawed it needs to be completely rebuilt (23 per cent).

As with other aspects of modern life, Canadians are willing to accept change in the health care system. Indeed, those who argue otherwise are looked upon as charlatans. The quo has very little status left. When all was said and done in Ontario, six out of ten respondents disagreed with the statement "If we just changed things back to what they were before the Harris government was elected, our health care system would be much better than it is today." Canadians are seeking assurances about their quality of life. They want to maintain the high standards they believe existed in the past. They seek certainty, not necessarily constancy.

A plan—a good plan, a plan that respects their values—counts big-time with the public. As we have shown before, Canadians are patient investors in their country if they can be convinced governments or corporations are moving in the right direction. They don't demand instant gratification. But they want to be satisfied their public and private sector leaders are anticipating the future. In health care throughout the Nervous Nineties, they had a keen sense the future was not well in hand. That is the wellspring of their search for certainty.

Let's move back to Alberta and its penchant for private solutions. Alberta has been a leader in public policy innovation over the past decade and has been at the forefront of the health care issue. The Klein government began hacking away at provincial health care costs long before Ottawa's celebrated 1995 budget took a national machete to social transfers to the provinces. Alberta was one of the first to close hospitals and curtail services, winning kudos for its efforts from the editorial board of the *Wall Street Journal* and providing a role model for Mike Harris. In 1996, the Klein government went so far as to champion private for-profit clinics for such procedures as laser surgery and magnetic resonance imaging, arguing they would ease demand on the public system. The federal government—and most Albertans—disagreed. They felt Alberta was ushering in an American-style, two-tier health care system. Ottawa levied penalties on Alberta under the Canada Health Act. Eventually, the province backed down.

Then in the spring of 2000, the Klein government pushed through the highly contentious Bill 11, the so-called Health Protection Act, amid howls of protest. It allowed profit-seeking private clinics to perform minor surgeries and keep patients overnight, but it did not permit user fees or private payments for medically necessary procedures. The costs were to be covered by the public treasury. The government argued that the private sector can deliver these services more efficiently. Critics, in turn, charged that Bill 11 is the thin edge of the wedge of private medicine. Premier Klein steadfastly maintained the act was perfectly within the ambit of the Canada Health Act in that it did not deny universal access to health care under public administration. Ontario premier Mike Harris has talked up a similar approach, even floating the idea of private hospitals.

Polling on Bill 11 was consistent with our other findings. The public framed it, like so much else in health, as a follow-the-money issue. Fully 77 per cent of Albertans said they would not even be considering this matter if only governments had put enough money into health care. And despite its reputation as a private-sector haven, more than nine out of ten Albertans—a slightly higher proportion than in any other province—wanted to preserve the intent and spirit of the Canada Health Act, even though they never got over their confusion over whether Bill 11 imperilled those principles. By 2001, the Alberta government had changed tack and was pouring its petro wealth into the public health care system.

So when it comes to health, even Alberta, with its frontier spirit in public policy matters, opts to preserve what we've already built. Moreover, as Alberta residents looked in the rear view mirror at the measures taken by their government in the 1990s, they were more, not less, disturbed over what took place. According to the Alberta Advantage Studies discussed earlier, they had no patience for the classic governmental approach in Canada of trying to control spiralling health care demand by limiting hospital beds, staff, and services. Opposition to these tactics was rising, not falling.

In 1999, half a dozen years into the Klein government's health restructuring initiatives, 93 per cent of Albertans opposed longer waiting times for health care; 93 per cent opposed restrictions on the number of doctors and nurses; 88 per cent said the system needed fixing; 81 per cent said availability of health services had declined; and 68 per cent said quality of service had fallen. The only place Albertans seemed willing to tolerate some limits, if absolutely necessary, was elective surgery. But that's just a snapshot. The interesting finding is the trend line. As with other polling on the subject, the Alberta Advantage Surveys show Albertans had become less receptive to private solutions. Only 23 per cent in 1999, for instance, supported the creation of private-user clinics in the province. That was down from 37 per cent support in the early stages of the Klein government reforms. Meanwhile, opposition to hospital closures grew from 61 per cent to 88 per cent.

First the Klein government cut. Then it tried to reform. Then it replenished its health care spending and brought it up to record levels. As far as public opinion goes, the later years of mea culpas have accomplished, as in Ontario, absolutely nothing. In 1996, 75 per cent of Albertans said the province was worse than before for the ill or sick. In 1999, 74 per cent still thought it was worse.

So what solutions are Canadians prepared to consider? What sort of plan are they willing to entertain, especially given their conditioning to think salvation can only be found in a big, fat cheque? In politics, someone once told me, the choices are usually between the bad and the worse. That's probably as true in health care policy as anywhere else. Unless governments are willing to defend and expand the current system, which they seem convinced is unaffordable, there is no good answer. The worst answers, at least in public opinion terms, would be those that either peddle the benefits of two-tier medicine (by which we mean differentiated service based on ability to pay) or preach continued patience with having to wait for treatment. The first would be rejected by Canadians in their role as citizens, the latter by Canadians as consumers.

Late last year, after Prime Minister Chrétien and the provincial premiers signed their health accord, Pollara surveyed the public as to what changes they considered acceptable or unacceptable. The message on bureaucratically imposed constraints was compelling: Eighty per cent opposed decreasing the number of services covered by medicare; 75 per cent opposed limiting choice; 67 per cent opposed limiting the introduction of new health technology; 59 per cent opposed increasing taxes and directing the revenue to health care; 56 per cent opposed increasing the burden on individuals for items already outside the ambit of medicare, such as prescription drug costs. Respondents were open to putting more emphasis on health promotion and diverting funds into health care from areas such as transportation and defence, but little else.

The solutions that really fall off the table are the ones that entail acceptance of anything less than the best. Canadians are resoundingly opposed to the assertion that "patients will just have to learn to make do with limits in the availability of health services." Forget it, they say. Same with curtailing choice or learning to live with waiting lists as a means of rationing services. It is probably one of the great ironies of our times that the thing Canadians most value in their country, their health care system, is the only thing for which they have to wait in line. They are not going to stand for it indefinitely. Compromising on quality is simply not on.

Nor are they willing to let Granny go without her medicine. Restricting government financial support for drug benefits for the elderly and the poor is a complete non-starter, regardless of the age of the respondent. Much chatter attaches itself to the potential in Canadian society for inter-generational conflict over health care costs. So far, no evidence exists at all to support that contention. The Tory touch holds firm: We aren't willing to sacrifice the sick, the poor or the elderly in order to save the rest of us. Health care is a deeply ideological subject, and that's just not the Canadian way.

As for fixing the system with private money, polling from the 1990s periodically suggested a level of receptivity to the idea. Moderate support could be detected at times for user fees (payments designed to deter demand for medical services) and for two-tier medicine, the creation of a parallel system that would allow those with the means to purchase extra services. Proponents of a parallel approach, as exists in many European countries, contend it takes pressure off the public system. Critics say it undermines public health care. We've examined the polls on these supposed solutions and generally find the research unpersuasive. These surveys generally place the question in a "no-alternative" context, such as "If timely access to care is impossible, would you accept the option of individuals using their own money to purchase treatment?"

In a major review of all the available public polling on health care, the Conference Board of Canada concluded that "privatization is not a primary goal for reforming health care." The report noted that "support is stronger for purchasing private services if the question is worded that people should be allowed to pay for services that the public system is unable to provide than if the question asks if people should be allowed to purchase services for the purposes of receiving faster or better service." We agree that as an Alamo-type defence of a failing public system, Canadians would be prepared to look at private money. Obviously they would prefer private health care to no health care. In other words, their allegiance to a public system, while profound, is no match for their search for certainty. Certainty trumps even universality. As one of the participants in the Merck Frosst study said about private solutions, "As a last resort I'd pay the money, but there's got to be some better approach than that."

Certainly, if the health care system is seen to be failing, the public would lose one of the great glories of Canadian citizenship. That's one of the reasons that right-wing critics of medicare are as intent as those on the left in describing the system as being in crisis. Having said that, Canadians strongly prefer public solutions to private ones. In fact, they would have to be firmly convinced that everything reasonable had already been tried before they would accept any serious intrusion of private money into this most public of domains. And this necessity defence will be difficult to establish given the surpluses accumulated in recent years by the federal and most provincial governments.

The common retort to private solutions from individuals in focus groups comes down to "yeah, but" as in yeah, but there are alternatives. Canadians are deeply wedded to a public, single-payer system. The only way they would accept private money as the answer to the system's perceived woes would be if every other possible alternative (especially more money and improved efficiency) had been tried first and shown to have failed.

The changed reality of post-deficit Canada limits the choices of governments as they move forward on health care. They can't easily plead poverty. Nonetheless, just about every provincial government in the country, regardless of partisan affiliation, has been moaning about the "sustainability" of a health care system that commands a greater and greater share of the spending pie with each passing year. The provinces estimated last year that new technologies and an aging population will drive their share of health care costs from $55 billion to $85 billion within a decade and $186 billion twenty-five years from now.

Which leaves us with the question of how the policy-makers can craft an approach that addresses the very real pressures on the system and yet passes the public sniff test. Ensuring sustainability—that the health care system of the future can cope with the cost pressures from aging baby boomers and new technologies—is written right into the terms of the federal government's Romanow Health Commission, which is to report before the end of 2002. Commissioner Roy Romanow, the former NDP premier of Saskatchewan and someone who reveres Tommy Douglas, views his job as saving medicare. But as a former premier, he has been as alarmed as Ontario premier Mike Harris about the way health care demands are crowding out education, social services, highways, and the myriad other programs governments must provide.

We will distinguish in a moment between the potentially competing visions of Mr. Romanow and more radical reformers. But for the moment, it's important to recognize that they share the public opinion challenge of convincing Canadians that change is required beyond greater spending, that the system truly could be overwhelmed unless reformed. In the absence of a fiscal crisis, they have to persuade Canadians that our existing approach to health care is, in fact, unsustainable. The trick lies in linking the change agenda to the search for certainty. The one advantage these policy-makers have is the general acceptance Canadians display to arguments that the status quo alone won't produce a better future. Canadians are not unalterably opposed to change, but changes proposed in the health care field must conform to their values and perceived interests.

Two avenues present themselves. The first is the one Mr. Romanow is most likely to travel. It is the road already taken by Ken Fyke, a former deputy minister of health and hospital administrator commissioned by then premier Romanow to produce a diagnosis of Saskatchewan's health care system. Fyke's report, released earlier this year, was scathing in its condemnation of a health care system it found to be balkanized, inefficient, and almost indifferent to quality. Fyke found everything from the way general and family practitioners organize themselves to prescribing practices badly wanting. "Without eliminating unnecessary and inefficient utilization, without reforming the delivery of everyday services and without realizing the effects of successful prevention and health-enhancing social and economic programs, expanding medicare will be unaffordable, however desirable it may be."

Fyke, probably foreshadowing Romanow, argued that a dose of rationality must be injected into the system before it makes sense to throw in more money or to expand the frontiers of medicare. Throughout his report, he talked of "quality"—a management concept that swept manufacturing and other service industries in the late 1980s and early 1990s. Remember the slogan "At Ford, Quality Is Job One." It meant getting things right in the design and manufacturing stages rather than dealing with expensive defects in the future. The old idea of quality control was to test a product at the end of the assembly line; the new idea was to head off quality problems before they could be introduced into a product. Fyke catalogued all kinds of quality deficiencies in the health care system, such as bad prescribing practices and lack of communication between general practitioners and other service providers.

He recommended bringing the front lines of the medical community—family doctors, nurse-practitioners, physiotherapists, pharmacists, nutritionists, etc.—together in so-called primary-care teams.

A lot of what he said conforms to the new Canadian mindset. When the public is informed in focus groups of the amount of money—and the proportion—devoted to health care, they also marvel at what they figure must be the inefficiencies in the system. They see the irrationalities whenever they interact with the health care system. They love the principles, but can imagine it operating more efficiently.

Most analysts probably share in the Fyke diagnosis, but not necessarily the treatment regimen. The answer to Stalinism is not more Stalinism, scoffs my friend, Brian Crowley, head of the Atlantic Institute for Market Studies. More radical reformers, while offering up a wide variety of solutions, generally feel patients themselves must take greater responsibility for their health care needs and that market disciplines should predominate. Many reformers prefer user fees—outlawed since 1984—as a way to curb runaway demand for medical services. The argument goes that any commodity or service provided seemingly for free, like health care, will be abused, just as dirt-cheap energy was overused and wasted in the old Soviet Union, contributing to the despoilment of the environment. Even social democratic Sweden allows user fees.

A clear trend is developing toward some form of co-responsibility for health care costs. The Clair commission in Quebec recommended a personal savings plan in which residents would put money aside for non-urgent care, a form of self-insurance for old age. Saskatchewan's experience with drugs is instructive. For two decades until the early 1990s, the province covered drug costs, a natural extension of the physician and hospital coverage provided under health care. But the system proved unsustainable in the fiscal crisis of the early 1990s. Today, the province covers drug costs only for low-income families and those with extremely high pharmaceutical needs. In his report, Fyke comments that drug costs are "medically necessary by any common-sense definition" and therefore should be covered under medicare. Indeed, they often produce savings by replacing the need for surgery and long hospital stays. But he is troubled by the runaway costs of the past, which can occur when neither doctors nor patients feel any personal stake in controlling costs. Under those conditions, drugs are commonly over-used or prescribed inappropriately. The answer seems to lie, as with the Quebec drug plan, in some form of co-payment, except perhaps for the poorest and most vulnerable.

We aren't talking here of user fees per se. These have been studied from the Hall commission forward and generally have been rejected by policy-makers for the simple reason that to work as a deterrent they would have to be sufficiently high to also act as a barrier to access for some people. Co-responsibility differs in two ways: The cost is not levied at the time the medical service is provided; and certain people can be exempted. It is not a perfect solution, but could fly with the public in that it doesn't contradict the underlying principle of universal access to medically necessary health care.

Indeed, Darrell's focus group research shows that patients accept that they, too, must be accountable in producing a well-functioning health system of the future. Canadians agree with Fyke that the health care system is inefficient and they accept some of the responsibility. Wherever you go in this country, Canadians will shake their heads over people tying up emergency rooms for runny noses. They are receptive to any approach that would cause people to think twice about their quick resort to care, but only if it can be designed so as not to block or discourage access to those truly in need. That would be too high a price to pay, which is why classic user fees at the point of delivery are not the answer.

Despite what we've said about private money in health care, delivery of services by private providers could be made to fall within acceptable public opinion bounds. The key here is not that the provider is a private operator—after all, doctors are largely private operators, so are diagnostic labs—but that they don't have the power to extract payment from individuals. They will have to continue to work through the government system. By and large, Canadians continue to oppose having to pay out of pocket for medical care. They certainly won't tolerate a system that runs credit checks on them in the admissions department of a hospital. Private operators can work within the system so long as they aren't operating privately.

After poring over volumes of survey material on health care, Darrell and I have constructed our own five principles of medicare: the five public opinion principles. Any future reforms of the health care system can succeed only if they are mindful of these citizen-based principles.

1. **CERTAINTY** Governments will never again get themselves into a position where my health care system is put in peril. They will manage the budgets carefully so the future is assured. They will fund the essentials before the frills. They will build for the future, training the requisite numbers of doctors and nurses. As part of this effort, I expect them to develop a guaranteed and forward-looking formula for financing health care.

2. **SOCIAL COHESION** My values as a Canadian dictate that our health care system must cover everyone, regardless of economic, social, or cultural circumstances. We're in this together. Medicare will remain a wholly public program, run by the government for the people. Health care will be delivered on the basis of need, and nothing else. Ours will be a single-tier system.

3. **QUALITY** Governments will squeeze waste out of the system. They will ensure that I get top value for my hard-earned tax dollar. An efficient system is a prerequisite for a quality system. And a quality system is one that offers me choices. As a knowledge consumer, I rightfully expect to be able to see the doctor of my choice and to participate in treatment decisions. It makes no sense that my surgery is covered but a replacement drug therapy is not; that my drug costs are covered while I'm in the hospital, but not when I'm recovering at home; that I am discharged early from hospital, but left with no system of home care. If decisions need to be made as to what is medically necessary, I expect to be fully consulted as a citizen. And by the way, don't ever try to restrict my right to see the doctor of my choice.

4. **AVAILABILITY** My health care will be there for me when I need it, without bureaucratic or economic impediment. The old principle of equal accessibility is worthy but insufficient. Equality without quality doesn't suffice. I need to be able to receive treatment on a timely basis, so that illness or injury does not unduly hinder my quality of life. I never again expect to be sent out of the country for radiation treatment nor told that I will have to wait while operating rooms lie idle. And I expect to be eligible for treatment wherever in Canada I may fall ill. This represents one of my rights of citizenship.

5. **PUBLIC ACCOUNTABILITY** I don't care if my food is prepared by a public-sector employee or a private-sector employee. And I support the efforts of any government to eliminate waste by resorting to private-sector disciplines or even private-sector operators. But I need to have faith that the system is a public system—financed publicly for the public

good and therefore wholly accountable to me as a citizen. I can't unelect a private hospital corporation, but I can a public one. In order to live up to my responsibilities as a knowledge citizen and a knowledge consumer, I will need access to publicly available and comprehensible information on which to make informed choices about the performance of my health care system. The system must be transparent if it's to truly be accountable.

A final thought on the search for certainty. Darrell was conducting a focus group earlier this year in Whitby, Ontario, on the large issues swirling about health care, weighty matters such as costs, funding, the aging population and emergency room overcrowding. One woman in the group expressed impatience with it all. Don't talk to me about millions and billions of dollars, she interjected. All I want to know, the woman continued, is that if something happens to my child and he is rushed to hospital that the ambulance will not be redirected on its way there. That's her personal search for certainty: the comfort that her child can get to hospital without losing precious time because of overcrowded emergency rooms. Her message was simple: Make sure that what my family needs is there when we need it. At the end of the day, the public health care system is a very personal matter.

CHAPTER 7

THE HEALTH CARE REVOLUTION

So much for the patient as citizen. Now let's look at the patient as consumer.

Two upheavals are occurring simultaneously in the health field. The first revolves around the significant issue, discussed in the previous chapter, of getting our collective act together on medicare. The second is more individualistic, much less understood, and probably of more enduring importance. It involves the incursion of the knowledge consumer into the health care field, particularly the previously cloistered world of the medical practitioner.

The first health care debate, the macro debate, focuses on "big money, big interests, and big issues." This high-altitude discussion, which attracts the lion's share of governmental and media attention, relates to "wholesale" issues, ones generally beyond the influence of the average person. The more subversive debate, the one we explore in this chapter, is emerging at the "retail" level—in the places where the health care system intersects with our everyday lives.

The decline of public trust in Canadian society, which has levelled the Berlin Walls of almost all institutions, is reaching as well into the medical profession. A well-educated and increasingly self-confident Canadian population can be seen clambering over old authority barriers and issuing heretofore unknown challenges to front-line medical personnel, most particularly doctors. For most of the past decade, physicians and surgeons were preoccupied with fending off government bureaucrats hell-bent on containing costs and, in so doing, limiting medical freedom. But the emerging challenge from below is the one with real revolutionary potential. Armed with printouts from the Internet and expectations of higher standards of service, knowledge consumers are knocking down the walls of medical privilege.

I heard a wonderful story a few years ago about a speech that Tom Peters, the American management guru, delivered to a large gathering of airline executives. Peters was scheduled to kick off the proceedings at nine in the morning. At ten to nine, the organizers realized they hadn't seen him yet. At five to nine, their casual observation turned to worry. Where was he? What if he didn't make it on time? At nine o'clock, as the crowd began moving into the conference hall, their thoughts turned to contingency plans. By five after nine, the delegates were shuffling impatiently in their seats like passengers forced to wait on the tarmac; the organizers were frantically phoning around trying to locate Peters. At ten after nine, their guest suddenly burst through the doors at the back of the hall and strode purposefully to the stage. A hush fell over the large room. Peters reached the podium, looked out at the assembled airline chiefs, and without missing a beat boomed: "By the standards of your industry, I'm on time this morning." Then he proceeded to lecture them on their industry's poor quality of service.

Imagine if he had been invited to a medical convention!

In a world in which service providers have been forced to reckon with the age of consumer sovereignty, the medical profession has stood out for its old-style sensibilities. Long delays, inconvenient hours of service, waiting rooms still stocked with dog-eared copies of the *Reader's Digest*—all reflect an industry bypassed by the standards revolution. In other respects, technology has forced phenomenal change on the medical profession over the past decade. But the core patient-doctor relationship remains mired in a bygone mentality, neither the personalized service of the 1950s nor the attention to customer satisfaction of more recent times. No one-minute check-in. No same-day delivery. No satisfaction guaranteed or your money back.

The winds of change blowing through other industries have carried with them refreshing new approaches to customer service. But the medical profession, insulated from consumer demands by a bureaucratized delivery system and an apprehended health care crisis, has largely escaped this quality revolution. Imagine asking your doctor for an appointment to suit *your* busy schedule? How about a telephone consultation? A house call? None are impossible, but all happen to be more the exception than the rule.

Earlier this year, Cancer Care Ontario determined that it needed to keep its radiation equipment at Toronto's Sunnybrook Hospital operating in the evening in order to help whittle down a politically unacceptable waiting list for treatment. The entrenched health care establishment—from hospital administrators to doctors to unions—wanted nothing to do with after-hours work and refused to cooperate. Now let's consider the context here. For several years, provincial health care systems have found themselves totally incapable of keeping up with demand for radiation. Unable to service Canadian patients at home, the provinces shipped them off to radiation treatment centres across the border—places such as Plattsburgh, Buffalo, Detroit, and Bellingham. At the most vulnerable moment in their lives, these patients were warehoused for weeks on end in Spartan hotels far removed from their support networks. Some patients have experienced serious income deprivation and even job loss to add to their woes of ill health. Radiation therapy usually lasts just a few moments a day, and then it's back to the hotel for endless hours of "Oprah" or gin rummy with fellow cancer patients.

Charged with correcting this intolerable situation, the Ontario government's cancer agency finally contracted with a private operator to use Sunnybrook's public facilities after hours. The private provider hired staff who already worked daytime shifts but wanted to earn extra money (members of the uncooperative unions) as well as former radiation specialists who had left their jobs in frustration over inflexible working arrangements. The obstacles to introducing even this most rudimentary service flexibility makes for an interesting story in itself. But the agency's motivation is also of interest. The objective of working off a serious treatment backlog is obviously commendable. But why not think as well of methods of broadening options for radiation treatment so as to offer better convenience to those patients who might have to work during the day or would rather not spend hours in Toronto traffic? Hopefully, greater consumer choice will turn out to be an unintended consequence, but it should be an intended consequence.

The medical profession is arguably the last bastion in Canada in which the producer still holds sway, thus the durability of the nine-to-five mentality. But the consumer revolution so familiar in other areas of the economy is battering at the door of the health care industry as well. It's huffing and puffing—and sooner or later is bound to blow the door down.

The implications are huge. The knowledge consumer will increasingly challenge the assumptions upon which health care is delivered. Empowered patients will demand to know why health care authorities systematically discriminate against certain desired treatments. The current demarcation between traditional medicine, which tends to be public, and alternative medicine, which tends to be private, will come under enormous pressure. So will the working arrangements of health care professionals. So will the increasingly blurred lines between hospital care and home care. Once the high fever over the search for certainty subsides, this health care revolution from below—a revolution grounded in knowledge and all about choice—will really take off.

Few groups in society have traditionally enjoyed more authority vested in them than medical practitioners. For generations, the doctor served as a modern deity. Indeed, the initials M.D. may well stand for modern deity. There's an old joke that asks what's the difference between a doctor and God. The answer: God doesn't think he's a doctor.

Medical practitioners not only earned great incomes, they also commanded enormous respect in their communities. They were imperial masters of their workplaces, stars of television dramas from "Ben Casey" and "Marcus Welby" to "St. Elsewhere" and "ER," stalwarts of the community. They made life and death decisions and still slept at night. They even had special licence plates on their cars, the original vanity plates, although in this case they reflected the high calling of being easily identifiable in the case of an emergency. The doctor appellation merely conferred an added layer of authority upon a group of individuals who already impressed with their crisp white lab coats (or, better yet, slightly rumpled surgical greens), antiseptic stethoscopes, and the young shiny faces that followed them on rounds.

I've always been amazed at the deference with which older people treat their physicians. My dad, who suffered from multiple sclerosis and had more than his fair share of dealings with doctors, would never have dreamed of calling any by their first names, even the interns and residents. My mother never once in her life referred to my pediatrician by anything other than Dr. Surchin—in his presence or otherwise. I asked her about this recently. She said that even when Dr. Surchin would sit down for a cup of coffee after a house call, a wall of formality persisted. He was a doctor and she wasn't. She also reminded me that years after my sister and I were born, she and my father began socializing with her obstetrician and his wife. But even then, my parents would always refer to him as Dr. Weisberg.

In an era when only a small minority of the general population attended university and even fewer went on to graduate school, the years of study put in by doctors elevated them to an exalted status. Today, they're being brought down to earth along with the rest of us. The pronouncements of medical doctors, while still carrying great weight, no longer exist beyond the bounds of reasonable interrogation. The self-regulating nature of the profession, especially when it comes to matters of inappropriate behaviour, has become yet another matter worthy of public scrutiny. The doctor-patient relationship is moving, in the words of McGill University ethicist Margaret Somerville, from a blind trust to an earned trust.

Let's consider a single statistic to start. Ninety per cent of Canadians now prefer that their doctor offer many treatment options rather than a single course of action. What that means is that Canadians want to be fully involved in weighing their options and making choices. They expect to have input—in light of their own personal circumstances and inclinations—into whether it's best to pursue treatment path X or treatment path Y. Do they prefer to combat their migraines through prophylactic measures or by ingesting powerful drugs at the first onset of symptoms? Which mix of heart treatments

suits them best? What approach to cancer? Does drug therapy or herbal therapy make more sense for their ailment?

Doctors no longer always know best. Patients listen carefully, to be sure,
to their advice. Doctors are still held in high esteem for their expertise and
professionalism. In a 1997 survey, doctors were respected "a great deal" by 59
per cent of respondents and "a fair amount" by 35 per cent. Three years later,
doctors were considered a "very believable" source of information by 63 per
cent of Canadians. Patients obviously value the opinions of their doctors, but
they are becoming accustomed in all walks of life to shopping around for
information. And so doctors are being reinvented as health care consultants.

To put it another way, the era of the patient, a passive recipient of medical truths, is drawing to a close. The age of the health consumer, a full participant in his or her own health care strategy, has dawned. Health consumers
impose demands and make choices. They are like other knowledge consumers. They squeeze the grapefruits themselves. They ask questions about
the offerings on the menu. They return merchandise if they find it doesn't
match the decor when they get home. They expect the car rental company
to honour undertakings given over the phone. The health consumer is an
actively involved individual.

A few more numbers:

- I usually ask my doctor many questions about procedures:
  86 per cent.

- I am more likely now to question my doctor than in the past:
  76 per cent.

- Most doctors can't keep up with the latest treatments and
  breakthroughs: 67 per cent.

- I always ask my doctor about medicines he or she prescribes:
  69 per cent.

Year by year, patients are becoming emboldened in involving themselves
in their treatments as health consumers. Between 1995 and 1998, the percentage of Canadians admitting they didn't really know enough about medicine to make informed choices about treatments fell from 80 per cent to
56 per cent. The sharp downward trend continues, driven especially by the

easy confidence of younger people and the never shy and retiring nature of baby boomers, many now entering their fifties and becoming increasingly focused on health issues.

Not to get too carried away. This is a revolution in its infancy. And it is not one aimed at overthrowing established medicine or its practitioners. Rather, it is a revolution in favour of inclusiveness, greater choice and more robust consumer involvement. Canadians are no more interested in healing themselves than they are in being passive witnesses to the healing process.

The majority of Canadians still believe it is important to do everything a doctor tells you. But such majorities are wilting. Canadians are federalists at heart; they are uncomfortable when too much power resides in one place. When it comes to doctors, they are seeking their own power-sharing arrangements—a highly developed form of health care partnership. Even within more deferential groups (such as older Canadians and lower-income earners), a streak of independence can be discerned. Between 1994 and 1998, the number of patients fifty-five years and older saying they do everything a doctor tells them to do fell from 50 per cent to 42 per cent. Those wanting to be presented with options jumped sharply. As for baby boomers and the younger generations, only about one-third faithfully follow their doctors' advice and three-quarters expect to be presented with options on how they will be treated.

Fifty-six per cent of Canadians report that they looked up information themselves on a disease or condition over the last year. Increasing numbers declare they have challenged their doctor's diagnosis and/or have switched doctors because of unsatisfactory treatment. One-quarter freely admit to being "two-timers"—they go to two doctors at the same time and tell neither. Three in ten say they've asked their physician about a specific condition without the doctor initiating the discussion. One in three even think they know more than their family practitioner about a particular illness from which they suffer.

But they aren't deluding themselves into thinking they have a medical degree. They feel well informed and entitled to ask questions. But their ready access to information is meant to be supplemental; patient knowledge is by no means intended as a substitute for physician knowledge. Indeed, three-quarters of Canadians reject the suggestion they will visit their doctor less frequently given the information at their disposal.

Doctors are not blind to what's going on. They are slowly and often grudgingly coming to understand that the traditional doctor-patient relationship cannot withstand the battering being administered by information-empowered health consumers. Eighty-five per cent of doctors recognize their patients are getting more health conscious and are becoming more actively involved in their own treatments. And in a surprisingly candid admission, six out of ten physicians told the *Medical Post* that sometimes their patients know more than they do about a specific health matter.

Understanding and acceptance are, of course, different matters. It is never easy to see your authority diminished, especially for more established doctors. Michael Decter, one of Canada's leading authorities on health care matters, attributed the growing unhappiness among Canadian doctors in the 1990s as much to their loss of authority vis-à-vis their patients as to their loss of independence vis-à-vis health bureaucrats. There's a bit of a cold war going on in the examining rooms of the nation. Four out of ten Canadians say their doctor doesn't like it when they ask questions about prescriptions or other treatments. But they keep on asking. Two-thirds complain their physicians don't provide enough information about the drugs they prescribe. Among the millions of Canadians using the Web to better inform themselves on health matters, just one out of nine says his or her doctor encourages these efforts.

The frustration of doctors with the rise of the new health consumer can be readily gleaned from behind a one-way mirror in Darrell's focus groups. Ask doctors about the rights of their patients to second opinions and the discussion starts out politely enough. ("I think everyone has the right to a second opinion.") It then quickly degenerates into the horrors of "doctor shopping." For physicians, doctor shopping occurs when patients make the rounds of medical offices comparing the information they are receiving, as if, egads, they were purchasing cars or life insurance. The doctors view this as hugely wasteful, not to mention insulting. The patients consider it, well, kind of like kicking the tires or buying life insurance.

In the classic tones of monopolists losing their grip, the doctors also gripe in focus groups about the enhanced access patients enjoy to medical information. The physicians complain they are being pressured into providing the most expensive and leading-edge treatments, regardless of the prospects for success. Again, they consider this development both a drain and a pain.

They may be right. But it doesn't matter. The knowledge consumer will not be denied, especially not when it comes to something as precious as health. Consider the reaction of patients when a researcher let the cat out of the bag in the spring of 2000 that he was onto something interesting in his laboratory. As recounted by Dr. Miriam Shuchman in *The Globe and Mail*, pandemonium broke out even though the treatment in question had only been tried on mice.

The episode concerned the highly regarded work of University of Toronto scientist Robert Kerbel, which involves the application of a cocktail of drugs to choke off the blood supply of a cancer, thereby stopping the growth and spread of the cancer. His preliminary findings were reported early in 2000 in the *Journal of Clinical Investigation*. His novel approach and apparent success with laboratory mice intrigued cancer doctors, but their occupational conservatism dissuaded them from extrapolating these results to humans. Scientists have their protocols, and this research remained at an early stage. But knowledge consumers feel no such constraints. On Saturday, February 26, an article about the new cancer treatment regimen and its seemingly miraculous results appeared at the top of the front page of the *Toronto Star*. By Monday, phone lines to cancer clinics throughout the city were jammed. Cancer patients appeared at the doors of these clinics, Dr. Shuchman describes, clutching their copy of the *Star*. One breast cancer specialist related how some of his patients arrived and demanded specific drugs in specific doses.

Dr. Kerbel and his associates were deluged with requests for information. They used the Internet to distribute a layman's guide to the experimental treatment, even spelling out which drugs would be effective in blocking the cancer's blood supply. Now this may or may not have been beyond the bounds of medical ethics given that human clinical trials had not even been attempted, but that's not our concern here. Rather, we are interested in how these patients behaved once they possessed information with which to challenge and prod their own doctors to take actions with which they may not have felt comfortable. In time, Dr. Kerbel's findings might prove a great breakthrough or a great disappointment. But in the immediate term, they underline the way in which previously untouchable information can be accessed and put to use in today's world by knowledge consumers. The Internet, in particular, alters the role of the patient. The lot of doctors becomes correspondingly more complicated.

Perhaps the best guide to the difficulty many doctors are experiencing in adjusting to health care's new consumer age concerns those wonderful honorifics bestowed upon medical practitioners. Increasingly, patients are calling their doctors by their first names. The authority barrier of old is giving way. And many doctors, especially older ones, don't like it one bit. In a poll in the *Medical Post,* just 52 per cent of doctors found it acceptable for a patient to call them by their first name. (Conversely, 81 per cent of Canadians feel it is all right for their doctor to call them by their first name.) No wonder seven out of ten doctors also told the publication in 1998 that they've become less satisfied practising medicine over the last five years. First the government encroached on their space. Then the patients.

Better consumers demand more choices. As passive patients become active consumers, this axiom will apply to the health care field as much as any other. The Internet is reinforcing trends toward greater consumer choice and knowledge. Patients can buy drugs on the Net. They can research their diseases or conditions on the Net. They can even seek medical advice on the Web. They can form communities with the similarly afflicted no matter where they live. Then they can compare treatments.

Health care is one of the main engines of growth on the Internet. A gaggle of sites provides medical information and even mail-order products. As contributing writer Jack Hitt noted in *The New York Times Magazine* last February, the temptation for anyone to obtain drugs like Viagra can be more easily satisfied than ever before because "medicine is decentralizing, slipping the reins long held by doctors. There is already telling evidence that these new sex drugs may well do for medicine what porn did for the Internet— constitute the killer app that reshapes the industry in an age of patient choice and turbo-consumerism."

In an era in which so many big drugs are going to be "lifestyle" related (Viagra being the most noteworthy, but the baldness treatment Rogaine providing another example), consumers can be expected to insist upon more and better access to information about these medications. Sixty-one percent of Canadians—up sixteen points in five years—feel pharmaceutical manufacturers should be allowed to advertise their products directly to consumers, a practice currently outlawed in Canada. At the same time, though, these same respondents express strong doubts that they would trust what they read.

The World Wide Web is making a huge contribution to empowering patients, but credibility is its Achilles heel. Nobody, not even doctors, can keep pace with the explosion of medical knowledge, which by some measures is doubling every nine to eighteen months and is likely to pick up even greater pace in the wake of human gene mapping. Consumers are doing their best to remain informed. More than half of Canadians with Internet access report having visited a health site. Half of those, in turn, judge themselves more knowledgeable because of their research. When they visit health sites, Canadians are usually conducting research into specific diseases, their preventions, and their cures. They also tend to look up information about nutrition and exercise and prescription drugs. Those inclined to go health information surfing tend to be devotees. Three out of ten report having visited a health site at least once in the past week and another 45 per cent at least once in the past month.

The Internet has become a powerful force in health care, but it remains an immature one. When it comes to health information, the Web suffers from the same trust deficit we discussed in Chapter 3. Library reference books are considered "very believable" sources of medical information by 47 per cent of Canadians. Web sites clock in at just 13 per cent. More than half of Canadians strongly agree with the statement that the problem in assessing medical information is knowing who to trust. Still, this doesn't stop them from bringing their printouts to the doctor's office. But the lack of Web quality distresses them as much as poor physician service.

In the midst of negotiations in January 2000 between the province of Ontario and its doctors, *Globe and Mail* columnist John Ibbitson portrayed an Internet-driven health care future—virtual doctoring—that would put the consumers in the driver's seat and thereby render meaningless such negotiations between producer and regulator.

"The Internet doctor's office will probably be staffed with nurses, nurse practitioners and doctors," he wrote. "They will listen to you describe your symptoms. Then you will apply a wireless monitor that will take your temperature and blood pressure and analyze your heart rhythm, transmitting the information to the computer. One of the miniature analyzers either already on the market or in development—some do not even require a pinprick—will analyze your blood.

"The nurse practitioner or doctor will consult your medical records, examine the test results, perhaps feed the information to a diagnostic program and offer a diagnosis. If only medication is needed, it will be delivered to you. The computer will monitor your progress and alert the office if it detects a problem."

Ibbitson's point concerned the role technology will play in busting up the public health monopoly regardless of the desires of policy-makers. The same logic applies to the impact of these information technologies on the influence doctors wield over the system. In both cases, power is flowing slowly but steadily from bureaucrats and traditional producers to consumers and new alternative health care competitors.

The natural outgrowth of an ability to exercise choice is the desire to expand one's range of choices. Empowered health consumers are experimenting with their fundamental approaches to health care by ordering from a wider menu of services than ever before. They have dared to cross the continental divide between conventional medicine and so-called alternative therapies. Health increasingly is viewed not just as an absence of illness, but as the capacity to enjoy life to its fullest. As such, traditional medicine and new alternatives represent a continuum in the public mind, not a divide. And so health consumers, indifferent to the blandishments of self-interested doctors, are building bridges between the two spheres.

If there ever was an era when a taste for alternative treatments was something you didn't tell your friends or boss about, those times have clearly passed. More than half the Canadian population—and climbing—has turned to some form of alternative treatment. Estimates of spending on alternatives range from $1 billion a year to $4 billion, most of it out-of-pocket payments by highly motivated users. Ninety per cent of them report being either very satisfied or somewhat satisfied with the results, a performance rating conventional health care professionals might look upon with some envy. While women tend to be more inclined toward alternative approaches than men, the gender differences are not as great as is generally assumed. Rather, the greatest variation in usage is based on income: Those with higher incomes tend to experiment more with alternatives than lower-income individuals—a key finding to which we will return later.

The rise of alternative medicines has been well documented in a series of studies by the Angus Reid Group. Darrell's personal introduction to the trend occurred about seven years ago, when he was moderating a focus group in Vancouver on the North American free trade agreement. After he got everyone seated, he proceeded to put them at ease by explaining the procedures and then asking his standard round-the-table ice-breaker question: "What do you do in your spare time?"

After a few responses along the lines of "Hi, I'm Fred. I work as a contractor. I've got a wife and three kids and I like to play golf," it was the turn of a slight, curly-haired woman in her late thirties. She gave her name and replied that her hobby was "crystals." Ever quick on his feet, Darrell responded how nice that was. "Do you collect glass figurines like in *The Glass Menagerie*?" The woman looked puzzled.

"I mean crystals, like gemstones and other types of valuable rocks."

He still didn't get it, remarking, "Oh, you make jewellery."

Again, she said no. She looked baffled. (This was, after all, Lotusland. British Columbia has the highest incidence in Canada of turning to alternative treatments. The moderator obviously came from somewhere less exotic.)

Finally, another participant came to the rescue. "No, not for jewellery," she explained. "She uses them for medicinal purposes." The curly-haired woman nodded in agreement. At this point, Darrell was thoroughly mystified. He had never heard of anyone using rocks for health reasons. He wondered how she did it. Did she swallow them?

The woman proceeded to explain that she placed the crystals on parts of her body particularly receptive to conducting a special energy flow. Different crystals were used to treat different problems: some physical, others emotional or spiritual. Most of the other participants sat there nodding in agreement as she elaborated on the benefits of crystals.

The medical profession has historically been situated well outside this crystal consensus. It spent years and years either sneering at or conspiring against alternative treatment providers, periodically applying its self-regulating powers to chill out competitors it considered lacking in scientific gravitas. Take the case of Dr. William LaValley of Chester, Nova Scotia, who was subjected to a high-profile investigation by the province's medical society in 1991 due to his use of acupuncture and herbal medicines in his treatment regimes.

LaValley had become intrigued by alternative treatments while a Ph.D. candidate studying brain function at the Baylor University in Houston, Texas.

In 1982, he secured a grant from the American Medical Association to go to China and look into the effects of acupuncture on brain chemistry. "It blew apart my medical Western scientific paradigm—the model I had for what made sense and what didn't make sense. Either 1 billion Chinese over thousands of year were insane or our Western approach was incomplete." LaValley, a Texan, would subsequently meet a veteran Nova Scotian surgeon named David Baker at an acupuncture convention and be lured to work with him in the south shore community of Chester. Their practice drew patients from all over the province, usually chronic sufferers or the terminally ill who had hit a dead end with conventional medicine. The old guard in the medical establishment viewed the innovators as threatening and dangerous and went after them with the vigour of an inquisition. Four hundred and fifty of their medical charts were seized. They stood accused of "quackery."

Ultimately, the medical society, the medical board, and the government were found by the courts to be in collusion in improperly charging the pair with operating outside the conventions of the profession. A cold peace ensued. "The best I could call it was medical apartheid," LaValley reflects.

Since then, attitudes have changed within the Nova Scotia medical establishment, and in other provinces as well. The bull-headed prosecution of one of their own led to a great deal of soul-searching. More and more young doctors came forward to express their own interest in broadening the range of health treatment. Health consumers also became less timid about pushing for a more complete medical menu. In the mid-1990s, Nova Scotia's medical society became the first in Canada to establish a so-called complementary medical section. Today, LaValley has taken the offensive, advising the federal government on the regulation of natural health products and pushing for further health care integration to replace the medical apartheid of just a few years back.

Ordinary Canadians didn't bother taking sides in what they consider an artificial and unnecessary war. Nearly three-quarters believe that using both conventional and alternative therapies is better than using either alone. Seven out of ten agree with the statement that "just because alternative medicine hasn't been scientifically tested and approved by Canadian and provincial medical bodies doesn't mean it isn't effective." The new health consumer is not ready to bow to doctors who seek to restrict their choices. They'd rather just blow past them. Most say they simply don't bother keeping recalcitrant doctors fully informed of their treatment decisions. In fact, just one-third say they would even listen if their doctor recommended against alternative medicines.

Although acceptance remains uneven and resistance is still strong in some quarters to making truck or trade with the alternative providers, the tide seems to have turned in favour of health care dualism. A 1998 survey of family physicians on behalf of the Canadian Medical Association found that one-third provided alternative treatment of one kind or another, slightly more than engaged in anaesthetic services and a bit less than the number who treated HIV and AIDS patients. The word "complementary" used to describe physicians such as Dr. LaValley who combine traditional and alternative medicine is increasingly justified. Indeed, the Canadian Complementary Medical Association, founded in Alberta in 1996 by six crossover doctors, boasted a complement of 150 members within four years.

The walls are definitely coming down, as was evident at the autumn 2000 Canadian Cardiovascular Congress, a major medical conference involving fourteen health associations. The 2000 gathering included a session on alternative treatment for heart disease. Organizers, who had been concerned about the response from the scientists, researchers, and policy-makers in attendance, needn't have worried. The hall overflowed with interested observers. They listened intently as a Hong Kong doctor and herbal medicine specialist outlined the risks from mixing certain drugs and herbal treatments and an American specialist detailed the anti-oxidant qualities of dark chocolate.

Another example comes from the University of Alberta, whose medical faculty includes a geriatric and family physician named Stephen Aung. Dr. Aung has trained in both Eastern and Western medicine and serves as director of Medical Acupuncture and Oriental Medicine in the university's school of medicine. Dr. Aung is far from realizing his dream of having a complementary medical hospital and complementary medical department to rigorously test alternatives and teach them professionally. But his acupuncture course represents the proverbial foot in the door.

After decades on the ramparts, the conservative medical establishment appears to be adjusting to these new facts of life. Six out of ten doctors now report routinely inquiring whether their patients are taking herbal or alternative medicines. The dangers lie in those who neither ask nor want to hear.

Their patients go ahead without them—running the risk of creating a noxious brew of homeopathic and chemical remedies.

Canadians are employing a bewildering array of these alternatives. By far the most popular is chiropractic care. It is followed by relaxation techniques, massage, prayer or spiritual practice, herbal therapies, special diet programs, folk remedies, acupuncture, and yoga. The list also includes homeopathy, imagery techniques, energy healing, naturopathy, aromatherapy, hypnosis, biofeedback, and chelation.

Why do Canadians turn to these treatments? The best answer they provide is why not? They believe that alternative medicines can't hurt you and may help. Three-quarters will tell you that conventional medicine doesn't offer all the answers and that alternatives have been around for centuries in other countries so there must be something to them. Other popular explanations include the opinion that regular medicines on their own haven't worked for them; alternatives are more natural; they are concerned about side effects from prescription drugs; and they get better service from their alternative medicine providers than from their physicians. That final point is worth pondering; physicians are going to have to study the quality of service their more market-oriented alternative competitors are already providing. Less waiting and more empathy would be good lessons to pick up.

Still, consumer acceptance of alternatives should not be misinterpreted as a rejection of traditional medicine. Only one in five Canadians will go so far as to say alternative therapies are superior to conventional ones. Once again, they view them as complementary, not competitive. And they want to be able to choose for themselves without fear or favour.

The levelling of the playing field between conventional and alternative medicine has important public policy ramifications for the future. Generally speaking, conventional medical practices are taxpayer financed in this country while users of alternatives have to fend for themselves. Don't expect health consumers to tolerate this double standard for long. Our polling already shows that 70 per cent of Canadians think alternative medicines and practices should be covered under medicare and that 66 per cent feel governments should encourage their use.

These sentiments, it should be pointed out, soften considerably when hard trade-offs are raised. In a 1997 poll, support for public financing of alternatives fell to 39 per cent when respondents were told the funds would be diverted from conventional medicine and even further when challenged that taxes would have to rise to pay for this extension of medicare. But with the deficit eliminated, such scenarios may not be as relevant today as they were back then. Governments are awash in cash. Billions are being pumped into health care. Taxes are coming down. The zero sum era in which we can afford only one priority at a time is drawing to a close. Pressure to tear down the remaining wall between alternatives and conventional medicine is mounting. This is especially so given the popularity of complementary approaches within two key constituencies in Canadian society: baby boomers who view good health as a social entitlement and have become accustomed to not paying for their health care rights; and ethnic communities, particularly the Chinese, who have a long history with alternatives.

Just as important is the point we made earlier about the impact of income on alternative usage. Access to alternative treatments currently appears to be unequal, violating one of our five public opinion principles of medicare—the social cohesion principle. Unlike with most other physician services, the costs of alternatives are borne partly or entirely by the consumer. Some people can afford them and others cannot. This may have been acceptable in a period in which they were viewed as exotic interventions. But this differential access will come under pressure in an era of increasing health care eclecticism. Once the search for certainty is reasonably satisfied in health care, count on a movement arising to level the playing field.

So how will the advent of the new health consumer play itself out? Several points leap to mind:

- For policy-makers, it means the emphasis of recent years on de-listing services could shift toward the listing of new services. In the period of fiscal crisis, governments could reasonably make the case against expanding the range of medically necessary procedures. Those conditions don't exist any more. Health consumers can be expected in the next few years to lobby to add alternatives to the list of publicly insured services. Same with private insurance plans, some of which now offer a measure of coverage. Policy holders will wonder why prescription drugs are covered but not natural health products. Policy-makers, already fearful of the rising health costs associated with new technologies and aging populations, will be loath to knuckle under. But the political pressure on governments to justify their inclusions and exclusions is bound to increase.

• The flow of physicians offering alternative treatments will continue to grow until it becomes routine. Practices will cross over. There was a time when patients generally went to either the chiropractor or the physiotherapist. They were rivals. You didn't tell your physiotherapist that you were getting your bones cracked. My chiropractor in Ottawa, Patrick Faloon, shares premises and patients with a physiotherapist. Or take the Life Spring Clinic in Victoria. It brings together four medical doctors with practitioners of such alternative treatments as acupuncture, naturopathy, massage, and chiropracty. Increasingly, we will see clinics that bridge the conventional/alternative divide.

• As pressure builds to list alternative treatments, many doctors will fight to keep them outside the public medicare sphere for business reasons. Now that many doctors are offering alternative treatments such as chiropracty, they will not want to lose the lucrative privately financed revenue stream from their business mix.

• At some point, a smart entrepreneur will convert small alternative health enterprises—if they remain in the private realm—into consolidated businesses. Canadians will have a chance to invest in the growth industry of alternative treatment.

• Medical schools will learn to accommodate themselves to the changing face of health care. As Bud Rickhi, a University of Calgary professor of medicine and alternative treatment champion, says, "Given the choice of Western or alternative medicine, why not choose both?" Students, he feels, are more likely to push the agenda than their professors "because they don't have the same preconceived notions of medicine and healing."

• Canadians will continue to go to the Internet for health information and medical solutions ranging from drugs to diagnostics. This will open up more choice and introduce yet more competitive pressures into health care. It will also lead to demands for greater regulation of the quality of information or, at the very least, open up opportunities for information providers with established trustmarks.

• Increasing political power within ethnic communities will contribute to pressures to have "their" medical traditions legitimized. An important milestone was passed almost unnoticed last year in British Columbia when the provincial government became the first in North America to hand the title "doctor" to practitioners of traditional Chinese medicine. More than a century after Chinese immigrants brought their knowledge of herbal treatments and acupuncture to Canada, they finally won acknowledgement as a profession, which brought with it the welcome responsibility of regulation. The decision may well have been sound, but it couldn't have hurt that British Columbia has one of the highest concentrations of Asian immigrants in the world.

• The legitimate practitioners of complementary medicine will join B.C.'s Chinese medical practitioners in pushing for licensing in order to freeze out charlatans who give the entire movement a bad name. Health consumers will be looking for standards and order. This push for licensing will feed on efforts to have the public system cover alternatives.

• As always, the public will look to governments to protect them. By a margin of more than two to one, Canadians say government should regulate the emerging field of herbal remedies and alternative treatment. The perception exists in some places that governments should not impede access to new treatments with slow approval processes. That's probably true. Nobody likes inefficient government. But negligent government is even worse. The lessons learned in the Walkerton water disaster should not be lost. Canadians, without hesitation, expect governments to look out for their health and safety. It remains just as true for the new health consumer and for new patterns of health consumption.

• Finally, the challenges new knowledge-based, demand-emboldened health consumers are currently posing to the medical establishment will pale in comparison with the complexities to come when patients arrive in doctors' offices with expectations of genetically modified designer babies.

CHAPTER 8

HARD HEADS AND
SOFT HEARTS

Margaret Thatcher once famously declared there is no such thing as society. Canadians would dispute that assertion. They are made uncomfortable by the mutually exclusive pronouncements of hard right or hard left. Canadians believe in themselves, their family, their community, their country, their world. Individual and family come first. But to use the title of Harvard University academic Robert Putnam's groundbreaking work on social capital, Canadians are not prone to "Bowling Alone." How could a people whom distance and the elements threw together in a rigged survival course do that? We learned early to rely upon one another even while guarding our private prerogatives. A barn raising represents a good metaphor for the Canadian way. We are good neigh-bours, but we believe in strong fences as well. Self-reliance and mutual responsibility make up the twin leitmotifs of the Canadian mindset.

Through the twenty-five lean years from the early 1970s to the late 1990s, Canadians battened down the hatches and turned their focus inward to the increasingly harsh economic challenges they confronted. In poll after poll, year after year, they cited unemployment and the economy as their top priorities alongside, initially, inflation and, latterly, the deficit. The social agen-da that had so illuminated public policy discussions in the 1950s and 1960s—when Canada adopted universal health care, the Canada Pension Plan, and the Canada Assistance Plan, among other groundbreaking initiatives—found itself crowded out as economic fear eclipsed social hope. To the extent social issues garnered interest, it usually flowed from the sacrifice of yet another layer of protection in order to restore the fiscal bottom line to health. Canadians accepted the need to secure the economic base even at some expense to the social superstructure.

At times in the Nervous Nineties, it may have looked like the legacy of a compassionate Canada had succumbed to the imported tenets of neo-conservative ideology. Certainly, Canadians expressed deep reservations about the course their fabled social system had journeyed. Skepticism abounded about past policy approaches that in retrospect often looked indulgent of fail-ure and indifferent to the cause of getting people back on their feet. But the essential Canadian commitment to a greater social good never really faded. Chastened by our perilous economic state, the country merely took a time-out from social activism. The bedrock values upon which Canada was built continued to gurgle away just below the surface of public opinion. In the lyrics of a sixties song, the dream never died, just the dreamer. And so, as a new millennium dawned with renewed economic confidence, social policy concerns—health, education, and poverty—once again rose to the surface of public opinion.

Consider what Canadians had to say about poverty at the end of 1999. Six out of ten respondents told the Angus Reid Group they felt poverty had worsened in the previous five years. Only one in ten thought the situation was better, with the rest judging it about the same. Moreover, the harsh critique of social policy levelled by some neo-conservatives—beer-swilling single mothers, sexually irresponsible teenagers, able-bodied young men unwilling to take starter jobs—had garnered little following. Just 30 per cent of Canadians held individuals themselves, through their own choices and actions, responsible for their poverty. Only a tiny minority agreed it fell to the poor alone to pull themselves up by the bootstraps. More than three times as many thought government must take the lead. This continued compassion notwithstanding, a strong majority embraced a concept of workfare in which able-bodied welfare recipients are obliged to perform community work or attend training programs so as to break their cycle of dependence on government handouts.

All this underlines the persistence of the so-called Tory touch in Canadian politics, the idea that we are not different groups in a society pitted against one another so much as parts of a common organism—and that if one part is hurt so are the others. Canada has from its very beginnings combined the liberal individualism so characteristic of the United States with a more developed sense of order, tradition, and state intervention. Writing in the 1960s, political scientists Louis Hartz and Gad Horowitz labelled this latter trait "the Tory touch," tracing it to a fragment of our political culture probably brought north with them by the United Empire Loyalists. Attitudes toward social policy, even in the aftermath of the Nervous Nineties, are best understood with reference to this essential Canadian quality.

Even as we see ourselves getting richer, we reach out to those falling behind. We don't blame them. We feel a responsibility toward them. But we don't owe them a living. We expect them to take opportunities to help themselves. In her exhaustive 1995 study of Canadian values, social policy researcher Suzanne Peters noted a "hard-headedness on the fiscal side" that had emerged alongside our traditional tender-heartedness. "We accept the need for cuts in principle, but we do not want to lose cherished social programs. We see individual effort as ideal and necessary, but we accept collective responsibility when that effort fails or is impeded," she wrote.

Whatever our sentiments, though, it is clear that we've moved on from the ethos of the post-war welfare state. We now believe instead in the self-help state. Our attitude has switched, in the jargon of the social policy world, from one of handouts to hand-ups, from a safety net to a springboard. A 1999 report by the Senate Standing Committee on Social Affairs, Science and

Technology captured the new reality of social policy well. It noted that in the era of the welfare state, security used to mean protection from change. Today, it means building the capacity to change. That means reorienting social policy from a traditional welfare approach (focused on protecting individuals from change) to a social investment model (focused on investing in one's capacity to change). In a nutshell, that is the story of the past dozen years with regard to both public opinion and policy.

Quality of life supersedes all else for Canadians. Shortly before the November 2000 election campaign, Ekos Research asked a group of respondents to choose an overarching goal for the country to achieve by the year 2010. Their first choice in a list of sixteen was best quality of life in the world, nudging out even the best health care system. Their second to last choice—beating out only the best transportation system—was highest standard of living among industrialized nations. In other words, money isn't everything; it can't buy you happiness. And when Canadians think of quality of life, they think social issues. The Canadian Policy Research Network conducted forty discussion groups across the country in the fall of 2000 in order to find out what Canadians considered the vital ingredients of quality of life. The social issues all came first—health, education, social programs, environment—both in terms of the things participants felt are most important and the ones they judged most in need of improvement.

That is not to suggest that Canadians remain unmoved by their brushes through much of the 1980s and 1990s with economic decline and social stagnation. Arthur Kroeger, a former deputy minister of employment, once ruefully cited Ronald Reagan in remarking on the halcyon days of social programs: "We had a war on poverty—and poverty won." That pretty well sums up the verdict of the broader population as well. In the aftermath of their experiences, Canadians now exhibit a healthy skepticism about grand schemes. They will want to measure the success of programs not by how much generosity (money) goes in, but by how much poverty goes down.

Despite their renewed attention to social policy, Canadians aren't inclined to revisit the failed approaches of the past. The misplaced generosity that paid young people unemployment insurance benefits in the 1970s to ski in the Rockies no longer has a place in the Canadian mindset. Neither does the "victim pathology" so popular through the 1980s and early 1990s: the one that portrayed poor people as ennobled victims of one power structure or another and therefore deserving of transfers of tax dollars. Social policy often became more a vehicle to work out liberal guilt than to get people back to work. Canadians came to understand the incentives were all wrong in a system that made it economically irrational for single mothers to leave welfare for work or encouraged young men to forsake an education for seasonal work accompanied by long stretches on the dole. From such thinking arose a culture of dependence, not independence, and resentment, not generosity. The old ways have discredited themselves.

Ekos, which has delved deeply into the social thinking of Canadians, also asked respondents in early 2001 to rate a variety of different challenges the federal government could take on. Redistributing wealth in order to promote social equality, the core policy of the social safety net for more than a generation, ranked at the bottom. Moreover, by a two-to-one margin, they judged that the inadequacy of social programs could be blamed far more on poor design than on inadequate finances. In other words, they felt the system needed fixing, not funding.

Canadians increasingly concluded that collective responsibility kicked in only when personal effort failed, and that even then it should be accompanied by a renewed personal effort. Six out of ten rejected the statement in the mid-1990s that "we don't give everyone an equal chance." Meanwhile, by a four-to-one margin, they said individuals should take more responsibility for providing for themselves. And, by three to one, that there should be greater incentive for individual effort.

The public has given up on the poor generalship of past wars on poverty, but remains committed to the overall cause. In its study at the end of 1999, the Angus Reid Group asked respondents for their assessment of the government's handling of poverty issues. One-quarter judged the effort to be proportionate to the problem. Only five per cent thought the government was doing too much. The rest—seven out of ten—felt government wasn't doing enough. And, in stark contrast to their optimism about the country's economic future, they expressed deep pessimism about the ability to meet the challenges on health care, education, and poverty.

The persistence of the connection Canadians felt to one another shouldn't really come as a great surprise. Even in the most anxious moments of the 1990s, classic Canadian compassion could be seen flickering in the window. Social policy analyst Judith Maxwell, whom I once described as the Mother Teresa of the policy wonks, caught a glimpse of the candle during a conference at the Chateau Laurier hotel in October 1993. As the former head of the Economic Council of Canada, she herself unhappily accepted the need for a time-out to put the country's fiscal house back in order. But she also refused to sweep the social wreckage under the carpet. Whole categories of Canadians were finding themselves ill-equipped to compete in the new global economy. Maxwell was no pushover. She had called for anyone under twenty-five to be disqualified from receiving unemployment insurance, lest the siren song of poor-paying, insecure work lure them from school and into the dependency cycle. They would be forced instead into some sort of training or schooling—a kind of "trainfare" for our troubled youth. She personified that mixture of soft-heartedness and hard-headedness to which her friend and colleague Suzanne Peters later alluded. The country had a responsibility to ensure all comers could avail themselves of the opportunity to prosper, she felt, but in an intelligent manner and within reasonable fiscal bounds.

That October, she participated in a panel discussion at the downtown Ottawa hotel alongside Michael Walker, head of the neo-conservative Fraser Institute. Walker eclipsed the quiet-spoken Maxwell with his boisterous presentation in favour of deficit reduction. Frustrated by his single-minded perspective, she finally blurted out that governments had to be mindful not just of the fiscal deficit but also a social deficit. The phrase "social deficit" struck a chord. A wave of applause rippled through the room.

I witnessed first-hand the appeal of the term a little over a year later. The Liberal government was edging its way toward its historic deficit-busting February 1995 budget, distressed by the need to take measures contrary to its political persuasion, but convinced it had no choice. I wanted to illustrate the tension between what I viewed as two wings of Canadian liberalism—social progressives who generally accepted the need for deficit reduction and fiscal conservatives who generally believed in a role for social policy. I was looking for "thinkers" to illustrate the two points of view, but ones also actively engaged in shaping decisions. I settled on Peter Nicholson, a brilliant ideas guy then working as a special adviser to Finance Minister Paul Martin, and Maxwell, who had served on an advisory panel to Human Resources Minister

Lloyd Axworthy. My selections were influenced by the delicious fact that both of them had attended the same small school as teenagers in Annapolis Royal some forty years earlier, even sitting in the same row in Grade 12.

In the article, I referred to Maxwell's social deficit concept. Over the next several days, I was deluged by about a hundred phone calls and faxes from readers—an extraordinary number for a print journalist, particularly in the days before e-mail became commonplace. Everyone wanted to know how to get in touch with Maxwell so they could enlist in her battle to shine a light on the social deficit. She had touched a nerve—a nerve that has been implanted in the Canadian mindset from the very beginnings of the country.

In 1919, Canadians were given a remarkably accurate sneak preview of the social safety net that would be strung after the Second World War. In a visionary policy resolution at the convention that selected him Liberal party leader, Mackenzie King pledged to institute "so far as may be practicable, having regard to Canada's financial position, an adequate system of insurance against unemployment, sickness, dependence in old age, and other disability, which would include old age pensions, widows' pensions, and maternity benefits."

Little progress on the social policy front was recorded in the 1920s and even the Dirty Thirties. Canada experienced no equivalent of Roosevelt's New Deal. That spirit of creativity would await the Second World War, which ushered in an unprecedented era of activism in Canadian politics. Canada's population of 11.5 million entered the war with the scars from the Depression still fresh. The combination of these two seminal events—depression and war—thoroughly transformed the country and its frame of mind. Unemployment virtually disappeared as 1 million men and women joined the armed forces and others flowed into factories producing all-out for the war effort. The country's productive capacity doubled in the course of the war, as did national income. The wartime economy demonstrated to the public service elite that government actually possessed the tools to manage the economy. A new breed of bureaucrats, seared in their formative years by the Depression and now emboldened by the war effort, found in John Maynard Keynes's General Theory of Employment, Interest, and Money the intellectual justification to carry on managing the economy in peacetime.

Another transformation was also underway, this time in public opinion. The Canadian population—particularly the 1 million men and women who served in the armed forces—could not imagine a post-war society in which they would ever again suffer the privations of the Depression. Nearly everyone had put their lives on hold; many had placed them at risk. Canadians itched to embrace the future, but a future complete with a system of social security to offset the terrible insecurities they had already experienced in their young lives. In an early opinion poll taken in October 1943, 71 per cent of respondents said they wanted to see reform rather than having things remain as they were before the fighting began.

Canada hardly held a monopoly on such sentiments. In Britain, too, the political debate turned to the post-war order long before D-Day. In 1942, Sir William Beveridge published his famous blueprint for the welfare state. Expectations ran rampant over the good things that would happen once Hitler's defeat was secured. A.P. Herbert, a British parliamentarian and humorist, satirized the mood in a poem in *Punch* magazine:

> Oh, won't it be wonderful after the war
> There'll be no more war, and there'll be no more poor
> We don't have to work if we find it a bore
> We'll all get a pension about twenty-four
> The beer will be better and quicker and more
> But, Sir William, there's a problem I'd like to explore
> Why didn't we have this old war before?

King, arguably the greatest political tactician in Canadian history, sensed the new mood forming earlier than most and determined to do something about it. In 1940, he had steered through a constitutional amendment that allowed him to establish a national unemployment insurance program. His timing was typically clever: Unemployment hardly rated as a concern in the wartime economy, but he still looked like a champion of the little guy to a country smarting from the Depression. As the early 1940s progressed, he watched with fascinated horror as the Cooperative Commonwealth Federation (the forerunner to today's NDP) almost snatched electoral victory in an Ontario provincial election and then actually routed the established parties in Saskatchewan. King intended no such fate to befall himself.

Intent on outflanking the CCF, King appointed Leonard Marsh, a McGill University professor and social reformer, to produce a Canadian equivalent of the Beveridge report. The 1943 Marsh Report on Social Security hearkened back to the Depression experience and warned that the lessons must not be forgotten. March outlined a comprehensive package of income-maintenance benefits for the unemployed, disabled, elderly, unhealthy, and anyone else falling on hard times, an approach in keeping with King's unrealized 1919 blueprint. "Security has become accepted as one of the things for which the peoples of the world are fighting," Marsh wrote. "It is one of the concrete expressions of 'a better world,' which is particularly real to those who knew unemployment, destitution, inadequate medical care and the like in the depression periods before the war."

King went on to promise "a charter of social security for the whole of Canada" and "useful employment for all who are willing to work." He chose to start with a universal family allowance program. The legislation was passed in 1944 with the first cheques set to go out in 1945, which happened to be election year in Canada. Through his clever machinations, King dodged the bullet that felled Winston Churchill's government that same year in Britain. The Liberals dropped 58 seats in the 1945 election, but maintained their majority in the House of Commons. The Conservatives formed the Official Opposition with the outmanoeuvred CCF relegated to third place. King termed the outcome a "very near run thing," but he had created the template of Liberal electoral strategy for decades to come. Run from the left by stealing the policies, where necessary, of the CCF and later the NDP.

The Marsh blueprint took a generation to put in place, the fiscally conservative post-war Liberal governments ever mindful of the 1919 caveat "so far as may be practicable, having regard to Canada's financial position." Nonetheless, the pieces gradually fell into place. The social policy consensus in Canadian politics was sufficiently broad that the Conservative government of John Diefenbaker picked up the torch on health insurance and other measures when the Liberals went down to defeat in 1957. Back in power under Lester Pearson in 1963, the Liberals took advantage of a strong economy to kick into high gear the completion of the welfare state.

Their rendering turned out to be a largely passive patchwork of income-maintenance programs for people who fell from the economic train but maintained the capacity to clamber back aboard. The system was designed for an epoch of relatively low and short-lasting unemployment. The economy was regarded as self-correcting; it would take care of adults in the medium term. The social safety net would be required only for the unemployable—seniors, widows, the disabled—and to smooth over short-term dislocations. Children would get a boost through their family allowance cheques. The typical profile of an unemployed Canadian was someone either on temporary layoff or between jobs in the same industry. Recall notices were common and skills lasted a lifetime. A case could not be easily made for more active intervention. And so Canada in fact never boasted the full-employment policies whose supposed demise the left so frequently laments.

By the time Pierre Trudeau came to power in 1968, the fabled social safety net was well strung: old-age pensions, hospital and medical insurance, the Canada Assistance Plan, grants to post-secondary education, the Canada Pension Plan, public housing, family allowance, and unemployment insurance. In his first term, Trudeau sought to put some substance on his Just Society rhetoric with an ambitious and futile effort to overcome regional inequities, an approach based on the idea that jobs should move to where people lived rather than vice versa. He also gave his blessing to his labour minister, Bryce Mackasey, to preside over one final orgy of misplaced generosity in the form of a massive overhaul of the unemployment insurance system.

Mackasey's 1971 reforms represented the last blast of the era of plenty. The extraordinarily upbeat mood of the times was captured in a government White Paper that preceded the bill. Canada, it declared, stood on the threshold "of many brilliant changes and developments . . . marking us as a community capable of realizing the full promise of the post-industrial era—developments which single us out as one of the world's most affluent peoples, with a spiraling gross domestic product and a rising standard of living."

The Trudeau government's UI legislation made it possible to collect forty-four weeks of benefits after just eight weeks of work—year after year after year. Payment levels were increased to as high as 75 per cent of insurable earnings, providing a real incentive to stay on pogey. And the reforms relaxed penalties for voluntarily leaving a job, giving rise to the so-called UI ski team, composed of young ski bums who passed their winters on the slopes financed by working stiffs.

The boom, of course, was about to fall. Mackasey's reckless reforms flowed out of the same mentality that put us on the road to nearly three decades of deficits. Indeed, UI benefits doubled in the year after his legislation, even though unemployment itself fell. Before the seventies reached the halfway point, the government found itself in less "brilliant" circumstances than forecast. Mackasey's successors moved to roll back aspects of his reforms in 1975, 1977, and 1978. But it was difficult. Lotto 8-44 quickly morphed into a social entitlement in regions of high seasonal employment, often Trudeau government strongholds. The late 1970s Liberals found themselves hoisted with their own petard. They had succeeded too well in marketing the moral goodness of the post-war safety net. As the economy slowed and deficits mounted, they lacked the stomach for a sustained program of retrenchment. In 1984, the year Trudeau left office, party pollster Martin Goldfarb reported that "the principle of universality of social assistance programs is fairly well ingrained in the Canadian psyche." He added that any attempt to reduce the deficit by curbing social welfare spending "will not be well received by the public."

Goldfarb's analysis was spot on for its time and place, as Brian Mulroney would quickly discover when his deficit-afflicted finance minister, Michael Wilson, tried to remove a degree of inflation protection from old-age pensions. A sixty-three-year-old widow named Solange Denis accosted Mulroney outside the Centre Block as he nipped home for a quick lunch in the middle of the parliamentary day. "You lied to us," she shouted at the helpless Mulroney, the television cameras rolling. "You made us vote for you, then goodbye Charlie Brown." Within eight days, Mulroney forced Wilson to back down.

Such rearguard actions aside—and pensions existed in a totally different head space for the public than welfare payments or even UI—the grinding down of social benefits proceeded apace. Once burned, Wilson turned to cuts by stealth rather than frontal assaults. He also sought to target his limited resources on the most needy, ending the universal nature of such programs as family allowance.

Wilson was mostly motivated by fiscal imperatives, but there was more to it than that. The best social policy analysts—and increasingly the public at large—understood the system wasn't merely broke; it was broken, too. The safety net had been designed for an era of low and temporary unemployment. But with each successive wave of bad economic times— the stagflation of the seventies, the deep recession of the early eighties, the brutal restructuring of the early nineties—unemployment would reach new highs and then fail to recede to its previous lows when the economy recovered. Both the economic and social pistons were misfiring—the economy lacked the strength to sustain the social safety net and the net itself entangled potentially productive people.

Globalization threw up a very different set of challenges. There was nowhere to hide any more—the income redistribution programs of old simply weren't suited to the times. Canadians implicitly understood that the recession that had swept them off their feet had differed in substance from earlier such occurrences. In the early 1990s, they told pollsters they weren't experiencing an ordinary recession, but that something more fundamental was afoot. Technology had landed in their midst in its uneven way, creating high-paying jobs for those lucky few engaged with silicon chips but destroying job security for the larger crew working with wood chips. Intensified international competition could eliminate whole plants and employment categories with the certainty and swiftness of a tidal wave. The Economic Council of Canada had illuminated this polarizing trend well in an influential study called Good Jobs, Bad Jobs. As the Senate committee on social affairs would conclude at decade's end, coping with the new global economy called for active adjustment policies—job training, continuous education, literacy and numeracy upgrades—not the passive support programs of old. Income distribution by itself, Judith Maxwell argued, "provides palliative care but offers no remedies."

A new consensus was taking shape—that the social safety net had become an outmoded hammock, even a straitjacket. Redistribution policies were seen as not only unaffordable but as ineffective. The previous year, 3.7 million people had cycled through the unemployment insurance plan at one point or another. In total, joblessness touched the lives of 6 million family members. Another 3 million Canadians collected social assistance, twice as many as a dozen years earlier. Welfare rolls went up in bad times and failed to come back down in good times. Nearly 1.5 million children lived in low-income circumstances, an increase of 500,000 from 1989, many of them the children of working Canadians in unstable and low-paying work.

Between 1975 and 1992, federal and provincial spending on social programs, excluding health and education, rose from $12 billion to $75 billion, an increase of more than 50 per cent even after discounting inflation. Many programs spawned perverse results. In rural Atlantic Canada, the system encouraged young people to quit high school and work a couple of months a year. In some provinces, welfare mothers discovered they would be worse off in work than on social assistance—the so-called welfare trap. Taking a job would amount to a betrayal of the best interests of their children. A report by the National Council on Welfare found that a single welfare mother in Ontario could fall behind $4,165 a year by leaving welfare for a minimum wage job. Her benefits would be gone and with them benefits for her children (kids went on welfare, too) as well as dental, pharmaceutical, and optical coverage for the family. Meanwhile, she would be burdened with added costs for clothing, transportation, and day care. Better to remain a ward of the state. Both social assistance and unemployment insurance had been designed as stop-gap measures, but both systems had become overwhelmed with long-term and repeat users. A Quebec study of welfare cases between 1975 and 1993 found that nearly half of recipients had been on assistance for more than five years, 29 per cent of them for ten years or more. And these long-term cases included many recipients who could be considered employable.

Moreover, the protections designed for a bygone era increasingly sowed division. Often the lines between work and welfare were blurred, as people moved on and off social assistance. But a large contingent of low-paid workers never partook of government assistance. In a constant struggle to make ends meet and ward off joblessness, they became increasingly resentful of their welfare neighbours. The times were dividing low-income Canadians into the working poor and welfare poor.

Darrell was sent across the country in this period to probe attitudes to unemployment insurance on behalf of the federal government. He encountered a young single mother in Vancouver typical of the era. She unleashed a tirade against the unfairness of working and being poor. She suggested that if she were on welfare, like her neighbour who also happened to be a young single mother, she would have her rent subsidized, free dental and optical care for her kids, and a state-supported drug plan. And best yet—she could stay home all day tending her children and watching television! Obviously, she didn't feel that state intervention accorded her fair treatment.

These were the same sentiments that would be so ruthlessly exploited by

Mike Harris and the Tories in the 1995 Ontario election. The provincial Liberals in 1990 had raised welfare rates by 16 per cent. After their election later that year, the NDP added on another 9 per cent hike. Naturally enough, welfare caseloads shot up in the recession—from 315,000 in 1990 to 533,000 in 1992. But even after the economy began coming back, welfare rolls continued growing—623,000 in 1993 and 669,000 in 1994. Premier Bob Rae joined the growing group who thought something had gone awry with the welfare state. In early 1993, he openly questioned the wisdom of "transferring money to people so they can sit at home," a brave statement from a New Democratic politician. He was being swayed by arguments for a more active agenda of supports rather than just income assistance, what some called workfare. But his left-of-centre government didn't do much about it. The Harris Conservatives were unencumbered by the political constraints preying on the NDP. They prepared to campaign on deep welfare cuts and mandatory workfare programs, which would win them support not just in the high tax-paying suburbs around Toronto, but also in the struggling and stewing working-class neighbourhoods.

In Ontario as elsewhere, the country's massive $75-billion poverty pacification campaign had become mired in the muck. Policy was stuck in a quagmire. Poverty was winning the war. Canadians sought new rules of engagement.

For a generation, the ultimate dream of social policy planners had been to achieve the nirvana of a guaranteed annual income—that is, a level of social support that would ensure a minimum standard of living to all Canadians, regardless of circumstances. Marc Lalonde, one of the most powerful ministers in the Trudeau era, pushed the idea hard in the 1970s before watching it founder on the shoals of the sagging economy. Throughout the 1980s, polls showed strong support for the concept. But by 1994, having passed through the worst moments of the Nervous Nineties, public support dropped precipitously to just 33 per cent. The GAI, the purest of income redistribution policies, would never mount a comeback.

Resistance to an entitlement mentality strayed far beyond the country's small band of neo-conservatives. In her 1995 study of Canadian values, Suzanne Peters watched in fascination as Canadians hotly debated the issue in group discussions across the country. A minority held fast to the traditional view that a guaranteed income scheme represented a right of all Canadians.

But a larger segment of the population felt it would be too expensive, that it would reduce the motivation to work, and that the "undeserving" would receive the benefits regardless of their actions. "The perceived lack of effort and dependency of recipients of income support triggered negativity and hostility in group discussions," she observed. She added that many Canadians were hearkening back to the 1940s view of social programs as remedial measures for the unfortunate few.

A new mindset was emerging from the hard times. Canadians were hurting and their sense of cohesiveness buckled under the pressure. But it never broke. Three-quarters of respondents told Ekos Research in 1993 that "more and more people are going to have to stop depending on our federal government and learn to fend for themselves." They felt that individuals must take more responsibility for their predicament and that social programs often exacerbated rather than solved problems. But they refused to turn away from the view that the government had a responsibility to ensure all Canadians enjoy access to at least the basic necessities of life (84 per cent in 1993). They were ripe for a new approach, but devoted to the old values.

In October 1993, Canadians sent the Conservative government packing and returned the Liberals to power. But, by and large, these weren't the same Liberals. They, too, understood something had to give. In mid-campaign, Sheila Copps, the party's deputy leader and a charter member of the self-described Trudeau Liberal wing, received a plain brown envelope containing a secret Conservative blueprint for the social safety net. The Tory human resources minister, Bernard Valcourt, had wanted the plan to form a major plank in the election platform. He had advocated a break with the "liberal entitlement" psychology he felt had so corroded work incentives in his native New Brunswick, favouring instead an approach emphasizing self-reliance and individual responsibility. But other factions in Kim Campbell's cabinet judged the subject too incendiary for an election campaign. The Tories wouldn't be seen as reformers, they argued, but as hackers and slashers. Valcourt's action plan was hidden away, but now it had fallen into enemy hands. Copps intended to release the secret plan and paint the Tories as mean-spirited. But the prime minister's top adviser, Eddie Goldenberg, nixed the idea. The Liberals were cruising to victory anyhow. Goldenberg was looking ahead. "We might be doing that ourselves," he told Copps. The new consensus had gained an influential new adherent.

The new human resources minister, Liberal Lloyd Axworthy, was primed for the challenge. A natural-born reformer, he sought to pick up where Valcourt had left off—and then some. Axworthy was one of the brightest politicians in the country and despite his Trudeau Liberal label, his penchant for new ideas and new approaches outweighed any obeisance to the status quo. He understood that new pressures had come to bear on the social welfare system—and that these demanded new responses. He wanted to jettison the old passive approaches and engage instead in active measures to help the country's workforce keep a step ahead on the globalization treadmill. The job of government was not to protect people from the labour market nor to employ them directly, Axworthy argued. It was to make them employable.

He accepted neither the view of the left that society owed a living to anyone other than the truly disadvantaged, nor the view of the right that government should retreat from social engineering and help the private sector create jobs by cutting taxes. He accepted instead the policy course of active measures to help the millions of Canadians falling through the cracks of the economy to become employable. The private sector wouldn't want them if they couldn't read, write, or count, he reasoned. Unfortunately, the new-style employability policies he favoured didn't come cheap. It costs less to give someone a fish than a fishing rod and training course in how to fish. And the treasury, as Axworthy was soon to discover, was too bare to afford these new-style human investments. The reformist minister nonetheless marched gamely into the line of fire with sweeping proposals for reform.

On the week Axworthy brought down his action plan in 1994, I interviewed a smattering of Nova Scotians doing their best to become employable in difficult circumstances. Among them were Garnald Hendsbee, his daughter Mary, and her boyfriend, Doug Murray. Hendsbee was forty-seven and had just come off thirteen months on UI. Like his father before him, he had quit school at the end of Grade 9 and gone to work in the fishing industry. But the work hadn't sustained him and he eventually drifted into carpentry—nothing steady, but always dribs and drabs of work punctuated by periods on UI. He'd just landed a job building a Subway sandwich shop in Port Hawkesbury and hoped another project would come his way after that. But he felt resigned to a life of itinerant work "There's no hope down here," he said. "Never was and I don't think there ever will be."

Mary was twenty-four at the time and had just exhausted her UI benefits after failing to get into a secretarial course. She'd finished Grade 12, but hadn't ever been able to land anything steady. Doug, seven years older, felt even greater frustration. A high school dropout, he'd eventually gone back to get his Grade 12. He'd also trained as a shipmaster and taken a forestry course. "I wanted to better myself and get ahead in life," he said. "You can't get anywhere without some education today." But he could never land a job with any kind of security. He looked back at the second half of his life with astonishment. "I was out in the workforce for sixteen years and I tried to get a steady job. I was always, always applying for jobs to various places and there was just nothing there."

Father, daughter, boyfriend—none could attach themselves in a normal way to the labour market. They had been done in by a confluence of circumstances—the long-term weakness of the Atlantic economy, the slow growth of the period, their educational choices. But they hadn't given up, at least not the younger couple. They constantly sought out opportunities to improve their prospects.

In fact, when I first encountered Mary and Doug, they were staying with friends in Burlington, Ontario, and trying to start over. I caught up with them and with Mary's dad in the winter of 2001. Garnald was still struggling on, a classic east coast survivor. He continued to bounce back and forth between short-term carpentry gigs and the dole. "It's something you don't want to be on, but you have no choice," he philosophized.

He'd managed over the years to set aside enough money to help put his youngest child, Todd, through university. The whole family was proud of Todd, who was finishing up his final year of an undergraduate business program at St. Francis-Xavier University in Antigonish. "I want him to have more than I ever had, I'm sure about that." Garnald noted that even the nearby pulp mill, which had once hired kids out of Grade 9, now required a university education for entry-level positions.

As for Doug and Mary, they were doing well, but still not well enough to feel fully satisfied. The poor economy of 1994 notwithstanding, they had found work in Burlington. She enjoyed her job as a chambermaid, but was taking a course to become a pharmacy assistant when her first child came along in 1996. Doug worked in a scrap yard. Mary decided to stay home with baby Jamie. Then in 1997, a steel plate fell on top of Doug at work. He went on compensation while his back healed. He tried going back, but he now lacked the requisite physical strength. They eventually made their way back to Nova Scotia. With the help of the safety net, Doug enrolled in a program to train as a stationary engineer working with boiler systems. He couldn't find a job in his field, but he found a decent job as maintenance chief at a local hotel. Their family had grown to three kids by the time I phoned, and they were content, but still not complete. Their opportunities had never been great and they would probably always live with a high degree of insecurity. They thought of their kids and grimaced at their own education levels. "Grade 12 doesn't mean anything," Mary said. "Not today. You need post-secondary education." They plan to push their kids to follow Todd's example, not their own. But they worry about rising costs. "I worry that by the time our kids are ready, only rich people will be sending their kids to college. I can just imagine the place, what it's going to be like then."

Axworthy's proposals were rooted in the sort of active measures Garnald and Mary and Doug have always sought out. But his package proved hugely controversial with poverty activists and assorted other vested interests, both because of their general aversion to change and the impossible arithmetic of reforming social policies in a period of government cutbacks. Critics had accused him from the beginning of dressing up a slash-and-burn exercise in reformist garb. Now with Finance Minister Paul Martin insisting on a major contribution from social policy to his February 1995 deficit-slashing budget, Axworthy's ability to pay for active measures—and his credibility—flew out the window.

Still, his philosophical approach resonated with a changed public. The COMPAS organization found that 91 per cent of respondents strongly or somewhat supported his view that social assistance recipients should take training courses or do community work. Three-quarters supported the further targeting of child benefits on needy families. Two-thirds supported a two-tier system of unemployment insurance—one that would force frequent users into programs intended to prepare them for more stable employment. Furthermore, Angus Reid found that 84 per cent of Canadians felt their social programs were in need of reform. Nor were they cowed by the rampant economic uncertainty. Three-quarters figured this period of high unemployment and deficits represented as good a time as any to act.

Remember Goldfarb's 1984 conclusions that "the principle of universality of social assistance programs is fairly well ingrained in the Canadian psyche." By the time of *The Globe and Mail*'s Family Matters series fifteen thought-provoking years later, only 32 per cent of Canadians still stood by that principle. His admonition that Canadians wouldn't tolerate social cuts as a price of deficit reduction also experienced a quick death in the Nervous Nineties.

Even as the economy continued to bump along in low gear, job-anxious Canadians told public opinion researchers for the federal Department of Finance the government should keep its powder dry. In the wake of the deep cuts to social transfers in the February 1995 budget, conventional wisdom decreed the Liberal government must be in trouble with the public. But expectations had changed. Only one-quarter of respondents actually judged the government to be doing a poor job of maintaining "a responsible level of social programs." When it came to the jobs issue specifically, they scoffed at the idea of government spending to create employment, as it had in the 1980s recession. They accepted a role for government not as a direct player, but as a catalyst, partner, and regulator. "What Canadians are looking for from government," the Earnscliffe Strategy researchers wrote Martin, "is not job spending but a jobs strategy." The new Canadian mindset had gelled.

In January 1996, Axworthy hired the Angus Reid Group to test reaction to a new set of unemployment insurance proposals. The new frame of mind came through loud and clear. Three-quarters of respondents said, "People need to take more responsibility for their own job security. It's not the government's responsibility." But the most popular aspect of the Axworthy package—at 85 per cent—was the fact that low-income families on UI would receive some extra assistance. Then again, 93 per cent said UI should encourage people to take work rather than collect benefits. Even if it didn't look obvious, the new consensus couldn't have been clearer: People should be helped to help themselves rather than looking to clumsy, big governments for salvation. But government should be more generous with the worst off.

The surest sign of changing attitudes occurred in late 1997 when one of the country's foremost child advocacy groups, Campaign 2000, embraced the idea of sound fiscal management as part of a pro-children strategy. The organization pragmatically plugged into the new mood of fiscal conservatism abroad in the land and its own newfound wariness of ever having to re-experience the agony of a fiscal correction. If "reckless fiscal practices" recur, the group said, social spending will certainly be vulnerable again. "The social policy community in Canada has a high stake in becoming public interest guardians of the fiscal stability of federal finances," it concluded.

As we've seen, confidence in a more optimistic economic future showed the first shoots of renewed growth in late 1997. Gradually at first but with growing force, Canadians turned their attention back to social priorities. First health and then education pushed their way to the top of the public policy agenda. Then issues like poverty and homelessness found a foothold.

After years on the defensive, social policy-makers began turning their attention to the deferred challenges of the Nervous Nineties: all those children living in low-income households and the vexing phenomenon of single welfare mothers. Their direction, however, would differ markedly from the road previously travelled. A new concept of social policy was emerging, one consistent with the values of the past but designed for the hard-headed and results-oriented mindset that had emerged from the lean years.

The first major articulation occurred in July 1998, just months after the country finally kicked its deficit habit. After years of fruitless squabbling over who should bear the brunt of cuts, federal, provincial, and territorial governments agreed to the most significant social policy initiative in a generation. They designed a program intended to achieve two interrelated goals: get more money into the hands of poor families with kids and end the financial incentives to stay on welfare. The national child benefit accomplished the latter goal by paying benefits to all low-income families, regardless of whether they were working or non-working poor. The net result was to leave welfare families in roughly the same shape as before and improve the lot of the working poor, therefore lowering the so-called welfare wall. The approach was perfectly in keeping with the new Canadian desire to continue to support those who can't support themselves—poor children—while creating incentives for their parents to work. As such, it appealed to politicians on both the left and the right.

Governments also began taking an interest in an experimental social program called the Self-Sufficiency Project, which sought creative solutions to the vexing problem of single welfare mothers getting back into the workforce. The SSP is part of a movement in social policy called "making work pay," the underlying principle being to create incentives to re-enter the workforce. In this case, the idea was to supplement the wages of welfare mothers for a transitional period so as to offset the loss of benefits such as child care. But from the word go, participants would have to demonstrate self-sufficiency. They would receive the supplement only if they found full-time jobs. And the benefit would disappear if they couldn't sustain at least thirty hours of work a week. The supplements lasted for up to three years and then the recipients were on their own. By then, it was hoped, they would have broken free of the dependency culture and worked their way far enough up the job ladder to remain off welfare when the supplements ended. The point is to help them become self-sufficient, not dependent.

Early returns have been encouraging, albeit not miraculous. About 35 per cent of welfare mothers in the program made it back into the workforce, double the ordinary number. And, in keeping with the fiscally conservative, value-for-money times the net cost to the government is $150 a month (the cost of supplements less welfare payments and taxes paid). What's more, the costs actually turned into a profit of $29 a month when the project drew upon a sub-sample of single parents who had been on welfare for just one year—and therefore were less disconnected from the labour market.

In 1995, I interviewed one of the mothers who had taken up the challenge, a woman named Charlene Ukrainetz, who lived in the lower mainland of British Columbia. At that stage, she was two years past her last welfare cheque and feeling pretty good about it. A high school dropout, Ukrainetz had gone through a rapid series of jobs once she enrolled in the program: working as a security guard, handling the cash register at a fast-food restaurant, cleaning cages at a dog kennel, and assisting an electrician. Finally, she landed a decent position with a customs broker in Abbotsford, where they taught her how to use computers and underwrote a correspondence course.

Ukrainetz wasn't completely sold on the program. She thought it would have been better if the government had sent her back to school to study criminology, preparing her for a job as a prison guard. And she worried about what would happen when her supplements ran out. But she also told me about her pride on reading her name on a pay stub and of the satisfaction she received by contributing taxes to help support someone else. She felt she now provided a better role model for her two children, Amanda and Brandon, then aged six and four. "I don't want to be a welfare bum. I want to be a working mother," she said. "The program gave me a kick in the butt and I got a job. If it wasn't for the program, I wouldn't have even looked."

Throughout our research on this book, Darrell and I were struck by what we came to call "the 30 per cent exception." In poll result after poll result, the dominant mindset we uncovered didn't seem to apply to a group that ranged anywhere from 20 per cent to 30 per cent of the population. Whether economic optimism or support for free trade or participation in the Internet or anxiety about holding onto one's job, two realities co-existed—the majoritarian one on which we concentrated our efforts and a minoritarian one that we duly noted and mulled over.

The most fascinating aspect of this 70:30 phenomenon is the attachment that the majority doing all right—the Canadians who had bounced back from their own bouts of doubt and anxiety—continued to feel toward the insecure minority. The story of the Nervous Nineties is two-fold: Canadians abandoned their previous opinion about what worked best for them and their country, but they didn't abandon each other.

Social cohesion, the degree to which a society sticks together, represents one of the most fertile areas of investigation in social policy circles. In his 1995 essay, "Bowling Alone," Harvard University professor Robert Putnam wrote about a concept he called "social capital," which existed alongside financial capital (investment) and human capital (skills). Social capital represents the connective tissue of a society—the bonds of common participation through voluntary activities, religious attendance, political participation, and family ties that create trust and caring among citizens. Putnam calls this civic engagement. British scholar Tom Schuller has commented that "social capital is both a consequence and a producer of social cohesion." In other words, societies that play together stay together. And those that stay together play together. Putnam's analysis of the United States suggests a serious erosion of civic engagement and therefore of social capital. "The most whimsical yet discomfiting bit of evidence of social disengagement I've discovered is this: more Americans are bowling today than ever before, but bowling in organized leagues has plummeted in the last decade or so."

We would argue that social cohesion, although severely tested in the

Nervous Nineties, has held fast in Canada. Canadians share with our southern neighbours a strong belief in self-reliance, one that has become more pronounced over the past ten years. But it exists alongside the added Tory gene
we've discussed in this book. Canadians boast one of the highest rates of vol-
unteerism in the world. We like to bowl alone—*and* in leagues. We love to
windsurf at the lake, but we're still up for a game of pickup shinny at the local
rink. Increasingly, Canadians believe in rewarding excellence, but they see no
gain in punishing defeat. We prefer a country in which the poor will be lifted up, not in such a way as to ensure an equality of outcome, but certainly
not left behind without the opportunity to change their circumstances.
Canadians are naturally attracted to the argument that a society in which
people care for one another is a society that will be more productive and
more secure.

In *The Great Disruption,* American social commentator Francis Fukuyama
wrote, "The tendency of contemporary liberal democracies to fall prey to
excessive individualism is perhaps their greatest long-term vulnerability."
We've already seen in recent history ample evidence as well of the dangers of
excessive collectivism in engendering economic inefficiency and therefore an
ultimately poorer and less stable society. The challenge lies in getting the balance right—in promoting efficiency while retaining a reasonable degree (certainly not an absolute one) of equity. No society ever strikes a perfect balance,
but the reading from Canada early in the new millennium is encouraging.
Our stock of social capital remains relatively high.

An argument could even be sustained that our experiences through the
Nervous Nineties brought Canadians closer together rather than driving us
apart. Daniel Yankelovich, the dean of polling in the United States, has put
forward the notion of a three-stage "affluence effect." In the first stage, when
people have recently become wealthy but still harbour memories of economic insecurity, they remain too concerned with day-to-day survival to
indulge in quests for personal growth and exercises in self-gratification. To us,
that speaks to 1950s and 1960s Canada—the era in which our parents, with
the shadow of the Depression and war forever hanging over them, demonstrated an astounding work ethic. In the second stage, as people increasingly
take prosperity for granted, self-indulgence rises and self-sacrifice erodes.
Think of the Me Decade of the seventies, so well captured in the title of

Christopher Lasch's jeremiad, *The Culture of Narcissism*. And the Go-Go Eighties, whose essence was best distilled by director Oliver Stone in the film *Wall Street*, particularly Gordon Gekko's pronouncement: "Greed is good." These were second-stage manifestations.

In the third stage, people encounter life's vicissitudes and realize they can't take affluence for granted. Their thoughts turn more to the long-term and to the broader society around them. Yankelovich argues that many Americans reached this third stage in the 1991–92 recession and that this may explain a decline in the United States in the 1990s—also noted by Fukuyama—in measures of social dysfunction.

In a Canadian context, the wonder of the Nervous Nineties lies not in the anxieties and tensions they spawned but in the staying power of our social cohesion. As the country finally emerged at decade's end from its long gloom, Canadians did not turn away from each other but back toward one another. In early 2001, Ekos Research probed Canadian attitudes toward the causes of poverty. It gave respondents a choice between "People have not had the opportunity to improve themselves through things like education or training" and "People are just born this way." The more generous—and socially engaged—interpretation found favour by a wide margin—82 per cent to 11 per cent. Canadians shunned the blame game and opted instead for the active approach of the employability agenda. For the 70 or 75 per cent of Canadians confident they can make it in the global economy of the future, the search for certainty extends well beyond their own households and neighbourhoods to those being left behind.

That is not to say that Canadians had not been affected by their roller-coaster ride through the seventies, eighties, and nineties. They may have returned to the social policy menu, but they're demanding different dishes. They look back on the programs of the post-war era both in admiration for their good-heartedness and in frustration over their soft-headedness. Huge reservoirs of government money were thrown at regional development, Aboriginal advancement, single mothers, seasonal workers—with no real cure for the underlying problems. Canadians have been through a lot over the last quarter-century and romantic calls for a just society no longer resonate in and of themselves. Canadians will want to know justice for whom. They will want to know at what cost. They will want to know how governments intend to turn rhetoric into effective and measurable actions. From now on, we'll want greater transparency of program performance and real accountability for results.

In the Nervous Nineties, economic efficiency trumped social equity for an anxious population. But Canadians never ceased believing in society. Social equity is back in the picture. The Tory touch lives on, with a hard head balancing our soft hearts.

In his 2001 book *State of Minds,* Canadian economic theorist Thomas Courchene, never a social policy softie, wrote, "In the post-war period, Canadians collectively toiled long and hard and creatively to marry key aspects of a continental-European social contract with an Anglo-American approach to the economic sphere. Arguably, it is the collective achievement in generating American-style economic outcomes alongside European-style social outcomes that perennially results in our earning top ranking in the United Nations' Human Development Index as the most livable nation on earth. Moreover, we distinguished ourselves from the Americans on the social policy front in precisely the same period that we progressively integrated with them on the economic and trade fronts."

Striving to succeed in a global economy while remaining true to our social selves will continue to mark one of the country's great challenges in the new millennium. We're off to a decent start.

CHAPTER 9

WHOSE BODY IS THIS?

The woman trapped in the wasting body expressed it best. Long before the advent of teenage Internet entrepreneurs and dot-com mania, the wizened forty-two-year-old appearing before a darkened parliamentary committee room on November 24, 1992, served as the harbinger of a new Canadian mindset for a new century.

True enough, she could hardly get her words out. Amyotrophic lateral sclerosis, commonly known as Lou Gehrig's disease, had sapped the strength from her voice box. True as well, she would not even survive to see the dawning of the age for which she serves as a tragic but exquisite symbol. She would be dead within six months.

But the spirit of Sue Rodriguez is really the spirit of this book. She appeared on videotape that day before a committee of parliamentarians to share the details of her personal anguish. Her purpose was to gain the right to terminate her life. She came to decry a paradox she saw in the law, even a perversity. It would be legal for her to kill herself right then and there. But if she waited to squeeze out the last moments of quality living with her eight-year-old son, then it would be too late. She would be too weak to even swallow the barbiturates to end her life. And a penalty of fourteen years in prison remained on the books for those who "aid, abet or counsel" suicide, even though the Criminal Code had been amended by the Trudeau government in 1971 to remove suicide itself as an offence.

"I want to ask you gentlemen," Ms. Rodriguez told the transfixed assemblage staring uncomfortably at two television screens, "if I cannot give consent to my own death, then whose body is this?

"Who owns my life?" Her challenge echoed off the stone walls of a Parliament overflowing with empathy but unable or unwilling to accommodate her needs. She had summoned the strength from some hidden reservoir to confront the nation's lawmakers on their turf. She had petitioned them to change the law that made doctor-assisted suicide a criminal offence. She had fought through the courts for control over her own destiny.

Her suffering was terrible. She was too ill to even make the journey to Ottawa, as planned, on that late autumn day. Her hands were misshapen. She could barely write her name in a scrawl. She was having trouble breathing and swallowing. She was about to begin instruction in how to communicate through blinking. She felt entitled to a dignified end, one of her chosen timing. She didn't want the indignity of being kept alive with feeding tubes and respirators. She didn't want her son to witness her inevitable downward spiral into a drooping, motionless, and helpless body.

"The deterioration which I am undergoing is acceptable to me, up to a point. Beyond that point, my life will have degenerated to a mere biological existence. I will become a helpless victim of my illness and have to suffer prolonged suffering, lasting many months or even years.

"This is not acceptable to me. But when I sought legal advice as to my options, I was told that it is legal for someone to commit suicide in Canada—but it is not legal for someone like myself, who lacks the motors skills to terminate my own life, to ask or receive any assistance in ending my life."

Sick as she was, she simply couldn't accept the notion that the state had the right to trump her wishes.

"Whose body is this?" she implored.

Her question still hangs in the air nearly a decade later. But the answer is apparent all around us. From the plaintive plea of a desperate but pioneering woman, we've arrived at a point as Canadians where choice and self-reliance trump deference and social control. Whose health is this? Whose education is this? Whose retirement income is this? Whose identity is this?

Who owns my life?

"Please listen to what I have to say," Ms. Rodriguez continued in her articulation of the new Canadian frame of mind. "A law which states or implies that Canadians are not masters of their own fate, but belong somehow to the State or some other hypothetical authority, simply won't be tolerated much longer."

She would argue a month later before the British Columbia Supreme Court, in a voice quavering from her further medical deterioration, that she wasn't ready to die yet, but that she also wasn't ready to die without dignity. "I want to be in charge of my life and my death. I feel it's a choice I should make for myself."

The Sue Rodriguez story lives on as an emblem of many of the qualities we've discussed in this book. She demanded choice and self-control so she could satisfy her search for certainty—in her case, the ultimate certainty. She wanted society to respect her for who she was and support the course she set out for herself. Others would have different viewpoints, come from different moral backgrounds. But a liberal society, she felt, must always give the benefit of the doubt to the individual to make the choices most suitable for themselves. It was the same debate in legalizing abortion and decriminalizing homosexuality. In asserting her rights, Sue Rodriguez merely stretched the limits of Canadian tolerance into uncharted territory.

One could imagine Pierre Trudeau and Sue Rodriguez engaging in an interesting discussion. Despite the collectivist bent of many of his policies, he never deviated from a core belief in individual rights. In *Toward a Just Society*, a 1990 reflection on the Trudeau era, he noted that he and his friends had chosen in 1950 to name their new political magazine *Cité libre*. The opening line of his essay in the collection of articles read: "I have long believed that freedom is the most important value of a just society, and the exercise of freedom its principal characteristic." He allowed, though, that by the time he entered politics in the mid-1960s, he had felt that freedom was sufficiently secure that the greater priority for a just society lay in the pursuit of equality of opportunity, no matter where one lived or whether one spoke French or English.

But the pursuit of freedom is never complete. There's always one more mountain to climb, one more river to cross. In Trudeau's generation, the struggle for freedom consisted of overcoming the forces of conservatism in Quebec personified by the autocratic premier, Maurice Duplessis, and a clergy that discouraged independent thought. Trudeau's remarks notwithstanding, the Quiet Revolution did not halt the push for an ever more tolerant society. Indeed, in one of his earliest acts in politics Trudeau himself ushered through highly controversial Criminal Code amendments permitting therapeutic abortion and decriminalizing private homosexual relations between consenting adults. "I believe," he stated, "that the Criminal Code amendments are good because they will try to install in our legal concept that there is a difference between sin and crime, and that it's not the business of the lawmaker or of the police to check sin. This is a problem for each person's conscience, or his priest, or his God, but not for the police."

Or, as he put it more succinctly on another occasion: "The state has no business in the bedrooms of the nation."

In the period after his death in the fall of 2000, Canadians exhaustively catalogued Trudeau's legacies—the good and the bad. In this book, we've been highly critical of his stewardship over the economy and more generous to other aspects of his leadership. But we feel his greatest legacy can be found in the ethos of tolerance he inspired—by personal example, legislative initiative, and, finally, by the adoption of the Charter of Rights and Freedoms for Canada. "In the grand tradition of the 1789 Declaration of the Rights of Man and the Citizen and the 1791 Bill of Rights of the United States of America, it implicitly established the primacy of the individual over the state and all government institutions, and in so doing, recognized that all sovereignty resides in the people," he wrote of the achievement several years later.

The Charter, enshrined in 1982, confirmed for Canadians that they possessed individual rights that could not be taken from them by the state. And if governments so attempted, citizens had recourse to take the state to court.

Rights in the post-Charter world were to be asserted, not conferred, and certainly not restricted, at least not unreasonably. It's hard to quantify the impact this has had on the Canadian mindset—other than to say that the charter mentality has most assuredly reinforced the decline in deference in Canadian society and the rise of individualism. From a docile nation of sufferers-in-silence, we've matured into an independent-minded, even assertive country, one in which the good of the group rides high, but the rights of the person come first and foremost.

"Whose body is this?" The new Canadian mindset would certainly conclude it is Sue Rodriguez's body. Even back in 1993, shortly after Ms. Rodriguez issued her plea, three-quarters of Canadians told the Angus Reid Group that "as a moral question" they supported a terminally ill person's right to die. And by 70 per cent to 24 per cent, they felt doctor-assisted suicide for terminally ill individuals should be legal in this country. Five years later, with the issue less in the public eye, another Angus Reid poll uncovered precisely the same level of support.

The advent of the Charter age and the rise in Canada of a culture of tolerance represent developments of historic proportions. Racism and sexism, once a casual part of the Canadian frame of mind, have been pushed to the margins. Homophobia is under similar assault. But that is not to say that tolerance is absolute, nor to deny that it ebbs and flows with the times and circumstances. As we shall see in this chapter, the tolerant society, while very real, should not be misconstrued as anything other than a relative phenomenon. It is conditional on all sorts of influences having to do with economic and cultural security and, perhaps most importantly, with an equally powerful current in Canadian society, the principle of equality. Even when it comes to tolerance, Canadians have their limits—perfectly in keeping with the spirit of the Charter of Rights itself, which enables governments to place reasonable limits on rights "as can be demonstrably justified in a free and democratic society."

Let's probe deeper into mercy killing. About the time of the death of Sue Rodriguez, a Saskatchewan farmer named Robert Latimer took the life of his severely disabled twelve-year-old daughter, Tracy. The young girl was unable to walk, talk, or feed herself. In her short life, she had suffered through operations on her legs, hips, and back and was waiting for another operation for a dislocated hip, which was causing her pain. Neither her father nor mother could bear the thought of subjecting her to further surgery. They felt they had no reasonable alternative but to end her suffering. On October 24, 1993, Latimer put his daughter in the cab of his pickup truck and piped in the exhaust fumes. She died of carbon monoxide poisoning. Euthanasia advocates explained Latimer's action as a mercy killing. His detractors branded him a murderer.

The response of the greater Canadian public provides a vivid illustration of the limits of tolerance and the conditions attached to it. Unlike with Sue Rodriguez, the public does not view the Latimer case in easy black and white terms. In a 1999 survey, respondents felt by a three-to-one margin that Latimer had acted out of compassion for his daughter and therefore should be subject to a more lenient sentence. The other quarter felt he had murdered an innocent child unable to protect herself and therefore should be subject to the full weight of the law. The desire for leniency for Latimer was most pronounced among older Canadians and the university educated, but extended to all segments of society. But these lenient leanings did not mean that Canadians felt Latimer should go unpunished.

Sue Rodriguez gave her consent; Tracy Latimer was in no such position. Support for mercy killing in the latter case, therefore, fell from seven in ten Canadians to four in ten. But roughly the same proportion—two out of ten—held to the position that mercy killing of any type amounted to murder. The missing 40 per cent felt that mercy killing should remain illegal, but that those responsible, like Robert Latimer, should be treated with leniency and compassion. In other words, he should be punished, but not excessively. They didn't seem to feel that the Criminal Code, with its mandatory ten-year minimum sentence for murder, adequately covered all the awful circumstances life can throw one's way. Their liberal mindset toward Sue Rodriguez suddenly fills with qualifiers when it comes to Robert Latimer.

Over the past twenty-five years, tolerance has become one of the most cherished values of Canadians—as much a part of our self-identity as the Maple Leaf itself. Some observers have looked at our cultural diversity and social harmony and concluded we must be the most tolerant society on the earth. Eighty-eight per cent of Canadians certainly think so. And when the Angus Reid Group asked respondents in 1996 to volunteer a single adjective to describe Canadians as a whole, tolerant came first. It even beat out polite by a wide margin.

Canadian unity minister Stephane Dion holds up Canada's cultural diversity as a beacon for the other countries of the world. In his pre-political life as an academic, Dion travelled and studied in Europe and never ceased to be amazed by the relative tolerance of his home country. We're even tolerant of our separatists, a realization that turned one-time sovereigntist lawyer Guy Bertrand into a crusader for federalism. A nation prepared to debate its potential demise so openly and civilly is a nation worth preserving, he reasoned.

If we think we're tolerant, we should consider the generation currently growing up. Darrell recalls the day his daughter, Emily, came home from school all delighted that she had made a new friend. His wife, Nina, asked Emily to tell her about her new playmate. She told her mother that the girl was really nice, also liked Pokémon, and had the same length hair as her own. Only the next day when Nina took Emily to school and was introduced to the new friend did she discover the girl was black.

Emily, apparently, is colour blind. Nor, I can assure you as the father of three, is she alone in her generation.

Darrell and I both consider ourselves Trudeau's children when it comes to this great legacy of the emergence in the northern half of North America of one of the most tolerant societies in the history of the world. My mother used to marvel at how liberal my friends and I were on matters like homosexuality, religion, and race. In my parents' generation, it would have been almost unthinkable to marry outside the faith. When my wife and I married, a rabbi and a minister co-officiated at the wedding.

But Darrell and I are also products of rather uniform communities compared to today's rich cultural stew. I grew up in an area of Montreal that we used to describe as having the highest concentration of Jews this side of Tel Aviv. I can count on one hand the number of gentiles in my grade at elementary school—Andy and George and David. The latter also happened to be black. Darrell spent his early school years on an Air Force base in Greenwood, Nova Scotia. He also recalls only one black family living there.

In our generation, we would never think of excluding anyone, let alone fearing or hating them, because of their race or religion. Our self-image was resolutely liberal, but we were not colour blind. We resembled Archie Bunker's liberal son-in-law Mike "Meathead" Stivic, who needed to show the black neighbour that he felt his pain. In our generation, we wouldn't hesitate to describe someone by an obvious characteristic like their skin colour.

Emily fits the profile of the most tolerant Canadians—younger, urban, and better educated. Their attitude can be best summed up by the old proverb: "Live and let live." They are post-liberal, exhibiting an almost libertarian point of view on everything from cultural diversity to gay marriage. For them, visible minorities have become invisible. Check out a university campus near you. Young and educated Canadians represent the leading edge of the tolerant society. Slowly but surely, as we become a more educated society, they are sweeping sexism and racism from our midst. And their mood is infectious. When pollster Allan Gregg asked Canadians at the turn of the millennium to assess whether Canada was better or worse today than twenty-five years ago in fourteen different areas, the two we felt best about were our treatment of gays and lesbians and our treatment of visible minorities. He also put forth twenty-five propositions on which to assess the values of Canadians: The one that elicited the most virulent disagreement was a ban on homosexuals teaching in schools.

Canada was not always as tolerant as today, and therefore tolerance should not be taken for granted. Prime Minister Jean Chrétien once told me how he has it easier than his political hero, Wilfrid Laurier, because Laurier had to contend with the divisions between both French and English and Protestants and Catholics whereas Chrétien felt he only had to manage French-English relations. Most Canadians of his generation can tell you about their experience of exclusion based on religion.

It's far too easy to forget that not too many years ago in Canada even the two great strands of Christianity represented a major social dividing line. Nor should we think such minute differences—what Freud called the narcissism of the small difference—are necessarily relegated to the history books. In the mid-1990s, the small Ontario community of Pembroke was racked by old-fashioned divisions over which of its two hospitals would survive health cutbacks—the Catholic one or the Protestant one. We have not yet fully escaped the shadow of the Canada described in such convincing detail in John Porter's classic sociological study, *The Vertical Mosaic*.

There is nothing absolute or immutable about our current levels of tolerance. They are a product of their times, subject to the winds of change and often conditionally given. But measures of tolerance do seem to be moving in a single direction.

Tracking public attitudes on gay issues over time provides a good insight into the way in which social mores are evolving in Canada. Gallup Canada reported in February 2000 that for the first time in the seven years it had been asking the question, less than half of Canadians opposed same-sex marriages. Few would have even contemplated such a question when Trudeau decriminalized homosexual behaviour. While the Gallup numbers showed support at 43 per cent still below opposition at 48 per cent, the truly interesting finding was the movement over time. Subsequent polls have found up to two-thirds support gay marriage. Seven years earlier, when Gallup had first posed the question, only 24 per cent of Canadians expressed support versus 61 per cent against. And the trend line is strongly in favour of further liberalization. Among eighteen- to twenty-nine-year olds, same-sex marriages found favour with 67 per cent versus just 29 per cent opposition. The numbers more than reversed for senior citizens—14 per cent pro and 79 per cent con.

A battery of further questions on gay rights reveal the same general pattern, as well as the limits of tolerance. Some issues are no-brainers for Canadians. Ninety-two per cent believe homosexuals should enjoy equal rights in job opportunities and 61 per cent say gay couples should have access to the same benefits as heterosexual couples. But only 38 per cent think gays should be allowed to adopt children, with 55 per cent opposed. (A June 2001 Leger marketing poll found majority support for gay adoption, indicating another milestone.) Once again, even that figure is headed in a liberal direction. As recently as 1988, gay adoption garnered only 25 per cent agreement. Today, a strong majority of respondents under thirty-nine are perfectly comfortable with homosexuals adopting children.

It is interesting also to look at support levels for gays working in various occupations:

- Salesperson: 93 per cent vs. 72 per cent in 1988

- Member of Parliament: 86 per cent vs. 62 per cent in 1988

- Armed Forces: 82 per cent vs. 60 per cent in 1988

- Doctor: 82 per cent vs. 52 per cent in 1988

- Prison officer: 75 per cent vs. 44 per cent in 1988

- Junior school teacher: 67 per cent vs. 45 per cent in 1988

- Clergy: 63 per cent vs. 44 per cent in 1988

As you can see, the acceptance of gays as full participants in society grew between 20 and 30 percentage points in a little over a decade. And acceptance has become almost commonplace among the post-liberal generation of younger Canadians. But acceptance remains far from complete.

The same pattern of rising tolerance within proscribed limits occurs over and over. The vaunted generosity of Canadians is a relative concept. We are arguably more tolerant than most agglomerations of people in the world, but, unlike our Charter of Rights or young Emily's viewpoint, we are not colour blind. And our tolerance tends to express itself more strongly in good times than bad times.

Attitudes toward immigration provide a vivid illustration. As we've seen in the previous chapter, Canadians consider our multicultural make-up one of our proudest and most defining features by a factor of about five to one. But support for the famous Canadian mosaic is neither universal nor irreversible.

The good news is that even in the worst moments of the Nervous Nineties, Canadians never lapsed into intolerance. A major Angus Reid study in April 1993 noted that "events and conditions in recent years have served to strain the climate of tolerance." But the spirit of a modern, cosmopolitan Canada held fast for the vast majority of Canadians. At times, the knees looked set to buckle, but they never gave way. Even in that 1993 study, 77 per cent of respondents cited multiculturalism as one of the best things about the country and seven out of ten rejected the suggestion that Canadian society is threatened by non-whites. When it came to the notion that Canada was changing too fast because of minorities, the public again turned thumbs down by a two-to-one margin, as they did to the idea that immigrants take away jobs.

Still, there is no doubting that for one reason or another Canadians became concerned in the early 1990s about immigration levels—a consistent finding by all pollsters. The low point for generosity was reached in early 1994, when a study for the federal immigration department by Ekos Research generated headlines across the country with its finding that 53 per cent of respondents thought Canada had too many immigrants. That marked the first time in anyone's memory that a majority had expressed such a sentiment. The figure had been 44 per cent two years earlier and 31 per cent at the end of 1989.

The depth of economic pessimism at that point can't be forgotten. The economy continued to scrape across the bottom in the aftermath of the recession. The so-called jobless recovery was upon us and Canadians felt less generous than they had in better economic times. But Ekos president Frank Graves also felt attention had to be paid to rising cultural insecurity—an inchoate sense that our Canadian way of life was disappearing. The public was just beginning to come to terms with globalization. Canadian identity had yet to prove its resilience or adaptability. Immigration levels had been relatively high for some years, with the trend toward non-European immigration just making itself apparent in the major cities. Absorption in some cases was proving difficult, and more so as governments introduced austerity measures to cope with their deficits. In light of the new economic circumstances, Canadians were placing greater stock than ever in education. But they fretted about whether an influx of English-as-a-second-language students into neighbourhood schools would retard the progress of their own children. And what if these programs were curtailed?

These theories are lent some credence by the fact that the anti-immigrant attitudes were strongest—at 67 per cent—in Toronto, the place in the country where economic insecurity probably reached its highest level and where immigration had its greatest impact. Nowhere was the pressure greater than in Canada's largest city.

What to make of all this movement? The curious part is that the Canadian numbers began to correct themselves well before the restoration of economic confidence in the late 1990s, albeit past the worst moments for the economic downturn. As with support for free trade, the shift has to be explained by more than just economic determinism. Perhaps the real, on-the-ground experience of Canadians, particularly those hyper-anxious Toronto residents, calmed their nerves. All sorts of studies of French-English relations in Canada and other crossings of solitudes show that nothing promotes understanding quite like actual experience. Canadians apparently discovered that though visibly different, the new immigrants were essentially the same.

Their communities did not degenerate into race riots; their workplaces did not break up into Towers of Babel. Rather, their kids started playing with the Chinese kid down the block.

Certainly, our positive perceptions of multiculturalism remained high even as support for immigration fell. Indeed, in the same Ekos survey that uncovered the 53 per cent figure, three-quarters of respondents felt that a mix of cultures made Canada a more attractive place. They were driven more by anxiety than hate—a sense of too much change occurring too quickly. By late 2000, the percentage of Canadians thinking immigration levels were too high had fallen to 30 per cent. To put that into perspective, 45 per cent of Americans in 2000 felt their country was taking too many immigrants, even though the United States proportionately accepts half the numbers of Canada.

The only question on which a strong majority of Canadians have displayed a consistent streak that can be considered illiberal concerns whether they should adjust to take account of the different customs and languages of newcomers or whether the newcomers should be the ones making the adjustments. The assimilationist viewpoint was favoured by 57 per cent to 34 per cent in 1993. By decade's end, Canadians were more evenly split at 50 per cent to 46 per cent, but assimiliationism still remained dominant.

We pride ourselves in Canada on our idealized "mosaic" in contrast to the "melting pot" to the south. In large measure, the Canadian mosaic is a myth. Canadians are comfortable enough with racial and ethnic differences, but they seem to prefer that the customs and languages of new Canadians be confined to the private realm. When it comes to public interactions—in the workplace, schools, city councils, and the like—the public prefers that Canadians operate from a common and familiar platform.

The road to tolerance is full of potholes. Remember the imbroglios in the early 1990s over Sikhs wearing turbans in the RCMP and within the hallowed halls of the Royal Canadian Legion. By and large, these represented rearguard actions by older and cranky Canadians disturbed by the rapid pace of change around them. But they touched a deeper nerve as well. The Nervous Nineties were fraying the goodwill of Canadians. The economy was bad; globalization sowed uncertainty; governments had become consumed by the politics of national unity blackmail; and the look of the country was in transition due to the changed composition of our immigration intake. This was also a period in which certain Ontario communities, fed up with Quebec's domination of the national agenda, passed English-only bylaws. And successive Canadian governments quaked in the face of judicial pressures to add protection of homosexuals to the Canadian Human Rights Act.

Tolerance was tested. But it prevailed. The turban issue came and went. As did anti-bilingual sentiments. And the vast majority of Canadians, despite government timidity, stood up for their gay compatriots. A 1994 survey for the federal Justice Department showed that more than 80 per cent of Canadians believed homosexuals experienced discrimination at work. Three-quarters of respondents said they would not feel uncomfortable working with gays and more than half said they would "speak out in support of the gay or lesbian employee" facing discrimination. Still, the Liberal government in Ottawa hesitated before finally, in May 1996, permitting a free vote in the House of Commons amending the Canadian Human Rights Act to prohibit discrimination against homosexuals. The measure passed by 178 to 53, another milestone on the way to the tolerant society. It is worth noting that the political damage from the vote fell largely upon those opposed to the legal protection of homosexuals.

As we say, the road to tolerance is full of potholes. But the experience of the 1990s, in which the cause of tolerance slowed but did not truly go into reverse in the most pessimistic period and then accelerated in better times, suggests we are travelling on a one-way street.

Remember that 1993 Angus Reid survey on multiculturalism. After probing attitudes on a range of questions, the pollsters divided the country into four segments.

- The highly tolerant made up the largest group at four out of ten Canadians. They were highly liberal on all the questions and were the only group in which a majority actually felt that settled Canadians should be the ones to accept the customs and languages of minorities rather than vice versa.

- The second group, at three out of ten Canadians, made up the moderately tolerant. They also tended to be quite liberal, with 83 per cent disagreeing that the fabric of Canadian society was threatened by the influx of non-whites. But they worried a bit about the pace of change and split with the highly tolerant on the melting pot question.

- Next came the moderately intolerant at 20 per cent, perhaps the most interesting group of all because we don't know if they are truly intolerant or just insecure. They exhibited a consistent cautious streak in assessing the impacts of immigration and multiculturalism. But still a strong majority of them felt that multiculturalism represents one of Canada's finest qualities.

- Finally, one in ten Canadians was classified as highly intolerant. Between 80 and 90 per cent of them felt that immigrants were taking jobs away from Canadians and that the fabric of Canada was being threatened by non-whites. They were the only group to speak out against the ideal of multicultural Canada. Unsurprisingly, this highly intolerant group tended to be older and poorly educated. The highly intolerant also tended to live in rural areas or smaller communities, places where they were less likely to have any actual interaction with new Canadians.

Generally, our analysis suggests that these groupings remain valid, although the drift of opinion is blowing in the direction of ever greater tolerance. In May 2000, just 35 per cent of Canadians viewed new immigrants as a drain on the economy and only 26 per cent agreed with the proposition that they take jobs away from Canadians, numbers slightly lower than seven years earlier. And, as we've seen, support for immigration had been restored. As for gay rights, the agenda of a decade ago has been secured and the battle now has moved onto new terrain.

In more recent years, observers of the Canadian scene have encountered difficulties with the nuances and conditionalities attached to tolerance. These are not black and white issues. The Canadian mindset was widely misinterpreted when several waves of illegal arrivals of Chinese migrants arrived in British Columbia in the summer of 1999. Frustration over the arrivals led in many quarters to charges of rising intolerance. The facts didn't support that analysis. A series of Angus Reid Group surveys taken between 1987, when groups of Tamils attempted to land in Canada on the east coast, and the 1999 refugee "crisis," tell a consistent tale. While Canadians in both cases evinced little sympathy for the boatloads of illegal migrants, they remained increasingly receptive to refugees in general. A humanitarian impulse, despite the hand-wringing of some refugee advocates, lives on.

The lesson of the Chinese migrants was not that Canadians are anti-immigrant or even anti-refugee, but that they are anti-disorder. The public was offended by what it perceived as queue jumping as well as by the calculated and illegal nature of the smuggling operations. The arrivals did not conform to the most common definition of refugees. Rather than appealing to our generosity in light of political persecution or war, they tried to slip into our midst under cover of darkness. That's why more than half of Canadians said at the time that gaining refugee status was too easy.

Canadians still believe strongly in the historical record of immigrants who come to the country and make good. They are proud of our refugee tradition. But they also believe in due process. While more than half felt refugee status in Canada was too easily obtained, they didn't want the doors barred. Given a choice between doing more or less than other countries when it came to refugees, Canadians preferred the more generous course by a three-to-one margin.

As evidence, take the case of the Kosovo refugees who came to Canada in the spring of 1999. Their airlift out of harm's way in the former Yugoslavia was described as a temporary refuge. The vast majority of Canadians not only supported this approach, but felt we had a moral obligation to accept refugees. They also bought into the argument that the Kosovars wanted to return to their homes once the fighting stopped, which made their support for refugee status easier since it would be temporary. But "if it turned out they could never return to their homes in Kosovo, would you support or oppose allowing them to stay in Canada permanently?" Eighty-one per cent supported their staying here.

As for the costs and the fact the same money could be spent on homeless people or other Canadians living in poverty who are getting no help, respondents were unshakeable: The Kosovars deserved our assistance. We should not become distracted by the genuine but unrelated concerns of "our own poor." The naysayers are wrong. The same spirit that moved Canadians to take in Hungarians in 1956, Czechs in 1968, Ismailis evicted by Idi Amin at the start of the 1970s, and Vietnamese boat people in 1979 lives on. The Chinese refugee issue reflects not our intolerance but our sense of order.

To the extent that Canadians exhibit intolerant traits, these need to be separated into two different streams—first there are the shrinking ranks of the truly intolerant and then there are the situationally intolerant. The first group is genuinely racist and stuck in its ways. In focus groups, the truly intolerant will complain about Chinese people spitting in the street or the smell of Indian cabbies or other such examples. But they are almost invariably tamed by the unwillingness among the tolerant members of the group to allow such conversations to persist. The truly racist segment of the Canadian population tends to become troublesome only when they find one another.

It is the situationally intolerant, a far larger and more impressionable group, that interests us here. Proper distinctions are generally not made between these groups. The latter one is not consumed by hate; its motivation often has more to do with its overriding belief in equality of treatment and opportunity for all. In fact, this group perhaps can best be described as equality worshippers. Its adherents cannot abide anything that smacks of special status for any social group, including such icons of the seventies and eighties as affirmative action and employment equity. Equality worshippers, whether we're talking about the working poor or the unilingual, have too often seen themselves losing out to such social engineering.

In the course of the 2000 federal election campaign, I spent a morning canvassing with Ontario Liberal candidate Paddy Torsney in a working-class section of her Burlington riding. On one doorstep, I met a woman who fell into the latter category of intolerance. She worked in an office and just happened to be home for lunch. After the candidate moved on to the next house, I asked her how she viewed the campaign so far. She quickly dashed off on a tangent about immigrants—how the country had too many of them, how they exploited the system—coming over and going on welfare. Then she veered off in a different direction, relating how her sister had recently explained to her that immigration was necessary because the country wouldn't otherwise have enough young workers to cover the pension costs of baby boomers like herself when they hit retirement age. She suddenly slowed, adding it all together in her head. "So I guess we need immigrants," she shrugged, and then paused. "But I still don't really get it because they're all on welfare anyhow, right?"

Strip it all away, and the woman's essential complaint boiled down to her perception that immigrants somehow were receiving preferential treatment. She spoke to me also about high taxes and how the middle class "always gets it in the neck." She obviously cared about value for money and felt her hard-working family hadn't been getting a great bargain in recent years. She wasn't really racist in the sense of being filled with hate. Rather, she bridled against what she considered, rightly or wrongly, to be the offence of special status for one group over others.

Her sentiments were the same ones that helped propel Ontario premier Mike Harris to power in 1995—a strong sense among the insecure and struggling middle class that some people were getting an easier ride than others. It expressed itself very strongly both in its opposition to employment equity policies that placed gender or colour over competence and in resentments the working poor felt toward the able-bodied welfare recipients. Jaime Watt, a public opinion researcher working for the Harris Tories, vividly recalls how favourably workfare proposals tested with working-class Ontarians. They felt that they were having to wake up early in the morning, get the kids ready, and then take three buses to work—why were other people getting to stay home, sleep in, and collect welfare cheques that, when all the benefits were calculated in, often exceeded minimum wage. It offended their sense of equality. They didn't want special status conferred on anyone. He found the same sentiment among mothers of young boys who had always dreamed of becoming firefighters, only to discover a quota system now favoured some young girl down the street. These mothers wanted their kids competing on an equal footing, without state favouritism.

These same sentiments are expressed in working poor and lower middle-class households across the country. Remember Mary Hendsbee and Doug Murray from Nova Scotia—the couple who had moved, coincidentally, to Burlington in the mid-1990s in search of opportunity, only to return home to Nova Scotia after Doug hurt his back. Doug had enrolled in a vocational course to become a stationary engineer. According to a story Mary told me, he was at the head of his class. But one day an employer came through looking for a woman, of which there happened to be one in the entire class. She got the job. Two years later, Mary still bristled at the very idea that her guy failed to secure a job she felt he deserved on merit because of some gender quota somewhere. It violated her sense of equality.

Darrell can recount similar tales from focus groups across the country. He was once moderating a focus group in Newfoundland when the participants got into a dust-up over the emergence of a new privileged group in their midst—Romanian refugees. The way the locals saw it, these Romanians would land in Gander, declare refugee status, and then get put up in motels by the government, along with three square meals a day. They viewed these refugee claimants as living in the lap of luxury, receiving more largesse than any of the focus group participants could ever expect.

The bottom line on this equality principle is that its worshippers can imagine being tolerant and generous toward individuals in need, but not toward groups. You can see this equality principle at play when Canadians are asked about groups that are disadvantaged in the education system or where the emphasis should be placed in fighting poverty. They are not at all reluctant to say that low-income earners don't receive a fair shot in the educational system, but they are quite reluctant to so describe an identifiable group like blacks or Aboriginals. The same pattern applies when asked their preferred focus for combatting poverty. The number one target would be adults with dependent children followed by children under five and youth between eighteen and twenty-four. Their least favoured targets for help would be visible minorities, Aboriginal peoples, and recent immigrants and refugees. That's simply not the way they want to categorize problems.

Nowhere does the conflict between the tolerant society and equality worship become more nettlesome than in Aboriginal policy. The issue has blown up in recent years in the Atlantic and Pacific fisheries, where Aboriginals believe they enjoy historic rights to the resource and white fishermen complain they are getting the short end of the rod. Both sides, firm in their competing principles, have demonstrated a disturbing intractability.

Aboriginal inequities have been around for so long that Canadians largely don't think of them any longer within a tolerance frame. Certainly, the challenges have not changed. Rated by incomes, health, life expectancy, suicide rates, educational attainment, incarceration rates, and just about any other measure of economic and social standing, Aboriginals remain well behind the Canadian norm despite decades of effort at narrowing or eliminating these gaps.

Despite the seemingly intractable nature of Aboriginal problems and the billions expended in efforts to resolve them, Canadians still retain a strong desire to encourage economic and social equality for native Canadian populations. And they don't blame natives for their difficulties. Only 29 per cent of Canadians agreed in a 1998 Angus Reid survey with the suggestion that "most of the problems of Aboriginal people are brought on by themselves." Fifty-two per cent disagreed. And 58 per cent felt that settling land claims is important to righting past injustices.

But any hope of a consensus on an approach to this area breaks down when the tolerance instinct runs into the equality principle.

Research suggests that Canadians can be divided into a smaller group open to special status for Indians and a larger one hostile to the idea. The first group, which accepts that special status is necessary in order to preserve Aboriginal culture and heritage, tends to be a bit younger, a bit better educated and more concentrated in Ontario. The larger segment is united in a general distaste for special status, but divided on overall attitudes toward Aboriginals. Some are clearly hostile to Aboriginal aspirations for self-government, while others are hopeful of pragmatic solutions so long as their sacrosanct equality principle is not violated in the process.

The strength of the equality principle can be discerned by the following responses from the 1998 study. They show that Canadians are quite open to full Aboriginal participation in society and even special status when it comes to preserving their unique character. Respondents are willing to bend the equality principle but not to break it.

- Aboriginal people are capable of earning their own way if given a chance: Agree, 84 per cent vs. Disagree, 9 per cent.

- Canada's Aboriginal people are too dependent on government: Agree, 61 per cent vs. Disagree, 22 per cent.

- Canada's Aboriginal people would be better off if they just joined mainstream Canadian society: Agree, 49 per cent vs. Disagree, 31 per cent.

- Aboriginal people should have the rights and status they need to protect their culture and heritage, even if it means they may have certain rights that other Canadians do not have: Agree, 52 per cent vs. Disagree, 34 per cent.

- It isn't fair to displace people and businesses who currently depend on the land just to make up for wrongs committed against aboriginal peoples many years ago: Agree, 57 per cent vs. Disagree, 25 per cent.

- It's time for Aboriginal peoples to benefit from land claims through jobs and economic development even if it means some non-Aboriginal people might be worse off: Agree, 43 per cent vs. Disagree, 31 per cent.

- When treaties are signed, Aboriginal people should have the same rights as any other Canadians, no more and no less: Agree, 84 per cent vs. Disagree, 9 per cent.

As you can see, Canadians want Aboriginals to become full participants in society while possessing the tools to preserve their heritage. They have confidence in the ability of native Canadians to make it in society, but don't hold them responsible for failures up to now. Respondents still believe that past wrongs should be righted. But they grow hesitant when that process may impinge upon the established rights of others. And, at the end of the day, Canadians want us all to come out on an equal footing.

Incredibly, when it comes to attitudes toward Aboriginals, we end up where we began on tolerance—with Pierre Trudeau. Here's the best summary we can offer on the state of Canadian thinking on the issue:

"The government believes that its policies must lead to the full, free and non-discriminatory participation of the Indian people in Canadian society. Such a goal requires a break with the past.

"For many Indian people, one road does exist, the only road that has existed since Confederation and before, the road of different status, a road which has led to a blind alley of deprivation and frustration. This road, because it is a separate road, cannot lead to full participation, to equality in practice as well as in theory. In the pages which follow, the Government has outlined a number of measures and a policy which it is convinced will offer another road for Indians, a road that would lead gradually away from different status to full social, economic and political participation in Canadian life."

The quote is taken from the foreword of the Trudeau government's 1969 White Paper on Indian Policy, which was abandoned under heavy criticism from native groups that it amounted to assimilation. Perhaps Trudeau, like Sue Rodriguez, was simply ahead of his time. A generation on, the insistence of Aboriginals that they enjoy special rights because of their unique character continues to clash with the equality priniciple so deeply ingrained in a society whose tolerance knows *some* bounds.

CHAPTER 10

THE NEW CAN-GLOBAL IDENTITY

Nobody who visited Parliament Hill over the magnificent autumn weekend in October 2000 could fail to be impressed by the rich tapestry of Canadians in attendance. Tens of thousands of people lined up before dawn and shuffled along into the wee hours of the morning to view the casket of Pierre Elliott Trudeau. They formed a kaleidoscope of faces, a wonderful reflection of the diversity of twenty-first-century Canada. A similar scene played itself out in front of the Trudeau home on the slope of Mount Royal and in countless legislatures and town halls across the land as old Canada and new Canada, both, came out to pay their respects.

The mood on the Hill was subdued but not solemn, the autumn air suffused with only the warmest memories. Trudeau proved to be better loved in death than in office, but there was no denying his drawing power. One of his press secretaries, Patrick Gossage, had entitled his memoir *Close to the Charisma*. Even Trudeau's most ardent critics lauded him as a worthy foe and indisputably the most captivating personality of his generation.

The hushed procession inched forward over many hours, with nary a complaint from the mourners. The woman standing in line in front of our family and me had arrived here in the 1970s to escape political repression in Chile. As for so many new Canadians who made the pilgrimage to Parliament Hill, for this woman, Trudeau personified the decency and humanity of Canadians in embracing her during the most vulnerable period in her life. The stories that poured forth on the Hill and across the country in the days after his death demonstrated the uniqueness of the Canadian experience. We are a land whose human diversity marks a stunning historical achievement. Parliament Hill provided a fitting stage to show off Trudeau's greatest legacy: the multicultural society that had evolved so peacefully in this difficult country of ours.

In Montreal, a forty-seven-year-old woman named Marcella Thompson told Canadian Press of her appreciation of Trudeau opening the immigration doors that allowed her to come to Canada in 1975 from Jamaica by way of Britain. She shared a birthday—October 16—with Trudeau and had named her son Eliot in honour of him (although losing the second "t"). "Because of him we really say we've been given a new lease on life, a new opportunity." Another first-generation Canadian, fifty-nine-year-old Zeyad Haidar, recalled the day in 1982 when he received a copy of the Charter of Rights and Freedoms. He had been in this country eight years since emigrating from Iraq. He worshipped Trudeau for the charter, for opening up immigration, and for promoting multiculturalism. "When I received the charter in the mail I felt very proud," he recounted. "It spelled out for the first time the rights of all Canadians." These were his rights, too, he realized. "I felt like a somebody, frankly."

On Parliament Hill, journalist Roy MacGregor spoke to a man named Jimmy Chang, who had driven with his wife, Audrey, through the early morning fog from Toronto to pay his respects to a man he called "the father of modern Canada." He and Audrey stood and wept openly as they read the notes of tribute attached to red roses at the Centennial flame. Jimmy had arrived in Canada in 1968, the year of Trudeau's election as prime minister. "It all comes from him," he commented, wiping away the tears. Then there was Samson Young, a captain in the Canadian army, who poured out his heart over an entire page in the tribute books laid out beyond Trudeau's flag-draped mahogany coffin. "Although you do not know me, you have given me, who was once a refugee, a chance to live in this magnificent country, which I now call home. You have restored my once lost dignity of being a man without a country and have instilled in me a great sense of pride to be a Canadian, for which I will be forever grateful."

Canadians have never had an easy time with their identity. The country was founded by two competing European peoples—one of whom conquered the other—on a land mass already populated by Aboriginal peoples. From there, we've added another two centuries of complexity—capping it all off with the challenges wrought by the globalization of our economy and population. It is a natural wonder of the world, as impressive in its own way as Niagara Falls, that the 32 million people residing north of the 49th parallel continue to believe in this concept called Canada. But believe in it they do—as the rainbow society gathered on Parliament Hill attested.

Two great challenges have long buffeted our national unity and Canadian identity—one outward looking and the other inward looking. The first was situated along an American-Canadian axis; we defined ourselves in relation to our differences from the United States, the colossus that threatened to overwhelm us. The second revolved around a domestic French-English axis, the fact of two founding nations co-existing in the bosom of a single state. On the former, we occupied ourselves in overstating our differences. On the latter, we bent over backwards to overstate our similarities. Efforts to forge a coherent national identity in a united Canada resembled a two-dimensional game of chess: It required unrelenting concentration and martial discipline, but the process was manageable. Our identity toolkit served us well for decades: from institutions like the CBC and the NHL, which basically remained frozen in time from its formation in 1917 until expansion in 1967, to symbols such as the red-coated Mounties and our own belated flag.

But today the identity game is multi-dimensional. The rise of a global

economy has raised the challenge posed by residency next to the most dominant cultural and military power in the history of mankind to a new order
of magnitude. And the intricacy of maintaining unity in a country of two
dominant languages and cultures sometimes looks like child's play next to the
intricacies of managing with a plethora of languages and cultures.

When Pierre Elliott Trudeau became prime minister in 1968, the Canada
of the day was regularly described as a white and Christian country populated by two founding peoples of European origin. By the time he died, Canada
had developed an acute case of multi-polar personality disorder—except that
it's all so orderly. As Alberta Premier Ralph Klein once said, we are "severely
normal." Toronto, our largest metropolis, resembles a modern Tower of Babel,
with the important difference that it functions smoothly. The intake in one
year alone in the 1990s included individuals who among them spoke 122
separate tongues. People of vastly different origins—coming, as they do, from
169 different countries—work and live together harmoniously. Former premier David Peterson once quoted Peter Ustinov in describing Toronto as
New York City run by the Swiss. In cosmopolitan New York, however, immigrants make up just 28 per cent of the population. In Toronto, they account
for half the population. Toronto provides the true role model for the global
cities of the future.

Same story in Vancouver. Canadians used to talk of Winnipeg as the place
where east meets west. That was true of old domestic Canada. But in global
Canada, Vancouver sits at the crossroads between the Orient and the
Occident. A third of its population originated outside the country, with a
heavy Asian flavour. Canada's first cabinet ministers of Chinese and Indian
origin came from Vancouver. Same with the country's first Indo-Canadian
premier, Ujjal Dosanjh. When he was premier, Mike Harcourt liked to
remark that he travelled more frequently to Hong Kong than to Ottawa.

Even in Trudeau's home city, Montreal, the French-English conclave
(with a convenient east-west dividing line at Boulevard St. Laurent) of his
formative years is giving way to a multi-racial polyglot. Walk along St.
Catherine Street or Rue St. Denis on a Saturday night and watch the faces
from around the globe. And listen to their conversations in French. They are
different and yet the same.

In a typically insightful article in the January 2001 issue of *Canadian*

Geographic, journalist Gwynne Dyer turned his analytical brain to the phenomenon of Canadian immigration. The captivating cover reflected the mood of the piece well. "Welcome!" it read. "How Canada became the world's most spectacularly diverse country."

In keeping with the sentiments expressed on Parliament Hill, Dyer chose to lionize Trudeau as the inscrutable mastermind behind this transformation of Canada. He certainly warrants credit for propelling a white-bread country in that direction, but the elimination of race-based criteria in Canadian immigration policy actually occurred in 1962 under Conservative prime minister John Diefenbaker, who also spearheaded our first Bill of Rights. I happened to attend his funeral, as well, while I was a student at Carleton University in 1979. I recall a more contained but similar outpouring of emotion outside the church from a clutch of women gathered beside the church steps. They told me they were of central and eastern European origin and that Diefenbaker, half-German himself, had instilled in them the confidence they were just as Canadian as anyone else in the British-dominated culture of their day.

Slowly but surely, multiculturalism is eclipsing the French-English fact as the defining domestic aspect of our national identity and unity. A couple of years back, Pollara asked survey respondents a simple question: What does Canadian culture mean to you? The answers are instructive. They cited multiculturalism and diversity first. Bilingualism and the French-English fact came well down the list in fifth spot. In the winter of 2000, the federal government commissioned a study into the factors that contribute most to the sense of belonging Canadians have in their country. Nearly twice as many people selected the diversity of our society as the presence of two official languages.

In great swaths of the country, the vaunted French-English fact takes a back seat today to our multicultural reality. The first time I ever met former British Columbia premier Glen Clark, on an outdoor terrace at the Jasper Park Lodge during a premiers' conference, he boasted to me in his insouciant way about his ignorance of Quebec. He proudly told me how he had only been to the province twice—once to change planes at Mirabel airport and once to attend a one-day finance ministers meeting in Quebec City. I asked him if he thought that perhaps he was missing something. He replied that he felt he reflected his constituents in east Vancouver well. "When people think of bilingualism in Vancouver or British Columbia," he said, "they are thinking

Chinese-English, not French-English. Parents are wondering if they should teach their kids Chinese, not French."

Clark was too cocky by half, a tendency that contributed to his downfall. Over time, he came to rethink his indifference to the French fact in Canadian life, as will happen to any leader exposed long enough to the national stage. But that didn't render his initial analysis wrong. Although French immersion education stands out as one of the Trudeau era's great triumphs, official bilingualism looks from a place like British Columbia or Alberta like one of those policies dreamed up 30,000 miles away.

In fact, in early 2001, school boards in both Edmonton and Calgary announced plans to launch publicly funded Spanish bilingualism programs. Edmonton, which led the way by already offering such alternatives to French as Arabic, German, Ukrainian, and Mandarin, had 2,250 children enrolled in these other languages last year versus just 1,895 in French immersion. "We promote French to the extent we can, but we don't think Canada is just limited to that," Emery Dosdall, then superintendent of the Edmonton board, told *The Globe and Mail.* "Canada is a multicultural country."

Alberta views itself as an international geological and petroleum hub with the need to communicate with far-flung resource economies. British Columbia's destiny is tied increasingly to the American states to its south and to its position as a Pacific gateway. Asia, and particularly China, matters far more than Quebec. The streets of Vancouver are filled with Cantonese speakers, not French speakers. Our multicultural character increasingly shapes our identity. The French-English debate, while still crucial, has been relegated to secondary status for increasing numbers of Canadians.

Ideologically speaking, this represents a huge break with the old national consensus. Remember Catherine Annau's film *Just Watch Me.* It depicted a generation of Trudeauphiles, who travelled across the country in zealous, and often libidinous, pursuit of their hero's ideal of a bilingual, bicultural Canada. We were a nation of two solitudes and these Trudeau children felt inspired to reach out to the other side.

The most poignant scenes of the film tell the story of a Quebecois nationalist named Sylvain, who falls for one of these idealists, a young woman from British Columbia named Maggie, who has come to Quebec to learn the French language. Sylvain first lays eyes on Maggie in a bar where he works. He sees her across the room and immediately concludes from her perfect teeth that she must be English. They overcome their language barrier, move in together, and ultimately have two children. The quintessential Canadian story. But the 1995 referendum almost destroys their relationship. "We talked about it for weeks on end," recalls a tearful Sylvain. "Instead of discussing the referendum itself, I'd say, 'If we win, are you staying?' And she'd reply, 'If we lose, are you coming with me?'"

The Yes side, as we know, loses by a hair. Our quarrelling lovers cancel out each other's vote. On referendum night—*le pire de ma vie,* he tells us—he goes to a bar to watch the results on television. As the inconclusive tally becomes apparent, he shouts at the television set, "Never again!" This must be the last time. At the end of the film we see Sylvain and Maggie back together with their children on a beach. They have moved across the country to Victoria, where both are teaching French. Nothing is straightforward in Canada except, it seems, that the heart usually prevails.

Multicultural Canada is composed of many solitudes. French and English remain the most prominent, but they compete, especially in our major cities, with an array of upstarts. We are also Italian, Jewish, Somali, Chinese, Ismaili, Greek, and Vietnamese. Another of the characters chronicled in *Just Watch Me* is John Duffy, a semi-reformed Trudeauphile who has remained an active Liberal nonetheless. The referendum changes him, too. "I've started to think that the real achievement of this country may be more the way that people from all over the world can live together," he concludes. "That may be more important than the way two groups of white western Europeans may or may not be able to get along together."

The unity politics of the Trudeau age were dominated by the French-English fact. In post-Trudeau Canada, the solitudes are far more numerous but the divisions not nearly as profound. The romantics of today travel not merely to the Saguenay, but to the four corners of the earth, where they teach English as a second language and taste-test different cultures. Today's Maggie and Sylvain may well be Maggie and Hu, a Canadian romantic and Vietnamese nationalist. In what circumstances will they raise their children?

Back home, multicultural politics have grown well beyond the allocation of folk dancing grants and heritage language programs. Today, the national health minister finds himself grappling with the regulation of Chinese herbal remedies and the revenue minister puzzles over the taxation of the foreign assets of new Canadians.

From the first settlements in Port Royal and Quebec, Canada has been a nation of newcomers. In the twentieth century, the country experienced three major immigration waves, each of them challenging our collective identity in one way or another. The first wave occurred in the years before the First World War. The Liberal government of the day adopted policies aimed at settling the vast expanses of the Prairie region. Between 1900 and 1914, according to a sweeping Statistics Canada review, nearly 3 million people entered Canada. The high-water mark came in 1913, when 400,000 newcomers arrived in this country, a figure unsurpassed in the ensuing nine decades. The 1911 census showed that immigrants accounted for 22 per cent of the population of the country. Many of these people were the fathers and mothers of the women I encountered at John Diefenbaker's funeral.

The myth of the men in the sheepskin coats is a compelling chapter of Canadian lore, but the more typical immigrant profile of the day was an indigent English boy. Still, the first immigration wave broadened the ethnic base of Canada considerably, beginning the long erosion of the country's dominant British character. The late nineteenth century and early twentieth century saw increasing numbers of European nationals from outside Britain: Doukhobors and Jewish refugees from Czarist Russia; Hungarians; and Ukrainians. Chinese labourers were brought in under strict guidelines to work on railroad expansion.

The period was replete with impassioned public debate about the impact of this diversity on a young country. The government of the day introduced the notorious Chinese head tax, designed to ensure that Chinese coolies could not afford to bring brides or wives to Canada. In 1903, the authorities raised the tax to an insurmountable $500. Odious as it was, it worked as a measure of public policy. The 1911 census recorded 2,790 Chinese males in Canada for every 100 Chinese females. For immigrants overall, the ratio was 158:100.

Ours was not the record of a welcoming country. In 1906, Canada adopted its first Immigration Act. It prohibited paupers and criminals as well as persons defined as "feeble-minded," having "loathsome or contagious diseases," "likely to become public charges," or simply "of undesirable morality." A couple of years later, amendments were introduced to outlaw the landing of anyone who did not come directly to Canada from their country of origin. Sounds innocent enough. But the measure represented a cynical ploy to exclude the entry of people from India, who had no choice but to book passage on ships through a third country because no direct routes existed to Vancouver. In 1919, regulations were promulgated to deny entry to wartime aliens and to explicitly bar Doukhobors, Mennonites, and Hutterites. The 1923 Chinese Immigration Act erected further obstacles in the way of Asians. Canadian immigration authorities continued to apply their energies to exclusion rather than inclusion in the 1930s and 1940s—barring specified occupational groups and adopting new regulations at the outbreak of the war that took no notice of the difference between enemy nationals and genuine refugees. Jews fleeing Europe were thus turned away. And Japanese-Canadians living within 100 miles of the British Columbia coastline were forced to relocate inland, often to detention camps.

Despite this panoply of illiberal measures, the first wave of immigration succeeded in laying the early foundations of multicultural Canada. Roy Romanow, who resigned in 2001 as the long-serving premier of Saskatchewan, is the son of Ukrainian immigrants, the first member of his ethnic group to rise to such high office. Gary Filmon, the ex-Premier of Manitoba, is also descended from East European stock, as was Don Mazankowski, Canada's deputy prime minister during the Mulroney years.

Conservative leader Joe Clark tells a moving story about the success of this first immigration wave. In 1985, while Canada's foreign affairs minister, he visited the Soviet Union and raised the case of a Ukrainian prisoner of conscience named Danylo Shumuk, who had relatives in British Columbia. Eventually, Shumuk was released and came to Canada to live with his relatives. Before heading out West, he stopped in Ottawa and visited Clark. Parliament was on its Easter break, but Clark wanted to show him the Commons chamber.

"I took him into the House of Commons, which was not sitting and had him sit in the Speaker's Chair of our free Parliament. As we walked out of the Chamber, I pointed out the seats of the Leader of the Opposition, some ministers, and the Prime Minister. He said to me, through a translator, "I know where the prime minister sits. He sits next to Mr. Mazankowski."

I asked how in the world he knew that. He replied, "During all my years in the Soviet prison, my Canadian relatives wrote telling me about what could become, in Canada, of people with names like Mazankowksi, and Hnatyshyn, and Paproski."

As early as 1911, immigrants constituted 41 per cent of the population of Manitoba, 50 per cent of Saskatchewan, and 57 per cent of Alberta and British Columbia. In contrast, they made up just 20 per cent of Ontario's population and less than 10 per cent each of the Atlantic provinces and Quebec. Today, Toronto is Canada's most diverse city. But cultural diversity was invented in western Canada.

The two world wars and the Great Depression put a severe crimp on immigration flows. The 1930s actually produced a net outflow from Canada. The second great wave of immigration exploded out of the starting gate almost as soon as the last guns were silenced in 1945. The government struck a more generous posture, passing orders-in-council to admit people who had been displaced from their homelands and for whom return was deemed impossible. The flow of immigrants surged over the next decade, peaking at 282,000 in 1957, many of them the skilled workers required by a modern industrial economy. The United Kingdom still accounted for the largest number of immigrants, but other European countries, such as Italy, Poland, Germany, and the Netherlands, made an increasing contribution. Canada's refugee tradition was well in place before Pierre Trudeau came to power. In 1956, the country admitted 37,000 Hungarians in the wake of the Soviet invasion.

Canada's immigration policies became far more generous in this post-war period, but remained rooted in the premise of this being a white country. The 1952 Immigration Act confirmed a policy of restricted admission, particularly relating to national origin. The ranks of the admissible were to come from the United States, the United Kingdom, Australia, New Zealand, the Union of South Africa, and selected European countries. It was this national origins criterion that the Diefenbaker government removed in 1962. By the time of the 1971 census, Statistics Canada tells us, less than one-third of Canada's foreign-born population had been born in Britain. Half came from elsewhere in Europe, with Italy leading the way. We had grown beyond our British base, but remained very much a European country.

Sometimes it is difficult to fathom the recentness in our history of multi-cultural Canada. In January of 2001, Toronto MP Charles Caccia, in his capac-ity as the longest-serving member of Parliament outside the cabinet, presided over the election of the Speaker of the House of Commons. In the course of watching the proceedings, I learned that Caccia, born in Milan and having emigrated to Canada at twenty-five, was the country's first MP of Italian descent. And he didn't enter the House until 1968. The longest-serving mem-ber of Parliament is Herb Gray, first elected in 1962. In 1969, he became Canada's first Jewish cabinet minister. Canadians of Asian descent didn't begin breaking into the upper ranks of politics until the 1990s.

But perhaps the best illustration of how far we've come in such a short period of time originates in the world of music. In 1969, the National Arts Centre named Mario Bernardi as the first music director of the NAC orchestra. A member of Parliament rose in the House of Commons to ask the govern-ment why the federal institution had chosen a foreigner rather than a Canadian as conductor—the assumption being that the Ontario-born Bernardi must have been Italian. We don't make those stupid mistakes any more.

The third wave of immigration really took off under the new colour-blind system of immigration determination adopted in 1967 by the Pearson government, with Trudeau as its justice minister. (It wasn't, mind you, discrimination-free; homosexuality was not officially removed as a prohibit-ed category until 1978.) Over the next three decades, these liberalized immigration rules opened the country to the multicultural inflow that has revolutionized the look and feel of Canada. From the 1970s onward, the proportion of Canadians born outside the country took off. They came from all over the map.

At the time of the census in 1996, immigrants represented 17 per cent of Canada's population, the highest proportion in half a century. More tellingly, the influx of new Canadians accounted for more than half the country's pop-ulation growth from the previous census. The 1996 population snapshot pro-vides a head-spinning portrait of a country in transition. The top five places of birth for immigrants arriving in the first half of the decade were Hong Kong, China, India, the Philippines, and Sri Lanka—all non-white countries. Vietnam sent more people to Canada than did our neighbour, the United States. In the 1950s, 80 to 90 per cent of immigrants came from Europe. By

ंं

1994, that figure had fallen to 17 per cent. English and French, while still the dominant languages of the country, are actually both in decline. Sometime before 2006, we are set to pass a demographic and psychological line in which 51 per cent of Canadians will report at least one parent is of neither French nor British origin. Then the two founding nations theory will truly be stripped of its supremacy.

In 1971, Trudeau passed the country's first Multiculturalism Act, which set out to help different cultural groups retain and foster their identity, overcome barriers, become greater participants in society, and promote a sense of equality among all groups existing in Canada. In introducing the act, Trudeau stated that "Canadian identity will not be undermined by multiculturalism. Indeed, we believe that cultural pluralism is the very essence of Canadian identity." A quarter-century later, you didn't need an act of Parliament to make the point. The country was multicultural, plain and simple.

Today, there are three dimensions to the perpetual unity-identity challenge of the Canadian state. Each is in transition.

THE FIRST DIMENSION: THE QUEBEC WEDGE

Five years ago, Canada looked to be on the brink of breaking into at least two, and perhaps more, pieces—the vision of Macdonald and Cartier on the precipice of betrayal. Quebeckers had come within 30,000 votes of opting to depart Canada on October 30, 1995. The results had been in their favour most of the night, only swinging back to the No side late in the counting. But the momentum clearly lay with the separatists. They had mustered only 40 per cent of the vote in the first referendum in 1980. Now they had reached 49.4 per cent, within a whisker of fulfilling their national dream. It was only a matter of time, and probably not long at that.

The deep pessimism of that period sometimes seems today like a million years back. But they were just a short half-dozen years ago. At the end of 1995, one in three Canadians—and one in two Quebeckers—told veteran pollster Allan Gregg that Canada, as they knew it, would cease to exist by the end of the decade. Moreover, even in the cold light of the post-referendum period, Canadians outside Quebec held fast to their conviction that the country constituted a partnership of ten equal provinces, affording Quebec no special privileges.

Darrell's polling for Angus Reid also tapped into a dark cloud of despair enveloping the nation, only occasionally relieved by a ray of sunshine. It found that only one in twenty Canadians believed the country "is as strong today as it ever was" with regard to national unity. The rest were pretty evenly divided between those who thought the situation could still be salvaged and those who had concluded "the future of the country is threatened."

Outside Quebec, opinion was hardening, with 41 per cent owning up that they felt it would be better in the long run if Quebec separated—a far higher figure than even in the worst days of the Meech Lake debate. By a five-to-one margin, they described themselves as more hard line and less sympathetic to Quebec rather than more sympathetic and flexible. Canadian idealism had certainly not withered altogether. A strong majority within and outside Quebec disagreed completely with the statement that "it is not possible for francophones and anglophones to live together in the same country." But they couldn't seem to identify a way to reconcile themselves to each other and were running out of patience about even making further efforts. Eight out of ten Canadians outside Quebec felt that whatever they offered, Quebec would always want more.

The state of our political leadership also was in disarray. Prime Minister Chrétien, desperate to close the referendum wound quickly, seemed to lose his bearings in the days and weeks after the referendum. His adrenalin level had jumped off the chart as he frantically searched for solutions. Chrétien is a tough operator, but in the week before the referendum vote, he had broken down and cried in front of his entire caucus of Liberal MPs and senators. That, as much as anything, spoke to Canadians about the desperate times in which they lived.

Worse yet, Bloc Québécois leader Lucien Bouchard, who had waved his magic wand during two weeks of spell-binding campaigning for the Yes side, had decided to return home from Ottawa to be anointed the premier of his province and president-in-waiting of the Republic of Quebec. Conventional wisdom called for another referendum within eighteen months, the one in which St. Lucien would carry his sovereigntist brethren over the top.

In April 1996, as the dust from the referendum settled, 61 per cent of Quebeckers told Ekos Research that they thought their province would separate from Canada within ten years. In the rest of Canada, four out of ten felt that way.

What a difference six years makes. In January of 2001, a mournful Bouchard stepped down from the position of premier, admitting he had failed in his mission and that he could discern no foreseeable future for the sovereignty option. The federal government of Jean Chrétien had hardened its line in the aftermath of the referendum, going so far as to argue that Quebec could be subject to partition if it tried to separate. Ottawa sought a ruling of the Supreme Court of Canada on the legality of unilateral secession. The court set out a complex process for separation, one that required negotiations with the rest of Canada and, ultimately, a constitutional amendment. Then the Chrétien government adopted a law, the Clarity Act, which stated it would negotiate after a future Yes vote only if it agreed that the question and result had been clear.

Bouchard had waxed indignant at these developments, but was secretly pleased. He felt the humiliation of Ottawa dictating terms would incite Quebeckers to rally to the sovereigntist cause. But in the federal election in November 2000, the Chrétien Liberals won more votes in Quebec than the separatist Bloc Québécois for the first time. Shortly thereafter, Bouchard threw in the towel.

This reversal in fortunes, while impossible to credit as permanent, is nonetheless impressive. By January 2001, only 18 per cent of Quebeckers thought their province would separate from Canada within ten years. The figure was down to 14 per cent outside Quebec. With the ascension to the Parti Québécois leadership of Bernard Landry, a far more deeply committed *indépendantiste* than Bouchard, the proverbial trip to the dentist of referendum politics cannot be considered definitively over. But the sovereigntist option is not currently touching a nerve.

The return of economic optimism in Canada has been accompanied by a restoration of hope that the never-endum, which intervened in our lives so insistently and incessantly through the 1990s, might finally be petering out. In both cases, the tipping point was reached late in the decade, and only three or four years after public opinion hit its nadir. While it is pointless and foolhardy to forecast the death of something as emotion-laden as Quebec sovereignty, the new optimism appears to be built upon a reasonably solid foundation.

The caveat should be stated that Quebec public opinion, while in constant motion at the margins, has been surprisingly stable on the choice between Canadian federalism and Quebec independence. A third of the population (overwhelmingly francophone) can be characterized as strongly nationalistic and therefore more open to the separatist agenda; a third (significantly anglophone and allophone) is strongly federalist; and the final third constitute the ambivalent nationalists over whose hearts and minds all the political battles are fought. They are the inhabitants of middle Quebec to whom Yves Deschamps' great joke applies of the desire for an independent Quebec within a strong and united Canada.

These ambivalent Quebeckers can generally be swayed one way or another depending on how the issue is characterized. For instance, in 1980, Quebeckers possessed a high degree of respect for Canada's successes. That's why the convoluted referendum question—109 words long and never reaching a crescendo—actually referred to Canada almost as many times as Quebec. "The word Canada was all over the place because it was a magic word," Daniel Latouche, an adviser to Quebec premier René Lévesque, recounted years later. By the second referendum in 1995, Canada had lost its magic. Its debt was five times larger than a decade and a half earlier and its unemployment rate was three percentage points higher. Canada was seen no longer as a beacon of opportunity and saviour of lost souls, but as a sick and dysfunctional entity. In mid-campaign, for the first time ever, Quebeckers told pollsters they foresaw no economic cost in separation, blunting one of the federalist side's most potent arguments.

Two polling results tell the story. At the time of the 1980 referendum, 52 per cent of Quebeckers told pollsters they felt "profoundly attached to Canada," with just 21 per cent declaring otherwise. By the 1995 referendum, only 36 per cent of Quebeckers expressed the same level of attachment versus 37 per cent shaking their head no. The concept of Canada had lost traction in middle Quebec. The economic renaissance that has put the spring back into the step of Canadians arrived later in Quebec, which had fallen into even worse disrepair than the rest of the country. So its tipping point arrived later. In the fall of 1998, just 43 per cent of Quebeckers expressed optimism "for the future of the country." But by the spring of 2000 that figure was up to 56 per cent, suggesting the recovery of Canada's economic health has brought relief as well on the unity front.

Federalists also have demographic reasons for encouragement—and these relate to the multicultural phenomenon that is playing such a huge role in changing the face of Canada. Increasingly, the so-called ethnic vote is emerging as a critical factor in retarding growth for the sovereignty option. Jacques Parizeau knew of what he spoke when he famously blamed the October 30, 1995, loss on "money and the ethnic vote." And didn't Lucien Bouchard strive to reach out to "ethnics" to the point of citing the anti-Semitic rantings of retrograde elements within the Parti Québécois as one of his reasons for quitting as leader.

Like the rest of Canada—a little more slowly perhaps and a lot less assuredly—Quebec, too, is being transformed by the multicultural revolution. Immigrants make up about 10 per cent of the population of Quebec, less than many other provinces, but the fastest growing segment of the population nonetheless. This multicultural factor is intersecting with the rise of the Internet generation to make for a powerful new force in Quebec politics.

The youth of a generation ago had personal acquaintance with the era of the Anglo bosses, the leitmotif of old industrial, pre-*maîtres chez nous* Quebec. They'd suffered in silence as they bore witness to the humiliation of their parents.It was this psychic vein that Lucien Bouchard so brilliantly tapped into in the 1995 referendum campaign. His generation had a score to settle and succeeded marvellously in settling it. First they took over the professions and government. Then they infiltrated and overwhelmed industry and finance. And along the way, they put in place policies and built institutions to train a future generation of Québécois leaders, and ensure the supremacy of their embattled language within the borders of a future state.

Among the building blocks was Bill 101, the language law that mandated, among other things, a French-language education for all but the established minority. It succeeded brilliantly in its objective of absorbing immigrant children into the French language milieu, but, as so often occurs in social policy, with unintended consequences. Indeed, Bill 101 may well have undermined the larger dream of an independent state.

Today, the *pur laine* Quebecker intermingles easily at university or in the nightclubs with the immigrant newcomer. The wall of the mind—the psychology of separation—has fallen for these young people. The "ethnics" have broadened the world view of their *pur laine* friends, who already are linked by the Web and a globalized mindset to a world beyond La Belle Province, a world, incidentally, that operates almost exclusively in English.

Gwynne Dyer makes the point well in his *Canadian Geographic* article. "Never mind the political debates," he counsels. "Listen to the news programs and the commercials. It is the sort of thing that is almost impossible to measure, but the symbolic content of the word 'nous' (we) has changed significantly in Quebec's French-language media in the past five years. It used to mean 'nous,' the heirs of Cartier and Champlain, the victims of a cruel history, the beleaguered standard-bearers of values, traditions and a language forever on the brink of extinction. It was politically loaded, and the message was implicitly nationalist if not separatist.

"These days, in the common run of news reporting and ads, it has come to mean just *nous*, the sort of people who watch this channel or read this paper. They obviously speak French or they wouldn't be here, but it is an inclusive *nous* that doesn't leave out francophones of Italian or Lebanese or Haitian or Vietnamese descent.

" ... As the tone of the debate changes, even separatists are compelled to insist that theirs is a territorial nationalism, not an ethnically based one. It fails to convince most of the new francophones. They will defend the status of the French language in Canada as fiercely as any previous generation, for it is now their working language, too, but they cannot be persuaded to care about Louis Riel. It's just not their history."

How all this affects their commitment to an independent Quebec remains to be seen. But when it comes to identity, this younger generation is neither narrow nor inward-looking. The graduates of a CEGEP animation program in Montreal are no less likely to dream of a Hollywood gig at Disney or DreamWorks than similar graduates in Toronto. And they are significantly less political than previous generations, for whom politics served as a means of collective expression. Their worldliness and comfort with multiple identities, one can reasonably infer, probably works against the development of an exclusionary nationalism.

THE SECOND DIMENSION: THE MULTICULTURAL WEDGE

The triumph of multiculturalism in Canada lies in the wonder of its becoming more of a unifying symbol of Canadian identity than a force of divisiveness. We have given birth to a remarkable cosmopolitanism, a fact that can only work to Canada's advantage in the global economy of the future.

But multiculturalism, although firmly established, remains a very uneven development. Perhaps counterintuitively, concerns about the threat immigrants pose to Canadian identity are greatest where immigrants are the least numerous—like the phenomenon of anti-semitism without Jews. Our cities have adapted remarkably well to immigration. There are tensions, to be sure. Established families have expressed frustration at the impact of non-English-speaking students on the school system. Likewise, the importation of ethnic politics into Canada, witnessed in the Air-India bombing and again in the rival protests surrounding the various hostilities in the Balkans, try the patience of many Canadians.

These challenges could deepen in the coming years—it is hard to know. The government is moving toward a target of 300,000 immigrants a year, nearly 50 per cent higher than the levels of the 1990s and three times the relative rate of absorption of the United States. Canada has always promoted itself as an ethnic mosaic, but in reality the melting pot was kept at high boil, integrating new Canadians into a common set of values. Increasingly, immigrants are moving into established sub-communities and, through the wonders of modern communication and transportation, they are maintaining as much connection to their homelands as to Canada. One immigration observer has said we live side by side but not together. In that light, the task of integration—if that is the goal—could become all that much more difficult to achieve.

That is the pessimistic outlook. The positive scenario can be witnessed in our high schools, where interracial couples are more a norm than gang fights. Between the school system and modern communications, the walls between immigrant and native-born can be knocked down in half a generation these days. Moreover, the government is moving toward the immigration of more knowledge workers into the country. Given their level of educational attainment and probable language proficiency, this, too, could ease the task of integration.

Canadians remain positive about immigration but wary. In a 1999 poll for the Canadian edition of *Time* magazine, six out of ten said the country's cultural diversity enhances Canadian identity, twice as many as felt it is eroding our identity. Likewise, by the same two-to-one margin, Canadians consistently told Ekos Research over the past five years that immigrants coming from many countries strengthens rather than weakens our culture. That said, Canadians are reluctant to pick up the pace. Only 14 per cent told *Time* they would like to see more immigration in future versus 43 per cent who like the current levels and 41 per cent who would like us to scale down. And looking ahead, only one in eight Canadians is prepared to countenance a language other than English or French ascending to official language status. We want immigrants, we celebrate diversity, but we want them to adapt to Canadian realities, not vice versa.

All this aside, Canada's experience with immigration absorption represents a remarkably successful experiment in cultural harmony. Once again, Toronto provides the most instructive laboratory. In 1961, when most of Canada's baby boomers were growing up, non-whites represented just 3 per cent of Toronto's population. At the start of the 1990s, they accounted for 30 per cent. By the end of the 1990s, they were in the majority. Scottish-Presbyterian Toronto was no more. The whites now constituted the visible minority.

In fact, in 2001 the number of Toronto residents born outside of Canada was on track to exceed those born in Canada for the first time. Toronto stands out as perhaps the earth's first global city not merely in the sense of being connected to the world, but of actually containing the world. And with 70,000 new arrivals a year, 83 per cent of them non-European, the trend continues to build. The wonder is not the odd flash of racial tension, but the everyday ordinariness of this extraordinary situation.

The experience of metropolitan Canada, however, does not extend beyond the outer fringes of the suburbs or into less dynamic parts of the country. Out there, old, white Canada harbours resentments about how all this is changing who we are. Toronto's "immigration problem" looks far more daunting from far away than it does in Parkdale or Mississauga, where whites and non-whites have established a capacity to live among one another without much ado.

In 1991, Darrell undertook a massive research project into multiculturalism and Canadian identity for the federal government. The study involved nearly thirty cross-country focus groups and a major telephone survey. The Mulroney government commissioned the study in the wake of the failure of the Meech Lake accord. Canada was approaching its 125th birthday, and the powers that be in the federal government, worried about nation-building, felt a need to better understand Canadian attitudes to the changing face of the country.

Darrell visited every province of the country at least twice over an eighteen-month period and discovered a great deal about the diverse nature of this country, even when it came to views on diversity. In case he might have missed the point, an older woman participating in a focus group in St. John's, Newfoundland, was kind enough to drive it home. Darrell asked the group about their personal encounters with immigrants. Apart from the odd professor at Memorial University or the community Chinese restaurant owner, they were hard-pressed to come up with examples. But the helpful older woman chimed in that one of her neighbours was an immigrant. She volunteered that the neighbour had lived on the same block for about fifteen years, but that she still didn't really fit into the community. Darrell asked her where the woman was from. "Nova Scotia," came the reply.

Looking at the numbers, her narrowness is not surprising. Only 7 per cent of Canada's immigrants settle outside major metropolitan centres. St. John's is just one of dozens of mid-sized communities in Canada where the proportion of visible minority residents remains lower today than the Toronto of 1961. Interestingly, it is these people—with the least first-hand experience with immigration—who most fear its consequences for Canadian culture and identity.

Still, the overall picture is pretty attractive. In each of 1993, 1996, and 1998, about eight in ten Canadians agreed that the country's multicultural make-up is one of the best things about Canada. Our record on diversity and tolerance also stands as one of the main attributes young Canadians find most attractive about our country versus the magnetic republic to the south.

THE THIRD DIMENSION: THE AMERICAN WEDGE

The struggle over English-Canadian nationalism has been just as animating a part of our history as that of Quebec nationalism. Whereas Quebec national-ists have tended to define their distinctiveness vis-à-vis the rest of Canada, English-Canadian nationalists defined theirs in relation to the behemoth to the south of us. We were not as blindly patriotic as the Americans. We were not as militaristic or violent. We were not as prejudiced. We have universal health care; they've got guns. We were kinder and gentler long before it became a cliché. George W. Bush probably met his first compassionate conservative on a Texas Rangers road trip to Toronto.

If the United States didn't exist, we'd have to invent it. Otherwise, how could we explain ourselves. Without them, we'd be like Laurel without Hardy or, in the interests of Canadian content, Wayne without Shuster. We need a straight man.

It's instructive to read the actual words spoken in the now famous Molson beer ad featuring Joe Canadian. It's a truly subversive piece of work, representing on some levels as much a satire on the desperate need of English Canadians to define themselves by the misperceptions and slights of Americans as an assault on those American misperceptions. On another level, it lays out many of the significant policy differences that give Canadians comfort. You'll notice it doesn't say "I am Canadian. I prefer waiting lists before surgery and a lower standard of living." Read the words:

> I am Canadian
>
> I'm not a lumberjack or a fur trader
> I don't live in an igloo, or eat blubber or own a dog-sled
> I don't know Jimmy, Sally or Susie from Canada. Although I'm
>   certain they're really, really nice
> I have a prime minister, not a president
> I speak English and French, not American
> I pronounce it about, not a-boot
> I can proudly sew my country's flag on my backpack
> I believe in peacekeeping, not policing
> Diversity, not assimilation
> And, that the beaver is a truly proud and noble animal
> A toque is a hat
> A chesterfield is a couch
> And, it is pronounced zehd, not zee, zehd
> Canada is the second largest landmass, the first nation of
>   hockey, and the best part of North America
> My name is Joe, and I am Canadian

Living next door for so long to the American colossus has made Canadians the most practised people on earth in the art of coping with globalization.

We've recognized the daily chore of preserving a national identity ever since Hollywood began producing movies in bulk in the 1920s; then, in the 1950s, someone got the clever idea of putting rabbit ears on the top of television sets.

Yet globalization has added a further layer of complexity to the ongoing identity battle—both in the pervasiveness of the cultural bombardment and the constraints imposed on the standard remedial responses of old. Canadian nationalists argue strenuously that our identity is imperiled by the universal- ization of American culture and the weakening of national governments. By all rights, we should be in the midst of a profound identity crisis. But the steadfastness of our attachment to Canada perseveres through every imagina- ble assault on the old markers of Canadian identity. We've gone into the cor- ners with some of the toughest goons in the global league and come out still proudly Canadian. In its own less dramatic way, it reminds us of the resolve demonstrated in the 1940 Battle of Britain. Military strategists were con- vinced that the terror of concentrated aerial bombing would break civilian morale. But the civilians defied the logic of the German general staff and became, with each succeeding raid, more, not less, determined.

Among the most fascinating snapshots in the annals of Canadian public opinion are a pair of identical questions posed both in 1964 and again in 2001. Respondents were asked first if they favoured or opposed a union with the United States. In 1964, a period in which the Walter Gordon Liberals had begun beating the drum about American economic domination and long before the Nervous Nineties, 29 per cent favoured a union and 62 per cent opposed it. A generation and a half later—a span that included all the famil- iar American economic and cultural encroachments—support had fallen in half to 15 per cent and opposition had grown to 81 per cent. Moreover, those disputing the assertion that such a union was, in any case, inevitable had grown from 59 per cent to 68 per cent.

The Trudeau generation proposed a strong and interventionist central government—able to talk up Canada at home and erect barriers to unwant- ed influences from abroad—as the guarantor of our national identity. Thirty years on, unreconstructed Canadian nationalists, seeing the withering of the old interventionist state, argue strenuously that globalization imperils every- thing distinct about our country. In fact, it has produced a paradoxical result. Even as power has flowed away from the state and national institutions and into the hands of individuals (with a large assisting hand from Trudeau's Charter), the persistence of national belonging has held fast. Somehow, our sense of ourselves—and our will to be unique—has proven amazingly resilient in the face of the external pressures from economic globalization and American cultural domination and the internal pressures inherent in a country of ten provinces, two founding nations, and a multitude of cultures. Our emotional attachment to Canada draws on a vast reservoir, one that even the disappointments of the past twenty-five years failed to drain.

For most of our first century, Canadian identity was tied to economic and engineering achievements—from the building of the transcontinental railway to the St. Lawrence seaway. As recently as a quarter-century ago, Canadians still turned to economic measures as a main means of nationalistic expression. Trudeau gave us the Foreign Investment Review Act to screen out unwelcome foreign investors. Canadian ownership of the strategic oil industry was among the prime objectives of Petro-Canada and the National Energy Program. Tariff walls protected scores of inefficient industries, putting undeserved profits in the hands of corporate Canadian nationalists-by-convenience rather than conviction.

This is all changing—mostly. Canadians moderated their economic nationalist impulses over the course of the 1990s, the decade in which Wal-Mart made its move into Canada. But they didn't dispose of their nationalistic sentiments altogether. Today, our nationalism is less reflexive and more situational. It is largely a nationalism of inclusion, not exclusion.

Take the sale of the Montreal Canadiens to American entrepreneur George Gillett Jr. The mere thought of foreign ownership of a cultural icon like the Canadiens would have been imponderable a generation ago. Non-local ownership, even corporate ownership, formed a radical concept back then. But let's listen to cultural commentator Yvan Cournoyer, the former Montreal Canadiens captain who came out to see the changeover of ownership in January of this year. "It is always sad," he commented succinctly, "but the times they are changing."

The times had indeed changed. No longer was domestic ownership a proxy for the public interest. For fans, the question of Canadian ownership took a back seat to the prospect of Canadiens' winnership. Molson, the previous owner and the sponsor of the famous Joe Canadian ad, had done little over the previous ten years for the cause of firewagon hockey. Maybe George Gillett Jr. could do better. The foreign sale of the Habs reinforced the principle that the quality of the product now matters more to Canadians than the passport of the owner. All things being equal, domestic ownership is still preferred. But not at the price of inferior service. In this way, the Canadiens were little different from Eaton's.

That's not to say that Canadians are indifferent to domestic success. It is only to say that ownership is no longer the determining variable. Naturally, Canadians still worry about the hollowing out of our corporations, and the loss of job opportunities that would entail. William Dimma, a former president of Torstar Corp. and Royal Lepage, wrote in *The Globe and Mail* last year about how in his young days in business in the 1950s, a Canadian reaching the third rung in a branch plant operation faced a choice between moving to head office in New York or watching his advancement stall. Today, he said, that choice occurs at the fifth rung because so many decision-making jobs have gravitated from regional offices to head office. His solution was not to screen out foreign investment, but, sensibly, to foster the growth of more Canadian-based global corporations.

Willard "Bud" Estey also penned a heartfelt article at about the same time over his profound disappointment that Nova Corp., the Alberta chemical giant founded by the provincial government in the 1950s, planned to move sixty-five senior head office jobs from Calgary to Pittsburgh. Estey, a former Supreme Court justice and one of the country's leading corporate lawyers, also refrained from demanding the erection of old-style protectionist measures. Rather, he called for resolute governments and sober examination of how to ensure the attractiveness to foreign companies of processing Canada's natural resources at home. "It is," he said, "our own weakness that threatens our existence."

These laments were published at a time when the strong American stock market and the chronically weak Canadian dollar were encouraging U.S. companies to snap up assets at bargain basement prices. Even members of the corporate elite seemed genuinely spooked by the fear the country might be in the midst of a closing-out sale.

Among the Canadians jewels falling into American hands was the British Columbia forestry giant, MacMillan Bloedel. Mac-Blo presents an interesting case study in the evolution of economic nationalism. In the late 1970s, two central Canadian corporate giants, Canadian Pacific and Domtar, both attempted to take over MacMillan Bloedel. But B.C. premier Bill Bennett, an economic conservative and British Columbia chauvinist, fended them off by declaring, "B.C. is not for sale." Those were the days when politicians still carried tremendous weight in business matters. It was also a bygone era in which Canadians still extracted large quantities of identity from logs and fish.

Fast forward two decades as the Mac-Blo board submitted to the advances of the American-based Weyerhauser forestry giant. One might have expected a re-mounting of the ramparts. But the transaction barely caused a ripple outside a small circle of interested parties. Jeannie Southam, the octogenarian daughter of founder W.R. MacMillan, attended the shareholders' meeting, voted against selling out her family's legacy, and wept at the outcome. "I was absolutely bowled over," she said. "I never dreamed such a thing was possible, that MB, that beautiful Canadian company, could be taken over by an American firm. It was like an earthquake. It was like the Rocky Mountains falling down. I very nearly had a heart attack."

The grande dame of the woods simply hadn't kept up with the times. The Rocky Mountains had fallen long ago. But it would be wrong to dismiss her lament about foreign ownership simply as the ramblings of an out-of-touch, old-moneyed lady. Canadians still care deeply about the ownership of our economy. It's just that their caring is muted by other considerations—and is, in any case, highly selective.

A *Globe and Mail* poll taken at the time of this takeover mania found 70 per cent approval for Ottawa exercising the power to halt an American purchase of a Canadian company if it believed the deal was not in Canada's best interest. Foreign investment controls to further the public interest remain a durable concept. Then again, an equal number applauded the benefits of Canada's growing integration with the United States. Even while desiring some kind of action in smoothing the rough edges of greater economic integration, Canadians didn't want to see the baby thrown out with the bathwater.

The old solution would have been for the state to create and coddle national oligopolies, giving them preference over other comers regardless of performance. Ownership would have been the prime consideration. The new solution lies in fostering Canadian-based global champions in the mould of Nortel and Bombardier. Even our railways, the original ribbon of steel of Canadian identity, are judged today by a different standard than even ten years ago. Canadian National has been privatized and Canadian Pacific freed of its public policy obligations. They are corporations now, expected to provide a service of value to their customers but not in defiance of such realities as the north-south pull of the integrated North American economy. Our hope is that we will prosper at this game. The aborted 1999 merger of CN and Burlington Northern, with its promise of an integrated North American carrier with a Canadian headquarters, provided the kind of model the public can probably support.

Canadians clearly accept the economic benefits in the integration of the North American economy, and they want to capture these. But they don't want to give up their identity—or their economy—in the process. Given a choice, 37 per cent would opt for even closer economic ties with the United States, 45 per cent would keep relations as they are, and 16 per cent (the nationalist hard core) would weaken ties. But they are strongly opposed to further cultural integration. They implicitly understand that culture is the best bulwark against being overwhelmed.

The dominant mindset is still forming on these questions and therefore figuring precisely where Canadians will draw the line is tricky. A strong majority, for instance, think it inevitable the Canadian dollar will give way to a common currency with the Americans some time in the next ten to twenty years, even though they aren't pleased by the thought. The message, in essence, is this: We're willing to join together economically if that's what it takes to enjoy a higher standard of living and thereby a better quality of life. But don't ask us to give up those things that give us meaning as a people. Three-quarters of respondents, in fact, told Ekos Research that it is "very important" to maintain a unique system of values and national identity in the context of increased globalization and international trade. Another 20 per cent thought it was moderately important. Respondents were not overly daunted by the challenge either. Nearly six out of ten thought it was "very possible" to achieve this goal.

Some things are simply beyond the pale, though, even for an economically tolerant people. The epic battle that raged throughout most of 1999 over the Canadian airline industry was a testament to the limits of our economic open-mindedness.

At a Toronto press conference on August 24, 1999, financier Gerald Schwartz officially launched the Onex bid to take over Air Canada and merge it with Canadian Airlines. The top Air Canada brass gathered expectantly that morning in the executive boardroom of their Dorval headquarters to watch the proceedings on a large monitor television screen. They had known for several weeks something was up and were happy at least that the shadow boxing was over. Canadian Airlines, their long-time rival, had obviously reached the end of its financial rope. But the government, understanding that patience for the old ways of private-sector bailouts had worn thin in Canada, expressed an unwillingness to pay out again to keep Canadian in the air. Canadian had few choices but to throw in its lot with Onex and its partner, American Airlines.

The Schwartz press conference completed, the Air Canada braintrust reviewed the situation and quickly reached several conclusions. First, the bid was illegal under the provisions of the Air Canada Act, which didn't permit anyone to own more than 10 per cent of the airline. On that point alone, the courts would bring down Onex, they felt. Perhaps just as importantly, they couldn't imagine the takeover gambit flying with Canadians at large. They would view it as the destruction of the Canadian airline industry itself.

As far as Air Canada was concerned, Onex was merely the Trojan horse for American Airlines, which already had a partnership arrangement with Canadian and would increase its presence. The press picked up the theme with little prompting—that the Americans were going to take over our national airline. "The ugly American idea," an Air Canada strategist would later comment with some satisfaction.

Air Canada had been privatized in 1988. The Canadian people no longer owned it. But they still felt pride of ownership. Air Canada (and its predecessor Trans-Canada Airlines) played an integral role in the country's development. It remained one of Canada's best-known brand names, perhaps its best-known international brand. Wherever Canadians travelled in the world, the red maple leaf symbol of Air Canada painted on an aluminum tail (a close cousin of the flag) provided a comforting reminder of home.

Air Canada knew from its market research that Canadians regarded it as a national and international success story—at least before the merger mess changed opinions. We imagined it as more than a mere business providing a return on investment to shareholders. Psychologically, it still belonged to all of us. We didn't want our national airline run out of Dallas for ideological as well as practical reasons. The onus fell to Gerry Schwartz to prove he wasn't an American Trojan.

Schwartz had cards to play, but the hand he held was weak. Ironically, Robert Milton, the Air Canada president, happened to be an American citizen, whereas Don Carty, the American Airlines president, is a Canadian. One of those odd outcomes of a global economy. But it didn't play in Portage la Prairie. Air Canada's obvious Canadian credentials overwhelmed Robert Milton's citizenship. As the battle dragged on, Schwartz worked hard to downplay the role of American Airlines, eventually amending his bid to formally reduce its influence. But by then it was too late.

The nationalism question wasn't Onex's only public opinion vulnerability. It also suffered from the widespread perception that the federal government had altered the rules of the game to favour Schwartz, a prominent Liberal fundraiser. He also couldn't escape his image as a corporate buccaneer, a financial wheeler-dealer who doesn't really get his hands dirty running companies but makes billions raiding going concerns and then breaking them up. The charge is unfair—Schwartz actually boasts an enviable track record of adding value to his companies and generating good jobs in Canada—but it was a hard label to shake.

Public opinion polling about the takeover battle tells an interesting story about contemporary Canada. In the early fall, *The Globe and Mail* surveyed 1,500 Canadians. They strongly preferred a market-based solution, saying any airline restructuring should be a private-sector matter. At the same time, though, the numbers saying it would be unacceptable for the federal government to provide financial assistance to save Canadian Airlines constituted a bare majority.

What Canadians really found unacceptable—by 77 per cent to 22 per cent—was the notion of allowing a U.S. carrier to buy up a Canadian airline. In fact, a strong majority (57 per cent) deemed the suggestion very unacceptable. A merger was judged quite acceptable, even if it meant shutting down unprofitable routes, so long as Yankee Doodle didn't end up in the pilot's seat. The poll also showed that public trust for the concerned players

varied greatly. The more Canadian you were and the more closely connected to the actual operation of an airline, the more trust you earned. Nearly
nine out of ten people trusted Air Canada. More than eight out of ten trusted money-losing Canadians Airlines. Even the federal government, which
respondents felt had handled the issue badly, was trusted by six out of ten. But
only half of respondents trusted American Airlines and just four out of ten
trusted its perceived stalking horse, Onex Corporation.

The federal government's own polling on the airline wars also showed a
strong preference for made-in-Canada solutions. Respondents strongly preferred fostering competition through the nurturing of small Canadian airlines
over an influx of American carriers and were almost evenly divided when
asked to choose which was more important to them: lower fares or Canadian
ownership. Mind you, those who never flew were the more likely to support
the Canadian ownership option. Looking over the whole body of research, it
seems that Canadians probably ranked consumer issues first, nudging out
nationalism. Trailing behind were equity issues, such as maintaining service to
remote locations.

Looking back, Douglas Port, then Air Canada's communications chief,
didn't think the takeover battle brought out any real anti-American feeling in
the country. It's just that Air Canada, as a people's company, was held to a different standard. The takeover crossed some kind of line in the sand in the
Canadian mindset. "You can touch a lot of things, but don't touch this," Port
succinctly put it.

So beware. The new Canadian identity is no more fixed or predictable
than the location of the North Pole. We suspect there are a couple of principles at play here. The first is that all things being equal Canadians prefer a
Canadian alternative. But not to the extent of paying a penalty for their
Canadian choice, whether in higher prices or inferior service or greater
environmental damage. The second principle is the famous Canadian exception: Notwithstanding principle one, the public prefers to reserve certain
areas of activity for continued Canadian control, as long as the pain threshold remains within reason. As Port says, you can touch a lot of things,
but don't touch this. The "don't touches" can only be inferred. But it would
be safe to guess they include health care, our water resources, education,
some of our cultural institutions, and, as it turned out in 1999 at least, our

national airline. Pretty much everything else, even Mac-Blo, is judged by a more pragmatic standard.

In December 1999, for the third time in three years, Ekos Research asked Canadians if they felt Canada has become more like or less like the United States over the previous ten years. By almost a six-to-one margin they felt we had become more similar. But asked whether they would like us to become more or less like the United States in the future, the story changed. Nearly half wanted us to be less like the United States, four out of ten wanted us to remain on the same keel and just 14 per cent wanted us to be more like the United States. Pollster Allan Gregg tapped into similar sentiments in his annual pulse-taking for *Maclean's* magazine at the end of 2000. Seventy-two per cent of respondents disagreed, most of them strongly, with the notion that we should move closer to the United States in our laws and attitudes. It marked the strongest disagreement among twenty-five propositions he put forward. Mainstream Canada would still say: *Vive les differences!*

Classically, the tools of identity have been wielded in Canada by the state. Graham Spry, one of the country's great nationalist intellectuals, famously declared, "The State or the United States." In other words, if we didn't marshal the powers of the state to accentuate our differences from the Americans and vigorously promote our common identity, we would wither away as an independent entity. In his excellent book, *Nationalism Without Walls,* Richard Gwyn covers the same territory. He describes Canada not so much as a nation-state but as a state-nation, by which he means our identity and very being as a country derive from the will of the state to make it so. "Our state," he tells us, "has formed us and shaped our character in a way that is true for no other people in the world."

Many Canadian intellectuals argue that as a "state-nation," we are particularly vulnerable to the national thinning agent of globalization. We lack the natural cultural cohesiveness of the Japanese or the powerful ideological glue of the Americans, with their revolutionary past and sense of manifest destiny. We should therefore suffer a greater identity crisis since the state upon which we have relied has supposedly been crippled, with its powers either moving upwards into supra-national bodies like the WTO, downwards to provincial or municipal levels, or outwards to the private sector.

The argument makes good intuitive sense. But it is flawed. First off, the state has not been enfeebled to the extent usually depicted, and certainly not in the non-economic areas from which Canadians increasingly draw their identity. Remember, the greatest source of national identity for Canadians in recent years has been our universal health care system. Second, the available public opinion data suggests that against all the odds, the attachment of Canadians to Canada is growing stronger, not weaker. Thirdly, it is becoming more and more apparent that we are finding other hooks, beyond the state, upon which to hang our sense of being Canadian.

On the first point, there is no denying that the process of globalization has usurped some of the traditional economic policy levers employed by governments to promote our distinctiveness. Trade rules and new communications technologies have done their job. That said, we believe governments retain the capacity to govern, especially in the human resources, social policy, and cultural areas so close to the hearts of modern electors. Nothing yet prevents the Canadian government from restoring our health care system to the top ranks in the world or underwriting a well-trained workforce or pouring public money into a televised thirty-hour people's history of Canada. Both the Marxists and the neo-cons have got it wrong: The state has not withered away. It is merely in a Schumpeterian process of creative destruction.

The trade constraint on governments lies in preventing viewers of a CBC history series from changing channels to also watch a PBS documentary on jazz. And a good thing at that. Canadians are past the point of having their choices circumscribed in the name of identity politics. Policies that promote a sense of Canada are fine; those that interfere with the flow of information from elsewhere not only won't stand up to the scrutiny of free trade agreements, they won't be tolerated by domestic consumers.

The greatest obstacle to activist governing over the past twenty years has not, in our view, been globalization but the cul de sac of chronic deficits. Fiscal weakness is what truly hobbled governments. The path to greater activism—smart, focused activism—therefore has reopened in the age of surpluses. All it takes is imagination—and public confidence that governments aren't returning to their bad old ways.

In his 1993 book *Preparing for the Twenty-first Century,* social historian Paul Kennedy argued that the nation-state remains for most people their primary locus of identification "and no adequate substitute has emerged to replace it as the key unit in responding to global change."That view remains valid eight years later. In our country, even to the extent the national government might be inclined to evade responsibility for, let's say, a deteriorating health care system, the public would refuse to let it off the hook.

Point two: Despite the logic that regional and supra-national identities will replace the nation-state, the opposite appears to be happening in Canada. Ekos Research asked Canadians in 1998 to which group they would say they belong first of all: the locality or town where they live (21 per cent); their province or region (19 per cent); their country (41 per cent); North America (4 per cent); or the world (12 per cent). Their country, Canada, led the next popular choice by a 2:1 margin. Canadians, it turns out, are more inclined than Europeans or Americans to cite the nation-state as their primary source of identity. This sense of national belonging actually increased in the decade during which globalization made its greatest advances. So has the connection Canadians feel to the world. In contrast, local identity has declined.

In a major poll in the winter of 2000, the federal government uncovered similar sentiments, with 79 per cent of respondents reporting a strong sense of belonging to Canada and 75 per cent a strong sense of belonging to their province. In western Canada, the source of so much angst over alienation from the central government, the sense of belonging to Canada registered in the high 80s, well above the national average. Country scored better than provinces everywhere except Quebec, where neither country nor province are held in great esteem.

Canadians are so enamoured of this land of ours that even the disappointments of the 1990s—while bringing our politicians and many of our institutions into disrepute—have failed to shake our faith that we live in the best country in the world. International comparisons show us to be almost smug about the supposed superiority of Canada. Dissatisfaction with the state of our health care system does not deter Canadians from rating it more highly than anybody else's. Indeed, in a twenty-three-country survey at the low point of the Nervous Nineties, 78 per cent of Canadians judged their country the best place to live. Only half of the more circumspect citizens from the other twenty-two countries displayed similar chauvinism. Canadians also were twice as likely as others to believe the world would be a better place if others were just more like us.

These are not the attitudes of a country suffering an identity deficit. It may well be that the action of globalization has produced an opposite and equal reaction—a new outward-looking nationalism. In many parts of the world, globalization has spawned the re-assertion of tribal identities, a kind of localism. In the cultural stew that is Canada, we know that tribalism and localism won't fly. Could it be that globalization is enhancing rather than diminishing our sense of national identity? The experts may be wringing their hands over the attachment of Canadians to their country in a global age, but ordinary people appear too busy sewing the flag on their backpacks or enjoying the splendours of our national parks to be bothered.

With or without the state, globalization or no globalization, Canadians are maintaining their sense of who they are through their own devices. They clearly aspire to something greater than a weak imitation of Yankee Doodle Dandy. They appreciate the distinctiveness of their country, even revel in it. Even in a globalized era featuring the triumph of private markets and the growth of individualism, they want the sum of our parts to amount to more than the gross national product.

But the old identifiers aren't sufficient. Economic nationalism doesn't cut it in a world in which our economic space is so much broader than our political space. The classic economic identifiers were gradually superseded through the 1980s and 1990s by what economist Thomas Courchene called the social policy railway, particularly our national medicare system. Today, our identity markers are once again in transition.

Increasingly, we are cultural Canadians: Canadian by willpower rather than by policy. We feel attached to Canada because we like the smell of it. It is an affair of the heart. The process is ephemeral, not mechanical, but no less real. Get used to it. We live in an age of intangibles and our love of country is as intangible as it is profound. Identity, like so much else, no longer is the singular purview of the state. It cannot be contained in a government program. Today's identity is a bottom-up affair. "Ours is a quiet anarchy," says a perceptive Canadian friend who tracks the changes in his home and native land from Europe.

Who says globalization and national identity are incompatible? They are not mutually exclusive spheres, but overlapping ones. They throw up new challenges—both domestically and internationally—ones that require new sets of answers. But despair is unwarranted.

Darrell recalls test marketing the federal government's "Canada 125" TV ads in 1992, a few months before the Charlottetown referendum. The purpose of the campaign was not so much to celebrate our 125th birthday as to soften people up on national unity so they would be more accepting of the eventual constitutional deal. One of the ads that garnered a lot of attention from the media came to be known as "Little Mila." It depicted a girl (who many felt looked uncomfortably like Mila Mulroney as a child) singing the national anthem. The ad featured a montage of scenes of Canada—fishing boats, cowboys, the Chateau Frontenac hotel—and ended with a massive nighttime fireworks display from a previous Canada Day celebration on Parliament Hill.

Of all the ads Darrell has tested in the last fifteen years, this one spot elicited the most emotional response. No matter where he took it across the country at least a couple of people were moved to tears. And, when he asked them why, they had a hard time explaining. This was the "smell" in action. This being Canada, once they wiped their eyes clean, each group bitched about the under-representation in the ads of images from their region. But the emotional impact was undeniable.

This continued affection for Canada is striking, but we would guard, as well, against complacency. The knowledge citizen does not grant his or her approval unconditionally. Love of country can carry you a long way, especially among older Canadians, but eventually love must be requited. That 1995 survey that showed Canadians nearly twice as likely as citizens of other nations to rank Canada better than the others also found them half as likely to say they would support their country, right or wrong. Canadians are increasingly pragmatists. The old nostrums left them stuck in the muck for a quarter-century. They love their country, but they insist that it must work for them.

The Department of National Heritage is mandated to puzzle over the question of Canadian identity. Its research has tapped into the paradoxical co-existence of tremendous pride in Canada—among the highest levels in the world—alongside a readiness to pull the plug and emigrate elsewhere to improve living conditions. These are the same sentiments former University of Toronto president Robert Prichard discerned in his final round of convocation ceremonies. "Younger and more highly educated Canadians are, generally speaking, as attached to Canada as older and less highly educated Canadians," the department says. "However, these people are more prepared to let their heads rule their hearts when considering the economic consequences of their physical ties to Canada. . . . Our findings would also suggest that if citizens cannot realize their expectations in Canada, they will move abroad to improve their conditions."

Canada appears well on its way toward the development of what we call a Can-global identity—a multiple, diverse, evolving identity rooted in a set of values drawn from Canada's Tory tradition. This Can-global identity mixes a well-placed pride in the achievements of the country with an expectation that individual Canadians deserve access to the best opportunities the global economy offers. The young and multicultural, in particular, won't allow their attachment to Canada to stand in the way of personal development. They are well educated and therefore globally mobile. They've grown up in a world of niche marketing and global marketing, narrow-casting and broadcasting. They are open to the world. Their sense of diversity goes beyond appearance. The baby boomers all grew their hair long and tie-dyed their shirts at the same time. They stopped smoking dope and settled down with a single partner as if on cue. This new generation exhibits far less uniformity in its attitudes or lifestyles—from fashion to music to sexual orientation. They can change identities as quickly as Clark Kent. Three hundred of them work at Cisco Systems in San Jose, California. They have their own club, which meets on the third Wednesday of every month. They call it the Digital Moose Lounge and it serves Canadian beer. Its denizens keep close contact with Canada through the Internet and with one another. They entertain Canadian visitors and help them understand the ways of Silicon Valley. They put out alerts of new places where you can find Coffee Crisp chocolate bars ("brown gold"), Smarties, Shreddies, and Sour Cream 'n' Onion chips. Theirs is a different experience than the hundreds of thousands of Canadians who took up residence in the Los Angeles area in the decades after the Second World War. When expatriate Canadian businessman Jack Kent Cooke started the Los Angeles Kings in 1967, he was shocked at the sparseness of the crowds. There are several hundred thousand Canadians in the greater Los Angeles area and they all moved here because they hate hockey, he groused. Not the San Jose Canadians. They remain Canadians wherever they are.

The worldliness and education of young Canadians make them less susceptible to chest-thumping and myth-making about Canada being the best country in the world. They are the Show Me generation. They will demand that Canada deliver on their high expectations of offering top-tier work and lifestyle opportunities. There will be no keeping them down on the Canadian farm if we fail to challenge and reward them. A generation or two ago, the most precocious among them might have taken off for the bright lights of Toronto or Montreal or Vancouver. Today, they look upon all of North America as their back yard. Through the Internet, they have already stretched the concept of community beyond the confines of geographic space. The community of Canada matters to them, but they also know how to connect into communities of interest wherever they exist.

They won't settle for a middle-tier existence replicating technological breakthroughs made elsewhere or satisfying themselves with research two steps behind the cutting edge. Well-educated Canadians, particularly the young, are three times more likely than others to express a readiness to leave Canada if opportunity dictates. They prefer our high level of tolerance over what they consider to be American moralism and so their strong preference would be for the best of the world to be available to them in our global cities. But if we fail to deliver, they will vote with their feet. Opportunity no longer knocks. It walks.

Remember Joe Canadian. His origins and message make for an interesting story, and one far more nuanced than "the rant" might suggest. Think about the slogan that underlines the campaign: I Am Canadian. Most of the attention has been paid to the last word—Canadian. But "I Am" tells just as interesting a tale. The "I Am" campaign began in the mid-1990s, bouncing off the same research about Gen-Xers that we presented in Chapter 4. The data contradicted the pervasive media image of the time of a lost and loutish generation, instead showing Gen-Xers to be ambitious, opinionated, and individualistic. The "I Am" was no accident; it spoke to their individualism.

The guy who came up with the rant for Molson was a young Canadian named Glen Hunt. He worked at the Bensimon, Byrne, D'Arcy agency and had recently returned from a stint on Madison Avenue. Inspired by the things that turned him off about living in the United States, he pretty well delivered up the script out of a spontaneous soliloquy at a creative meeting. Interestingly, the rant, despite its great media success, garnered a fairly neutral reaction within the young (nineteen to twenty-four) target audience for Molson Canadian—the I Am crowd. Where it did much better was among more nationalistic twenty-five- to fifty-year-olds, not a bad thing for Molson in that it extended the reach of the brand. But for our purposes, what should be remembered is that the slogan says *I Am* Canadian and not *We Are* Canadian.

Incidentally, the young actor who played the patriotic Joe Canadian, Jeff Douglas, has moved to L.A. He continues to love Canada, plans to be back to do some theatre in the summers, but has found the career opportunities in Hollywood impossible to resist.

Earlier this year, shortly after he became Canada's industry minister, Brian Tobin went to speak to a class of Canadians at Oxford University in Britain. A great Canadian patriot with a poetic tongue, Tobin paid heed to the emergence of a new class of global workers for whom border hopping is second nature. But he also implored them when all was said and done to return home to Canada and make it a better place. "Take advantage of this special place you're at now," he said. "But for God's sake, come on home when you're ready."

For at least one woman in the audience, though, it was too late. "I love Canada and all," she said afterwards. "But these days it is just too small a country."

The challenge, of course, is to try to reverse such sentiments or, failing that, at least maintain the kind of continued connection with Canada displayed by our Digital Moose ambassadors in San Jose. Remember the 14 per cent of respondents who want us to be more like the United States in future. The young and multicultural and super-talented are strongly over-represented in that group. They don't necessarily want to emulate the values of the United States—they prefer the smell of Canada—but they are attracted by the energy and opportunity down south. These young people represent the vanguard of our new Can-global identity. The Canada-in-decline of the 1990s had too little to offer them. Mediocrity doesn't grab them. The only strategy with any hope of keeping them at home over the coming decade is one based on excellence.

NAVIGATING THE NEW CANADIAN MINDSET

A DOZEN RULES OF THE ROAD

1. IT'S ALL ABOUT TRUST

The future will be dominated by the competition for public trust. Canadians are increasingly turning to "trustmarks" to sort through the cluttered marketplace of an information economy. For organizations interacting with individual Canadians, trustmarks will supercede the trademarks of old. A trustmark goes well beyond a good brand name. The brand provides the entry point to the product. Today, people are seeking guidance of a higher order. We want to be able to judge quickly if the information coming our way— about products to buy, decisions to make, causes to support—is authoritative, credible, and reliable. We aren't seeking a signal about the quality of the product as much as the trustworthiness of the producer—whether it be a corporation, charity, or political leader. The default position of the new Canadian mindset tends to be set on skepticism rather than trust. Therefore, the trust-mark holder possesses an asset as rare and valuable as platinum. Trustmark stewardship will become one of the top tasks of modern CEOs. Leaders must excel beyond the traditional management skills of finance, strategy, and marketing to master the political skills necessary to forge trusting relationships with the new knowledge consumers.

2. THE NEW KNOWLEDGE CITIZEN/CONSUMER IS KING

The marriage of the most highly educated generation in our history and the information technology known as the Internet places phenomenal power in the hands of a newly enfranchised class of knowledge citizens and consumers. Information has been democratized, giving rise to heretofore-unprecedented demands for choice in everything we do. The mentality of "there is no alternative" no longer suffices; we will create our own alternatives if the official offerings don't satisfy. Indeed, the motherlode wealth of information now available to individuals and groups is giving rise to a revolutionary power shift from producers to consumers. Producers and governments are under pressure as never before to deliver results and be accountable for performance. Combine this heightened consumer assertiveness with a diminution of brand loyalty and you will see the potential for businesses, voluntary groups and political parties, which may have taken decades to build, to be destroyed in the blink of a cursor. Witness our swift abandonment in the 1990s of long-standing institutions such as the Red Cross, Eaton's and the Progressive Conservative party. The challenges posed by the new knowledge consumer/citizen are obvious, but so are the competitive advantages for those who can relate to a more informed and wilful population.

3. WHAT I WANT IS CONTROL—WHAT I NEED IS CERTAINTY

What the new knowledge consumer most desires is a greater measure of control in an unstable and insecure world. Our craving for control is not an end in itself but a means of enhancing certainty of outcome. (Is this the best medical treatment for me? Am I receiving the training that will secure my career goals?) The new mindset demands to know how the story ends, and a means to intervene if the ending appears unsatisfactory. Canadians are less willing than ever to entrust the narrative to the powers that be. Producers and governments therefore are going to have to be able to articulate their vision and persuade consumers and citizens not just of their intended destination but of how they plan to get there. Those with a compelling vision and a convincing plan are best positioned to satisfy the search for certainty. Those, in contrast, who hide behind glib sales pitches will learn how swift and harsh public judgement can be.

4. MULTICULTURALISM IS THE NEW DEMOGRAPHIC MEGATREND

Our traditional view of the three founding nations (French, English and Aboriginal) is becoming less and less relevant, especially in the cities where most of us live. We have succeeded in establishing a genuine rainbow society in this country, a model for the world in the twenty-first century. It makes us a more complex land, but a richer one. Our marketplace has become both more heterogenous and global at the same time. One example: the increasing pressure on health-care regulators to recognize alternative therapies such as acupuncture that are standard fare among certain ethnic groups.

As this multicultural Canada become more firmly rooted, we are learning that diversity and tolerance are not just social goods, but also a national advantage in a world in which we all want to be judged on our abilities and nothing else. The implications of Canada's multicultural reality are huge for our concepts of citizenship, national unity, and commerce. Adapting to this new reality will prove one of the great challenges of the next quarter-century.

5. THERE IS NOTHING UN-CANADIAN ABOUT OUR NEW IDENTITY

A new Can-global identity is evolving hand-in-hand with multiculturalism, especially among our youth. The most noteworthy characteristic of this new identity is its easy blend of love of country with a conscious external focus. Plugged into the world through the Internet and other communications technologies, our new Can-global citizens are programmed to be the best at what they do, wherever they do it. They shun mediocrity, increasingly bench-marking themselves not against the person in the next cubicle or apartment block but against the best the world has to offer. Can-global citizens can no more easily accept being second best in the economy than accept being second class in society. The Can-global citizen therefore pursues excellence and insists upon having an impact. Comfortable in their skins, they are much less moved than previous generations—but not unmoved—by appeals to nationalism and parochialism. While clearly preferring excellence at home, they are prepared, if necessary, to select excellence over home. Unless we lift the pursuit of excellence to a national passion, the potential for Canada to lose its most talented young people to the best of the world is very real.

6. BEWARE THE NEW EQUALITY PRINCIPLE

The new Canadian mindset increasingly embraces a live-and-let-live philosophy, at least up to the point where it butts heads with the new equality principle. The stigmas attached a generation ago to homosexuality or mixed-race marriages have all dissipated significantly. We overwhelmingly embrace the unique qualities of individuals or groups of individuals, but anything smacking of special status—whether for a province or a demographic group—gets our backs up. That's where Canadians come face-to-face with the limits of their tolerance. Equality used to involve the intervention of government to lift up the disadvantaged. Today, equality increasingly entails not affirmative action programs but the assurance of equal access to all, regardless of circumstances. Canadians are consequently highly suspicious of initiatives that disadvantage certain categories of individuals in order to right historical wrongs or perceived group inequities. Bottom line for the new mindset—distinctions that can apply to all, such as income, are acceptable arbiters of policy, but exclusionary criteria will not cut it. The new mindset holds that all Canadians should be treated similarly because we all must face the same challenges.

7. THE PRIVATE SECTOR HAS LOST ITS PRIVACY

The concept of a "private" sector no longer exists in Canada. Canadians increasingly expect that corporations and professionals must be accountable to the public interest. Nortel merits no more of a free ride than the government of Saskatchewan. The professional misconduct of a doctor no longer is a matter between him and his College of Physicians. As knowledge citizens and consumers, we are prepared to enforce this accountability through whatever mechanisms are available; indeed, the collective actions of consumers are becoming just as commonplace as the collective actions of citizens. Moreover, this insistence that once-private players be held publicly accountable extends to what they do outside our borders as well.

8. GLOBALIZATION IS US

Globalization was once widely regarded as a business issue. No longer. Since all Canadians are deeply implicated in the globalization process, we obviously all have an interest in its shape and direction. The Gemini twins of globalization are Davos Man and Seattle Woman. Throughout the 1980s and 1990s, Davos Man was ascendant. Now, Seattle Woman's moon is rising. Canadians are troubled by the unrepresentative nature of globalization, its so-called democracy deficit. That doesn't make them sympathetic toward anarchists running amok or woolly theories of world government. But we do want to ensure that mechanisms are in place for citizens to see their values reflected in the global agenda. The concept of globalization without representation is untenable in a knowledge age. Demands will grow to get our political and economic space into alignment. Davos Man and Seattle Woman can be expected to beget Democracy Child.

9. WE LEARN A LIVING

As stated throughout this book, Canadians demand choice and seek certainty in all matters. This very much applies to the workplace. The surest way for workers to achieve choice and certainty, as Karl Marx preached, is by controlling the means of production. Except that in a knowledge economy, the means of production resides between your ears. Control therefore comes in the form of education and training, which have become a kind of gold reserve of the new economy (particularly for employees of choice). Access to education and training promises to be the key political and workplace issue of the next decade. These developments obviously have major implications for employers, unions, educational institutions and governments. Look for life-long learning to dominate our public policy agenda and to also become a critical component of employment negotiations. Earning a living alone no longer produces enough certainty. The new workplace compact, therefore, will sound like this: I'll work for you if you'll help me grow.

10. GOVERNMENT MATTERS AS LONG AS IT REMEMBERS ITS PLACE

In spite of the knocks that government takes, it remains the preferred vehicle for realizing our collective interests. However, our expectations of government have changed markedly as a result of our experiences with deficits, globalization, and the Internet. We expect our governments to be focussed on helping us resolve the big problems. We don't want them engineering one-size-fits-all solutions on our behalf or striving to be all things to all people. Our elected officials need to understand that certain principles prevail for the knowledge citizen. First off, deficits matter. Governments that tolerate renewed deficit-financing risk being tossed out of the game by voters. There is virtually nothing, including a major economic downturn, that would convince us to once again journey along any well-intentioned road to fiscal hell. Accountability also matters as never before. The new knowledge citizen expects results in place of rhetoric, which requires the development of an unprecedented degree of transparency and new accountability mechanisms that allow us to keep track of outcomes. We want government to work, but not in the old ways.

11. THE TORY TOUCH LIVES ON

At heart, Canada remains a compassionate society. Canadians don't like to view themselves in terms of winners and losers; we prefer to see ourselves instead as winners and those who, with some assistance, can become winners. This means that punitive attacks on the economically disadvantaged find little fertile ground in Canada. However, while Canadians are prepared to be compassionate, they are not prepared to be played for suckers. We are both tenderhearted and hardheaded. We prefer the hand-up to the handout. Ours is a self-help form of compassion. Canadians always stand ready to assist the truly needy. As for those who have fallen on hard times, we are willing to lend a hand to help them get back on their feet. But we don't think we owe them a living; we expect them to help themselves as well.

12. DON'T UNDERESTIMATE THE RESILIENCY OF THE PATIENT CANADIAN

Canadians are patient investors in their future. If we could be one person collectively, it would probably be Warren Buffet, the legendary value investor. We are not by nature attracted to quick fixes or get-rich-fast schemes. We don't demand instant gratification, but steady improvement and long-run returns. We love nothing so much as a long-term plan of action, articulated by a credible spokesperson. Canadians have been through a lot together over the past generation, not all of it pleasant. The process has imbued us with a remarkable resiliency. We've come out the other end of the tunnel a collection of quiet optimists, with an optimism based not so much on a confidence in the economy to perform well as a confidence in ourselves to endure whatever the economy throws our way. Our experiences in the economic trenches have cured us of the temptations of simple solutions. Today, we're prepared to weigh the trade-offs implicit in any decisions; if anything leaves us cold, it's being told there are no trade-offs. Like Warren Buffet, we're looking for the best return tomorrow rather than the fastest return today. Whether it's politics or the stock market, Canadians are neither bulls nor bears; we are instead a nation of patient owls.

ACKNOWLEDGEMENTS

Darrell and I wish to acknowledge the many people who generously shared their data, insights, and expertise in the course of our journey. Several of them were kind enough to read early versions of chapters and provide the sort of peer review that makes us happy to be in less rigorous callings than the academy. Our thanks go out to Judith Maxwell, David Pecaut, William Tholl, Owen Adams, Neil Nevitte, Peter Harder, Alex Himelfarb, Peter Nicholson, Andrew Sharpe, Frank Graves, David Crapper, Kevin Lynch, John Wright, Natalie Lacey, Andrew Grenville, John Duffy, Sheldon Ehrenworth, Jaime Watt, Brian Crowley, David Agnew, Dan Atlin, David Small, Peter Hickey, Doug Hart and David Livingstone, Evan Potter, Nathaniel Stone, Andrew Parkin, and Peter Cowan. This list is hardly exhaustive. We've both been fortunate in our careers at being able to rub shoulders with some of the keenest minds in Canada, an opportunity that has helped shape our understanding of the currents of opinion running through the Canadian public. The debt we owe therefore is broad and substantial.

Invaluable research support for our efforts was provided by Elaine Roberts, Justin Graham, Tricia Benn, and Alison Baldock of Ipsos-Reid and Dana McAllister, a fourth-year journalism student at Carleton University, who served as my indefatigable researcher in Ottawa. This marks the second time I've turned to Carleton's School of Journalism for research on a book, and the second time I've come away with a renewed faith in the quality of today's students.

A special thanks as well to the team at Doubleday. This project would never have got off the ground without the patient prodding of John Pearce. It might well have collapsed without the continued support of Maya Mavjee and Brad Martin. And it would never have been completed without our editor, Meg Taylor. Perry Goldsmith and Robert Mackwood, our agents, also proved indispensable in turning an urge into a book. Their support is greatly appreciated.

———

Darrell has a few acknowledgements he'd like to make directly:

I like to say that public opinion researchers are not born, they are made. With this in mind, I'd like to thank those who had a major impact on making me what I am today: Barry Kay and Steven Brown from Wilfrid Laurier University, Scott Bennett and Conrad Winn from Carleton University, and Ian McKinnon from what used to be Decima Research. I'd especially like to thank Allan Gregg, from whom I learned much of what I still practise today.

I'd like to acknowledge the contribution (both knowing and unknowing) of the clients of Ipsos-Reid, who, over the last ten years, have allowed me the opportunity to come into direct contact with the evolving Canadian mindset as I worked to help them manage their public issues. Much of what I brought to this book was derived through "on the job training" that they paid for.

I'd like to thank my colleagues at Ipsos-Reid who contributed both directly and indirectly to this book. Not only did they take a little Winnipeg-based company and turn it into Canada's most dynamic and respected research company, they made "Angus Reid" into a household name. When someone writes a history of market and public opinion research in Canada, they will have to acknowledge that this group of people, at this time, is the best that our industry has ever known. This is especially true of the members of the Public Affairs Division with whom I've had the privilege of working most closely over the last decade. Special thanks go to my partners and colleagues John Wright, Natalie Lacey, Mike Colledge, Bob Richardson, and Chris Martyn, to whom I owe very, very much.

One of my biggest supporters in this project has been Angus Reid (yes, there really is an Angus Reid). It was Angus who first encouraged me to write this book. He was also the first point of contact with both my agent and Doubleday. As well, throughout the writing of the book Angus was a constant source of encouragement and support. But Angus is much more than this to me. He is my mentor, my business partner, and a great friend. Thanks, Angus.

Finally, and most importantly, I'd like to thank my wife, Nina, and daughter, Emily, for all that they are to me. They are the ones who have sacrificed the most to allow me to chase my dreams. For this I dedicate my contribution here to them.

As for me, I'd like to single out the unflagging support of Phillip Crawley, publisher of *The Globe and Mail,* and colleagues past and present too numerous to name. Finally in this list but firstly in my life, there is my family. In the preface of my first book, *Double Vision,* I recounted the manner in which my young children participated in the project: from a companion autobiography (still incomplete) by my five-year-old daughter, Bailey, to Batman-themed title suggestions from my four-year-old, Joshua, to mad slapping on the keyboard from my two-year-old, Jacob.

As I submit this manuscript, the children are eleven, nine, and seven. Rather than joining me in the attic and lovingly watching me click away on the keyboard, this time out they agitated loudly for equal access to the computer, bemoaning the unfairness of my digital domination. It kind of makes you nostalgic for a time before their mindsets were so well formed. That said, their joyfulness alone is enough to leave one optimistic for the future. My hopes and dreams for them infect me with a rock-solid interest in Canada's welfare, an objective I hope this book will help further. I desperately want them to discover opportunity in close enough proximity for us to be able to shoot baskets together on the weekend.

Then there's my life collaborator, my wife, Janice Neil. She somehow is the only one who doesn't appear to have aged between the two books— despite my bombarding her with every excuse. More than twenty years have passed since we met in residence at Carleton University. Janice shares with me a passion for journalism and a commitment to family. As everyone who knows us understands, she's the one who holds things together, not just for herself but for all five of us. What can I say other than that our relationship, thankfully, isn't getting older but better.

INDEX

A

aboriginal policy (Canada), attitudes toward, 276–78

Adams, Bryan, 74

Air Canada, 305–7

Alberta Advantage Surveys, 192, 206

Alfredsson, Daniel, 70

American Airlines, 305

Amnesty International, 83

Angus Reid Group (polling). *See also* Ipsos-Reid, 2, 13,
  17, 32, 37, 45–46, 53, 61, 64–66, 71, 75, 92, 98, 105,
  108–9, 134, 140, 151, 156–57, 162, 168, 170, 173,
  177, 226, 235, 251–52, 263–64, 268, 271–72, 276, 291

Annau, Catherine, 284

AOL (America Online), 114

AON Consulting Inc., 136

"archie" (search engine), 97

Armstrong, Jack, 194

ARPANET (Advanced Research Projects Agency),
  96–97

Atwood, Margaret, 74

Aung, Dr. Stephen, 229

Axworthy, Lloyd, 240, 249, 251–52

B

Baker, David, 228

balance of payments. *See* debt, foreign

Ballard Power, 5

Bank for International
  Settlements, 79

Bank of Canada, 11

Baran, Paul, 95–96

Barlow, Maude, 80, 82–85, 104, 164

Barnard, Robert, 131

baseball-ization of the labour
  market, 136

Batsford, Eric, 142–43

Baynton, Fred, 153

Begin, Monique, 184–86

Behmenburg, Heinz, 154

Beliveau, Jean, 70

Bell Canada, 143

Bennett, Bill, 303

the Berlin Wall, 11, 45

Bernardi, Mario, 289

Berners-Lee, Tim, 97–99, 116

Bertrand, Guy, 265

Beveridge, Sir William, 241

bilingualism, 283

Bloom, Richard, 119–20, 146

Bolivia, 83–84

Bombardier, 5, 304

Botkin, Jim, 127

Bouchard, Lucien, 291, 294

Bouey, Gerald, 24

brain drain (from Canada),
  139–40

Branson, Richard, 102

Brazil, 58, 82, 84

Bricker, Darrell, 2–4, 38, 45–47, 66,
  71, 86, 90, 92, 108, 155, 194, 246,
  275–76, 297, 312

Bricker, Emily, 265–66

Bricker, Nina, 92

Brooks, David, 173

budget deficits, 13, 126

budget surpluses, 10, 14

Buffet, Warren, 322

Burgoyne, Terry, 146

Burlington Northern (RR), 304

Bush, George Sr., 55

Business Council on National Issues
  (Canada), 81

C

cable service, 94–95

Caccia, Charles, 289

Campaign 2000 (child advocacy
  group), 252–53

Campbell, Kim, 124, 248

Canada
  americanization of, 4

budget surpluses achieved, 10
diversity of, 280, 283
Canada Assistance Plan, 235, 243
Canada Health Act, 184–86
Canada Pension Plan, 235, 243
Canadian Airlines, 305–6
Canadian Broadcasting Company, 281, 309
Canadian Council on Social Development, 124, 127, 201
Canadian dollar, erosion of, 51–52
Canadian government, recent opinions of, 309–10
Canadian identity, America's proximity and, 298–99
Canadian Imperial Bank of Commerce, 145
Canadian Medical Association, 192–97
Canadian National (RR), 304
Canadian Pacific (RR), 304
Canadians
new status of, 10
tolerance levels of, 264–78
Canadian Tire, 63
Carrier, Roch, 64, 69
Carty, Don, 306
Ceausescu, Nicolae, 11
"certainty," the search for, 7, 115, 126, 149, 163, 165, 168, 200, 202, 204, 261, 317–18

Chang, Jimmy & Audrey, 280–81
change, attitudes toward, 74
Charlottetown constitutional accord, 28, 122–23
Charter of Rights and Freedoms for Canada, 262
Chartrand, Amy, 137
Chartrand, Ben, 136–38
chiropractic care, 230
Chrétien, Jean, 23, 27, 30, 55, 69, 72, 124, 139, 174, 183, 207, 266, 291
Churchill, Winston, 242
Cisco Systems, 41, 141, 313
Clair commission (Quebec), 211
Clark, Glen, 283
Clark, Joe, 287
Clark, Scott, 38–39
Clements, Craig, 35
Clinton, William J., 69
Cohen, Leonard, 32
commodity prices, 29
communications technology
globalization and, 60
increased speed of, 57
communitarianism, 5
COMPAS (polling), 3
Conference Board of Canada, 135, 197–98, 208
conservatism, fiscal, 2
control, the drive for, 317–18
Cooke, Jack Kent, 313

Cooperative Commonwealth
  Federation (CCF), 241

Copps, Sheila, 248

Corel Corp., 136

corporations, global, 56

Council of Canadians, 82, 84

Coupland, Douglas, 130

Courchene, Thomas, 8, 104, 258, 311

Cournoyer, Yvan, 301

Crawley, Phillip, 87–88

crime vs. sin, 262

Crombie, David, 184

Crow, John, 27, 30

Crow, Sheryl, 101

Crowley, Brian, 211

Crump, Tom, 28, 37, 40–43, 141

cultural industries. *See* free trade,
  cultural industries

currency trading, 54

D

d'Aquino, Thomas, 81–82, 84

Davis, Stan, 127

Davos Switzerland, 79, 82

Day, Stockwell, 193

debt

  Canadian national levels of,
    27–32

  effects on governments, 1

  foreign, 29

  public anxiety over, 37–39

reduction measures, national, 31

Decima Research (polling), 3, 90, 156

Decter, Michael, 222

deficit(s). *See also* debt

  Canada's fiscal, 25–26

  "democratic." *See* "democratic
    deficit"

  drawbacks of, 309–10, 321

  Ontario's fiscal, 37

  social, 239–40

"democratic deficit," 79–81, 320

Denis, Solange, 244

dependability. *See* "certainty," the
  search for

the Depression. *See* the Great
  Depression

Deschamps, Yves, 293

Diefenbaker, John G., 180, 242, 283

the digital divide, 111–12

the Digital Moose Lodge, 313, 315

Dimma, William, 302

Dingwall, David, 193

Dion, Celine, 74

Dion, Stephane, 265

diplomatic service, changing nature
  of, 55

disposable incomes, 40

Disraeli, Benjamin, 152

doctors

  authority of and respect for,
    218–19

customer service and, 216–18, 230

frustrations felt by, 222–24

Dodge, David, 17, 21, 33–34

dollar. *See* Canadian dollar,

Donolo, Peter, 15

Dosanjh, Ujjal, 282

Dosdall, Emery, 284

Douglas, Jeff, 315

Douglas, Tommy, 179–80, 182, 209

Drucker, Peter, 34

Duhamel, Ron, 175

Dulude, Fernand, 169

Duplessis, Maurice, 262

Durst, Fred, 101

Dyer, Gwynne, 283, 295

Dykeman, Scott, 155–56

E

Earnscliffe Strategy (polling), 3, 252

Eaton's, 64–65

Economic Council of Canada, 239, 245

economy

knowledge based, 17

public perception of, 17–18, 32–36, 42–43

service, 56

World War II and, 19

education. *See also* knowledge; schools, 6

adult, 170

attitudes toward, 2, 37, 151, 155–56, 162–73

as employment assurance, 150, 170–71

historic attitudes about, 153–54

historic levels of, 152–53, 158–59

importance of, 158, 320–21

perceived priority of, 151

perceived quality of, 156–57

as personal enhancement, 127, 129, 135

post secondary, 159–60

public vs. private, 161–62

results produced by, 160

social cohesion and, 172–73

testing and, 164–66

trends in, 148–50

egalitarian values, 274–76, 319

Ekos Research (polling), 3, 36, 74, 237–38, 248, 257, 268–70, 291, 297, 304, 308, 310

e-mail, 93–94, 106

employment, rewards for, 127–29

entrepreneurial attitudes among employees, 128

Environics Research (polling), 3, 34, 76

Estey, Willard "Bud", 302

European Union, 80

excellence, pursuit of, 319

Expo 3, 67

exports, Canadian, 72–74

F

Faloon, Patrick, 232

family allowance program (Canada),
    242–43

FedEx, 144

Filmon, Gary, 287

Fishman, Ted C., 121–22

food labeling, 110

Foreign Investment Review Act, 301

foreign ownership of Canadian
    companies, 302–3

Fortin, Pierre, 39

Frank, James, 198

Fraser Institute, 239

free trade, 2, 29
    attitudes toward, 68–69, 75–77
    cultural industries and, 73–74
    future developments in, 76–78

free trade agreement. *See also*
    NAFTA, 30, 46, 60–63, 65–66, 72

Friedman, Thomas, 50, 58, 104

Fukuyama, Francis, 256–57

Fyke, Ken, 210–12

G

Gallup (polling), 3, 17, 162, 166, 267

Geffrion, Boom-Boom, 70

General Motors, 30

Generation-X, 130–35

genetically modified foods, 109–10

Georgetti, Ken, 142

Gibson, Lib, 88

Gillett, George Jr., 70, 301

globalization, 2, 10, 29–30, 47–63,
    67, 69–86, 90, 127, 139, 245, 281,
    318–21
    affecting Canadian culture,
        300–301
    America's proximity and, 299–301
    anxiety about, 269–70
    attitudes toward, 74
    cultural identity and, 76
    its effects upon nationalism,
        308–15
    nature of, 54
    sans representation. *See*
        "democratic deficit"
    unemployment and, 67
    prior to World War I, 78

Gnutella, 102

Goldenberg, Eddie, 248

the Golden Mile (Scarborough,
    Ont.), 34–35

Goldfarb, Martin, 3, 36, 244, 252

Gordon, Walter, 300

government. *See also* Canadian
    government
    accountability and, 81, 321
    spending rates of. *See* spending rates

Graves, Frank, 74–75, 107, 269

Gray, Herb, 174–77, 188, 192, 289

the Great Depression, 18–19, 240

Greenspan, Alan, 16, 52

Greenspon, Bailey, 89

Greenspon, Edward, 2–4, 34–36, 87, 91–92, 164–65

Gregg, Allan, 32, 44, 90, 106, 266, 290, 308

Grimes, Patty, 146

Grove, Andrew, 136

Gruending, Dennis, 181–82

GST (Goods & Services Tax), 11

Guevara, Che, 84

Gwyn, Richard, 308

Gzowski, Peter, 164

H

Haidar, Zeyad, 280

Hall, Emmett, 181–82, 184, 186, 212

Hamilton, Lee, 25

Harcourt, Mike, 282

Harris, Mike, 168, 205, 247

Hartley, Bruce, 15

Hartz, Louis, 236

Haslam, Sir Robert, 121

health care. *See also* medicine, 6
    attitudes about, 2, 178
    costs of, 16, 186–88, 197–99
    extra billing and, 183–86
    knowledge consumer and, 215–19

origins of, 178–83

patient participation in, 219–32

private. *See also* Canadian Medical Assn., 196–97

private vs. public, 208–9, 212

public anxiety about, 187–92, 195–96

public expectations of, 213–14

public perceptions of funding for, 37–38, 199

reform/rationalization of, 210–12

search for "certainty" and, 210

voting behavior and, 202–6

wellness and, 200

Hebb, Tessa, 85–86

Hebert, Yvon, 62

Heinzl, John, 63

Hendsbee, Garnald & family, 249–51, 275

Herbert, A. P., 241

Heston, Charles, 5

Hitt, Jack, 224

Hnatyshyn, Ray, 288

hockey, globalization of, 69–70

Home Depot, 105

homosexuality, attitudes toward, 267–68

Horowitz, Gad, 4, 236

Horton, Tim. *See* Tim Hortons

Hosek, Chaviva, 61

Howlett, Karen, 145

Hull, Bobby, 70

Humber College, 147–48, 153

Hunt, Glen, 314

I

Ibbitson, John, 225

IMF, 48, 79

immigrants to Canada, origins of, 289–90

immigration

attitudes toward, 296–98

Canadian laws and, 286–89

multiculturalism and, 295–96

income, guaranteed annual, 247

income per capita, Canada vs. USA, 39–40

index, puzzling self-reference to, 334

individualism, 4–5, 7

inflation, 16, 19–22, 24

German aversion to, 38

monetary policy and, 16

rates of, 31–33

information, modern wealth of, 317

institutions, decline of public trust in, 6

insurance

coverage levels of, 5

medical, 20

unemployment. *See* unemployment, insurance for

interest rate policies, 27

International Monetary Fund.
See IMF

the Internet, 2, 6, 41, 57, 69, 83, 87–117, 135, 143, 232, 295, 314, 317–18, 321

medical knowledge and, 189, 223–26

origins of, 95

public approval of, 98–99

quality of life and, 107

rates of usage, 111

trustworthiness of, 113–15

uncertain credibility of, 225

investment, foreign, 73

investor psychology, 53

Investors Group (polling), 52

Ipsos-Reid (polling). *See also* Angus
Reid Group, 2–3, 71

Italy, life in, 12

J

Jacobs, Jane, 116

job anxiety, 14, 33, 36, 123–27, 137

public perception of, 17–18

job security, declines in, 14

"Joe Canadian" (advertisement), 299, 301–2, 314

John, Elton, 124

Johnson, Tod, 88

Johnston, Donald, 82

the Just Society, 3

K

Katz, Mike, 147–48

Kennedy, Paul, 309–10

Kenney, Jason, 193

Kent, Tom, 181

Kerbel, Robert, 223

Keynes, John Maynard, 240

King, Mackenzie, 13, 29, 240–41

Kirck, Harvey, 69

Klein, Ralph, 199–200, 205, 282

knowledge based economy. See economy, knowledge based

knowledge citizen(s), 6–7, 81, 86, 100, 312, 317, 320–21

knowledge consumer(s), 6, 64, 75, 89, 100, 162, 189

knowledge economy, 54, 320

knowledge society, 6–7

knowledge worker(s), 6, 75, 143

Koivu, Saku, 70

Krispy Kreme (donut shops), 73

Kristofferson, Kris, 113

Kroeger, Arthur, 237

Krugman, Paul, 78

L

Lacey, Natalie, 166

Lalonde, Marc, 247

Landry, Bernard, 292

Latimer, Robert, 263–64

Latouche, Daniel, 293

Laurier, Sir Wilfrid, 8, 18, 29, 266

LaValley, Dr. William, 227–29

layoffs. See job security; unemployment

Lee, Derek, 35–36

Leger (polling), 3

Lévesque, René, 184, 293

Lewis, David, 61

life, quality of. See quality of life

Little, Bruce, 62

Livingstone, David, 161

Lohr, Steve, 97

"Lotto 8-44", 244

Love, Courtney, 101

M

Macdonald, Donald, 29–30

Macdonald, Sir John A., 28, 47

MacGregor, Roy, 280

Mackasey, Bryce, 243–44

MacKinnon, Mark, 144

MacLeod, Robert, 148

MacMillan Bloedel, 302–3, 308

magnetic resonance imaging. See MRI

Maher, Bill, 113

Mandela, Nelson, 52

Manley, John, 71

market crash of 1929. See also the Great Depression, 18–19

Marsh, Leonard, 241

Marsh Report on Social Security, 242

Martin, Paul Jr., 13–14, 22, 24, 27, 30–31, 33, 38–39, 50, 80, 187, 239, 251

Martin, Paul Sr., 23, 179–80

Martin, Roger, 42

Matthey, Jeanette, 55

Maxwell, Judith, 1, 151, 167–68, 239–40, 245

Mazankowski, Don, 287

McCallum, John, 40

McClendon, Sarah, 72

McDonough, Alexa, 85–86, 203

McLeod, Ian & Norman, 180

McNealey, Scott, 120–21

medicare, 23

medicine. *See also* health care
   alternative, 226–33
   conventional, 230–31

Meech Lake
   crisis re, 122
   rejection of the Accord, 11

Mendelsohn, Matthew, 68, 76–77

MERs (investment fees), 89

Metallica, 101

Mexico, 67
   monetary crises in, 48–51

middle class, economic status of, 24–25, 33

Mikita, Stanislaus, 70

Miller, Dennis, 102

Mills, Rick & Diane, 56

Milton, Robert, 306

misery index, rates of, 26, 36

Moses, Barbara, 138

MRI (machines), 200

Mulroney, Brian, 26, 30, 81, 185–86, 244

multiculturalism. *See also* immigration, multiculturalism and, 2, 270, 280, 282–83, 289, 318
   in Quebec, 294

the Multiculturalism Act, 290

Multilateral Agreement on Investment, 80, 82

N

Nader, Ralph, 79, 83

NAFTA (North American Free Trade Agreement), 59, 67, 69
   opinion about, 46–48

Napster, 89, 101

national child benefit (program), 253

national debt. *See* deficit

National Energy Program Tariff, 301

National Hockey League, 281

nationalism, 310–12
   economic, 311

neckties, significance of, 118–19

Neil, Janice, 28, 91–92

Nicholson, Gary, 15

Nicholson, Peter, 21, 239

Nortel Networks, 5, 122, 304

O

Ohmae, Kenichi, 64

oil prices, 20, 23

Ontario Institute for Studies in Education, 156–57, 161, 166, 171, 173

Organization for Economic Co-operation and Development, 159

Oyshi Sushi (restaurant), 2–3

P

Paine Webber (brokerage firm), 120

Paproski, Steve Eugene, 288

parents, concerns of, 166

Parizeau, Jacques, 294

PBS (U. S. public broadcasting), 309

Pearson, Lester, 13, 177, 182, 242

Pecaut, David, 144

pensions, 20

Peritz, Ingrid, 169

Personal Security Index, 124, 127

Peters, Suzanne, 236, 239, 247

Peters, Tom, 134, 216

Peterson, David, 282

Petro-Canada, 301

Poland, 59

Pollara Group (polling), 3, 75, 107, 125, 140, 207, 283

polls, "30% exceptions" in, 255

Port, Douglas, 307

Porter, John, 266

Porter, Michael, 42

poverty, public perceptions of, 235–36

Prichard, Robert, 138–40, 312–13

private sector, accountability of, 319–20

productivity
individual's rewards for, 127–29
levels of, 20–23, 39

protectionist economic policies, 19

Provost, Claude, 70

Public Interest (org.), 83

Putnam, Robert, 234, 255

Q

quality of life. *See also* standard of living, 7
importance of, 237

Quebec City, 81–82, 84–85

Quebec referenda, 32

Quebec separatism
attitudes about, 290–93
politics of, 294–95

R

Rae, Bob, 36, 247

Reagan, Ronald, 27, 237

recession(s), 9–13, 24–28

refugees, attitudes toward, 272–76

Reich, Robert, 102, 115, 167

Reid, Angus, 4

resources, human vs. natural, 29

Richard, Henri, 70

Richard, Maurice, 64

Rickhi, Bud, 232

Rifkin, Jeremy, 33–34

Robillard, Jean, 146

Rock, Allan, 188, 200

Rodriguez, Sue, 259–61, 263–64,
    278

Rogaine (drug), 224

Romanow, Roy, 186–88, 209–10,
    287

Romanow Health Commission,
    209

Royal Bank, study of Canadians,
    130–34

RRSP contributions, 5

Russell, William Howard, 54

Russia, economic difficulties in, 52

S

Saint Pierre, Guy, 151

Schildroth, Ken, 148

schools. *See also* education
    discipline in, 166–69

Schuller, Tom, 255

Schumpeter, Joseph, 34, 64

Schwartz, Gerald, 305–6

Seattle, 79, 82

Self-Sufficiency Project, 253–54

Sharp, Mitchell, 23, 182–83

Sharpe, Andrew, 39

Sheppard, Jim, 55

Sholzberg-Gray, Sharon, 174–77, 187

Shuchman, Dr. Miriam, 223

Shumuk, Danylo, 287

Sierra Club, 83

skills enhancement, 127

Snobelen, John, 157

social capital, 255–56

social cohesion, 255–57

society
    compassionate, 321
    patient, 322

Somerville, Margaret, 219

Soros, George, 52

Southam, Jeannie, 303

spending rates. *See also* deficit, 26

Spry, Graham, 308

standard of living, 7
    changes in, 19, 40, 42

Starowicz, Mark, 102–3

Statistics Canada, 158

St. Laurent, Louis, 13, 179

Stone, Oliver, 257

Strategic Counsel (polling), 3

suicide, the law and, 260–61

Summers, Lawrence, 16–17

T

taxes, 6

  changes in, 1

Thatcher, Margaret, 27

Thiessen, Gordon, 20, 22, 50

Thompson, Marcella, 280

Thurow, Lester, 12

time stress, 167

Tim Hortons (donut shops), 73

Time-Warner, 114

Tobin, Brian, 315

Toffler, Alvin, 105

tolerance (social), 6, 11, 318–19

Torsney, Paddy, 274

Tory, John, 94–95

the "Tory touch", 4, 7, 149, 208,

  236, 256, 258, 321

trade, free. *See* free trade

travel, global, 71

Tremonti, Anna-Maria, 55

trucking, 143

Trudeau, Pierre Elliott, 3, 23, 25–32,

  28, 51, 57, 72, 174, 183–85, 243,

  261–62, 265, 278–85, 288

trust (public)

  corporations and, 53

  importance of, 316–17

trustmark(s) (brands), 115, 232,

  316

Tuck, Simon, 137

Twain, Shania, 74, 83

U

Ukrainetz, Charlene, 254–55

unemployment. *See also* job anxiety,

  14, 18, 22

  Canadian acceptance of, 25

  concern over, 122–24

  defenses against, 24

  disincentives for ending, 243,

    246–48

  insurance benefits for, 23, 142, 243

  insurance levels debated, 245–55

  rates of, 18, 23–24, 28, 31–32

United Nations Human

  Development Index, 9, 258

University of Western Ontario, 147

Ustinov, Peter, 282

V

Valcourt, Bernard, 248–49

Veterans Rehabilitation Act, 153

Viagra, 224

W

Walker, Michael, 239

Wall Street Journal, 51

Wal-Mart, 63–64

Watt, Jaime, 275

Weinstein, Richard, 57

welfare, philosophies of, 236–39

Wente, Margaret, 12

Weyerhauser (forestry), 303

Wilde, Oscar, 202

Wilson, Michael, 26–28, 45–47, 66,
86, 244

the Winnipeg General Strike, 18

Wolfe, Robert, 68, 76–77

Woods, Tiger, 105

work environment, importance of, 128

Workopolis (web site), 135, 167

World Bank, 48, 79

World Trade Organization, 77, 79,
83, 308

World War II, 240

World Wide Web, 98

Wright, John, 120

X

Xerox Corp., 144

Y

Yankelovich, Daniel, 256–57

Yankovic, Al, 90

Yashin, Alexi, 70

Young, Neil, 101

Young, Samson, 281